Reforming Mary

Reforming Mary

*Changing Images of the Virgin Mary
in Lutheran Sermons of the
Sixteenth Century*

BETH KREITZER

OXFORD
UNIVERSITY PRESS
2004

OXFORD
UNIVERSITY PRESS

Oxford   New York
Auckland   Bangkok   Buenos Aires   Cape Town   Chennai
Dar es Salaam   Delhi   Hong Kong   Istanbul   Karachi   Kolkata
Kuala Lumpur   Madrid   Melbourne   Mexico City   Mumbai   Nairobi
São Paulo   Shanghai   Taipei   Tokyo   Toronto

Copyright © 2004 by Oxford University Press, Inc.

Published by Oxford University Press, Inc.
198 Madison Avenue, New York, New York 10016

www.oup.com

Oxford is a registered trademark of Oxford University Press

Library of Congress Cataloging-in-Publication Data
Kreitzer, Beth.
   Reforming Mary : changing images of the Virgin Mary in Lutheran sermons of the
sixteenth century / Beth Kreitzer.
      p. cm.—(Oxford studies in historical theology)
   Includes bibliographical references and index.
   ISBN 0-19-516654-X
   1. Mary, Blessed Virgin, Saint—Sermons—History and criticism.   2. Lutheran
Church—Sermons—History and criticism.   3. Sermons, German—History and criticism
4. Sermons, Latin—History and criticism.   5. Mary, Blessed Virgin, Saint—History of
doctrines—16th century.   6. Lutheran Church—Doctrines—History—16th century.
7. Reformation.   I. Title.   II. Series
BT610.K74 2003
232.91'088'241—dc21   2003051789

9 8 7 6 5 4 3 2 1

Printed in the United States of America
on acid-free paper

To my parents

Acknowledgments

I have many people I wish to thank and to whom I must express a debt of gratitude. Many thanks to the members of my dissertation committee at Duke: Elizabeth Clark, Susan Keefe, Kalman Bland, and Thomas Robisheaux. I would especially like to thank David C. Steinmetz for his guidance and his example, as well as for his work on my behalf.

This study could not have been completed without the help and support of numerous people and organizations. I have used the collections of various libraries and received vital help from their staffs: Roger Loyd and the staff of the Duke Divinity School Library; the Rev. Terrance Dinovo at the Luther Seminary Library, who helped with the Lutheran Brotherhood microfiche collection; Dustin Strong and Ros Parnes, the intrepid interlibrary loan staff at the Bellarmine College Library, Louisville, Kentucky; and the library staff at the Southern Baptist Seminary library in Louisville. A special note of thanks goes to Gillian Bepler and the staff at the Herzog August Bibliothek in Wolfenbüttel: their help and access to their collections was a necessity for my research.

Funding for this research and writing was given to me by the following: the Duke University Graduate School; the Graduate Program in Religion; the Center for International Studies at Duke; the Center for Medieval and Renaissance Studies at Duke; and the Institut für Europäische Geschichte in Mainz. Funding along with emotional and mental support were also provided by my husband, Lucas Lamadrid, who read and commented on the majority of this study. He has helped me in numerous ways, even with occasional babysitting.

Contents

List of Abbreviations

ADB   *Allgemeine Deutsche Biographie.* 56 vols. Leipzig: Duncker & Humblot, 1875–1912.

Jöcher   *Allgemeines Gelehreten=Lexicon* . . . Hrsg. Christian Gottlieb Jöcher. 11 vols. [Leipzig, 1750–1897] Hildesheim: Georg Olms, 1960–61.

LW   *Luther's Works.* Vols. 1–30, ed. Jaroslav Pelikan. St. Louis: Concordia, 1955–86; vols. 31–55, ed. Helmut Lehmann. Philadelphia: Fortress, 1955–86.

NDB   *Neue Deutsche Biographie.* Hrsg. von der Historischen Kommission bei der Bayerischen Akademie der Wissenschaften. 17 vols. Berlin: Duncker & Humblot, 1953–.

RTK   *Realencyklopädie für protestantische Theologie und Kirche.* 3rd ed., ed. Albert Hauck. 24 vols. Leipzig: J. C. Hinrichs'sche Buchhandlung, 1896–1913.

WA   *D. Martin Luthers Werke. Kritische Gesamtausgabe.* 62 vols. Weimar: Böhlaus, 1883– .

Note: In the German and Latin texts provided in the notes no attempt has been made to standardize spelling, but the spelling, capitalization, and punctuation of the originals have been preserved to the extent possible. For ease of reading, many of the abbreviations have been spelled out, with the added text placed in brackets. The superscript letters, for example, "o" or "e" placed above other letters, have been standardized as umlauts.

Reforming Mary

Introduction

Few contemporary historians of the modern era seem to have noticed Henry Adams's fin-de-siècle proposition that in the Middle Ages "the Virgin had acted as the greatest force the Western world ever felt, and had drawn man's activities to herself more strongly than any other power, natural or supernatural, had ever done."[1] Medievalists may have always known it, and Catholic theologians may have believed it, whether they were embarrassed or empowered by it. But Adams himself, the author of *Mont-Saint-Michel and Chartres* (1904), was sure that the Virgin of the thirteenth century rivaled the "dynamo," or steam engine, which powered the nineteenth and twentieth centuries. However, historians of the sixteenth century have tended in other directions in their research, addressing the changing relationship between Christian Europe and the Virgin only obliquely, in the context of other topics, or more generally in discussions of piety, liturgy, and the saints. There is one question that has not been satisfactorily answered by modern historical scholars: if, as Adams believes, "all the steam in the world could not, like the Virgin, build Chartres," how is it that this most powerful force of the late medieval period should come to be so difficult to discover in the modern world?[2] Even if one can sense the Virgin as a force in Lourdes or Medjugorje, or among the throngs that gather there, no scholar would suggest that she is a recognizable force behind modern western culture. In the following pages, I hope to offer a small piece of the puzzle, through an investigation of the way Mary is presented in the sermons of Lutheran pastors in the sixteenth century.

The sixteenth century is a period uniquely poised for an investigation into the decline of Mary's power, for in this time not only Protestants but also some Roman Catholics such as Erasmus were rejecting the abuses and excesses into which the Marian cult had fallen, and were calling for a renewal of morality and spirituality in religious and social life. While Erasmus rejected what he saw as popular abuses but maintained Marian devotion, even pilgrimaging to Walsingham, Protestants criticized more than pious excess or popular misunderstanding, striking at the heart of many dearly held notions of Marian theology. Their rejection of any role for merit in human salvation in particular undermined Mary's cult. In this study, I will focus on the treatment of Mary and the continuities and changes in theological ideas concerning Mary and her presentation beginning with Martin Luther, and continuing with clergy in the Lutheran tradition. Luther, the earliest of the Protestant reformers and the most important reformer in the early years, is usually considered independently of the tradition he helped to found, but we will begin to understand the trajectory of Mary's image and her role in early modern life only if we investigate other members of the tradition throughout this period.

Lutheran Sermons and Postil Literature

In order to explain my choice of sermons as the source material of this study, let me first note that a number of other sources could have been (and still need to be) mined for their presentation of Mary, including more "official" publications such as biblical commentaries, confessional writings (which some assume are hegemonic for the Lutheran tradition and answer all questions), catechisms, or other treatises. Devotional literature and liturgical materials, along with artistic representations, could also have made interesting objects for studying how the Virgin Mary is portrayed in the Lutheran context.[3] These various media, whatever contribution they might make to filling out our picture of Mary more completely, have their own merits and demerits as subjects for study, and still beg the question of how they were received by their various audiences.

The sermon, it must be admitted, is not a perfect art form—or, in this case, historical source. The sermons drawn upon for this study were all published in the sixteenth century—they may be representative of the thousands of sermons that sit in archives, were lost, or were never recorded, but they are already at least somewhat exceptional in that they were not only recorded but also thought worthy of publication, that is, the publisher thought these works would find a profitable market.[4] Some sermons were published because their author was exceptional and popular, for example, Luther, while others were published because the sermons themselves were seen as better than average or in some other way significant. Some of the sermon collections were edited or at least overseen by the preachers themselves, but the majority were collected and edited by others, occasionally without the author's permission, which often happened to Luther, or after his death, as in the cases of Johann Spangenberg and Joachim Mörlin. The hand of an editor must almost always be assumed in the final work. The issue of censorship should also not be forgotten, for works were often censored before going to press or occasionally suppressed or even destroyed after publication. A number of scholars have argued that censorship was a major factor in the decline in sermon publication in other areas of Europe such as France and England, for both Catholic and Protestant authors.[5]

An even more basic question relating to sermons is how they were recorded. We know that preachers often did not write out their sermons ahead of time—Luther himself rarely preached from a manuscript, but usually only from an outline.[6] Luther and others did on occasion write out sermons for their published postils, for example, Luther's Wartburg Postil for Christmas and Advent, which he conceived as a book of model sermons to aid preachers. A "postil" (or "postill," from *postilla*) is simply a sermon collection arranged by and covering the Sundays and often festivals of the church year.[7] However, many of the sermons that appear in these collections were originally compiled by one or more note takers. The question of the reliability of note takers has bedeviled Luther scholars, not only with many of his sermons but especially for the contested authority of his *Tischreden*. Often the scribes would make their notations in Latin, even if the sermon was preached in German, which leads to a problem of terms, definitions, and interpretation. Some of the sermon collections were written in Latin and intended for a university or at least well-educated audience (of readers, if not listeners), while others were then translated into German and published in both forms. Many postils were published in German, although this is no guarantee that the individual sermons were not first given in German, transcribed into Latin, then retranslated into German. Several authors published both German and Latin postils that were unrelated texts, but it is not always possible to determine whether the sermons were actually preached or were intended simply to be instructional. Postils were often intended to be used as preaching manuals by clergy, and thus would indirectly impact their congregations, but could also be found in the libraries of literate lay people.[8]

These difficulties being noted, printed sermons are probably still the best means of discovering what many Lutheran preachers were teaching their congregations. While we cannot assume that any particular sermon appears in the form in which it was actually preached (if it was ever preached), we can assume that in its current form it reached a wider audience than any single congregation. Robert Scribner has theorized about how ideas were disseminated in the largely illiterate and oral-based culture of the sixteenth century. He suggests that printed media must be considered as only one element in the transmission of ideas: "the printed word was most often mediated by the *spoken* word, by reading aloud to oneself, by reading aloud to others, or by discussion of things in print."[9] The "major formal means of communication" was the pulpit, for "the religious reform was first and foremost a powerful preaching revival."[10] The centrality of the sermon both to the "preaching revival" of the Reformation and within evangelical services supports the importance of sermons as a genre of research, and the direct connection of printed sermons to what was preached (with the proper caveats noted earlier) and otherwise disseminated in the sixteenth century makes them an ideal source for investigating the ideas that Lutheran leaders wanted to teach to the lay population.[11]

Postils, while often conceived as model sermon collections, but not necessarily preached by their author, are a particularly useful source for investigating not only the ideas that a variety of sermons contain but also for finding sermons that reached a wide audience. Pastors in Lutheran regions were often required by ecclesiastical ordinances to own postils, in order, according to Patrick Ferry, to "enforce orthodoxy," and probably also to aid in improving the quality of the average sermon.[12] Gerald Strauss's research has shown that many pastors owned more postils than were required of them, which, considering the high cost of books in the period and the often quite small salary of pastors, was a significant investment.[13] In fact, many postils were so popular as to appear in a number of editions: for example, the postils of Johannes Mathesius went through ten editions between 1563 and 1593, while the postils of Tilemann Hesshusen had the same number of editions in the decade between 1580 and 1590.[14] Hans-Christoph Rublack notes that one or more new postils or postil editions appeared almost every year at the great book fair in Frankfurt, and they were not Calvinist or Catholic, but almost exclusively Lutheran.[15]

Printed sermons, then, are not only accessible to modern scholars but also appear to be located at a convenient nexus for research into what Lutheran leaders were trying to teach both other preachers and, more important, the people in the churches. They are, in a unique way, both the printed and the spoken word, accessible to both the literate and illiterate elements of the population. And, if clergymen can be assumed to be part of the "elite," sermons provide an important, if mostly one-way, connection between "elite" and "popular" religion.[16] Most reformers, as Harold Grimm asserts, "used the sermon to bring their doctrines directly to their followers in the vernacular and to apply those doctrines to the immediate and practical needs of the people."[17] Sermons were conceived as not only the means to present scriptural truths to the laity but also a very effective and public means to apply these truths pastorally to the specific needs of their congregations. Although printed sermons provide only the voice of the preacher, they are a result of the complex interaction between the preacher and his congregation, between the theoretical (theology and doctrine) and the practical (what they need to be taught, and in what ways they need correction).[18]

The State of Research

Luther's ideas and writings began to be evaluated usually very soon after they appeared in print, and such was the case with his ideas concerning the Virgin Mary and the saints. Early in his career, after publishing his famous commentary on the Magnificat, he was accused of teaching that Mary did not remain a virgin, and that in fact Jesus was conceived by Mary with Joseph. To silence these rumors, Luther published "That Jesus Christ Was Born a Jew" in 1523, denouncing these supposed statements. Luther was especially criticized for his new rendering of *gratia plena* as the more passive *holdselige* (see chapter 1 for a discussion of these terms) in the angel's address to Mary at the Annunciation. Various Catholic theologians wrote against his teachings on Mary and the *communio sanctorum*, while Luther himself, along with many of his followers, defended the new "Protestant" position on the proper role of the saints in the church.[19] Scholars have suggested that it was only in response to the criticisms of the reformers that Catholic "Mariologies" began to be written, such as the important works by Peter Canisius and Francisco Suarez.[20] Among Protestants, interest in Mary faded until the nineteenth century, but was most emphatically revived with the papal declaration of the dogma of the immaculate conception in 1854, and again with the declaration of Mary's assumption in 1950.[21]

In facing new questions about Mary—especially issues relating to the church and the authority of Scripture and tradition—and the older questions concerning soteriology and Christology, Protestant (and some Catholic) scholars turned to look again at the statements of the reformers on Mary. Very few of these works look beyond the main reformers—Luther, John Calvin, Ulrich Zwingli, and occasionally Philipp Melanchthon, Johannes Brenz, and Martin Bucer.[22] A number of these works, especially those written since 1950, were written in the spirit of a mostly positive contribution to the ecumenical movement. While the majority of scholars and theologians do not suggest that Mary as the mother of the church can be "the bridge and the road to true ecumenism" as did Charles Lees, quite a few paint Luther's views on Mary very positively, suggesting that Protestants and Catholics both might be surprised to discover what Luther and other reformers actually believed concerning Mary, and that such a history lesson may be beneficial for Protestants hoping to develop more, or at least some, Marian devotion in their traditions.[23] Other authors are less hopeful that Luther's views on Mary can help to bring about Christian unity.[24]

Among Protestant authors who treat Luther, several, in the interest of promoting Marian devotion, insist that Luther remained devoted to Mary throughout his life, indeed, that "in Luther there existed in newer evangelical form the German Marian veneration of the Middle Ages."[25] Friedrich Heiler claims that "Luther belongs in the ranks of the great devotees of Mary," for he was only trying to rid Marian piety of its excesses and aberrations.[26] For Heiler, it was the Enlightenment with its rejection of mystery and miracles that destroyed Marian piety in the Lutheran tradition. The works of Hans Asmussen and Reintraud Schimmelpfennig from the early 1950s follow in this same vein.[27]

Such positive presentations of Luther's views brought highly critical responses. Hans Düfel questions how one can even speak of a Protestant veneration of Mary, for "do not Marian veneration and Protestantism mutually exclude one another?"[28] Düfel, in contrast to these uncritical texts, wants to provide an evenhanded presentation of Luther's position on Mary, not burdened by external goals such as the desire to foster a liturgical space for the Protestant veneration of Mary or by an anti-Catholic reaction against any mention of Mary.[29] Albert Ebneter, a Jesuit priest, also criticizes the earlier works on Luther's views of Mary, not only for their extreme positions but also for mistakes in interpretation, for removing quotations from their contexts, and for generally twisting the evidence to support their own ends. The problems are most evident in the various presentations of Luther's stance on the immaculate conception: the authors who tend to see Luther as devoted to Mary present his adherence to the commonly held theory, while those who find that Luther's mind and practice changed concerning Mary present him as eventually rejecting Mary's immaculate conception.[30] Ebneter tries to maintain a more nuanced view, by suggesting that while Luther definitely held to the immaculate conception until the early 1530s, certain statements made after that time call into question his final views on the matter. Robert Lansemann, whose work is relied upon throughout this study, has the merit of being the only author who delves deeper than Luther and Melanchthon to try to discover Lutheran attitudes toward Mary and Marian festivals. He suggests that the christological emphasis in Lutheranism relegated Mary to a low and almost unimportant position, which is based to a large extent on a thorough investigation of sermon collections, polemical tracts, and ecclesiastical ordinances.[31]

Catholic evaluations of Luther's Marian attitude have also vacillated from positive to negative. Stephan Beissel, in his two-volume work on the veneration of Mary in the Christian tradition, cautiously writes that "Luther praises Mary's privileges with a certain warmth, especially in his later writings," but criticizes Luther's rejection of medieval piety.[32] Joseph Lortz, in his famous work *Die Reformation in Deutschland*, suggests that Luther did not renounce the veneration of Mary and the saints, nor did he cease preaching on Marian festivals. The medieval attitude of devotion that Luther maintained was rejected by later Protestants, to their impoverishment.[33] Saturnin Pauleser, in his book *Maria und die Reformation*, indicates that Luther remained a devotee of Mary his entire life, at least in essentials, and even suggests that Luther continued to call Mary *mediatrix*.[34] Ebneter, despite his attempts to present a balanced view of Luther's position on the immaculate conception, fails to consider the context of Luther's statements on the queenship of Mary and insists that Luther maintained a strong Marian devotion throughout his life.

More recent writings in support of the ecumenical movement still tend to suffer, albeit to a lesser extent, from the difficulty of making Luther, Calvin, and others speak directly to contemporary ecumenical issues.[35] Two major documents have been published in the context of Protestant/Catholic dialogue that discuss (among other related issues) the approaches of the major reformers to Mary, as well as the official doctrinal statements of Protestant churches. In France, an interconfessional body of forty theologians (the *Groupe des Dombes*) published a study entitled *Marie dans le dessein de Dieu et la communion des saints*, which as part of its study details both the positive and negative reactions to Mary among the reformers.[36] In the United States, the Lutheran/Catholic dialogue (1983–1990) produced the document *The One Mediator, the Saints, and Mary*, which also includes further essays on the topic. In this last study, Eric Gritsch portrays Luther as a Marian "minimalist" whose positioning of Christology firmly in the center of Christianity determines to a large extent his position on the doctrines concerning Mary.[37] Luther's views on Mary are Lutheran theology in a microcosm: we see law and gospel, unmerited grace over good works, the "hidden" work of God, salvation through faith alone, the authority of Scripture over tradition. While Gritsch presents, to the extent he can, a positive Lutheran view of Mary, David F. Wright is more determinedly Protestant in his evaluation of Luther and the other reformers on the issue of Mary. The Christocentrism of Luther, Zwingli, and Calvin determined their stance toward Mary, while allowing them to see her as an important example of faith and humility. That they maintained Mary's perpetual virginity and, to a certain extent, her sinlessness, shows only their own "limitations" in maintaining beliefs based on speculation rather than Scripture.[38] Heiko Oberman also presents a brief analysis of the reformers' perspectives on Mary to outline the necessity that "a truly catholic and evangelical Mariology is Christology."[39] Peter Meinhold suggests that the reformers did not reject the proper but only the improper veneration of the saints and Mary: they reinstated the "christological character of the veneration of Mary." The fact that the "churches of the Reformation" did not develop a tradition of Marian veneration has to do with other factors, such as a reaction to the increase in Marian piety in Catholicism.[40]

On the Catholic side, William Cole has contributed a long and generally balanced presentation of Luther's views on Mary to the debate, in which he concludes that "only a complex answer is possible" to the question of whether Luther was a devotee of Mary.[41] If one follows a contemporary Catholic notion of devotion to Mary, in certain respects of course Luther falls short: although he wished that Mary be honored, especially as the Mother of God, he denied any suggestion that she is a *mediatrix* or *coredemptrix*. While he encouraged Christians to imitate Mary, he eventually came to reject any invocation to her. That being said, Cole feels that a *description* of Luther's position and various statements is more useful than "an attempt to answer a loaded and unfair question."[42] Georg Söll's article in the *Handbuch der Marienkunde* maintains the traditional Catholic approach that Luther and the other early reformers were more Catholic in their attitudes toward Mary than their followers, which might surprise the readers of today.[43] A major work that takes an ecumenical approach to Mary is George Tavard's *The Thousand Faces of the Virgin Mary*, which treats ecumenism broadly, discussing Mary not only within various stripes of Christianity but also in Judaism, Islam, Hinduism, and Buddhism.[44] His chapter on "Mary in Protestantism" (Anglicanism merits its own chapter) treats Luther, who is painted as retaining a warm piety toward Mary despite his christological orientation; Melanchthon, author of the *Augsburg Confession* and the *Apology;* and Lutheranism, which holds to the *Book of Concord* rather than Luther and has lost both the Marian festivals and Luther's warm piety toward Mary.

Other scholarly attempts to evaluate the position of Luther and the other reformers toward Mary and the saints are few. Several Protestant authors have pointed out that Luther and the other reformers simply were not very interested in Mary as a theological issue, and in light of the volumes of their writings on other topics, this appears to be true.[45] Beyond those theological points that the reformers accepted (the virgin birth, Mary's perpetual virginity, and her title of *Theotokos*) and those few disputed mariological issues (her conception and assumption), the main *theological* interest in Mary was in the context of the *communio sanctorum*. How do the saints relate to the church and to the living Christian community? A number of works address the issue of the saints in the Lutheran Reformation, most notably Robert Kolb's *For All the Saints: Changing Perceptions of Martyrdom and Sainthood in the Lutheran Reformation*.[46] Kolb argues that, although Luther and his followers insisted that Christ is the only mediator with God, and saints do not have power over daily human life, this does not mean that saints and martyrs were excluded from the piety, including the liturgy and hymnody, of sixteenth-century Lutherans. In fact, saints could and did serve as strong models of faith, and many saints' festivals continued to be celebrated in Lutheran churches. Kolb points out in another article that in Lutheran postil sermons we do not find a great deal of fulminating against traditional medieval piety and pious practices: the authors he investigates do not seem "to have perceived the system of the veneration of the saints as a serious contemporary threat within their congregations."[47]

Several articles approach the issue of Mary in the Reformation from the context of late medieval spirituality. Elizabeth Johnson considers Marian doctrine and veneration in late medieval Europe, and concludes briefly that "the first generation of Protestant reformers, all originally Catholic and thus nourished in a spiritual environment that stressed the cult of Mary, did not abandon Marian devotion completely."[48] Rather, they criticized its excesses. It was only in later generations that Marian devotion disappeared, "a casualty of both the new form of evangelical spirituality introduced by the reformers and the continuing polemic with the Roman Catholic Church, which continued to honor Mary with ever-increasing fervor."[49] Peter Brooks considers Luther's response to the cult of Mary in more depth, stressing the development of his ideas over time. He concludes, like many others, that Luther's christocentric theology spelled doom for the medieval veneration of the saints and Mary.[50]

In the vein of what we might call feminist history, numerous authors have considered to what extent the attitude(s) of Luther and other reformers toward Mary, along with other female saints, had an impact, either positive or negative, on women in the sixteenth century. In light of the seminal work of Caroline Walker Bynum on religious symbolism and the saints in the medieval period, one must be extremely careful about assigning a positive or negative impact to changes in symbols and images. Even the effect that such changes have on piety or religious practices is very difficult to measure and interpret. Scholars such as Merry Wiesner and Susan Karant-Nunn have attempted to provide careful analysis and to investigate the changes in the situation of women in the sixteenth century, considering the alteration in the position of Mary as one factor among many. The general conclusion of these authors is that, considering as much information as possible, it seems that the position of women—in society, in law, in the church, in both Catholic and Protestant regions—did decline in the sixteenth century.[51] Wiesner suggests that Luther's views of women are no harsher than those found in medieval authors, but "they are not balanced by praise of the Virgin."[52] Even if, as Wiesner admits, "the [medieval] cult of Mary may have been detrimental to women's actual position," it did at least describe "one woman in totally positive terms."[53]

One final work that deserves mention here is the book by Jaroslav Pelikan on Mary, *Mary Through the Centuries: Her Place in the History of Culture.*[54] Pelikan provides a general history of Mary in Scripture, art, literature, theology, and religious practice, discussing the various strains of Christianity and even how Mary is presented in the Islamic tradition and the Qur'an. In his chapter on Mary in the Reformation, Pelikan emphasizes again that the reformers did not reject all veneration of Mary, but that the position of Mary (and the other saints) had to be adjusted in light of the theological changes introduced into the Reformation churches. This chapter title, "The Model of Faith," indicates what Pelikan thinks is the primary significance of Mary for the reformers.

Pelikan cites the "remarkable collection of texts from Luther, Calvin, Zwingli, and Bullinger" gathered by Walter Tappolet entitled "The Reformers in Praise of Mary."[55] This book documents "the continuing orthodoxy of the Mariology of the Reformers" as well as numerous examples of their continuing veneration of Mary.[56] Although the book does discuss the reformers' "orthodoxy" on theological matters concerning Mary, its title indicates what, in fact, so much of the literature under review here is occupied with: to what extent did Luther (or Calvin or Zwingli) venerate, honor, and praise Mary?[57] However, the question of where Protestant churches stand today in relation to Mariology or the veneration of Mary cannot be answered by attempting to assess the personal piety of the reformers toward Mary, or even their teachings on elements of Mariology. The answers to this question will rely on scholarship that researches both the context of the question and the developments in the various traditions.

The Context: Mary in the Later Medieval Period

The majority of authors in the previous section who address Marian veneration by Luther suggest that as a child and young man, Luther was steeped in the religiosity of the Germany of his day, which to a large extent was dominated by the saints and Mary. Hans Düfel characterizes the veneration of Mary and the saints as the "core of all piety" in the early sixteenth century.[58] In his book on western Christianity of this period, John Bossy paints "traditional" Christianity as intimately involved with the "kith and kin" of Jesus (i.e., Mary, Anne, his other family members, and the remaining saints), which to a large extent came to mirror the social and familial relationships of the time.[59] Mary and the saints were central to the system of merit and the search for salvation that so occupied late medieval Christians. Mary especially was of importance to the church and in the life of medieval Christians: the great cycle of Marian festivals punctuated the liturgical year, while other Marian elements (such as the Magnificat) were integrated into the continuous life and liturgy of the church; extra-liturgical piety and devotion to Mary could be found among Christians of all walks of life. In this section, I will consider the situation of Marian devotion and theology on what has been called the "eve" of the Reformation, and attempt to develop a context for the presentation of Mary by Luther and his followers, many of whom would have been raised in the same saint-saturated Catholic religious culture that was so formative for Luther.

Developments in Theology about Mary

Because the information given about Mary in the New Testament is fairly scanty—her most extensive involvement is in the infancy narrative of Luke, which places her at the center of the drama of the incarnation—Christian theologians have turned to the Jewish scriptures to find foreshadowing and prophecies concerning Mary and also amplified her image (based primarily on the incontrovertible biblical evidence) to meet the needs engendered by theological controversies and developments. Certain early, but apocryphal, texts such as the *Protevangelium of James* of the mid-second century compensate for the lack of biblical information about such important facts as Mary's parentage, her conception, and childhood, and flesh out the gospel stories of the annunciation, and Jesus' birth and childhood. Many elements of these stories, because of their legendary status, were not relied upon in theological arguments, but their impact on piety and devotion should not be underestimated. Compiled in saints' lives such as the popular *Golden Legend* of Jacobus de Voragine (what Bossy calls "a history of salvation in the West in the form of a dictionary of saints")[60] and appearing in various artistic representations, the extra-canonical information about Mary also provided such important details as her inviolate virginity in Christ's birth as well as his conception, and the explanation that the "brothers of Jesus" referred to in the Gospels were sons of Joseph from a previous marriage—both points that became part of the standard theological view.[61]

Much of the Marian theology in the early church was developed in response to christological questions. As with so many important theological developments, patristic Mariology came out of theological conflict—the fights over the borders between orthodoxy and heresy—and most particularly out of the debates over the nature of Christ. Numerous councils were convened to debate christological questions, and Mary's role in anchoring Christ's fully human nature was central. The use of the title *Theotokos* (literally "God-bearer," but usually translated as "Mother of God," *mater dei*, rather than *Deipara*) was the main controversy behind the council at Ephesus (431), which firmly established her role in orthodox Christianity. The council at Chalcedon (451), which reaffirmed the two natures of Christ defined at Ephesus, also affirmed Mary's virginity both *in partu* and *post partum*. Her paradoxical virginity, despite her motherhood, is the strongest Marian theme of these early councils, which has led feminist authors such as Marina Warner to rue that "the cult of Mary is inextricably interwoven with Christian ideas about the dangers of the flesh and their special connection with women."[62] Mary did indeed serve as one model of the Christian ascetic life: as an avowed virgin (already a development from the early texts), she was promoted as a model for female asceticism by a number of early Greek and Latin fathers. Her virginity was also a key element of her role as "second Eve," an important parallel found in Christian writings as early as the second century.

By the later Middle Ages, the period of most concern for this brief sketch, the image of the Virgin was vastly more complex, and was not limited to her relatively passive role in establishing the humanity of Christ. It is also important to note that theological ideas concerning Mary were tied to and influenced by popular piety; for example, the debate over the title *Theotokos* arose because the term was being used in devotion and liturgy. Also important to remember is that those figures who participated in the theological conversation concerning Mary often maintained a strong devotion to the Mother of God. One example can be seen in Anselm, who addressed issues concerning Mary in his *Cur Deus Homo* and in his treatise on "The Virginal Conception and on Original Sin," in which he provided the future justification for the immaculate conception of Mary, although he himself did not hold to it.[63] Anselm was also the author of several very popular Marian prayers: he addresses Mary as the "Mother of Salvation," whose function it is to pray for sinners, and calls Christ the "judge" who would both avenge and pardon sins, while he terms Mary the "Reconciler of the world."[64] Anselm maintains the distinction between Christ, who spares sinners, and Mary, whose role is one of intercession with her son, but stresses the graces and benefits of Mary's "divine motherhood," stemming from her title of *Theotokos* and forming a parallel with the fatherhood of God. The devotion to Mary as queen and patron, so characteristic of medieval piety, is understandable in light of Anselm's portrayal of Mary as the ideal of mercy, along with her powerful role of mother-intercessor, in contrast to the image of Christ as the judge.

What Oberman terms the greatest debate of the late medieval period, that over Mary's immaculate conception, was also to a large extent prompted by popular devotion.[65] It became a burning issue for theologians at least partly because it had been established as a feast in some areas, such as Lyons, which prompted Bernard of Clairvaux (1090–1153) to write to the canons there in opposition to the feast. The feast of Mary's Conception had been celebrated for centuries in the eastern church, and the popular legend of her "miraculous" conception stemming from the *Protevangelium* had also been frequently expressed in art.[66] The first Latin treatise promoting the immaculate conception, by a disciple of Anselm, Eadmer (d. 1124), was written in England most likely on the occasion of the reintroduction of the feast of Mary's Conception at the abbey of Bury St. Edmund's—the feast had been celebrated by the Saxons, but abolished after the Norman invasion.[67] Eadmer follows Anselm in arguing that the immaculate conception was fitting for the Mother of God, but also argues along lines later used by the Franciscans: "[God] certainly was able [*potuit*] to do it and He willed it [*voluit*]; if, therefore, He willed it, He did it [*fecit*]."[68] It was also around this time, or somewhat earlier, that new Marian hymns and prayers came into common usage: the *Salve Regina*, the *Alma Redemptoris Mater*, and most especially the *Ave Maria*. This prayer, which had appeared in briefer form in the East from at least 600, quickly became popular for both personal devotion and liturgical use. For example, in 1095, Pope Urban II ordered its use on Saturdays by both regular and secular clergy to gain Mary's assistance with the first crusade.[69]

In the thirteenth century, the debate over Mary's conception became more heated. Peter Lombard (d. 1160), in his highly influential and widely read *Sentences*, had rejected the immaculate conception in favor of a purification of Mary from sin at the incarnation. Even the *Mariale super missus est*, mistakenly attributed until recently to Albert, which otherwise is full of praise for Mary and even calls her "the helper of redemption through her compassion," which became a generally accepted mariological doctrine, denies the immaculate conception and instead holds the more commonly accepted view that Mary was sanctified in the womb at some point after conception.[70] Thomas Aquinas objected to the immaculate conception on the grounds that she could not have been purified from sin until animation, and then her purification was still redemption through Christ, although he taught, following the Augustinian tradition, that Mary was free from actual sin of any kind.[71] Near the end of the century, however, the Franciscan theologians William of Ware and, slightly later, his student Duns Scotus headed a strong defense of the immaculate conception, and inaugurated a bitter and long-lasting debate between Franciscans and Dominicans over this issue. William stressed Eadmer's axiom and argued for the preservation of Mary from any taint of sin, rejecting the notion that this would limit the universality of Christ's redemption, because "[Mary] needed the passion of Christ not because of the sin that was in her, but of that which would have been in her, if her Son himself had not preserved her through faith."[72] Duns Scotus developed and systematized this view, insisting that, as Christ would want to give his mother the most perfect redemption, he would choose to preserve her from sin rather than purify her from it.[73]

The debate over the conception of Mary continued unabated into the fifteenth century. The council of Basel (1431–49) considered the question, declaring in favor of the feast and the doctrine in 1438, but because the council had been officially dissolved by the pope several months earlier, this resolution had no legal authority within the church. Heiko Oberman points out that the debate continued so strongly that further discussion of the issue was forbidden by the pope "on pain of excommunication," first in 1482, and again in 1483 and 1503.[74] Theologians of this period of course continued to debate and write on the matter;[75] for example, Gabriel Biel accepted the Scotistic argument of perfection, and in addition asserted Mary's eternal predestination, which, Oberman notes, "helps to solve the problem that Christ would have honored Mary by preserving her from original sin before she had actually given birth to him."[76] Because Biel did not find these arguments in themselves completely convincing, he rested on the authority of church tradition, which he considered decisive, despite the unofficial nature of the Basel resolution, to support the doctrine.

Biel's writings also provide a good example of common mariological principles accepted by many theologians in the fifteenth century. Biel applied three "mariological rules" when discussing Mary in his sermons (which, Oberman points out, are not as careful to stress Mary's dependence on Christ as his other theological writings): the "superlative rule," or *regula convenientiae*, accords the highest possible privileges to the Virgin, with the condition that they cannot contradict Scripture or tradition; the "comparative rule," the *regula comparationis*, gives Mary a place second only to God, seen in the distinction between forms of worship due only to God (*latria*) and that due to Mary (*hyperdulia*) and the saints (*dulia*); the rule of "similitude with Christ," the *regula similitudinis*, stresses Mary's cooperation with Christ through her humility.[77] When used to describe her "heavenly status," these rules and her eternal predestination led Biel to accord Mary the titles of "*Coredemptrix, Mediatrix,* almost *Concreatrix,* and as we will have to conclude finally—to *Maria Spes Omnium*."[78] As *coredemptrix*, Mary, by her bond with Christ, is the mother of all saints, and therefore the church. She cooperates with Christ through her humility and maternity in the incarnation, and with her compassion in his sacrifice. Her role as the Queen of Heaven at the right hand of Christ allows her continual intercession with her son: "as mediatrix to the mediator she completes the work of salvation, she pleads the case of mankind and balances by her *misericordia* the *iustitia* of her Son."[79] In fact, Mary represents for medieval Christians the virtue of mercy detached from justice: as Caroline Walker Bynum suggests, "in keeping with the medieval view that women were above and below reason, [Mary] saves her loyal favorites, even if they fail to meet the standards of contrition and penance."[80]

We find that Mary holds a larger significance for human salvation than simply through her compassion with Christ. Her bodily assumption is an even greater guarantee for sinners that they can be saved, for while Christ is the God-Man, he is not "pure man" in the way that Mary is, and thus his ascension into heaven is not as representative for sinners. By thus contrasting Mary with Christ, her "pure nature" works to "define her position as the object of *fiducia* and hope of the world. . . . She represents love and pity in contrast to the severity of Christ the judge."[81] She is the hope of the *viator* not only in her preservation but especially as an example of the individual's means to heaven. Through her humility Mary received God's grace; the sinner also must do his best to attract God's grace, and his merits also depend on divine acceptation. For Biel and the medieval Christian generally, "in life and word [Mary] reveals the will of God; she is at once the example to be imitated and the staircase to be climbed [to Christ]."[82]

Medieval Piety and Mary's Presence in the Life of the Church

As has already been seen in the previous section, it is highly artificial to separate piety and theology when discussing Mary in the medieval church. Pious practices and liturgical events often preceded and influenced theological speculation or acceptance, and even ideas about Mary's titles and privileges often sprang from popular usages or worship. Theologians who might be concerned in treatises to defend or reject subtle differences of principle or doctrine often wrote highly devotional prayers, promoted popular devotions such as the rosary, and preached about both Marian doctrine and piety. Even the debate over the immaculate conception arose from and often reacted against popular practice and celebrations, although as a scholastic debate it had only limited effect on popular piety. In this section I will consider the liturgical and paraliturgical aspects of Marian devotion, as well as other popular devotions that characterize late medieval Christianity.

At the beginning of the sixteenth century, according to Robert Scribner, one of the most common ways in which people at all levels of society and in all walks of life experienced religion was as ritual practice. There were rituals to celebrate rites of passage, such as birth, marriage, and death, and the annual cycle of ritual that formed the church year.[83] The church's calendar begins at Advent, the four-week period that culminates in Christmas/Epiphany, while the next great sequence of feasts celebrates Christ's passion and resurrection, with the forty-day preparation period of Lent. The third stage is from Easter through Ascension, Pentecost, Trinity Sunday, and finally to the feast of Corpus Christi. This half-yearly cycle, known as the *Herrenjahr* (year of our Lord), is often called the festival half of the church year. A second kind of liturgical celebration, the saint's feast, is celebrated throughout the year, including the seven great feasts of the Virgin: Purification (February 2), Annunciation (March 25), Visitation (July 2), Assumption (August 15), Birth (September 8), Presentation in the Temple (November 21), and Conception (December 8).[84] These Marian feasts (along with the great feasts of Christ, and several other saint's festivals) were celebrated as solemn (full-day), obligatory feasts. These festivals would normally have begun on the prior evening with vespers and a vigil, and the singing of the *Salve*, which, Scribner notes, was a "form of popular devotion to the Virgin which had grown up outside the formal liturgy, and which consisted of singing the Marian antiphon *Salve regina* followed by a versicle and an oration."[85] The feast day itself included several masses (with a sermon) and numerous processions within and often outside the church, with the carrying of monstrances and relics, and would conclude with another vespers and a *Salve*, and finally matins sung at midnight. Even regular Sundays and lesser feasts included processions, the singing of the *Salve*, and various exorcisms and blessings (especially of holy water).

These festival and Sunday celebrations are what Scribner terms the "official" aspect of ritual, that is, "that which any churchman or theologian would unhesitatingly have recognised as the 'correct' form of worship."[86] This description, however, only outlines the "skeleton of religious ritual life," for it does not recognize the more popular and "complex body of observances," which would include *functiones sacrae* ("sacred performances") that dramatized events of Christ's life, death, and resurrection, and what Scribner calls "magical ritual," that is, the use of ritual or ritual/devotional objects for magical, protective purposes.[87] One example is the candles blessed on the festival of Mary's Purification, which were intended for use as devotional objects but were also thought to be useful as protective magic, especially for women in childbirth, to keep away evil spirits.[88] These "popular" practices had a complementary relationship with the official liturgy, even if they were often only tolerated by church officials, and occasionally were specifically condemned.

Alongside of these "paraliturgical" forms, we should also remember that religious life of the late Middle Ages would also often have included membership in confraternities (in the fifteenth century confraternities dedicated to the rosary were popular, and in the later sixteenth century these were often founded specifically for devotion to the Virgin),[89] pilgrimages to shrines or holy places, belief in miracles and apparitions, and other participation in the cults of various saints. Many of these practices and devotions were encouraged by the church, and, as Bernd Moeller points out, much of the "religious spirit" of the fifteenth century was contained within the bounds of the church: heresy had in essence died away in this period, and Christians were more interested in gaining access to the church's "treasury of salvation" than in attempting to find salvation elsewhere.[90]

Along with the liturgical and paraliturgical aspects of late medieval Christianity, in which Mary and the saints played a major role, we must consider the more personal, even mystical, devotion to Mary, and the development of her titles and privileges. In her book *Jesus as Mother: Studies in the Spirituality of the High Middle Ages*, Caroline Walker Bynum suggests that in the eleventh and twelfth centuries there was an outburst of mystical theology, and an increase in devotion to female figures and use of female metaphors. This shift in piety, from a more removed God, and Christ as a "judge and king" with Mary as his queen, to a more human Christ and a more motherly Mary (often pictured with a baby on her lap), was occasioned by basic changes in concepts of church, clergy, and the apostolic life (e.g., the rise of the mendicant orders).[91] With the emphasis on Christ's humanity, the image of Mary as his [human] mother increased in importance, although her image as the Queen of Heaven remained powerful. As a mother, Mary was seen as highly approachable, and the imagery associated with motherhood—nurturing, protecting, and feeding— became very popular, especially with male mystics.[92] Mary was also seen as the bride of Christ, and the lover of the Song of Songs, and in this connection was specifically associated with the church, whose union with Christ was often expressed in passionate or even erotic language. Female mystics tended to use bridal imagery to express their union with Christ, as well as motherly images.[93] Bernard especially used bridal language to express the soul's union with Christ, and his devotion to Mary as mother, bride, and queen became characteristic of his order, the Cistercians, who helped to spread the cult of devotion to the Virgin throughout Europe from the twelfth century.

One of the most popular forms of devotion to Mary, especially among the laity, was the rosary, which in its earliest forms stems from the twelfth century. Based upon the *Ave Maria*, which by this time included both the angel's salutation to Mary and Elizabeth's greeting, the early rosary devotion mimicked the 150 psalms of the Divine Office and was called the "Psalter of Our Lady."[94] The repeated words of the prayer were believed to weave a garland of roses for Mary, and the term "rosary" derives from *Rosencranz*. The rosary as it developed into its most popular form included meditations upon the lives of Christ and Mary, usually divided into fifteen mysteries (joyful, sorrowful, and glorious). It spawned a large body of literature, including legends, exempla, poems, and songs, and also had a great impact in the visual arts. One proof of its popularity is that the confraternity dedicated to the rosary, founded in 1475 at Cologne, had close to one million members on the eve of the Reformation.[95]

In the late medieval period, devotion to Mary came especially under the rubric of the sorrowing mother, the *Mater Dolorosa*. Several mendicant orders were instituted particularly for devotion to the Virgin, and the Servites of Mary, founded in the late thirteenth century, had for their special devotion the sorrows of Mary. Out of this order came a number of Marian offices developed from the hymn *Stabat Mater*, the *Planctus Mariae*, and the numerous *Marienklagen* ("Laments of Mary") so popular in this period. Mary's sorrows, fixed by this time at seven, included Simeon's prophecy of the sword, the flight into Egypt, the loss of Jesus in the temple, Jesus' arrest and trial, his crucifixion and death, the placement of her dead son in her arms, and their separation at his burial (sometimes these last two were collapsed, and the seventh became her sorrowful waiting after his burial).[96]

Mary as the *Mater Dolorosa* remained a powerful image throughout the later medieval period: in a time when there was an intense focus on death and a popular literary form was the *ars moriendi*, Mary's role at the death of the Christian was also emphasized. John Geiler of Keisersberg, a popular and influential preacher in Strassburg from 1478 until his death in 1510, in his *Das Schiff des Heils* (1501–1502) speaks of Mary as the "*kahn*" of this ship of salvation, that is, the small boat or canoe that the sailors use to move between the boat and the shore, and to load and unload all the wares and passengers. Mary is thus responsible for leading us "finally, after the difficult journey through the sea of this life, securely into the harbor of blessed eternity."[97] Mary is not only the one who has brought us the "Bread of Heaven" (i.e., Christ) that nourishes us upon the journey, she has also saved (*gerettet*) many who through doubt or other heavy sins had left the "ship of penance and the Christian life," for she is the "mother of mercy and a haven for all sinners who turn to her in trust."[98] For those guilty sinners who cannot expect anything from the righteous God, their pleas to Mother Mary cannot fail. For Mary is also the Queen of Heaven: her death and assumption into heaven, that is, the release of the boat from the ship and its safe arrival (with its pilgrims) at the shores of the new Jerusalem, is what places Mary in a position of power to help us through her intercession with her son. Thus, it is through her intercession and her merit that "we also arrive at the shores of the heavenly Jerusalem."[99]

Moving a step closer to Luther, we find in the *Himmlische Fundgrube* of the Augustinian Johann von Paltz a collection and expansion of homiletic material on the passion of Christ (including a *Sterbebüchlein*), with a special focus on the *mitleiden* or co-suffering of Mary at the cross.[100]Along with meditations on the five wounds of Christ, the blows that were given to him, and the words he spoke on the cross, Paltz devotes a special section to the *klein evangelium* (John 29:25–27), which recounts that Mary, her sisters, and John stood under the cross, and that Jesus recommended Mary and John to each other.[101] This text should be "carried in the heart of each Christian," according to Paltz, for it is at the cross of Christ that we find salvation.[102]And it is Mary who will help us find the cross, and support us through the suffering we experience there. Paltz paints Mary, standing at the "tree of suffering [*peinlichkeit*]," as the opposite of Eve, who stood by the "forbidden tree of [sensual] pleasure [*wollustigkeit*]," and recommends that we pray to Mary: "O Mary, most faithful mother, deliver us from the first mother, who stood by the forbidden tree. Draw us to you under the cross, where we cannot be deceived by the infernal serpent."[103] In his *Sterbebüchlein*, Paltz suggests that, in our hour of need, we pray to Christ that our sins might not be counted against us, and pray to Mary that she not see our great unworthiness, but come to help us: "I ask you through your eternal election, your holy conception, and your *kreuzstehung*, come to help me at my final end."[104] It is because of her faithful, willing suffering with Christ at the cross, her *kreuzstehung*, that she stands for us as an intercessor with Christ, and a helper in our time of need.

In Paltz's work, we see probably the most elemental aspect of late medieval Marian piety and devotion: although it is Christ whose sacrifice saves Christians, it is Mary who brings them to Christ and the salvation he provides. For Mary, the humble maiden, the gentle mother of the baby Jesus, the fully human, suffering mother who watched her innocent son die, is their nearest connection to the divine, even closer to them than Christ, who is the God-Man. Because of her relationship to her son, who is God, and because of her personal merits and faithfulness (shown in her *fiat* at the incarnation and her co-suffering with Christ under the cross), Mary also has power in heaven to intercede for sinners with Christ. Her power to aid in human salvation tied with her human motherly love and mercy are what made Mary the focus of such intense devotion in the later Middle Ages.

The Image of Mary: How Do Religious Symbols *Mean*?

After addressing the questions of method, context, and previous literature, it is important to situate this study within the discussion of religious symbols, what meanings they can have, and how the various participants in symbol production and usage experience symbols differently, especially those symbols that bring issues of gender to the fore, as Mary so often does. This section will be necessarily brief, although the theoretical literature on religious symbols, often drawn from the field of anthropology, is vast. Much of this literature has been influenced by the theories of Clifford Geertz, Victor Turner, and Paul Ricoeur, which will provide a convenient means of limiting the discussion.[105]

Caroline Walker Bynum, in her essay "The Complexity of Symbols," argues that "religious symbols point men and women beyond their ordinary lives," helping to give meaning to ordinary existence.[106]She draws upon an insight of Ricoeur, that a religious symbol is never merely "a sign of or statement about social structure."[107] It does not simply describe social order, or propose how things should be. Religious symbols are "polysemic," to use Turner's phrase, and possess a multiplicity of meanings.[108] Bynum critiques Geertz's theory that closely associates a symbol with that which it signifies: "to Geertz, religious symbols . . . give meaning to existence by providing a model of the world as it is and a model for the world as it ought to be—a template that shapes ordinary experience by reflecting it and, in the process, imparts value from beyond it."[109] While Geertz sees symbols as "historically created vehicles," Ricoeur, by contrast, theorizes that the symbol in some sense precedes meaning, rather than simply pointing to some already existent meaning: for example, "water may signify (i.e., point to) cleanliness, but it will never 'mean' cleanliness. For cleanliness itself will point to absence of or freedom from something else, something palpable and real but not communicable in a single word."[110] Bynum prefers Ricoeur's model, which allows room for the notion that "those with different gender experiences will appropriate symbols in different ways," an important element in much of her work.[111]

This insight, that men and women experience religious symbols and rituals differently, is the means by which Bynum critiques both Geertz and Turner. In contrast to Geertz's notion of how gender symbols function (i.e., mirroring the world of men and women, and presenting an ideal), Bynum finds that many gendered religious symbols are both about and not about gender—they have multiple and not mutually exclusive meanings. Turner discusses the usage of symbols, especially in rituals, as a process of movement from social integration, through crisis, to a reintegration, a process that Bynum finds fits very well with the experiences of men (e.g., male saints in the late medieval period, such as Francis), but is less adequate to explain female religious experiences and women's ways of talking about and symbolizing experience or self-understanding.[112] However, Turner and Ricoeur do agree on several aspects of symbols: they have a "capacity to refer simultaneously to many levels of human experience," and they allow "users to appropriate that to which the symbol points."[113]

Beyond the theory that religious symbols are polysemic, and the fact that men and women seem to experience such symbols (including rituals) differently, Bynum offers a suggestion highly relevant to this study of images of the Virgin Mary: "Gender-related symbols, in their full complexity, may refer to gender in ways that affirm or reverse it, support or question it; or they may, in their basic meaning, have little at all to do with male and female roles."[114] Gender-related symbols are "sometimes 'about' values other than gender," but, Bynum cautions, "all symbols arise out of the experience of 'gendered' users. It is not possible ever to ask, How does a symbol—*any* symbol—mean? without asking, For whom does it mean?"[115]

In light of these conclusions, we can begin to assess the significance, as well as the limitations, of this study's topic. What does it mean to say this book is a study of the images of the Virgin Mary in Lutheran sermons of the sixteenth century? First, the "images" are not visual or ritual-based, but are rather textual. Second, they are images presented by literate male clerics, presenting male viewpoints, in the context of a male-dominated society and tradition. One should not assume that Lutheran women (or laymen, especially of other classes) would or did talk about Mary in the same way. Third, these images of Mary are presented in dialogue with the medieval traditions concerning Mary, affirming some aspects, rejecting or even ignoring others, but are especially designed to teach and to explicate the texts of sacred Scripture. In Geertz's terms, the images of Mary in these sermons help to provide a "model of" the world as it is, that is, what is "natural," at least in the eyes of Lutheran preachers, as well as a "model for" the world as these preachers think it should be.[116] Fourth, these sermons, with their various images of Mary, were presented to a disparate crowd of people, men and women, young and old, married and unmarried, city dweller and rural inhabitant. However, we cannot presume to know from these texts how the audience experienced or appropriated the images of Mary presented to them. Finally, the images presented in the following six chapters are gleaned from many texts and authors, separated by space and time, but joined by a common adherence to Lutheran theology and principles, although even that is occasionally various. One cannot speak of "a symbol" of Mary that emerges from sixteenth-century Lutheran sermons, unless the definition of "symbol" includes the notion of multiplicity. One cannot even simply assume that because the Virgin Mary is a female symbol, her significance is always related to her female gender—it often is not. However, to ignore the issue of gender when discussing Mary and how she is presented (by men, and often specifically to women) would be to miss much of the complexity present in her image.

Overview of the Chapters

Each chapter in this study deals with sermons on a text or series of texts from the gospels in which Mary plays a role. The sermons are drawn primarily from published postils of Lutheran clergymen, although occasionally individually printed sermons have been used. The one exception is Luther's treatise on the Magnificat, which, although not a sermon, is important for understanding Luther's views on Mary and was influential on his followers. The earliest sermons used in this study originated in the 1520s, primarily in Luther's early postils, while the latest sermons were preached around 1580, at the time the Book of Concord, the official Lutheran confessions, was completed and accepted by most Lutheran churches. Some of these later sermon collections, such as those by Mörlin and Spangenberg, were not first published until after this date, but attempts have been made to use the date as a convenient terminus ad quem. Thus, two to three generations of Lutherans are included in the study, and we can more easily discover what continuities exist between the preceding tradition and Lutheran preaching, as well as what has changed. Many of the changes between the early devotional attitude toward Mary characteristic of Luther and what might today be thought of as a traditionally Protestant, deemphasized view of Mary happened in the sixteenth century and can be traced through the sermons across this period. In addition, I have attempted in this research to consult every printed Lutheran sermon collection from the period

1520–1580, and while there are certainly some extant texts that have been missed, the sermons here represent the great majority of Lutheran sermons published.

The sermons relied upon in this study can be divided into several categories. First, there are sermons on the traditional gospel readings for important Marian festivals, such as the Annunciation, Candlemas/Purification, and the Visitation. These three festivals in particular were retained after the Reformation in Lutheran areas, and preachers continued to give sermons on these texts throughout the period chosen for this study. Second, there are numerous sermons on other texts in which Mary plays a significant role, but are not special holidays, such as Luke 2:41–52 (the loss of Jesus in the temple) and John 2:1–11 (the wedding at Cana). Third, sermons on a number of holidays dedicated to Christ often mention Mary, who appears in the gospel narrative, such as Christmas, Epiphany, Innocents, and the Passion (i.e., Jesus' words on the cross). Finally, there are sermons on several holidays that were important in the late medieval church but were eventually rejected by the reformers, usually because of their lack of biblical basis, such as Mary's Conception and Birth, and her Assumption. Several sermons by Luther and a few colleagues were published for these festivals, so some comparison can be made with the previous tradition.

For the purposes of comparison with the later medieval tradition, each chapter also presents some material from the sermons of John Geiler (d. 1510), mentioned earlier as an important and influential preacher in the city of Strassburg who immediately preceded Luther. Geiler, besides his popularity as a preacher and even as a critic of the religious life of both clergy and laity, had a wider impact, both through his publications and through his personal and political connections (e.g., as a chaplain to the emperor Maximilian).[117] Geiler had taught at the universities in Basel and Freiburg am Breisgau, and was active in intellectual humanist circles. His sermons appeared in various editions in both Latin and German, but because he preached primarily in German, the sermons used in this study have been taken from his German postils, his *Das euangeli buch* (1515) and the 1522 version of his *Postill: Uber die fyer Euangelia durchs jor, sampt dem quadragesimal, vnnd von etlichen Heyligen.*

The first three chapters deal with sermons for the three great Marian festivals maintained in Lutheran churches: Annunciation, Visitation, and Purification. Chapter 1 presents some common themes found in Lutheran sermons on the Annunciation: responses to perceived Catholic threats and criticisms, especially on Luther's new translation of *gratia plena* in the angel's address to Mary, which emphasizes a passive rather than an active role for her; the traditional parallel between Eve and Mary; the importance of Mary and her sinless body for Christology; and Mary as a model for believers. For Lutheran pastors, sermons provided an important opportunity for instruction, especially moral instruction, and thus Mary, along with most other figures who appear in the gospel texts, is frequently used as an exemplar for Christians. In the Annunciation sermons, her piety, chastity, and humility are held up as model virtues, and her obedience despite her lack of understanding is highly praised. In another common thread that runs through many of the sermons on all the texts, Mary serves as a special role model for women and girls, which allows the pastors to promote a highly patriarchal and domesticating view of women's roles.

In chapter 2, considering sermons on Mary's visit to Elizabeth, we find an even greater emphasis on Mary as a role model for women, along with the importance of the Magnificat as a statement of faith. This meeting between Elizabeth and Mary, and John and Jesus in utero, and occasionally also including Zechariah, is frequently characterized as the first council of the church and the first preaching of the incarnation. The fact that Mary is this preacher makes her a doctor of the church and a prophet, but because of her uniqueness as the *Theotokos* she does not serve as a model for women to preach, and because of her humility she does not try to leave her vocation of housewife and mother. Instead, Lutheran preachers use her example to emphasize their rejection of the notion that a convent or monastery provides a higher way of life and to encourage their listeners to remain happily in their given social calling. They especially encourage girls to protect both their reputation and their virginity through good and careful behavior, portraying the opposites of Mary, the good girl, and the Old Testament Dinah, the girl who falls into trouble.

Sermons on the festival of Mary's Purification, or Candlemas, discussed in chapter 3, present several interesting themes related to Mary. Most important, many sermons address the rituals of churching for women after childbirth, and other customs surrounding childbirth and postpartum recovery. The reformers and their followers rejected what they saw as superstitious elements in churching (e.g., blessed candles) and in social practices relating to parturient women. Mary's obedience in following the Jewish law despite her freedom from it is often commented upon in these sermons. This chapter also considers sermons on the text immediately following the purification in Luke, which deal with the prophecy of Simeon and the example of the aged prophetess Anna. The image of the "sword" of Simeon, immensely important throughout the tradition, allows Lutheran preachers to stress Mary as a type of the church, suffering under the cross of Christ. This theme is taken in a new direction, however, for many sermons move from Mary to the church, to all Christians, finally deemphasizing Mary in favor of stressing the grieving of the community of Christians. This text also includes the prophetic figure of Anna, who causes some initial difficulties for Lutheran preachers, but is also made to fit the mold of the pious and domesticated female.

Chapters 4 and 5 present sermons on texts that were not associated with particular holidays: the loss of the twelve-year-old Jesus in the temple, and the wedding at Cana. The first text provided a special opportunity for Lutheran preachers to address a favorite topic, the values and importance of families, with a stress on the duties of parents and the obedience of children. The following text, although not strictly about marriage, was usually presented in the context of a mini-treatise on marriage and the married life, rejecting especially the Catholic evaluation of marriage as a lesser good than a life of celibacy. Both of these texts present Mary in a somewhat ambiguous light and give us the opportunity to evaluate certain changes in the presentation of Mary across this time period: the later preachers are much more willing to criticize Mary and to suggest that she erred, or even sinned, in some of her behavior.

Chapter 6 includes the remaining sermons that consider Mary, both from the gospel texts for the infancy narratives and from the Marian holidays that were eventually dropped from the Lutheran calendars. In Christmas sermons, Mary serves in a traditional fashion as the guarantor of Christ's humanity: it is in this context that Mary is affirmed as the *Theotokos*. Lutherans were concerned to emphasize their orthodoxy on this point. The obedience of Mary and Joseph to the emperor's decree is also praised, while preachers encourage their audience to obey temporal authorities. The difficulties and poverty encountered by Mary, Joseph, and Jesus is another common theme, which also can be found in sermons concerning the family's flight to Egypt. On the holiday of Epiphany, Mary is only infrequently mentioned, and in sermons on the text of Christ's circumcision she plays virtually no role. In sermons considering Christ's passion, often found in the popular *Passionals*, pamphlets containing sermons or meditations on the passion, Mary again plays a significant role in the segments that deal with Christ's seven words on the cross. In the medieval period, as we have seen, the sorrowing mother under the cross was a powerful and widely honored image, and some of this emphasis on Mary under the cross can be found in Lutheran sermons. The preachers stress that, although she suffered great pain and sorrow, she is a shining example of patience, constant faith, and fortitude. She is also held up as an image of the church, which, because Christ commended Mary to the care of his disciple, obviously is weak and powerless, and needs the care of all Christians, but especially pastors and secular authorities. Another very popular theme that stems from Christ's words to Mary and John is the fulfillment of the fourth commandment and a stress on family values.

The final sermons considered in chapter 6, on the holidays of Mary's Conception, Birth, and Assumption, are few. Beyond sermons by Luther, there are only a small number of other published Lutheran sermons to compare. The sermons tend to criticize Catholics and those who celebrate these holidays because the events that they celebrate are not attested by Scripture. The gospel texts read on these days have, for the most part, little to do with Mary. Those Lutheran sermons that do consider Mary stress that she is blessed because of her faith, not her physical connection to Christ. The preachers cautiously allow devotion to Mary, but insist that she is not a mediator or intercessor, and seem generally uncomfortable with what they consider the excessive praise and devotion given to the Virgin before the Reformation, and which sometimes they condemn as continuing within their own regions (at least among Catholics, if not among Protestants).

The concluding chapter draws together the common themes found in the various sermons and attempts to assemble a more complete picture of the "Lutheran Mary," considering the changes and developments throughout the sixteenth century. It clarifies both what the Lutheran view of Mary had in common with the preceding tradition and how certain traditional elements were changed or rejected as the century progressed. It also considers the image of Mary in a more social and normative context, what the Christian man and woman were supposed to learn from her example, and how Mary was used to support and model the preachers' image of the ideal woman, wife, and mother. Based on the evidence presented in the main chapters, the conclusion argues that while Lutheran preachers strive to remain orthodox, especially accepting the statements of the early church councils, they transform the traditional image of Mary: she no longer serves as the powerful Queen of Heaven, but is only held up and praised as a meek, pious, chaste, and obedient girl. Because of the theological changes inaugurated by Luther and the social conservatism of the Lutheran clergy, Mary could no longer be portrayed as an active figure, but rather must serve as a passive representative of the faithful Christian.

I

The Annunciation

"And now, you will conceive in your womb and bear a son, and you will name him Jesus. He will be great, and will be called the Son of the Most High, and the Lord God will give to him the throne of his ancestor David."[1] The angel's prophecy to Mary of Christ's incarnation is a focal point of the Christian gospel, a text that provides Christians the basis of their belief in human salvation through the advent of God's son. It is also a source of conflict within the Christian community, in that it brings a human being, a woman, into a pivotal role in salvation history. How should one think of Mary? What pride of place is to be given her? Interpreters have read this text to make of Mary a powerful mother-goddess in her own right, and conversely to lower her to a mere passive vessel. But even Protestants, who have tended to diminish the role and importance of Mary in the tradition and life of the church, must admit when faced with this text that Mary was and is in a special position, at the nexus of the divine and the human that Christians view as the incarnation of God. Her uniqueness is relevant not only to dogma but also to Christians' self-perception, to issues of faith but also to cultural markers such as gender. This chapter will explore how these issues were handled by Lutheran preachers in the sixteenth century, and how the image of Mary from the Annunciation text was delineated, received, and manipulated by a variety of authors, each one writing in his own particular context but part of a larger Lutheran tradition.

The festival of the Annunciation is one of the great Marian holidays of the church year: its authenticity and importance were recognized in all of the main Lutheran ecclesiastical constitutions (*Kirchenordnungen*) of the sixteenth century by maintaining the holiday as a full-day festival.[2] There were hymns and collects written for the liturgical celebrations, and even appropriate older Catholic hymns were included in Lutheran hymnbooks for the festival.[3] This is not to suggest, however, that Mary was always the focal point of the festivities. In fact, as Robert Lansemann points out in his important study on saints' days in the Reformation, the title of the festival frequently given in the church constitutions and sermon collections was *Conceptionis Christi* or *Empfängnis Christi* ("the Conception of Christ").[4] Rather than a Marian holiday, it appears that the Annunciation was often celebrated as a *Herrenfest*, or festival of the Lord, especially because of its importance for Christology. In the Lutheran postils examined in this study, we find an occasional sermon in which Mary is not even mentioned. This omission is not true for the majority of postils, however, and most Lutheran preachers continued to find in Mary a profitable example as well as a necessary topic in preaching upon this gospel lesson.

The gospel narrative itself revolves around the visit of an angel messenger to Mary, who, we are told, lived in Nazareth in Galilee, and was engaged to a man named Joseph, of the house of David. The angel, Gabriel, addressed Mary with a message from God, that she would conceive and bear a son whom she should name Jesus. Mary, quite naturally, wondered how this could be possible, since she was a virgin, but the angel assured her that the child would be sent from God, and she would conceive through the Holy Spirit. In proof of God's ability to produce such miracles, Mary was told that her elderly relative Elizabeth was also pregnant. Mary's response to the angel's message assured for her the admiration and praise of following generations of Christians: "Here am I, the servant of the Lord; let it be with me according to your word."[5] Upon hearing her assent, the angel departed.

The focus of the text is upon Mary's interchange with the angel. She is described in the modern translation as perplexed, pondering what the angel's greeting could mean. In the text of sixteenth-century Lutheran interpreters, she was "frightened" or "terrified" over the angel's speech (*erschrack sie uber seiner rede*). Her mental and emotional state had been a favorite topic of medieval interpreters: Bernard of Clairvaux stressed that she was troubled by her strange visitor, as is usual for virgins, who are always timid and on guard, but not distressed, which shows her courage.[6] John Geiler of Keisersberg suggests that Mary was not frightened by the angel, for she was accustomed to them. Rather, she was disturbed by his greeting, since she was a very humble girl.[7] She was also concerned how she could bear a child, since she was a virgin and wanted to remain one. The angel was able to assure her, according to Geiler, that she would remain a virgin both in the conception and during the birth of her son.[8] The exaltation of Mary's virginity in the sermons of Geiler and other medieval preachers does not find a strong echo in Lutheran sermons, but it is still present, in light of its purported preservation of Christ from original sin: "Everything which comes from a fleshly conception is impure, therefore Christ was born of a virgin."[9] The fact of her engagement to Joseph is seen as a welcome corrective to the Roman Catholic emphasis on virginity, in that God obviously wanted to honor the estate of marriage through Mary as well.

The themes that arise in the sermons of sixteenth-century Lutheran preachers from the text of the Annunciation are, for the most part, unsurprising. There are responses to perceived Catholic errors or threats: the prayer of the *Ave Maria* comes in for special attention in this regard. Several traditional themes receive a great deal of attention, such as the comparison of Mary with Eve, which provides insight into the importance of Mary's role in the Lutheran understanding of the history of salvation. The date traditionally accepted for this holiday, March 25, is shown to have a special place in salvation history, which points to an abiding interest in numbers, dates, and years that characterizes the period.[10] The christological importance of this day and event is stressed in all of the sermons, although it is not so much Mary as it is her body that generates most of the interest in the discussions of Christ's person.

Beyond these recurring themes, Mary comes to life most fully for her sixteenth-century Lutheran interpreters as an example of the faithful believer, a model for both men and women. She represents the Lutheran virtue of Christian faith over the "worldly" virtue of human reason, which in an age of increasing insistence upon acceptance of orthodox belief without questioning was a most highly touted quality. Many of the sermon writers under investigation also do not miss this opportunity to stress Mary's piety, chastity, and humility, in some cases particularly to their female audience, and in others to hearers and readers of both genders, all of whom they thought could profit from increased obedience, humility, and faith. Mary is seen not so much as the model believer—only Nicholas Selneccer and Georg Major explicitly mention her as a type of the church—but as a fruitful model *for* believers, whose real importance lies in her role in bringing Christ into the world.[11] For most of the Lutheran preachers of the sixteenth century, Mary recedes into the background of the "christological moment" taking place in this gospel.

Luther's Sermons on the Annunciation

"This is a happy and charming gospel, . . . for we will hear how the Virgin Mary had such a high faith, the equal of which we have not often found in the Scriptures."[12] For Luther, Mary exemplifies the newly "rediscovered" doctrine of faith alone, and it is in light of her faith that she is such a powerful figure. Her example should stimulate everyone to greater faith, for although this gospel provides an important lesson about the Christ who fulfills scriptural prophecies, it is also an exhortation to faith. In the sermon found in Roth's *Festpostille* of 1527 (preached in 1522), Luther insists that in fact this gospel is all about faith, its character and its manner, and we are shown through this story that faith can only be based on the "naked word of God."[13] The majority of the sermon deals with questions surrounding faith, its nature, and its relation to works, and does not address any questions concerning the incarnation and the person of Christ, a problem that comes to the fore for the next generation of Lutherans.

Mary's response to the angel reveals the essence of faith. Echoing Geiler, Luther insists that it was not easy for her to believe the angel's message that she, a virgin, would conceive a child. Even more, that she should remain an "uncorrupted" virgin: "That is a high and excellent faith, to become a mother and remain an uncorrupted virgin, that truly surpasses sense, thought, and all human reason and experience."[14] Luther remained convinced by tradition that Mary was "ever-virgin," but that is merely a side note in this text.[15] What interests him in this story is the necessity that Mary reject all human reason and experience, trusting upon the word of the angel that she would bear a son. It would have been no surprise if she had questioned this promise, and in fact, Luther declares, she did feel "a shot of unbelief in her heart."[16] But Mary was comforted and strengthened in her faith by the angel's assurance that such an incomprehensible wonder would be a work of God and she took heart at the example of Elizabeth. Luther is concerned to stress Mary's humanity and her need to rely upon God's word, in order that she might be a comforting and sustaining example for his listeners.

Among the "secret" meanings (*haimliche deuttung*) of this text, Luther discusses the meaning of Mary's name: "Mary is a Hebrew name and means for the Hebrews as much as for us a little drop of water that remains hanging on a bucket or pitcher," which can hardly be compared to the water in the sea.[17] This signifies that Mary and the other Jews who believed in Christ were only a little drop compared with the sea of those who did not believe. The fact that she was engaged to a man yet remained a virgin shows that the gospel will only be preached to those who are oppressed and "martyred" by the law, for "to be under the law is the same as to be under obedience to a man," as a wife must be.[18] And yet Christians must remain, as Mary did, both a wife and yet a virgin, subject to the law and yet free from it. Luther compares living in faith to virginity, and calls it a "spiritual virginity" that can be lost through sin and trying to do good works under the law: "then the bride will become a whore and lose her virginity."[19] Luther does not demand that women attempt to follow Mary's example literally, but rather that all Christians follow her spiritually, which according to his own theology may be just as difficult. His language, however, continues to underpin the cultural understanding of the connection between virginity and purity, on the one hand, and sexual maturity, impurity, and even prostitution on the other.

The explanation of the *Ave Maria* provided in this sermon may have been written by Stephen Roth, the editor of the 1527 postil, although Luther's contemporaries would probably not have been able to make that distinction. The themes found in this section are commonly repeated in other sermons: confidence and trust should not be placed in Mary, but only in God; the *Ave Maria* is not a prayer, but rather words of praise and honor to Mary; and using the angel's greeting as a prayer or invocation of Mary dishonors both her and her son. Mary should be highly praised, for God has protected her and lifted her above all other women, allowing her to conceive without sin. But it is through this "fruit of her womb" that the faithful are blessed, and it is only faith in Christ that will bring salvation.[20] In a sermon on this topic from 1523, Luther stresses that abuses are running rampant in the church: "If someone had said that it was not necessary for Mary to be adored, that person was [declared] a heretic."[21] But if we say that Mary is our mediator, we denigrate the salvific work of Christ. Because of all the problems associated with the use of this prayer and the adoration of Mary, Luther concludes, it would be better to leave her out altogether, and concentrate on believing in God and serving our neighbor.

In the sermon in Luther's *Hauspostille* of 1544 (the sermon is from 1532), we find more attention being paid to the incarnation and the person of Christ, but still a great deal of emphasis on Mary: of the three sermon parts, two parts concern the person of Mary and her faith. In the earlier sermon, Luther mentions that Mary was a poor young woman, probably around the age of thirteen or fourteen. The following section, which the editors indicate was probably added by Roth, even suggests that her parents Anna and Joachim were poor, not well-to-do as legend would have it. In this later sermon, Luther reminds us that Luke provided only scant information about Mary, although we can tell from her other appearances in Scripture that she was of lowly means. Luther supposes that she "served with a friend, and did the common housework like any other poor, pious, and upright maid."[22] In fact, it is quite likely that this is the work she was engaged in when the angel arrived, or perhaps she was hidden away in prayer.[23]

The angel's unusual greeting alarmed Mary: " 'Hail (he said) gracious one' or blessed one, 'the Lord is with you, you highly blessed one among women.' "[24] Her fear at this surprising message was allayed by the angel's comforting words, "Fear not, Mary, you have found grace with God." It is upon these words that Luther bases a strident argument against "the pope and his monks . . . who make a god out of the Virgin Mary."[25] Luther insists that grace comes from God through Christ, and neither Mary nor any other person can dispense grace, which he thought was implied by the words *gratia plena*. Mary herself, the poor maid, needed grace from God and comfort from the angel. The impact of Luther's words is to remove all the barriers between Mary and his audience. In fact, the angel's words are for them as well: "Therefore, although this pious virgin alone is the mother of this child, we also belong under this little one's regiment and kingdom."[26]

The differences between his audience and Mary sound almost minimal, which is quite the effect Luther was intending. Mary's response to the angel shows her great humility, her even greater faith, and a love toward all humanity, virtues that we all can and should emulate. She knows that this child will save the whole world from sin and death, "and through such faith alone is she holy and free from sin, and not through the work, that she brought the Son of God into the world."[27] In other words, although only she can be Christ's mother, she is saved in the same way as the rest of humanity: through faith. And it is faith in an orthodox Christ: Luther uses more than one-third of his text in explaining the nature and birth of Christ against heretical ideas. Although Mary is not better or more holy than we are (or than we can be), Christ is, and Luther thought it important in light of current debates that the doctrines concerning Christ and his incarnation be clearly stated.

The *Ave Maria* and False Catholic Teachings

A continuous thread running through the Lutheran sermons on the Annunciation text is a critique, occasionally implied although more often overt, upon the traditional Roman Catholic usage of the *Ave Maria* as a prayer, with its concomitant theological underpinnings. Luther and his followers rejected the notions of the intercession of the saints and Mary's mediation between believers and Christ. The veneration of Mary was to be either limited or redirected toward her son. The idea of a prayer addressed to Mary was extremely troubling and caused these preachers a difficult time in their exegesis of this passage: how could prayer to Mary and idolatry be avoided while continuing to give Mary the praise and honor that she herself said would be her due?

meaning of "gratia plena"

One of the first issues of importance for the Lutheran interpreters of this text was the language: the term *gratia plena* was a sticking point. Rather than using the German *voller gnade*, Luther used the term *holdselige* (lovely, gracious), in light of Erasmus's discussion of *gratia plena* in the *Annotationes* to his 1516 Greek New Testament.[28] Andreas Keller, in his *Sermon auff den tag der verkündigung Marie* from 1524, points out that the Latin term is not quite accurate: the Greek *kecharitomene* should be translated as *holdselige* or *begnadete*, and not *vollgnad*.[29] This new term gives a passive or received sense to the greeting: "the little word 'full of grace' should not be understood as if [Mary] was through herself full of grace or favor, but that all grace [and] favor come from God, for grace is nothing other than the favor of God"[30] The possibility that "full of grace" might imply that somehow through her own merit or service Mary deserved to be the Mother of God means that the term itself is dangerous and misleading. Who could ever deserve to be the Mother of God? Mary's own words reject this notion: "he has done great things to me," and further, "he has seen the lowliness of his handmaiden."[31]

The Latin sermons that discuss the *Ave Maria* also address the problem of language. The Württemberg reformer Johannes Brenz, in a sermon from 1541, broaches the question immediately: the angel said to Mary, "*Ave gratiosa*," which highly honors Mary with the "heavenly title" *gratiosa*, or, he also says, *gratia plena*.[32] *Gratiosa*, the Latin equivalent of *holdselige*, can be translated as "enjoying favor, full of charm, pleasing." Brenz obviously prefers this term to *gratia plena*, as he adds the caveat: "This [term *gratia plena*] should not be understood as the hypocrites explain, that Mary in herself is a 'chest' of graces and possesses as a goddess a kind of treasure of all heavenly goods, which she distributes to those whom she wishes."[33] The distributor of grace is, of course, Christ, which is why *gratiosa* more accurately conveys the correct meaning: that "God has recognized [Mary] through grace, and she has found the greatest favor with God."[34] The shift in language helps to ensure that the meaning of the angel's greeting will not be misconstrued. Luther himself in his famous *Sendbrief vom Dolmetschen* (1530) does not completely reject the traditional *gratia plena* or *voll gnaden*, but argues that, along with the possibility for misunderstanding, the translation is poor. Simply put, *voll gnaden* is bad German.[35]

But we should, according to Keller, realize the greatness and importance of not so much Mary's *act*, but the great gift that is given to her, and in turn to us. We cannot even comprehend, he insists, the great goodness of the gift: "she is a unique person in the entire human race to whom there is no one comparable, that she had a child with the heavenly Father, and such a child that has paid for the sins of the whole world."[36] If anyone wishes to praise her and give her all honor, that honor is contained in the name "Mother of God," which she did not earn although she was sinless. How are we to praise Mary, Keller asks, and yet "not remain in the error in which we have been up until now"? We have given her the honor that is due only to God, especially in the words of the *Salve Regina*, where Mary is named "our life" and "our hope."[37] This error, perpetuated by Rome, makes Mary into an idol, but we must only praise and honor her as a *creature*. The whole tenor of the approach to Mary is changed: she is not powerful in herself, but is chosen and blessed by God without any action on her part; she cannot help petitioners, for even her sinlessness is a gift of God's grace.

[margin: contra Rome]

Brenz also stresses the unique position of Mary. No other woman has ever conceived or borne a child in this manner, or been blessed with bearing the promised Messiah. But does this put her in the position of reconciling sinners with God or make her our comfort in the hour of death? Indeed not, says Brenz, for where else in the Bible do we find support for these "papist" ideas? "Now the angel did not commend Mary by such praises so that she might be offered to us as a mediator and reconciler before God's wrath . . . [but] that through these [words] faith might be awakened in her, that she might accept the following promise of Christ's conception and birth."[38] How else could Mary believe the astonishing idea that she, a virgin, would conceive and bear the Son of God? The "great crowd of hypocrites" who insist upon praying the Rosary mislead the faithful away from Christ.

The hymn *Salve Regina* receives special mention in a number of sermons: Luther had rejected the names "life" and "hope" being applied to Mary, although he does not seem to be troubled with calling Mary "queen."[39] The popular author and preacher Anton Corvinus (1501–1553), in his "Short Interpretation" of the pericopes "for poor Pastors and Housefathers," insists that calling Mary our "life, sweetness, and comfort, as the *Salve Regina* says," installs her as an idol and competition to Christ. "I can suffer it," he writes further, "and it is just, that Mary is praised, extolled, and commended as a blessed child of God, and put forward as an example of justifying faith for all Christians, but let her remain a creature" and do not place her over Christ.[40] Dresden pastor Daniel Greser (1504–1591) more generally rejects the notion that this festival is ordained for celebrating Mary, but particularly not for her propitiation and intercession for us before God, "as they sing of her among the papists."[41] So thorough is his rejection of these idolatrous ideas and practices that he does not mention Mary again in the remainder of his sermon.

[margin: Salve Regina]

We find in the sermons published after Greser's postil (1569 and later) an increasing number of complaints against Catholic practice and doctrine. Johannes Wigand (1523–1587) insists that although Mary is owed all honor and praise as the Mother of God, this does not mean that she intercedes for us with Christ: "In no way does the angel teach that one should call upon Mary, for invocation belongs to God alone . . . Therefore the Papists must be a mad and foolish people, who in the *Salve Regina* and in other little prayers call upon Mary as a mediatrix and a helper in time of need."[42] Catholic practice transgresses the first commandment, turning Mary from a creature into "the Almighty," which not only is not the proper way to praise and honor her but indeed shames and slanders her. It is a "foolish craziness" to make the *Ave Maria* into a prayer, as though we need to continue to announce to her that she will bear God's son.[43] This foolishness and idolatry continue to prove that the true nature of the papacy is the Antichrist.

A great deal of the "papist" idolatry stems, according to Johannes Heune (1514–1581), from the Latin text, *Ave Maria, gratia plena*.[44] The "prayer" of the *Ave Maria*, along with other "monkish" songs, has led people to turn to her in times of trouble, even expecting her help against the Turkish threat. "[Since] Mary is full of grace, they have decided, so one ought to call upon her justly for help, but Mary is not full of grace" and only Christ can give us grace and make us holy.[45] It is not Mary who is to blame, but rather the "papists," particularly the monks, who mislead people and convince them to place their trust in another besides Christ, especially in the hour of their death. This has even gone so far that people believe that wherever the bells are rung in service and honor to Mary at the appointed hour of prayer of the *Ave Maria*, no one can be injured or killed.[46]

The theme of the foolishness of those who pray the *Ave Maria* continues to receive elaboration in other sermons. University of Copenhagen professor Niels Hemmingsen insists that the silliness of those who call upon Mary "against the public word of God" will bring them to condemnation: "Cursed be all those who invoke creatures and falsely interpret the word of God in order to confirm their abominable idolatry, with high contempt for the Son of God, with great insult to the all-holy Virgin Mary, and with certain ruin for their souls' salvation."[47] Invocation of the saints, as far as Hemmingsen is concerned, is the work of the devil and was introduced by the devil himself into the church. The idolatry and error of invoking Mary was already noted, as Nicolaus Selneccer points out, by the early church father Epiphanius, who condemned the practices of the Antidicomarianites and the Collyridians.[48] Rather than leading us to place the emphasis upon Mary, the greeting of the angel should lead us to call upon God and celebrate the good gifts he has provided for his church.[49]

Christoff Mollen, in his *Predig von dem Aue Maria, vnd von anrüffung der Heyligen* of 1575, gives us a clue as to why his contemporaries express such a strong rejection of the invocation of saints and the usage of the *Ave Maria* as a prayer: the renewal of Catholicism through the work of the Jesuits has returned many of the "poor people" to the papist "error and abomination."[50] The townspeople do not care to send their children to learn the catechism, which contains all that is necessary for faith, but before the children even learn the Our Father they can pray the *Ave Maria* without stumbling. This "abominable

[handwritten marginalia: complaints against RC practice]

misuse" of prayer is an invention of the papists, and Mollen assembles numerous scriptural passages that support his view that prayer should be directed
to God alone. Mollen cites the Catholic catechism to show that the *Ave Maria*
is not simply the angel's greeting but also includes words from Elizabeth, as
well as others that have been passed down through tradition, and supposedly
prayed "by our blessed forefathers."[51] But this is not the kind of prayer that is
known in the Bible, according to Mollen, and the Catholic catechism does not
hide that the intent of the prayer is to gain the favor and intercession of Mary.
The pope and his monks have invented the "tradition" of prayer to Mary for
her intercession against both scriptural witness and testimony of the church
fathers, among whom Mollen is able to find pages of proof against the current
papist practices.

Mollen cites not only the catechism, he also transcribes in full several
prayers and hymns to Mary, calculated, perhaps, to shock as well as inform
his readers, at least those readers who were not aware of the extent to which
Mary was elevated in the Catholic tradition. Georg Spindler also includes a
Latin prayer, conveniently translated for his less educated audience, along with
a recapitulation of the language problem: it is the "old translation" of *gratia
plena* that, although it does not at all agree with the original Greek. has allowed
the papists to misinterpret the text completely. This misinterpretation has led
to the heights of idolatry in such lyrics as:

Per te mundus saluatus,	Through you the world is saved,
Per te sursum eleuatus,	Through you it is lifted up,
Per te mors damnata,	Through you death is condemned,
Per te uita donata,	Through you life is given,
Maria mater gratiæ,	Mary, Mother of grace,
Mater misericordiæ,	Mother of mercy,
Tu nos ab hoste protege,	Save us from the enemy,
Et hora mortis suscipe.	And receive us in the hour of death.[52]

However, we learn through the word *gratiosa/holdselige* that it is God who has
shown grace to Mary, and she did not earn or deserve it through any of her
virtues. We should take comfort in the fact that, according to Spindler, we have
all found grace with God through our faith in Christ, "and are as holy as Mary,
for Christ has won it for us, and shared it with us through his word and assured
it in the sacrament."[53]

Most of the remaining preachers repeat the warnings and criticisms we
have seen thus far: Mary is not our mediator or intercessor before God; the
angel's greeting is not a prayer and praying to Mary is idolatrous; rather, Mary
has received grace from God, and this story should make us thankful for God's
graciousness toward us. However, although their listeners and readers might
be in danger from "papist lies and superstitions," these preachers could not
reject or condemn this gospel text and the angel's greeting to Mary. She did
say that she would be praised and honored by all generations, and our Lutheran
preachers could not deny that. How then should she be praised and this festival
celebrated? Tilemann Hesshusen (1527–1588) suggests three ways: "that we

thank God for his gifts, that he allowed his son to become man; we should learn to understand the basis of our faith correctly; and imitate the excellent example of Mary's faith."[54]

Eve and Mary: Female Sin and Redemption Reinterpreted

The parallelism between Eve and Mary first appeared in the Christian written record in the mid-second century, in Justin Martyr's *Dialogue with the Jew Trypho*. Justin contrasted the virginity and obedience of Mary with the virginity and disobedience of Eve, who brought death into the world.[55] This parallelism was extended by Irenaeus, using the Pauline doctrine of the recapitulation of all things in Christ to make an explicit connection between Mary and human salvation: "Inasmuch as [Eve], having indeed Adam for a husband, yet being still a virgin, became disobedient and was made both for herself and the whole human race the cause of death, so also Mary, having a husband destined for her yet being a virgin, by obeying, became the cause of salvation both for herself and the whole human race."[56] In the medieval period, the comparison between Eve and Mary continued to be used, primarily to promote Mary as in some way a cause of salvation. Amadeus of Lausanne, a former novice of Bernard, transformed the Pauline phrase concerning Christ into a Marian teaching: "as in Eve all die, so also in Mary all shall be made alive."[57] Mary's connection with our salvation is here quite explicit, although theologians such as Bonaventure insisted that Mary's role in Christ's salvific work is *passive*, through her consent and her acceptance of the cross.

The text for the Annunciation is one of the traditional loci in the Bible for finding a connection between Eve and Mary. It was in consenting to the conception of Jesus through the Holy Spirit that Mary reversed the action of Eve, causing life rather than death to come into the world. It is also in this story that Christian theologians have understood God's curse in Genesis 3:15 to be fulfilled: "I will put enmity between you and the woman, and between your offspring and hers; it [*ipse*] will strike your head, and you will strike his heel." However, unlike many earlier interpreters, Luther and his followers did not see this text so much in a mariological as in a messianic vein, having corrected the Vulgate error that transposed "she" (*ipsa*) with the "it" (*ipse*) in the second part of the verse. Jerome's translation was already questioned in the fifteenth century, but while humanists and Protestants changed the pronoun, the Council of Trent confirmed this verse in the official biblical text of the Roman Catholic Church and it is one text that is used to support the dogma of the immaculate conception.[58] Although Mary continues to hold an important place in this text—in a significant parallel with Eve, she is also the "woman" and mother—it is her *seed* that engages in battle with the evil forces. It is in this context that some, though by no means all, of these sermon-writers discuss the parallelism between Mary and Eve.

"Blessed are you among women," the angel said to Mary. Through this phrase the angel indicated, according to Andreas Keller, that Mary had been freed from the punishment of Eve pronounced by God: "I will greatly increase your pangs in childbearing; in pain you shall bring forth children, yet your desire shall be for your husband, and he shall rule over you."[59] A number of feminist historians and theologians have suggested that it is this particularly female capability of bearing children that pushed the great fathers of the church—Jerome, Ambrose, Augustine—to identify the evils of sex and the body with women, allowing the ideal of virginity to take root in Christian tradition.[60] Eve did not maintain her virginity, but received the curse of God: she bore children in pain and was subservient to her husband. Mary, on the other hand, preserved her virginity, yet became a mother while remaining exempt from any "tainted sexuality." For the developing Marian cult, Mary's purity was her power, and Christian asceticism found in her a champion of virginity.

For the sixteenth-century reformers and their followers, many of the elements of the traditional Marian cult were no longer so idealistic: despite their inheritance of dualistic notions that associated sexuality with sin, marriage was to be preferred to a life of avowed celibacy or virginity. Luther, Melanchthon, and others agreed that, in accordance with Paul, "it is well for a man not to touch a woman" (1 Cor. 7:1). But the gift of chastity was in essence that—a gift. A life of celibacy was not a promise that could be made, something that could be vowed, and indeed it could not be required of men and women who desired to live a religious life. Life in marriage was better than life in a monastery, where one was forced to abrogate nature and promise to live in opposition to what was God's will for the vast majority of his creatures. In a number of the sermons under investigation, the authors suggest that Mary's own marriage to Joseph was meant to indicate God's strong support for the married life in opposition to life in celibate communities of monks and nuns, or under the rules of celibacy required of priests. However, in Mary's virginity there was more at stake than simply preserving a belief of the early church. The connection between Mary's purity—she had never had intercourse with a man—and Jesus' sinlessness and the purity of his body is maintained. It is quite clear that Mary's experience of motherhood was better than any other woman's, but this is not only because she bore the Son of God. She was freed from the woman's curse and was able to conceive a child without sin. It is also clear that Mary's virginity was seen as a vital part of her moral character: her chastity was both physical and spiritual, and evident to the Lutheran preachers in her behavior.

Keller proposes that the blessings heaped upon Mary were threefold: she was able to give birth without pain, having been freed from Eve's curse; she remained "a maiden before, during and after the birth," bearing Christ "without any stain;" and she conceived, through the Holy Spirit and without any sin, a unique and holy child.[61] Christ is exempt from the "curse" that is laid upon the rest of us "children of Eve" who are conceived in sin and are therefore "children of wrath."[62] He alone is holy as he is conceived, whereas we are made holy through him. The children of Eve are those who are conceived sexually, through natural intercourse, which forms the equation sexual conception=sinful conception. The child of Mary, the one conceived miraculously, without intercourse and therefore without sin, is the one who can take sin away from us and make us, by inference, into children of Mary. Mary is also preserved from sin, and preserved in her virginity; although Keller does not explicitly connect a life of virginity to a sinless state, the implied suggestion is that it can only help.

The opposition between the sinful mother Eve and the chaste mother Mary is even more strongly painted by Caspar Huberinus (1500–1553). Satan chose a woman to tempt and mislead Adam and all his descendants into the kingdom of Satan, while God chose a "daughter of Eve" to bring the "new Adam" into the world and return God's righteousness to the world.[63] Although she is Eve's daughter, the angel's greeting and blessing of Mary show "that Mary, unlike her mother Eve and other women, is not under the curse, displeasure, and wrath of God."[64] Mary, now contrasted with *all* women, is free from the curse and stands in God's favor. Eve was just like her before the fall, "still a virgin, a bride, and engaged to Adam," but Eve caused a curse to be placed upon all women, while Mary was lifted high above this curse, purified in "body, flesh, and blood," and made mother of the Son of God.[65] Huberinus continues to sing Mary's praise by enumerating each of fifteen "sweet-smelling, praiseworthy little blooms" in the blessed crown placed upon Mary's head by "the almighty God."[66] This highly flowery praise of Mary is somewhat unusual by Lutheran standards, but serves to spell out even further the great distinction between Mary and all other "daughters of Eve."

The long sermon of Johannes Drach (1494–1566) on the "Threefold Sermon of the Angel Gabriel" is more in keeping with the bulk of the sixteenth-century Lutheran homiletic tradition, in that he does not mention explicitly the Eve/Mary parallelism. For Drach, the phrase "blessed are you among women" indicates that Mary was chosen "from eternity" to be the mother of the Messiah. This is why Christ is named the "seed of the woman" in Genesis 3.[67] It is not surprising that much more is made of the Adam/Christ parallel, as in Brenz's sermon, while most preachers are content merely to mention the messianic prophecy as it refers to Mary, and leave Eve out of the discussion.

This does not mean, however, that the parallel is forgotten or rejected. It does mean that any active role is reserved for Christ, which also is a logical conclusion with the gender change in the referent in the Genesis prophecy. We find in Heune's 1570 postil the notion that Christ, the promised woman's seed, restored what Eve had destroyed: Mary is called blessed because she "brings the one who will trample the serpent to the world, who will set everything to rights that the hostile Eve has spilled, spoiled, and displaced through her disobedience and inquisitiveness, Genesis 3."[68] She participates in the salvation of the world in an important, but somewhat distant way, by being the mother of the savior. Heune is willing to preserve the negative and powerful, if destructive, picture of Eve, but not to make Mary into a heroine. Christoph Vischer makes this point explicitly: "Eve was hostile [*feindselig*] and brought us to [working] in the sweat [of our brow]; you are gracious [*holdselig*] and carry Christ, the fountainhead of all graciousness. [But Mary] is not the fountain of grace for us, out of which all grace springs forth . . . for that is suitable and proper to Christ Jesus alone."[69] The *feindseligkeit* of Eve is contrasted with the *holdseligkeit* of Mary, a term that we have seen was chosen for its completely passive connotation. Mary was chosen by God as his "instrument and tool," and for this reason the angel called her "blessed among women."[70]

Mary's blessedness and election, however, set her apart from other women, who are not correspondingly blessed by Mary's faith or behavior as they were condemned along with Eve. Niels Hemmingsen remarks, "[J]ust as Eve was cursed among women, and all women were cursed on her account, so are you [Mary] blessed through God's gift and grace."[71] This is the message that most of the sermons convey: it is not through Mary that women (or men) are brought into favor with God, but through Christ. The power of the parallelism between Mary and Eve is lost when Mary's role becomes completely passive. It is the seed of the woman, not the woman herself, who receives all the attention: "Today the seed of the woman has put to flight, expelled, conquered, and exterminated death, which a woman brought into the world."[72]

Despite the distance of Mary from Christ's work and human salvation, several sermons make good use of the Eve/Mary parallel. Selneccer, in explaining why Christ was born of a virgin, provides for one response the "reason of innocence: Eve was innocent before the fall. Mary, now having been sanctified, bore Christ, and thus *Ave* is opposed to *Eva*, the letters inverted."[73] Mary's participation in the incarnation, albeit passive, is still necessary and allows Nordhausen pastor Johann Spangenberg (1484–1550) to preach that through her faithful acceptance of the angel's message, "Mary brought back that which Eve had lost. And here is the Father become reconciled with the human race, here is all wrath given up and all grace and mercy, forgiveness of sins and eternal life are promised, Amen."[74] If Spangenberg is willing to give Mary a certain pride of place, future bishop Joachim Mörlin (1514–1571) will allow her even more: "[Mary] will help all women on earth out of their shame again to honor, and they will no more be cursed" for bringing unhappiness into the world. For Mary brought into the world the "heavenly Apple" who lifts the curse from all of us.[75] From Mörlin's perspective, Mary's honor affects all women positively, but the other sermon writers do not incorporate this theme.

Faith and Virtue: Mary as Example

As is not surprising for a movement that characterizes one of its main doctrines as *sola fide*, the faith that Mary expressed in the Annunciation text is one of the main themes of Luther and his followers in their praise of Mary. She not only had faith in the promised Messiah, she believed, against all reason and worldly expectations, the message that the angel brought to her: she, betrothed but still a virgin, would become pregnant and bear the Son of God. Luther indicates that when the angel came to her, she may have been completing household tasks proper to a poor maid, or perhaps praying in a quiet corner for the fulfillment of God's promises to Israel. She was not, as all his followers agree, a highly educated or wealthy young woman. That is clear from the biblical text. Rather, as if to counteract the excesses of devotion to Mary the Queen of Heaven in the medieval period, when it was even suggested that the angel should have been frightened of her because of her high status as "heavenly bride," Lutheran preachers of the sixteenth century seem particularly pleased to stress her lowly, humble position, unnoticed by the world despite her royal lineage.[76] Her humility of attitude, attested by her own words, makes her a powerful witness to the first and foremost goal of the Lutheran authors: showing that all work, grace, and glory belong to Christ alone.

This is particularly true when it comes to the question of Mary's sinlessness. The sinlessness, or moral purity, of Mary had been held by the fathers of the church from at least the time of Ambrose and Augustine, the latter even defending her special status in the face of the Pelagian controversy. A belief in her lack of sin did not necessarily imply holding to a belief in the immaculate conception, as there were many theologians who held the first but not the second.[77] It is unclear whether Luther held to the lifelong sinlessness of Mary throughout his career, although he does stress that she was purified from all sin by the Holy Spirit at some point before Christ's incarnation (see the discussion in chapter 6). In the sermon from Roth's *Festpostille*, Luther suggests that one reason Mary was addressed as "full of grace" is so that "she will be recognized as without sin."[78] This is, of course, due to God's grace, which protected her from all evil and harm. In the sermon from 1532 printed in the *Hauspostille*, Luther reiterates that her sinlessness does not come from her own work: "And through such grace alone is she also blessed and become free from sin, and not through the work, that she has brought the Son of God into the world."[79]

Luther's reform-minded contemporaries also occasionally remark upon Mary's sinlessness, usually in relation to her preparation for Christ's conception, although they do not usually specify a life-long condition. Andreas Keller wants to emphasize that all of Mary's gifts, even "that she was without sin," came to her through grace, which makes her unlike Christ, who was born without sin through his own power.[80] On the day of "Our Lady's Conception," Caspar Huberinus insists that it is the devil who is trying to promote the idea that "Mary, like other people, was conceived and born in sin." This fiendish idea, according to Huberinus, has led to many heresies in the church, such as the Eutychian notion that Christ's body must have had a heavenly substance, or he would not have been able to avoid having sinful flesh.[81] But the day's gospel teaches differently: "Blessed is the womb that bore you and the breasts that nursed you!" (Luke 11:27). And so, Huberinus asserts, "Mary must have had a pure, holy, blessed body," since Christ took his true humanity from her.[82] Of course, Mary was "full of grace" through God's mercy, not through her own work.

Huberinus does not clearly articulate a belief in the immaculate conception, although he implies it in this text. In the later sermon for the Annunciation, the implication is more clearly that "now [in the angel's greeting] out of the grace of God, the vessel, body, flesh, and blood of Mary is purified, blessed, and made holy."[83] It is not necessary that Mary have been immaculately conceived for Christ to receive purified and sinless flesh from her. Brenz places the purifying force in the Holy Spirit: all children of Adam are born "lacking the Holy Spirit and subject to the spirit of Satan. But Christ alone was conceived from the Holy Spirit and carried the Holy Spirit with him."[84] That is why we trust, says Brenz, that he will save us from our sins.

If, then, God is able to purify miraculously the material out of which Christ's flesh is formed, and there is no sin passed through his conception, it is not really necessary that Mary be sinless at all. In fact, Johannes Wigand announces to his hearers that Mary was a "weak, stupid human being, just like other people," and needed the comfort and strengthening of the gospel as much as anyone, although he is quick to assure them that her fear of the angel was no sin or stain upon her.[85] It seems clear that the many authors who write of Mary's blood or body being "purified" before Christ's conception assume that there is something (i.e., sin, weakness) that must be removed, but it is not until late in the period under investigation that this assumption is clearly stated, and even then, not by many authors.[86] Hesshusen in his 1581 postil explicitly states that the Holy Spirit purified Mary's blood from *sin*, which is the sin that we have inherited from Adam.[87] Christ is the only one who is born without sin. Martin Chemnitz (1522–1586) agrees: "Besides, Mary is a sinner, exactly like us, but the flesh that the Lord took from her was purified by the Holy Spirit, so that it would be pure."[88] The concern is to protect Christology from any heretical threat, not to preserve Mary's reputation.

Despite the priority that christological orthodoxy takes in these texts, most of the sermon writers also offered opinions about Mary as a good and faithful example for their listeners and readers. Even if Mary was sinful like the rest of us, she was uniquely chosen and blessed by God. Her response in faith to God's word is worthy of our praise and honor, as well as our imitation. Keller suggests that following Mary in faith will allow Christ to be "spiritually conceived in our hearts," and our hearts will be, like Mary, purified through faith in God's word.[89]

But what is it about Mary's faith that makes it such a wonderful example for Christians? There are several elements, according to Corvinus. Mary's first response to the angel was fear, which gave way to wonder, even disbelief. After hearing the angel's explanation, however, she believed God's promise "with great humility."[90] Mary portrays for us true "justifying faith," in that she "believes in the word, hangs on the word, and stays by the word," even when the message is incomprehensible to her reason. In fact, this is why it is called faith, since one cannot "see, feel, or comprehend it."[91] Mary had the kind of faith and trust in God's word that one must have in order to believe in the real presence of Christ in the Eucharist. In fact, it is especially this quality of her faith, that it overcame her reason, which receives close attention. She could not understand what the angel was saying by using her human reason or her senses, but, through God's gift, she was able to believe. Leonhard Culmann (1497/8–1562) suggests that "the angel recalls Mary to faith, and she believes the word," and then offers herself obediently to help accomplish God's will.[92]

In her incomprehension Mary is again fully representative of humanity.

Luther calls it doubt, but Culmann inclines toward innocence: "the questions of Zacharias arise from doubt and curiosity, but not Mary's." Her question arises rather from her virginal purity.[93] Drach informs his hearers what they should learn from the situation: "But Mary the Mother of God has an angel's sermon through which God himself speaks; from her own free will and ability she could neither understand nor believe: how then should you and I through our own free will and ability believe and be able to live the gospel[?]"[94] The Holy Spirit had to enter into Mary's heart so that she could believe. And, in the same way that she became the Mother of God through her belief, so we will be "children and heirs of God" when we believe his promises concerning Christ.[95] Mary's "gift" is available to all Christians; she is an example of great faith, but, these pastors hasten to tell their congregations, this faith is also a gift from God in which we all may share.

Although this argument could lead one to suggest that Mary deserves no praise for her faith since it was solely a gift of God, the focus in the sermons moves in a different direction. Lutheran preachers, especially beginning around 1570, stress that there are many Christian doctrines that are counter to human reason and worldly wisdom, but we must follow Mary's example of *obedience*: "Such things Mary could not grasp with her reason, but she stands on God's word and is well-contented with it."[96] God wants such obedience from Christians, the preachers insist. Luther had had strong reservations about the use of human reason in theological matters and was certainly opposed to idle speculation, but his later followers were even more concerned that the faithful not be misled.

In order to honor Mary truly, Johannes Heune preaches, we should follow her lead and believe in God's word, "for it is the greatest and highest wisdom to believe God's word, which never fails or deceives, for wisdom is of three kinds, a human or worldly wisdom, a diabolical wisdom, and a divine wisdom."[97] Mary's human reason was completely opposed to the angel's message of the incarnation, but she "took her reason captive, and put herself under the obedience of faith, for she heard that with God all things are possible."[98] We should follow her example of humble faith and leave all human reason behind. Mary spoke an "Amen" to God's word, giving a childlike and intellectually humble assent. It is *this* kind of faith that provides a good model for Lutheran laymen and women. Martin Chemnitz suggests that his hearers respond to God's word thusly: "With God there is no thing, no word [that is] impossible, etc. Therefore I will be an obedient servant, a humble maid, I will dispute nothing but rather believe, as you have promised and pledged to me in the Word."[99]

Mary's obedient and humble acceptance of God's word is not the only factor that makes her a suitable example. Several authors take the opportunity to portray her further as a good role model in her behavior, particularly for their female audience. While a number of authors repeat the traditional view promoted by Luther that the angel came upon Mary as she prayed for the fulfillment of the messianic prophecies,[100] several extend this image to include the vision of the pious and chaste young girl who appropriately stays quietly at home: "[She] is home-loving and secluded, for the angel came inside to her, *ex. for* not in the streets or at a dance."[101] Huberinus provides a further list of the *women* "pretty" example of Mary as a lesson to all "virgins and brides," and further to all females: "[Mary] is believing . . . [;] she is bashful, she is frightened and horrified by the angel; . . . she is also modest, pure, and chaste, for she says 'I know no man'; she is also humble, for she said to the angel, 'See, I am the handmaid of the Lord.' "[102] Her religious virtues (faith, humility) are intertwined with her "feminine," moral virtues (modesty, purity, chastity) in a way that gives added support to the image of the proper woman as both theologically humble and passive, and sexually chaste and domesticated. While men are encouraged to emulate Mary's obedience in faith, they are not urged in these sermons to imitate her chastity and sexual purity.

Huberinus is somewhat unusual among these Lutheran pastors in his effusive praise of Mary, but he is not the only writer to find in Mary's behavior and person an excellent role model for women. Christoph Vischer, notable for his very large postil with several sermons for each day, leaves hardly a stone unturned in his homilies. He repeats, for the sake of the girls and women in his audience, the point that the angel did not meet Mary on the street, adding that neither was she in the spinning-room, nor at a church festival among the young men. She was not to be found in a beer or wine garden, but was rather at home in her little chamber, occupied in earnest prayer to God.[103] Mary's example, according to Vischer, indicates to all women, young and old, certain standards for female behavior: they should not be "wild, insolent, and immodest," gadding about to all the drinking parties and "throwing down the glasses."[104] Such "loose" women are dangerous to honest society and threaten the very moral fabric of the community: "Beware of well-traveled young women and untraveled young men!"[105]

Mary represents an ideal in a Lutheran worldview where the domesticity of women is not only theologically correct, for women are *by nature* wives and mothers, but culturally desirable: women circumscribed within the home support the notion of the patriarchal family and complementary gendered spheres of activity.[106] Not only is the woman in the home occupied in her proper sphere, she is also *protected* from external influences and dangers. Mary's virginity, her sexual purity, is in some way associated with her staying at home. In fact, part of the reason that she was frightened of her angel visitor, some authors suggest, is that he appeared within her home, her safe haven, as a handsome young man. Georg Spindler remarks that it is "innate" in honest matrons that they become frightened "if a handsome man suddenly addresses them."[107] That he came upon her alone at home was even more frightening. However, she soon recognized that he was a special and unique messenger, sent from God (despite her unworthiness), and she welcomed his message with the laudable virtues of faith, humility, and obedience.

The complexity of the image of Mary is evident in the final section of this chapter: we have seen the way in which Mary could stand as a shining image of faith. Indeed, Mary's faith was just the kind that Lutheran pastors wanted to instill in their congregations. She is portrayed as humble and obedient, willing to concede her own inability to comprehend God's plan and to lean on God's goodness and grace. The association of humility with Mary is not new, but the emphasis is: she remained humble and lowly in spite of the fact that she was chosen to be the *Theotokos* (a name retained in Lutheran doctrinal formulations). The great gift of Christ's incarnation did not rely in any way upon Mary's value or merit, but rather was completely and totally the work of a gracious God. Even Mary's acceptance of God's plan, her *fiat*, was not a meritorious work, for her faith that it would be possible came from God. Therefore, Mary's election did not bestow upon her any special merit or power to administer grace to others. The Lutheran sermonists were adamant that Mary, although uniquely blessed by God through the physical bearing of his son, was thoroughly human, even to the point of implying, and then in the later period openly stating, that she was a sinful human being, no better than the rest of us. This shift in the status and power of Mary's image from the late medieval period is quite dramatic.

We have seen that this shift was accomplished in several different ways. As a reaction against Roman Catholic "error," Luther and his followers instituted a linguistic change in the biblical text of the Annunciation. Because *gratia plena* somehow allowed Catholics to see Mary as particularly meritorious and endowed with special powers, a much more passive term, *gratiosa* or *holdselig*, was substituted in translating the angel's greeting. Mary could only be the purely passive recipient of God's graciousness; that the term can be translated as "pretty" or "charming" effectively substitutes a feminine domesticity for female power and action. Consequently, it is both silly and idolatrous to pray to someone who has no real power. The *Ave Maria*, in the eyes of the Lutheran preacher, was not to be taken out of its christocentric context, and certainly should not be used as a supplication to Mary that would take attention away from the one true mediator. Even the usage of the Eve/Mary parallelism, more diminished in scope than in earlier theological texts, served to undermine any action and power in the image of Mary. Eve, still portrayed as the active destroyer of the original human happiness and the one who brought the punishment for sin on all humankind, but with a special burden for women, was not balanced so much by Mary as by Christ. It was Christ, the "seed of the woman," who mended the damage caused by Eve and who repaired the relationship between God and humanity. Mary, although necessary for the task, was kept at a distance from any sort of efficacious participation in human salvation. This imbalance meant that the onus placed upon women by Eve's fall could not be lifted by Mary. Several authors were willing to ascribe to Mary the regeneration of women, but most seemed comfortable with resigning all "daughters of Eve" to bearing the shame of their Ur-mother.

If Eve is powerfully and actively sinful, Mary is passively faithful and obedient. Her humility in faith and her obedient acceptance of God's promise against all human reason make her, in the eyes of Luther and his followers, a prime example of a faithful Christian. In this regard she is held up before both men and women as a model and exemplar. One might argue that the male audience is encouraged to adopt traditionally female characteristics such as passivity, submission, and obedience in their lives as faithful Christian laymen. No doubt this would, if effective, serve to keep the churchly power structures in place; the "priesthood of all believers" did not mean that every man (much less every woman) could function as his own biblical interpreter and religious authority. But if men are required to be submissive to religious authorities, they are not bound by the image of Mary in their social behavior. The significance of her example for women is much wider: along with exemplifying Christian faithfulness, she provides a model for proper feminine behavior. In fact, her passivity and docility in the religious sphere underlie and give a theological legitimization to her domesticity, social reticence, and sexual purity. How could God choose any other kind of woman? Of course, for Protestant defenders of marriage, her virginity is somewhat of a double-edged sword. But the sermon-writers remain fully traditional in their association of sexuality with sinfulness: they could still use Mary to affirm marriage (was she not betrothed to Joseph?), while celebrating her virginal purity and Jesus' protection from original sin.

We can begin to discern the development in Mary's image that takes place among Lutheran writers in the period from Luther's first postil to around the promulgation of the Formula of Concord. For Luther and his contemporaries, the requirements of the "rediscovered" gospel meant that certain aspects of Marian piety were to be discredited and removed from the life of the church. Mary could no longer be an intercessor, the most powerful mediatrix between God and humanity, but she remained a uniquely blessed, highly praiseworthy, even sinless (for many early authors) young woman chosen to be the Mother of God. But what seems now to be an inherent contradiction between a high veneration of Mary and the principle that all gifts, even faith itself, come from God, eventually led to a complete toppling of Mary from her pedestal, so much so that by mid century a number of preachers did not devote more than a phrase or two to Mary, and by the later period authors were positively asserting her sinfulness. Maintaining the proper anti-Roman stance, especially in the days of increased threats from Jesuits and other papal incursions, took priority over addressing Mary's special position as the blessed *Theotokos*. The resulting image is cloudy and complex: more must be added to the picture before we can claim to know the "Lutheran" Mary.

2

The Visitation

The story of the Visitation occurs immediately after the angel's annunciation to Mary that she would conceive a son and that her elderly relative Elizabeth, childless for many years, was also pregnant. Mary set out to visit and went "with haste" to the home of Zechariah and Elizabeth, the expectant parents of John the Baptist. As it is expressed in the Lucan narrative, when Elizabeth heard Mary's greeting, "the child leaped in her womb" (1:41) and she was filled with the Holy Spirit. Elizabeth blessed Mary, recognizing her as "the mother of my Lord." Upon receiving this blessing, Mary sang a joyful hymn of praise to God, traditionally known as the Magnificat, from the first word in the Latin translation: "My soul *magnifies* the Lord [*magnificat anima mea*]." The hymn is modeled upon other hymns and psalms found in the Bible, and has been an important text in liturgical use from the time of the early church. The narrative closes with the information that Mary remained with Elizabeth for about three months, and then returned to her home.[1]

This pericope for the church festival of the Visitation was a popular and important text for Lutheran preachers in the sixteenth century, although the holiday was not preserved in the ecclesiastical constitution of every region that became Lutheran, at least not as a full-day festival.[2] One should also not assume that the holiday was primarily celebrated because of its Marian significance. Robert Lansemann lists several foci of importance, not the least of which was Luther's love for Mary's hymn, the Magnificat, and its importance as a statement of faith. The text recounts the first public preaching of the incarnation after it was announced to Mary. Also, many preachers suggested that this gathering (consisting variously of Jesus, John, Zechariah, Elizabeth, and Mary) constituted the first council of the new church.[3] The text was also considered important in that it gave evidence against Anabaptist tendencies: John's movement in his mother's womb was thought to indicate both his faith and his participation in this early council, thereby proving the validity of infant baptism. Preaching on this text provided an opportunity to excoriate the perceived Roman Catholic abuses of the holiday, especially its supposed effectiveness against the onslaught of the Turks and its recent institution by the pope.[4] Luther even suggested reading and preaching on the Visitation text on the traditional holiday of Mary's Assumption, as that event could never rest solidly on scriptural support.[5]

Although the theological content of the text remained the central focus of all the sermons, the opportunities for moral instruction were also readily seized upon by the majority of preachers, certainly more often than polemical issues were raised. At least two-thirds of the published sermons used in this study, including those by Luther, explicated the moral lessons contained in the story for their audience. Often the moral import was directed to all Christians, men, women, and children: Mary's faith and example of humble service were to be followed by *everyone* as true Christian virtues. However, as often as Mary was presented as a model for all Christians, she was also elevated as a shining beacon of proper feminine behavior, both for women and for unmarried girls. Even her more general virtues could teach something especially to the female audience. The "school" of Mary was open for business.

Comparing Mary's virtuous behavior to a school for the female sex, as several pastors do, is in fact entirely appropriate to sixteenth-century Lutheran notions of the proper education for girls.[6] Doubtful questions concerning whether Protestant leaders actually desired universal education for boys and girls do not alter the fact that where such schools for girls were established, a primary goal was instilling correct morals and virtues. As noted by Gerald Strauss, sixteenth-century Hamburg established schools for girls in each parish, where they learned "reading, writing, sewing, and the fear of God, good manners and honorable conduct."[7] Both girls and boys, even in the most basic of schools, were expected to learn the catechism and some psalms, but where boys might be expected to use their instruction in a trade or business, it was hoped that girls' training would help them "grow up to be Christian and praiseworthy matrons and housekeepers."[8] Although they might need to use their reading and writing abilities to run the household or help in the family business, and certainly would be expected to help educate their own children, it seems that even the more academic aspects of a girl's education were expected to help inculcate Christian values and morals in her, for the benefit not only of her own soul but also of society. A new genre of edifying literature for girls gradually developed. The publications by pastors such as Conrad Porta were intended, as he states, to teach girls about both "Christianity and motherhood."[9] Christian morality and social responsibility overlapped, and Lutheran pastors felt it their duty to remind and instruct their female listeners and readers of this fact whenever they had the opportunity. It is not surprising that they often took advantage of Sunday and holiday sermons for this instruction, as they provided a regular means of addressing their parishioners.

Luther's Preaching on the Visitation and the Magnificat

When Luther describes the primary goal of this gospel text, he remarks that it displays a truly Christian existence in the examples of Mary and Elizabeth: they represent both faith and love.[10] Mary showed a model Christian love in not succumbing to pride, but rather serving others, as Christ did. Her example destroys all "classes and orders" that, Luther asserts, are established only so that their holders can serve and help themselves, or serve others only to gain glory for themselves and "become pious."[11] Mary was not interested in gaining such self-important "piety" through good works, but rather her piety led her to serve and care for Elizabeth, and she did not allow her blessings to puff her up with pride. Elizabeth was sensible of the great honor Mary bestowed upon her by this visit and was astonished by Mary's great humility. The fact that she recognized that Mary was "the mother of my Lord" expresses the nature of Christian faith: it runs counter to human nature and must be impressed upon our hearts by the Holy Spirit. If Elizabeth had been thinking according to human reason, she would have rejected the notion that Mary was pregnant ("she is too young"), and certainly could never have guessed that Mary was carrying the Son of God.[12] But her reason was "blinded" by her faith, and she was able to see beneath the surface to the *rerum non apparentium*.[13] It is in the nature of faith, argues Luther, to find life in the midst of death, to see righteousness under the cover of sin. Also, Elizabeth's joyous response to Mary shows that faith is not simply a matter of belief but bears fruit in one's heart, words, and actions.[14]

A further virtue exemplified in this text, according to Luther, is humility. Mary's example and Elizabeth's as well provide a true image of Christian humility, in contrast to current false presumptions concerning this important virtue. Mary's "humility" is not what caused God to give her the blessing of his son, but rather, in Luther's translation, God "looked upon the *lowliness* [*nidrigkeyt*] of his handmaiden." Her humility is not some sort of self-created possession for which God blessed her—a situation that would not give sinners much hope. Instead, her election provides hope to all those who are poor, troubled, and unimportant: "the lower you are, the smaller you are, the more clearly God's eyes look upon you."[15] Her *humility* is something else altogether and is expressed in all of her words and actions: she came immediately to serve Elizabeth, she acted appropriately and modestly upon the way, and she did not consider herself at all but instead turned to God, giving him all the glory for the great blessings she had received. Her hymn of praise expresses the proper knowledge of true humility and teaches all Christians how they should hold themselves before God: "[a man] is nothing and God is all things, [a man] receives nothing from himself but everything from God."[16] It is impossible for our human natures to understand this truth on our own, remarks Luther, and it is therefore necessary that we are instilled with the knowledge of the fullness of God's grace and our own lowliness.

This story also shows us how such grace and the knowledge of it is provided for us: it is announced through the spoken word of the gospel, found here in Mary's greeting to Elizabeth, "Peace be with you." Such words, received by a heart "thirsting after peace," bring with them the Holy Spirit, who teaches believers to know Christ and conquers "all human reason, sense, wit, and understanding."[17] This *Evangelion* announced by Mary supports Paul's insistence that the Holy Spirit is not received "through the works of the law, but rather through the preaching of faith"; it serves as a "tube, through which the Holy Spirit flows in and comes into our hearts." Luther emphasizes the *preached* word in opposition to those who expect the "unmediated" intervention of the spirit in their hearts: "God does not want to give his Holy Spirit without the external word."[18] Any "Spiritualist," whether his former colleague Andreas Karlstadt or any other, must learn from this example, read through the lens of Pauline theology: the Holy Spirit will not be found where the "corporeal [*leiplichen*], external word" is not spoken.

Mary the "Good Girl"

"Mary stood up and went with haste through the mountains." The Vulgate uses the phrase *in montana festinatione*—a phrase that had received a moral interpretation in the western biblical tradition from the time of Ambrose: "[L]isten, virgins, do not run around to others' houses, do not linger in the streets, or get together in public to gossip. Mary was earnest at home, hurried in public, and stayed at the home of her relatives."[19] In his earliest sermons Luther followed this phrasing, but in his 1523 sermon on this text and after, he favored the words *züchtig*, which can be translated as chaste or modest (related to *artig*: good, well behaved, polite), and *endelich*, a now archaic term that became standard in Lutheran sermons upon this text, meaning "chaste, fine, pure."[20] The haste with which Mary traveled now became only one aspect of her behavior, out of which a larger picture emerged. Rather than her quickness, Luther insists that Luke was commending Mary's modest and chaste manner of travel, which was very shy and retiring (*fein eingezogen*), such that "no bad example" could be taken from her.[21] She was "chaste with [her] eyes, ears, [and] conduct"—an example for all "women and virgins."[22] Mary may have been outside, but she remained enclosed within herself, exhibiting the behavior appropriate to a young woman—of this Luther had no doubt.

In the alternate sermon from the 1527 postil, Luther stresses further that in this text, the Holy Spirit is teaching women how to behave "in the streets and lanes": they should be *züchtig* and not bother anyone with immodest behavior.[23] For "a chaste life and honorable behavior" are a woman's "best jewel": if she loses this "treasure," she is done for.[24] In fact, although Luke does not record it, it is likely that Mary had a companion on her journey, either Joseph or a servant, as this is more seemly than that she traveled alone.[25] The Bible is full of examples, Luther suggests, of the honorable and chaste conduct of the saints, which counteracts the claims of those who think that being a Christian frees one from restrictions upon actions and thoughts. Mary's good example is provided by the Holy Spirit to oppose just such ideas; in Luther's eyes, a

Christian life must include both religious virtues (faith, love, and humility) and social propriety (*zucht und erbarkeit*). In fact, these elements are inseparable and must be inculcated in people from a young age.

Luther uses the traditional image of the rose garland to enumerate the virtues that Mary is teaching "to us all, but especially to the women-folk": "a garland, which is bedeckt with three especially beautiful and lovely roses." These "roses" represent the virtues of faith, humility, and "fine and chaste conduct."[26] If a woman has such "jewels," she outshines the greatest queen or empress with all her gold, precious stones, and silks. Mary's faith in God's word teaches women that they should "rather be found in church, in prayer, or at a sermon, than at a dance, at the market or elsewhere."[27] From the second rose, humility, we all should learn to respect and serve our elders. Mary did not succumb to pride (a special vice of women, according to Luther), although she is the Mother of God and "the greatest woman in heaven and on earth," but rather had a humble heart and served in the lowliest position, as a maid to the baby John. Servants, Luther remarks, should take a special lesson from this, and not be proud and unwilling to serve their masters and mistresses: a truly Christian servant will obey and serve, following Mary's example.[28] The third rose, chaste conduct, shows young women that they should not be irresponsible and nosy, gossiping and flitting here and there, but should rather stay at home, and when out in the streets, should behave modestly, focusing on their tasks and not idling.[29] Girls should not say to themselves, "Why should I always stay at home, like a nun in a cloister, and not go out walking like the Virgin Mary did?"[30] For Mary did not take a frivolous trip to see how things were out of doors. Rather, she traveled to serve Elizabeth, and did not stop to count the trees, or stand here and there thinking of things to do.[31]

Unfortunately, Luther says, today's girls fall far short of the measure. While Mary shows all of us that we foolishly pride ourselves on material possessions or our place in society, her example highlights in particular the faults of young women. In fact, he laments, girls seem to think that one cannot be happy and chaste or proper at the same time. He paints a dismal picture of young womanhood: "They are insolent and crude in their words, immodest in their behavior, they scream and rage as if they were crazy, which is called a good thing to be."[32] They even curse like the young men, from whom they learn all sorts of foul language. And who is responsible for this poor behavior? Mothers, who themselves set bad examples and do not make an effort to instill modesty and propriety in their daughters. Things have proceeded so far, complains Luther, that in his time "neither decency nor honor remains," the divine punishment for which will not be long coming.[33] He can only hope that the virtues shown in the examples of Mary and Elizabeth and celebrated on this holiday can have some effect, especially on young people and women: "Such virtues are worthwhile, that people, especially the young folk, consider them on a special holiday, and learn to be pious and God-fearing, and especially the women-folk should learn to conduct themselves in all decency [*zucht*], respectability, and humility."[34]

Mary's Song: The Magnificat

In 1521, Luther sent his recently completed translation and exposition of the Magnificat to the young prince John Frederick of Saxony. In it, he urged that its lessons in humility and trust in God be taken to heart by the young ruler, to preserve and protect the welfare of the people. As he writes, "in all of Scripture I do not know anything that serves such a purpose so well as this sacred hymn of the most blessed Mother of God, which ought indeed to be learned and kept in mind by all who would rule well and be helpful lords."[35] Mary's hymn, inspired by the Holy Spirit, but born out of her own experiences of God's grace, offered a view of a just and divinely sanctioned society that Luther wanted to promote. Although some of his emphases changed in later interpretations—for example, inspiration by the Spirit is not stressed in the later postil sermons as a prerequisite for understanding the Scriptures—Luther remained attached to this hymn, and continued to promote its proper use and understanding long after his definitive break with Rome.

This being said, it is not surprising that for Luther the primary message of the Magnificat is not directly related to Mary herself; we do not discover a great deal about his views of Mary in his expositions of this text.[36] We should keep in mind, however, as Luther does, that Mary is the speaker of these words, and in that capacity serves as a teacher of the church and an important preacher of the Word. This factor is significant, even if it remains largely unexplored: Mary's preaching as an activity does not become an example for women the way her chaste behavior does. She serves rather as a unique messenger of God's word who nevertheless should not be overemphasized.

The first lesson that can be drawn from Mary herself is that she praised God with joy because he chose her despite her poor and low status in society. God does not choose those who are powerful, wealthy, or great, those who might think they had been elected by God because of something they did or possessed themselves. Mary came from "poor, despised, and lowly parents," simple citizens of the town who received no notice.[37] It was incredibly unlikely that a great and powerful king should be born of such a poor and simple girl, even though she was, Luther iterates, of David's lineage. However, God does not work in ways that make sense in the eyes of the world. This canticle has been greatly misused by those who do not understand this aspect of God's work; particularly dangerous are those who consider themselves important because they have been given many gifts. Mary herself, Luther asserts, would have been more than happy if another had been given her gifts, as she considered herself always unworthy of God's blessings: she claimed nothing for herself but saw herself as "no more than a cheerful guest chamber and willing hostess to so great a Guest."[38] Most of us would become sinfully proud and haughty at such an honor, but "Mary's heart remains the same at all times."[39] She appears simple and humble and thinks of herself as such, but she is spiritually stronger than most of us: her "wondrous pure spirit . . . is worthy of even greater praise" because she resists all such sinfulness.[40] Her humility,

[handwritten margin note: (9 does not choose the great!)]

which could never recognize itself as a high virtue, is an example of what all Christians should regard as true humility.

Although Luther has just painted a picture of an unrecognized (because of her poverty and lowly life) but great saint (because of her virtue, moderation, and understanding), telling us that she is deserving of great praise, he is again uncomfortable with the notion that Mary should be set upon a pedestal and praised for her greatness. This dilemma leads him to say that rather than be praised or called "blessed," as she herself said she would be, Mary is "despised, and she despises herself in that she says her low estate was regarded by God." What honor and devotion should then be offered to her? Luther remarks that she would prefer to be addressed in such a manner: "O Blessed Virgin, Mother of God, you were nothing and all despised; yet God in His grace regarded you and worked such great things in you. You were worthy of none of them, but the rich and abundant grace of God was upon you, far above any merit of yours. Hail to you!"[41] She considered herself unworthy and so would not be offended by such a remark. What does offend her, however, are those who see merit and honor in her, and thereby take away honor from God. We are deprived of her example by those who set her above all other people, when really she is the greatest example of God's grace to humankind.

Although she is an example for all and should be emulated, Luther also realizes that she is unique as the Mother of God: "for on this [becoming the Mother of God] there follows all honor, all blessedness, and her unique place in the whole of mankind, among which she has no equal, namely that she had a child by the Father in heaven. . . . Hence men have crowded all her glory into a single word, calling her the Mother of God."[42] She is unique and should be greatly honored, and is even without sin, yet as she ascribes all of her blessings to God's grace and not to her own merit, so should Christians. Luther criticizes the words of the hymn "*Regina coeli laetare*," which call her "worthy" to bear Christ: she was only worthy in that she was suitable and appointed to the task by God.[43] Since everything she received was from God, it is better, he remarks, not to "make too much of calling her 'Queen of Heaven,' which is a trueenough name and yet does not make her a goddess who could grant gifts or render aid."[44] In fact, even in calling upon her for help, we should recognize that God does everything and the power is not Mary's: "We ought to call upon her, that for her sake God may grant and do what we request. Thus also all other saints are to be invoked, so that the work may be every way God's alone."[45] Mary herself has no active power to help us, although Luther still maintains a pride of place for her, almost as a figurehead.

In the sermon from 1523 that appears in Luther's early postil, many of the same themes are repeated. In this sermon Luther addresses Mary's virginity as an important aspect of her character but insists that her true purity and virginity consist in that she recognizes that God has done everything for her, and takes no credit herself.[46] We should thus praise her, not for her possessions or blessings, but because she had nothing and God gives everything. This is the proper attitude to take toward honoring her and all the saints, Luther adds:

rather than singing the *Salve regina*, we should instead through Mary (and the saints) praise God.[47]

Luther also spends time in his later sermons criticizing Roman practices surrounding Mary and the use of the Magnificat. He feels it is appropriate to imitate the early Christian custom of singing Mary's hymn at evening prayers but insists that despite respecting this custom, "the pope, his priests, monks, and nuns . . . do not understand a single letter of it"; they instead have fallen into "abominable idolatry."[48] Their pride has led them to care less about God's mercy and place more confidence in Mary's "wisdom, power, and riches." The pope thinks that because Mary will be "called blessed" by all generations and was chosen to bear God's son, her intercession can provide comfort and help in times of need.[49] However, Luther argues, this is a shameful misreading of the text and does not do justice to Mary's words.

It is, finally, her words that lead Luther to his characterization of Mary as a teacher: he calls her variously "the great Doctor and Prophet, more learned than all the apostles and prophets" and a "special master" with the ability to speak of "high things," and refers to her "sermon," which along with her example teaches us to humble ourselves, trust in God, and live properly (*in aller zucht*).[50] She is great in her humility and worthy of praise because she did not think herself worthy but rather praised God. She humbles us because of our sinfulness and pride, as she did not crave attention or honor for herself. Even her status as a learned doctor of the church did not raise her in her own estimation, but she was willing to serve Elizabeth as a nursery-maid. As contradictory as this image might seem, Luther would suggest it is only contradictory in the eyes of the world, as is all God's work. He is not being disingenuous when he calls Mary great and learned, or insists that her hymn is more beautiful or important than any other, but these terms must always be understood within the context of Mary's lowliness, meekness, and *züchtigkeit*. Her example cannot empower women (or men for that matter) to become preachers or theologians, because her strength and virtue subsist in her weakness and humility. While some might argue that the medieval Catholic picture of Mary removed her from the realm of reality to the extent that she could not serve as a realistic model for women, Luther's image of Mary can serve as an example only to limit women to a domesticated, tightly controlled sphere of existence. It is true enough that within this sphere, Luther has raised Mary's activities to the level of a God-pleasing vocation: serving as a nursery-maid and doing housework are now also serving God with faith and charity, as well as humility. Raising traditionally female duties that had lacked status to the level of saintly activities was part of the recovery of respect for the married life, the life within a household, that Luther and his followers promoted, and it no doubt helped many women come to a new appreciation for their roles as wives and mothers. But Mary could not serve as an example of a woman of action: her preaching and teaching are considered by Luther as part of her uniqueness and cannot be duplicated. As no other woman can be the Mother of God, neither can she create such a hymn as the Magnificat, teaching God's highest truths.

Mary's Visitation in the Later Lutheran Tradition

The adherents of Luther sound, for the most part, similar themes in their explanations and expositions of the Visitation text. When Mary is discussed (and this is not the case in every sermon), she most often serves as a virtuous example for Christians to follow and is especially recommended as an example for women to emulate. Many preachers also address the theme of Mary's preaching and her status as a "doctor" of the church, finding in the gathering at the house of Zechariah the first "council" of the new church. We even find in the sermons of Georg Major a reference to Mary as representing the church, a traditional medieval Marian image that otherwise is not mentioned in these texts. A certain amount of anti-Catholic polemic remains, but generally less than we have seen in the sermons of Luther himself.

Mary's Virtues: An Example for All Christians

Mary provides a positive example of many virtues, according to Luther's followers in the pulpit. The pastors continue to stress the traditional virtues that she had represented in the church, especially faith and humility. Her posture of faith, gratitude, and praise toward God is the most important element in her service as a witness and exemplar for Christians. They also find other aspects of her words and behavior that are profitable for their listeners and readers to consider and emulate. Not wanting to lose a good opportunity, the Lutheran preachers use this text to make both "evangelical" points—for example, faith over works-righteousness—and social comments—for example, Mary is a model of good-neighborliness.

As Johannes Brenz suggests, Mary's great benefit to us and to the church is that she teaches us to pray to God, especially when we are rejected by the world: "There is no greater opportunity, time, utility, and necessity to pray, than when we are the most miserable and hated."[51] Other biblical figures, such as Joseph, Moses, and David are examples of how individuals receive material benefits from God through prayer, but Mary is the main example of how we may receive "spiritual and eternal" benefits through prayer. God will look upon us and listen to us as his children—not because of Mary's intervention, of course, but because of Christ. She does not reign, either in heaven or in this world, but she does take the highest place among women in the church, both here and in God's heavenly kingdom.[52]

Every sermon on the Visitation mentions Mary's faith as a defining virtue. A number of them also use this occasion to clarify the constituent elements of true faith for the benefit of their listeners. Anton Corvinus stresses that the examples of Mary's travel and service to Elizabeth teach that true justifying faith must always be expressed in works: "Justifying faith, without concomitant works through which one's neighbor is served, cannot exist. For faith in God which grasps the promise and recognizes the benefits, and therefore is a fervent, living, and burning thing in the heart, cannot and does not desire to be hidden."⁵³ Not only does such faith necessarily express itself in works, it also expresses itself in words and witness, as Mary did in her hymn of praise. Such faith, Caspar Huberinus insists, breaks out of the heart into the mouth, as Mary hurried to the home of her relatives "and shared such knowledge and joy with [them], for that is the way and characteristic of true faith." Mary did not, however, visit silly or irresponsible people, but went to God-fearing folk, "for a Christian should betake himself to pious, God-fearing, upright people."⁵⁴ Her faith was also expressed in her greeting to Elizabeth, for it is also "the way of faith, that Christians are welcoming and subservient to each other, and humble ourselves with respect."⁵⁵

Faith should be expressed through works of love and service not only to our neighbors but also to God. Leonhard Culmann emphasizes that Mary is an example of how we should show our gratitude to God: "Therefore we learn through the example of Mary to show our gratitude in turn to God for his gratuitous mercy to us, and this gratitude is an effect of faith, which is not able to be hateful."⁵⁶ In fact, one of the main reasons this holiday is celebrated in the church is to give us an opportunity to thank and praise God publicly for his great blessings to us by sending Christ into the world: that is why we sing Mary's "most sweet and erudite" song in church, according to the Freyburg preacher Hieronymus Weller.⁵⁷

A second reason that this festival is celebrated, according to Weller, is "that in the blessed Virgin Mary an example of faith, humility, and chastity is put before the people, that all men of all ages might imitate her piety and virtue." He repeats that her chastity should be an example for "all men," but especially the "feminine sex."⁵⁸ Both her humility (which is to recognize one's baseness before God) and her faith are also lifted up as proper examples.

This pattern, where her virtues are emphasized for all listeners, but certain virtues are directed especially to the female audience, is followed by many authors. A good example can be seen in Georg Steinhart's "Crown of Honor and Jewel of a Christian Lady," which contains his interpretation of the Visitation text. For Steinhart, one of the main goals of the gospel writer is to display Mary's virtues for us—"faith, love, humility, and good behavior [zucht]"—each of which leads to the next. Steinhart uses the popular image of the rose garland, or "garland of honor" (Ehrenkrentzlein), with "three little blossoms," to describe Mary's desirable virtues.⁵⁹ Mary is not given this crown for the sake of pride, but so that all "Christian and honor-loving people might imitate her example."⁶⁰ The first blossom, faith, bears fruit in acts of love, which Mary shows by visiting Elizabeth, serving her, and caring for the baby John. Her humility, the second blossom, is also displayed by Mary's service and her lack of pride. Both of these virtues show us that we should let our faith bear fruit in love and humility to serve our neighbor. But Mary's humility (demut), and especially her honorable behavior (ehrbare Zucht), should be especially taken to heart by the female sex, which is "somewhat inclined by nature to arrogance, which they inherited from their first mother Eve."⁶¹ Likewise, all Christians should imitate Mary's good behavior and respectability, but women in particular should take care to follow her, for it is especially troubling when a woman behaves inappropriately, walking either too slowly, "as though [she] were walking along on nails," or too quickly, "running like a hamster, casting her eyes around brazenly."[62]

Mary teaches us to find happiness within our domestic sphere, according to Christoph Vischer. While other authors see a special lesson for young women in happy domesticity (it is much safer for them to be at home), Vischer suggests that Mary shows all of us that we should be content to live quietly at home, working in our usual vocation. This statement rejects both traditional Catholic options for the religious life and the perceived threat to daily life, marriage, and family by the Anabaptists: "Mary did not run into a cloister or a desert, leaving her house, hearth, and possessions, like the Anabaptists, but returned home to her house, her calling and office. . . . [I]t teaches us that a Christian can be comfortable and obliging in serving God at home in his house with a good and happy conscience."[63] This domesticity is related to the importance of good neighborliness, as Simon Pauli suggests that Mary and Elizabeth's example shows us how important and respectful it is to give one another proper greetings. It is especially prideful—such a person is stupidly full of *Bauerstolz*—to ignore the greeting of another, as though one were too important to respond.[64]

In general, all the pastors would agree with Niels Hemmingsen, who finds three reasons to celebrate the festivals of the saints in the church: first, they give an example of repentance and the mercy of God; second, they show how Christians should follow the saints in faith; and third, they illustrate that the faithful might follow the saints' "conduct and good morals," leading them to an honorable life.[65] Mary is an excellent example of these three factors, both in her behavior and in the lesson that she provides in her hymn to God. Mary shows us that we should believe God's word, even when "all nature and creatures" seem to contradict it.[66] The Magnificat teaches us to recognize our own pitiful state and to humble ourselves before God. We should admit everything God has done for us, thank and praise him for his gifts, and encourage other people to do so.[67]

Zucht *and Virginity: Mary as an Example for Women*

In his sermons on the Visitation, Luther does not make a strict distinction between Mary's propriety and her chastity and is not concerned with her virginity per se, but it is no surprise that this concern makes an appearance in later sermons by Luther's followers. A popular parallel is set up between Mary and Jacob's daughter, Dinah, who was raped while out visiting the local women (Genesis 34).[68] Mary, of course, offers the good example, while Dinah shows what can happen when proper conduct is not followed. Corvinus, in his *Auslegung* of 1545, indicates to his young female listeners where their immodest behavior will lead them. Can anyone discover, he asks, any girlish immodesty or frivolity in Mary's trip to Elizabeth? Of course not, for she hurried, chastely and modestly, greeting no one and thinking only of her goal. If only, he solemnly intones, Dinah had gone visiting with such propriety, respectability, and such a good disposition, she would have protected her honor and her virginity.[69] The choice is clear: follow Mary's good example, or risk suffering Dinah's fate.

Huberinus suggests that young women cannot be too careful in protecting even their reputations from suffering any damage. We know from Mary's example that humility and service are proper virtues for the Christian young woman to emulate. Mary also shows that haste and single-mindedness in one's tasks will keep one out of danger, whereas gossiping, lingering, and carelessly wandering about can lead one into Dinah's fate.[70] If a young woman were to follow Mary's example, visiting only with God-fearing people and family, and returning home immediately, she would protect herself from prying eyes and wagging tongues that might be willing to spread rumors about a girl seen in the wrong company. But if, Huberinus remarks, a pious girl is defamed by any "false tongues and through false suspicions," she should be comforted in knowing that God sees the truth and will save and publicize her honor in the end, as Mary was also preserved from false assumptions about her pregnancy.[71]

Mary is a type of all young women, preaches Leonhard Culmann, and she teaches girls that they should serve and honor their elders. But more than this, from her example girls learn to recognize their own vocation: "she teaches that after accepting the gospel, [her] vocation is not to abandon [her family] and go running about the town, without being settled at home and among her own things, leaving behind parents, children, husband, relatives, and friends."[72] Rather, he implies, a girl's vocation is to serve at home, among family and friends. Later in the sermon he reemphasizes that young women should learn from Mary not to be seen frequently in public, but rather should join together privately for the purpose of discussing how better to serve and honor their elders, and encouraging each other in modesty and proper behavior.[73] Hieronymus Weller agrees, making a more explicit connection between Mary's piety and her chastity. Her virtues are faith, humility, and chastity, and her example is intended to attract "all people, but especially the female sex, to chastity and correct manners." For after piety, he remarks, "there is nothing greater to commend in this sex than chastity."[74]

All the Lutheran preachers agree: true piety, which is not only interior but is also displayed in external behavior and manners, is the best defense for protecting one's chastity. Likewise, one's behavior and demeanor are the best indicators of one's chastity: as the saying goes, Georg Steinhart reminds us, "one recognizes birds by their feathers and song, and people by their face and walk."[75] Christoph Vischer reiterates this fact: if a girl wants to be considered a virgin, she had better act like one. Mary did not make her long journey out of curiosity to see the road or a desire to be out dawdling on her walk, unlike today's girls, who "often disturb church services, dances and banquets, and, in spite of wanting to be [as well as] be considered virgins, are more than silly, inconsiderate, and impertinent."[76] Vischer repeats a popular saying: "Beware of well-traveled young women and young men who have never been anywhere!"[77] Mary, on the other hand, displayed a "spirit of chastity and purity" through her song, which was not a "shameful, wanton love-song," and through her speech, which was short and to the point. She gives the lie to the usual saying about women: "Women were made from a rib, which is why they rattle and chatter so much."[78] In fact, it seems that, outside of attending church, singing hymns, and saying prayers, it would be much better if young women just stayed quietly at home and learned to be the *custodes domus*, or guardians of the house, as Paul recommends. Through this behavior they will avoid Dinah's fate, protect their reputation, and complete all their household chores.[79] Like the proverbial snail, several pastors note, a woman should always be safely surrounded by her shell, the home.[80]

Mary as a Preacher in the Church

In the home of Zechariah gathered the "most saintly and excellent assembly" ever seen under the sun, which brought the news of the coming Christ to the world and confirmed it for all posterity, according to Johannes Brenz.[81] After it was established that Mary had conceived this Christ, the news had to be broadcast to everyone. However, since neither Zechariah nor Mary was authorized to send out envoys carrying this news, Mary composed a song that would publicly share the message of God's fulfillment of his promises, as well as express her gratitude and faith.[82] In fact, Simon Pauli insists that Zechariah was still unable to speak, so it was the women who held the council: "as the woman first sinned, so also women held the first Synod of the New Testament." This council is a symbol that the church is a "trifling and despised little band" before the world.[83]

Veit Dietrich, in his *Kinderpredig* of 1546, also mentions Mary's song, which he calls a "beautiful sermon, in which the Virgin Mary teaches us how we might come to God's grace."[84] Before arriving at the house of Zechariah, Mary was the only one who knew of the incarnation, but her sermon was not primarily meant to spread the word of the arrival of the Messiah—that was accomplished through the working of the Holy Spirit. Rather, her example teaches us how we should respond to God in the face of his gifts, praising him and avoiding all semblance of pride.

Huberinus, in his postil of 1554, remarks that the Magnificat can be called "a theological disputation and learned conversation of the Virgin Mary and the old woman Elisabeth." They were pregnant not only in body but also "in faith and spirit, with spiritual fruit, which is a true good work commanded by God."[85]

Mary's faith shows the importance of preaching in another way—according to Steinhart, such faith comes through the spoken word, as the angel announced to Mary that she would bear the Messiah.[86] Mary's example, along with the witness of Paul in his letter to the Romans, should encourage us, then, "with all diligence and devotion to hold to oral preaching and God's word . . . [against] the Enthusiasts and Anabaptists . . . who reject the spoken word."[87] It is not the same, Steinhart insists, if one stays at home and reads the Bible.[88] The spoken word has a certain spirit and fire that has a special effect upon its hearers, "like the rain on barren land," according to the prophet Isaiah (chap. 55).

Mary came to the house of Zechariah both to teach and to learn, insists Johannes Wigand. Mary wanted to join with the "correct, true church and school," where she could be taught about the "high things" that had happened, for reason cannot grasp these things. She also wanted to share the news the angel had brought her and to gladden her friends with her good news.[89] This purpose, along with the fact that her visit to Elizabeth was God's will rather than her own, is what makes Mary's travel "*endelich*," appropriate and honorable. From such a gathering, we learn that "pious and God-fearing people" should come together and discuss God's word, and God's spirit will be active among them.[90]

Mary is not the only preacher in this story. Christoph Vischer insists that *Elizabeth* is the first preacher of the gospel of Christ's incarnation.[91] Her greeting of Mary announces Christ's coming birth. Vischer also includes Mary and Elizabeth among the participants in the first council of the church, which is the model for all other "councils, synods, conversations, and gatherings concerning religion." He suggests that others also attended, including Zechariah, Simeon, and Anna, and that the women had "*vocem decisiuam*," authority of decision, along with the men.[92] Christ presided in utero over this "most holy gathering," according to Johannes Mathesius, and the basic articles of the Christian faith were decided upon and confirmed at this first council.[93]

Anti-Catholic Polemic in Visitation Sermons

Johannes Brenz remarks early in his 1539 sermon on the Visitation that although Mary was not sent into the public ministry of preaching the gospel either to the Jews or the gentiles, still the church can receive the "greatest utility" from Mary.[94] Of course, he hurries to add that although it is most proper that she be revered and celebrated in the church, the "hypocrites" who call her our intercessor before the stern and angry Christ bring her great dishonor. Although she is the mother of the "*corporalis Christi*," this does not mean that Christ must honor her above all other saints, granting her every petition; Jesus' question "Who is my mother, and who are my brothers?" (Matt. 12:48) shows that his earthly family has no claim on his heavenly authority.[95] Christians are not to look to Mary for her help in placating an angry Christ. Rather, Mary's usefulness is first, according to Brenz, that in her role as *dei genetrix* she bears the savior, "by which Mary exhibits to the church the most beautiful act of faith, through which faith believers come to justification."[96] Her faith was in the promises of God, although the promises seemed impossible to fulfill. Her further usefulness for the church is in the example of her many virtues, too numerous to recount, only one of which is her gratitude to God, expressed through her hymn of praise. This is as great a work, Brenz suggests, as if she had founded a hundred monasteries in Judea: such monasteries could be destroyed, but the Magnificat will remain until the end times.[97]

An especially important point for those authors critical of the Roman church is the interpretation of the word "humility," which Luther had translated as "low estate" to avoid any confusion. "Many interpret *humilitas* in this passage as a virtue, but they are in error," writes Brenz. "Mary is not glorying in her virtue or justice, or her merits before God. But *humilitas* in this passage means misery, affliction, scorn, and abjectness."[98] Humility is not a state or possession that will be rewarded by God, and the truly humble person will not expect any reward for such a "virtue."[99]

Mary's example also provides an opportunity to address the issue of faith and works. Anton Corvinus remarks that people should not confuse one with the other, "or one would make fruit out of the tree, and a tree out of the fruit, against the teaching of the gospel."[100] Faith comes first, he insists, and the Christian will do good works to confirm his faith, but without putting his faith in them. Likewise, one's faith should not be placed in the power of Mary or other saints to grant petitions and hear prayers. Corvinus adduces Psalm 150, "Got loben in seinen hailigen"—praise God in/through his saints—to affirm the proper way to approach the saints. We may praise and honor them, if we keep in mind that all they have accomplished is through God's grace. We must be wary, reminds Corvinus, and avoid calling on the saints or praying to them to make them into our intercessors or advocates—such a role belongs to God alone.[101] That is why Elizabeth praised God for his blessings to Mary, and especially praised the "fruit of her womb," rather than praising her for earning God's grace. In fact, our best method of honoring Mary, besides taking example from her piety and honorable life, is to have faith in her son. By believing in Christ, as Mary did, Daniel Greser reminds his audience, "we will all be mothers, sisters, and brothers of Christ, as Christ himself said [Matt. 12]."[102]

The Magnificat shows us, according to Huberinus, that it is far better to "call Mary blessed" and place her before us as an example, than it is to pray to or call on her: she should receive her appropriate praise, and God should receive what is appropriate to him, "so that we do not pray to and call on four people in the Godhead, against the first commandment."[103] Praying to Mary is not only against biblical command but also without precedent in the early church. Mary is not divine, or even without sin, as Georg Walther insists against "the great blindness of the Papists," or Elizabeth would not have said that she was blessed through her faith.[104]

Mary's criticism of the world's powerful people allows for more personal attacks against the Roman curia and clergy. Veit Dietrich paints the pope, cardinals, bishops, priests, and monks, along with kings, great lords, and learned doctors of the universities, as enemies of the gospel, to be included in the same list with Herod, Pilate, and the high priests of Jerusalem.[105] The "small little group" that holds to God's word, although despised by these great ones, is comforted by Mary's words that those who are proud and do not fear God will be thrown down from their places of power.

Several authors also continue to ridicule the pope for the association of this holiday with the fight against the Turks. Rather than celebrating this holiday as one in which the news of Christ's coming was first spread, the pope had instituted another significance for its celebration. As Mary "went over the mountain, stepping over it with her feet," so likewise she should be called upon so that she might "with the same feet want to tread the Turks under her."[106] As Christoph Vischer remarks, such "idolatry and blasphemy," that is, "invoking the dead saints," has been decisively rejected as opposed to God's word. Mary said she would be called blessed, not that she would be recognized as "a Queen of Heaven, a helper in time of need, [or] a mediatrix," for all such honors are intended for her son.[107] In fact, Simon Pauli suggests that the more people call on Mary, forgetting Christ the true mediator and "the one who treads on the snake and the Turk," the stronger the Turks will become.[108]

Summary

In the Visitation sermons studied in this chapter, we begin to see a more complete picture of Mary emerging. Both Luther and his followers emphasize Mary's ability to stand as an example for their audiences, especially in how she represents the three prime virtues of faith, humility, and good conduct. Mary's faith is a mainstay of Christian tradition—believing the message of the incarnation and sharing it with Elizabeth and the rest of the church in the Magnificat exceeds even the witness of Abraham. Her humility, attested by her own words, underscores her position as the greatest saint in the Christian tradition: her humility was seen as perhaps her greatest virtue in the medieval period, taking priority even over her virginity.[109] Her chaste conduct and good behavior had also served as a model long before the sixteenth century. Luther and his followers are not innovating in their praise for Mary or in their application of her virtues as examples to their listeners.

We can, however, see a specifically evangelical piety forming in these sermons. Sixteenth-century Lutheran pastors, wanting to portray the "proper" image of Mary to their congregations, are not content to leave the traditional image of her in place, or to concede control over her image to their opponents. Instead, Mary is used to show how it is true faith that justifies, and then leads one necessarily to good deeds. Her humility is not a cover for pride or high status, but a real humbleness of person, position, and attitude. Although she is the Mother of God, she always defers to her son, and is content to model the behavior of a true believer, praising and praying to God, rather than insisting on a role of power as intercessor.[110] Sermons on this text regularly reject such Roman Catholic practices as prayers for saintly intercession or emphasis on merits being required for salvation. Mary's exalted position within the Roman pantheon of saints is unacceptable to the evangelical preachers, and most follow Luther's careful approach to reorienting her status within the church: the conceit is that Mary herself, being a pious believer, rejects all such glory and is offended by those who would place her on a pedestal near or equal to her son's.

The sixteenth-century Lutheran picture of Mary is not that of a heavenly queen, a virginal goddess, or even that of a strong maternal protector, a "Mother of Mercy" in contrast to a righteously angry Christ. The dilemma facing Lutheran preachers is how to preserve the paradoxical aspects of Mary's image, while remaining true to the scriptural texts: she is to be highly honored, and yet she is humble and of low estate; she is the Mother of God, the blessed *Theotokos*, and yet she must be rescued from sin and death like the rest of us.[111] Luther, as fond as he is of paradoxes, has difficulty in maintaining this one:

he tends to stress the lowliness and humility of Mary over her glory. He is willing to deemphasize the uniqueness and power of her position in favor of emphasizing her role as a good example for all Christians.

Luther's followers complete this tendency. If Mary can no longer do anything for their listeners, and any excesses of adoration must be avoided, her primary purpose must be to show Christians how to live in relation to God and to other people. The later preachers follow Luther's lead: most of the themes raised in the later sermons are found in Luther's own texts. Anti-Catholic polemics, while significant in many sermons, do not seem to increase or decrease across the period under investigation. Issues of morality, too, with occasional variations, are consistent and repetitious. The one topic that deviates from this pattern is the stress on Mary's virginity in the context of her chastity and modesty: Luther himself does not stress this point, while it is taken up in the sermons of many of his later followers. Although he does not stress her virginity, Luther is as concerned as the rest of the preachers to emphasize and repeat Mary's example of good and honorable behavior, modesty, chastity, and social propriety—the words *zucht, züchtig, ehrbar,* and *endelich* are repeated over and over again. This good conduct is urged upon the whole audience, although almost every author is quick to point out the special lessons in this text for the female members. One is left with the impression that although a cheerful domestic lifestyle and polite social relations are the goal for the whole of society, it is particularly distressing and destructive when women and girls fail to follow the rules.

In Lutheran sermons on the Visitation text, Mary represents the faithful believer, the inspired witness to God's word, the humble Christian servant. Her goodness in the theological virtues is connected to and undergirds her role as a model of good social behavior (especially for women and girls). The complex nature of her image as developed in these sermons allows the authors to honor an ideal in Mary that is not only, in their eyes, true to the scriptural text, but also avoids the pitfalls of her medieval portrait, while making her useful for the improvement of their audience's spiritual and social lives.

3

The Purification of Mary, or Candlemas

The festival of Mary's Purification—usually referred to as *Reinigung Mariæ* or *Purificationis*—continued to be widely celebrated in German territories even after the introduction of the Reformation. Robert Lansemann suggests that the holiday was maintained primarily as a *Herrenfest* rather than a Marian holiday—thus the preference for the title *Opferung Christi*—however, the clear majority of sermons in this study refer to Mary in their title.[1] The history of this holiday indicates that in the early church it was also celebrated as a feast of Christ: the Greek name "*Hypapante*" refers to the encounter between Christ and Simeon, and thus to Christ's presentation in the temple. Along with the Annunciation, Purification was considered part of the Christmas cycle.[2] By the early Middle Ages, this festival, celebrated on February 2 to correspond with Christmas, honored the virgin and included the blessing and lighting of candles, as well as carrying them in procession.[3] It is commonly thought that the festival, introduced in Rome sometime between the fifth and seventh centuries, was intended to replace the pagan festival of Lupercalia, which had associations with ritual purification and included carrying torches in procession.[4]

The text for the day of Mary's purification, Luke 2:22–32, includes both the references to Mary's and Jesus' purifications according to the law of Moses, and Simeon's hymn of praise to God, often referred to as the *Nunc dimittis*, from the first words in the Latin translation. In this chapter I will also consider sermons on the text immediately following (Luke 2:33–40), normally read on the Sunday after Christmas. This text records Simeon's prophecy to Mary—"a sword shall pierce your soul"—and describes the prophetess Anna and her words concerning Christ. Jesus' parents, according to the gospel, "were amazed at what was being said about him." After completing the requirements of the law, Joseph and Mary returned to their home in Nazareth.

The sermons on these texts address a variety of themes, including anti-Roman polemic, the law and its fulfillment through Christ, purification, the behavior of parturient women and ritual "churching," even the art of dying. In fact, Lansemann thinks that the sheer variety of topics discussed in the post-Reformation sermons undercut the significance of the holiday of Purification; without a uniform content, it was not clear why the day should have continued to be widely celebrated.[5] He observes that the festival was maintained through a combination of adherence to tradition and the opportunity to explicate another biblical text to the people, one that was turned to focus more upon Christ than upon Mary. It is possible, however, to propose another explanation for its continued observation. The primary reason must still be the importance of the text, the prophecies about Jesus and the significance of the recognition of Christ in the temple in Jerusalem. Maintaining tradition, however, cannot be considered a motivation for its own sake—too many other traditions were discarded or rejected. This holiday was maintained because of the importance of churching and other rituals and behaviors surrounding childbirth and new mothers.[6] The gospel text itself places very little emphasis on Mary's actual purification, but rather stresses Simeon and his prophecies. Yet most of the sermons include discussions, occasionally quite long, of such rituals, the rejection of Roman Catholic ideas and observances, and the promotion of "proper" female behavior. Karant-Nunn and Scribner both note an "early Lutheran clerical and magisterial ambivalence toward the post-natal rite of purification," but also indicate that such rituals were maintained and eventually often required in Lutheran areas.[7]

As important as the theme of the purification is in these sermons, it is only one element relevant to our study. Another significant theme, taken from the second reading considered here, is the prophecy spoken to Mary of the sword that would pierce her soul. The meaning of this phrase, especially in contrast to medieval interpretations, was very important for Luther and his followers. It is also one location where the preachers were comfortable with promoting Mary as an image of the church. The final point of interest is the discussions engendered by the example and words of Anna, the prophetess.

Churching, Purification, and *Kindbettnerin*

The practice of churching in German-speaking lands was quite common by the fifteenth century, and liturgical evidence for blessings of new mothers can be found as early as the eleventh century.[8] The rituals, with local variation, included the attendance of the mother (often called the *Sechswöchnerin*, indicating the confinement period of six weeks) by the midwife and the women involved in the birth to the church door, carrying lit candles. Here the group would be greeted and led in by the priest, who would sprinkle the new mother with holy water, and read certain prescribed passages, prayers, and blessings.

med.

The ritual often included processing around the altar, kissing a gospel or reliquary, and other applications of holy water and incense. Although churching was technically not a process of purification—Gregory the Great and other theologians had specifically stated that parturient and menstruating women were not unclean and could partake of the sacrament—it is clear that many ordinary Catholics, and even many priests, felt that some element of impurity was present in such women, including an increased vulnerability to Satan.[9]

The changes introduced into the rituals of churching during and after the Reformation are, on the surface, not difficult to recount or explain. The "superstitious" elements were rejected, particularly those sacramentals—blessed candles, holy water—thought to contain salvific effect within the objects themselves. The attendance at church by the new mother, midwife, and other women, special readings, prayers, and blessings, and the offering made by the new mother were all retained.[10] Lutheran pastors couched their criticisms of this ritual in terms of anti-"papist" rhetoric: the notion that women were somehow made impure through pregnancy and childbirth, or that they were somehow more susceptible to the devil than usual were more of the same superstitious anti-woman beliefs and practices of the Catholic Church. The blessing and lighting of candles were seen as not only of recent vintage but also as pagan practices with only a Christian coating, and what, asks Luther, can a Christian learn about serving God from a pagan?

Luther criticizes the Catholic practice of requiring a new mother to come to church for a blessing, "as though she were impure and should not otherwise go to church or among the people."[11] The Mosaic law itself is what assigned impurity to a new mother, so that without this law, there is no impurity. The example that Mary gave in following this law has other lessons, Luther suggests. Mary did not need to be purified, even according to the law, because she was not impregnated by a man but remained a virgin. Despite this fact, she observed the law and went to the temple like other women. Her example of freely chosen obedience shames us, who are culpable under the law (that is, the law that is still binding upon Christians, not the abrogated Jewish law) and yet refuse to do even what is required of us. The significance of her example, and more important of Christ's example and the teachings concerning him, make this an important holiday to maintain. Luther rejects, however, the Catholic practices surrounding the festival, especially the blessing of wax and candles, which were thought to protect both women in childbirth and Christians on their deathbed from the power of Satan. It is a shameful thing, he remarks, that Catholics turn to such objects for help, when in fact Simeon's sermon shows us that the true power of protection and salvation comes from Christ, the light of the world.[12]

Luther did not condemn the practice of churching any more than he rejected the holiday of Mary's Purification, but he also did not provide arguments for why it should be maintained. We must turn to the sermons of his followers in order to discover why Lutheran preachers supported both the practice of confinement and the ritual of churching.[13] A period of confinement is especially recommended for women after childbirth, and for primarily practical reasons. Arsacius Seehofer suggests that Mary's obedience to a law of which she was free is a pious example for us all, but that women in particular should follow her example: they, too, are free of the law's ritual requirements and are not impure, but nevertheless "[both] the law of nature and [of] justice teach that they should care for their own good health, and remain at home for a time" while they are convalescing.[14] Not only the health of the mother but also that of the child is at stake in this convalescent period, stress several authors. If the mother leaves the home too soon, she might threaten the health of herself or her child, thereby sinning against the fifth commandment, "you should not kill." Such a command also applies to husbands, for certain "tyrannical men" insist that their wives return to their household duties before they are really ready.[15] Johannes Mathesius even suggests that this law was designed to mitigate the burden placed on women through Eve's curse: because of the difficult pains during birth, God ordained this period for women to recuperate, "and the men would have patience with them, until they had regained their strength."[16]

The theme of the demanding, tyrannical husband is often repeated in these sermons. Simon Pauli contends that, even though women are no longer under the Mosaic law, still observing the period of confinement is a *Zuchtgesetze*, a law of propriety. Men must remember that women need a full period of recovery; Pauli suggests that husbands remember the pain in which their mothers bore them and thus have sympathy for their wives. He even repeats the philosopher's dictum that it is easier to fight in battle than to bear a child, and insists that "there is no nobler creature and creation of God on earth than a fruitful woman."[17] But Pauli does not reserve his criticism only for tyrannical husbands: he also attacks women who do not observe a proper period of confinement. Such women may be stronger and not need an extended recovery, but they can only do harm to the weaker of their sex. If impatient and inconsiderate husbands see other women returning to their work sooner, they may demand that their own wives do the same, thus causing injury and perhaps even death. In such case, the fault lies not only with the *bösen Tyrannischen Kerlen* but also with the women who did not observe the traditional lying-in period.[18] All women, according to several preachers, should follow these recommendations for the benefit of the weak. In this observance, women are patterning themselves on Mary, who, despite her freedom from the law, was obedient for the benefit of others, and to avoid causing a scandal.

Although the observance of a period of confinement was of concern to many Lutheran preachers throughout the sixteenth century, the practice of churching was not often discussed and recommended until the later part of the period. In a postil dated 1567 (this edition was published in 1590), Simon Musaeus recommends that a woman come to church after her six weeks in order to give thanks to God for the blessings of her own health and that of her child. However, his recommendations follow a strict rejection of "papist" ideas, both about the holiday of the Purification, especially the blessing of candles, and the practice of churching. The Jewish law requiring purification following birth establishes a "levitical" rather than a natural impurity; that is, sex within marriage and childbearing are not sins and do not break any of God's commands. Since the New Testament abrogates this law, the pope is wrong to demand that new mothers come to church to be blessed.[19] The law exists now only to remind us that we are all conceived and born in sin.[20]

Christoph Vischer reiterates many of these points. He insists that it is blasphemous to attempt to "honor" Mary with blessed candles and wrong to teach expectant mothers that such candles will protect them in childbirth: it is not blessed candles, salt, or herbs that will keep them safe, but rather God's angels.[21] He rejects the notion that the "work" of marriage is unholy or impure, as the "accursed Pope" allows. He stresses that Mary's example of obedience in observing the law when she was free from its requirements is an important example for all Christians to follow: we should all gladly seek the company of pious folk and happily attend religious services.[22] Women, that is, "Christian, pious, honorable, virtuous matrons or females," should especially learn from Mary's example to observe six weeks of confinement, treating their bodies as "a temple of the holy Spirit," and then afterward to bring their children with them to church, to thank God for their health, safety, and protection from "the devil's storms and raging."[23] Vischer does not say specifically that women (and their babies) are more susceptible to the "raging" of the devil during childbirth, but he at least assumes that this is a time when Satan works hard to bring pain and trouble to women.

In another sermon we find the recommendation of churching as a "fine and Christian" practice, but also a reminder that it is a "free ceremony": if one is not able to bring the child along, that is acceptable. But it is also the case that a woman is "free" to do it: "if she wants to be allowed to pray publicly for herself and her little child, each one is also at liberty [to do so]."[24] Mathesius does not say, however, that one is free to dispense with this custom, although that is one conclusion that could be drawn from his statement. He is quite thankful that his community is finally free from superstitions such as St. Blasius candles and other "misuses," but Christian freedom does not give anyone license to refrain from church services, sermons, prayers, or raising their children properly in the church.[25] From Mary's "good example and teaching" we learn that, for the sake of "love, peace, forbearance, unity, and to avoid scandal," we should participate in and honor all "good manners, fine ceremonies, and praiseworthy customs" even though we are free of them.[26] Although Christians are free, they do not live for themselves but rather to honor God and to serve others.

Later preachers also stress the need for a period of confinement, for reasons both of health and of propriety. Many also recommend a special trip to church for the mother to give thanks to God after her confinement has ended. These pastors continue to condemn in strong words Catholic practices and superstitions surrounding churching, suggesting that at the least they worry that their listeners could be swayed by fears of the devil or persistent beliefs about the impurity of parturient women. Tilemann Hesshusen, often noted for his irascible and truculent character, vilifies the "pope and his monks" for conducting an "*Affenspiel*" under the guise of religious ceremony. The threats of Satan's power, the consecrated herbs and candles, the need to "purify" the *Sechswöcherin*, are sheer error and superstition. It is Christian and praisewor-thy, however, for "pious matrons," when their "weeks" are finished, to come to church to receive a blessing and give thanks to God.[27] Martin Chemnitz elaborates on the Lutheran ceremony of churching: in Braunschweig, after the six-week confinement has ended, mothers come with their infants to church; a sermon is preached, after which the mothers approach the altar and the pastor reads psalms and other Scripture passages, prays over the mother and child, and blesses them.[28] Such a service is a "fine Christian arrangement" (*Ordnung*), unlike the Catholic ceremony, which, although it contains the proper elements of thanksgiving, is "befuddled and corrupted" by "much godless conduct and superstitious abuses."[29] It is only in a stripped-away form that churching be-comes a truly pious and Christian ritual.

Karant-Nunn suggests that the ritual of churching survived in Protestant churches for a number of reasons: first, the laity refused to give up the practice, which they regarded as "a means of defeating those swirling, invisible forces that threatened health and well-being," a way to minimize the power of the devil at a dangerous time; second, it served to reintegrate the female partici-pants of the birthing process back into society; third, it functioned to reimpress upon such women their subordination to male authority, especially through liturgical reference to Eve's punishments of "conceiving in sin, bearing chil-dren in pain, and being subordinated to her husband."[30] Churching, a signif-icant "ritual of transition," was valuable enough to the various social groups involved—husbands and wives, clergy and laity—that there was continued interest in its maintenance. This latter point is no doubt the case, for it does not seem that Lutherans or other Protestants would have any overriding *theo-logical* interests in maintaining ritual churching. The message of female sub-ordination that Karant-Nunn sees so clearly articulated in the liturgy and some sermons—which she in fact calls the "context of concerted indoctrination" through which Protestant churching must be understood—is not so clearly seen in the Lutheran sermons used in this study. The practice of confinement occupies a much greater place throughout these sermons than ritual churching and seems to be as much a restriction on husbands as it is on wives. Confine-ment was thought to have important health benefits for mother and child, and stronger women were indeed encouraged to subordinate their own desires to the good of other women, and thus the community. Churching, however, seems from these sermons to be a ritual still strongly associated with Catholic (i.e., superstitious) practices and thus somewhat problematic for Lutheran min-isters. The element of subordination that is apparent is that of lay people (in this case, women) to God, and, by association, to those with divine authority, that is, clergy. The male authority/female subordination paradigm is definitely present, but more as a subtext under the desire of clergy to control and direct all religious and ritual aspects of life.

"And a Sword Shall Pierce Your Soul"

The passage that the aged Simeon spoke to Mary concerning the sword that
would pierce her soul has had a conflicted history within the tradition of Christian exegesis. Origen perhaps inaugurated this conflict by suggesting that the
sword of the prophecy would be Mary's own doubts during her son's passion:
"Why should we believe that, when the Apostles were scandalized, the Mother
of the Lord remained immune from scandal? If she had not suffered scandal
in the passion of the Lord, Jesus would not have died for her sins."[31] The
"sword" of doubt caused Mary's faith to waver, according to Origen. Although
a number of later Greek fathers, including Basil of Caesarea, incorporated this
suggestion, many others rejected the idea that Mary ever doubted Christ. Epiphanius, in his *Panarion*, suggests that the sword is Mary's possible death by
martyrdom, although he neither affirms nor denies her death. Ambrose, setting the tone for the western church, does not attribute any doubt to Mary but
rather indicates that the sword is "her foreknowledge of the passion, because
she is 'not ignorant of the heavenly mystery.' "[32] His picture of Mary at the foot
of the cross prefigures the medieval *Mater Dolorosa* and explicitly connects her
with the church as its type. Much later, Geiler preaches on the connection of
the prophesied sword to Christ's passion by indicating that it refers to the pain
Mary would feel at the crucifixion. Such pain, the *"mitleiden"* with Christ's
suffering, makes her the greatest of the martyrs, because her suffering was in
her heart rather than her body.[33]

Lutheran preachers in the sixteenth century primarily followed the tradition of Ambrose, finding in Simeon's prophecy a prefiguration of Mary's pain
at Christ's passion and expanding on her position as a "type" of the church.
Luther insists that Simeon is not here referring to a physical sword, "for we
do not read of Mary that she was physically martyred and tortured."[34] Rather,
the prophecy indicates the "grief and sorrow" that Mary would have to suffer
at her son's pain and death, without the comfort of her spouse, for Joseph
would not be there.[35] It is odd, concedes Luther, that Simeon would give Mary
and Joseph a blessing, and then immediately after pronounce such a prophecy
as this, but Christians should understand that these words were also spoken
for their benefit.[36] The situation indicates that, although the world appears to
have many wise, pious, reasonable, and honorable people, the gospel lays bare
such false appearances and shows the truth of sin in the world. Simeon told
Mary that a "sword" would pierce her heart because she would see and experience all the evil in the world, "and not her alone, but the whole Christian
church."[37]

Both of these elements recur frequently in later Lutheran sermons: Simeon's prophecy of the sword is a warning to Mary of the suffering to come;
and the prophecy applies as much to the church and all Christians as to Mary.
Anton Corvinus suggests that Simeon told Mary of her future suffering so that
she would not be surprised by seeing her son's passion.[38] Peter Artopoeus
insists that there is no great happiness that does not also include unhappiness:

Mary's great blessing at being the mother of Christ includes the great suffering of the cross. In fact, this is true for all Christians: "these two things cling together, having Christ, and bearing the cross, or the sword piercing one's soul."[39] Mary's suffering at Christ's rejection and cross is shared by all the pious, according to Culmann, for "how much pain afflicts the pious, when they see Christ condemned and scorned."[40] Mathesius also asserts the unity of Mary with all the faithful in her suffering: "Mary and dear Christianity will have great anxiety, misery, and sorrow, because the world will band together and rebel against Jesus Christ by force."[41] Mary is no longer the "great martyr" portrayed by Geiler, nor even the stoic representative of the church at the foot of the cross, having compassion with Christ's passion (which led some to the idea that Mary's suffering has salvific effect along with Christ's as coredemptrix—see chapter 6). Rather, she is one among many Christians who suffer at Christ's pain and death, her uniqueness subordinated to the community of Christians who grieve at the foot of the cross.

Along with what is, in effect, a de-emphasis of Mary's special position as Christ's mother and the one who receives this troubling prophecy, we also find in the later sermons a modified version of Origen's position that Mary doubted Christ. While explaining why Mary should be warned of the future suffering and rejection of her son, many preachers suggest that the warning is designed to keep her from despairing at Christ's passion—without this warning, she might well have faltered in her faith. Johannes Wigand intimates that Simeon forewarned Mary of her future suffering at Christ's persecution so that she might not "fall away, [or] become faint-hearted and discouraged."[42] Rather, she would understand that such things were ordained by God for human salvation. Christoph Vischer suggests that Simeon's prophecy was meant to disabuse Mary of the notion that her life would be "pure roses" and that she would never suffer any care or sorrow, so that when troubles came she would not be "knocked back" by the experience.[43] Good preachers should learn from this example to preach the cross rather than pleasure, for it serves the people better when hard times come. In yet another sermon, both Mary and Joseph were expecting great joy and blessings from their son, based on all the good things they had been told about him. But Simeon "glossed the text" for them: their "worldly" hopes for Jesus would not be fulfilled, but rather his very greatness would precipitate his rejection and condemnation by the world.[44] Mary had believed like the woman in the crowd, "blessed is the womb that bore [Christ]"; but although she was loved by her son, this love would not protect her, or any Christian, from suffering. For Mary, "that is, the church of God, will have a sword penetrate through [her] soul."[45]

Simeon's prophecy of the sword piercing Mary's soul, the first of her traditional seven "sorrows," is commonly interpreted by Lutheran preachers to refer to Mary's pain and suffering during Christ's passion. She is forewarned by Simeon of her coming suffering so that she will not be surprised, and so that she might learn that the life of a Christian always includes a cross to bear. The later preachers even intimate that, had she not been forewarned, she might have fallen away or despaired, as Origen had originally suggested. This is not the same Mary of whom the post-Tridentine St. Francis de Sales (d. 1662) instructs his readers that she did not grieve or show any "feminine" weakness at the cross, because she knew that Christ would rise from the dead.[46] The Mary portrayed by Lutheran preachers in sermons on the text of Simeon's prophecy also is not the medieval *Mater Dolorosa*, standing in grief at the foot of the cross, who becomes the mother of the faithful through her compassion and suffering. Rather, the Lutheran Mary is subsumed by the church and now is only *one* of the pious faithful who suffer in the world's rejection of Christ. In representing the church, she becomes less important than that of which she is the model.

[handwritten margin notes: Is the Lutheran Mary also the Zwinglian or Calvinist Mary too?]

Anna Reinterpreted: A Model of Moderation and Piety

The final element in the story of Mary and Joseph's trip to the temple in fulfillment of the law is the narrative concerning Anna, the prophet and widow who had reached the great age of eighty-four.[47] According to Luke, "She never left the temple but worshiped there with fasting and prayer night and day" (Luke 2:37, NRSV). Like Simeon, she praised God and spoke about the child "to all who were looking for the redemption of Jerusalem" (2:38). Unlike Simeon, however, Anna does not play a significant role in sixteenth-century Lutheran sermons. She is discussed in only seven of the sermons used in this study. However, she serves as an important foil to Mary in these sermons, for she, unlike Mary, was a married woman (i.e., not a virgin) and a widow. While Mary's virtues in this particular text were most often recommended to all Christians—her obedience, her glad attendance at church services, her humility—and women in childbirth, Anna was a good example for wives and especially widows to follow. She is portrayed as a model widow, which, for these solid Lutheran pastors, required a certain amount of creative interpretation to make the text fit their own notions of what that might be.

In a sermon from 1538, Johannes Brenz seizes on the phrase just cited, "she never left the temple and served God with fasting and prayer day and night," to explain that she was not superstitious, but rather simply pious.[48] Anna did not fast in order to "expiate" her sins, for here, Brenz suggests, fasting means "living moderately" rather than not eating.[49] Such "fasting" is in fact a great virtue and leads to better service of God. It also does not "give the body occasion to sin through luxury."[50] Anna's virtues lend weight to her faith, and Brenz suggests that she no doubt spoke of Christ's kingdom and how it would not be of this world. Corvinus, on the other hand, believes that Anna said nothing that had not already been said by Simeon, and thus there was no need for Luke to record her words. Because it is her faith that saves her, it is important for "all women, widows and virgins," to follow her in believing in Christ, but also in her other virtues: in good conduct and in righteous service of God. For while it is faith that saves, such faith must be "living and active."[51] Johann Spangenberg agrees that it was her faith and not her works that justified Anna: "This tree was good, thus it produced good fruit."[52]

In Mathesius's longer *Postilla*, we find a greater treatment of Anna than in earlier sermons. He explains that Anna stayed in the temple for safety's sake, as the land was full of soldiers and fighting, as well as to serve God. She lived "soberly and moderately" like a true "church widow," serving the tabernacle, teaching girls, and praying constantly for the salvation of Israel.[53] After hearing Simeon's witness and song in the temple, she believed "her priest's blessed words, and began to praise and thank God, and sing her psalms with the other women," and confess that this child was the Messiah.[54] Mathesius is careful here not to assign an extraordinary role to Anna: she served as a widow according to the law of Moses; although called a "prophet," she heard and believed the gospel through the preaching of Simeon; and her witness to Christ is placed in the context of the worship of other women. Mathesius encourages his listeners to follow these examples: men should be "Simeons, diligent hearers of the word of God," while women should be "pious Annas, [and] diligently go to church, live moderately and modestly, pray at home with your children and servants, . . . comfort each other with God's word, speak and sing of it in your homes, go to the holy Sacrament, [and] trust confidently in the Lord with patience."[55] Women, although encouraged to follow Anna, are instructed to do so *at home*, in the proper sphere of women, among children and servants. The example of Anna has been modified to fit a sixteenth-century Lutheran pastor's notion of the proper activities of women.

Anna is given the title "prophet," explains Johannes Wigand, because she "knew the promises and at the same time, with others, paid attention to the time of the future Messiah and reminded others about [the coming Messiah]."[56] She is praised first, however, because she is "pious and God-fearing." Her piety led her to avoid laziness and luxury, and to prefer hearing God's word preached. She lived in the temple, as was the custom of "some females," in order to serve the Levites by washing the clothes used in temple services.[57] Her role in the temple, he suggests, was not to serve as a prophet but rather as a washerwoman. She fasted and prayed, not in a "superstitious" manner, but rather to serve God. At the time when Jesus was presented in the temple, Anna was led by the Spirit to him and added her voice to Simeon's, "confirming his prophecy" and seconding his praise and prayer. Her role was rather to confirm and support than to preach the gospel herself.

Anna was one of that pious order of matrons that served in the temple, according to Paul Eber, by cooking, cleaning, and washing clothes for the priests. There must have been, he reasons, a great deal of blood and mess from all the slaughters and offerings, requiring much cleaning. These women, including Anna, loved nothing better than to "hear sermons, train themselves in God's word, pray to him, and what was foremost, maintain the girls' school."[58] Such a life was not, however, anything like a cloister or a monastery, for such widows' "fasting" was not existing on bread and water, then pursuing a life of lazy inactivity. Rather, their fasting was "living secluded and taking food and drink moderately" in order better to serve God and hear his word.[59] This lesson of moderation is for all Christians, for no glutton or drunkard can properly serve God.

For Martin Chemnitz, Anna serves an even greater function: she is proof for all women that, despite Eve's sin, they too can be saved. Without such biblical examples women might despair, since Christ was a man and not a woman. The fact that Anna was allowed, like Simeon, to preach and teach in the temple, both publicly and privately, should give comfort to pious women that "they also, as well as men, belong to the kingdom of Christ."[60] Chemnitz does not indicate that women should learn from this example to take on the role of public teachers or preachers, for he stresses that Anna had the office of prophet, which gave her a special and unusual status. Along with her duties of washing and cleaning, her main responsibilities were in the girls' school, where she would have taught Scripture along with proper behavior and modesty.

Along with her special comfort to women in the knowledge that they too are children of God, Anna is also a comfort to the elderly, especially widows. However, Chemnitz warns, widows must remember to care first for their own families, children, grandchildren, and parents. Only if they are alone without such family responsibilities should they take on the role of serving the church, and then only if they meet the moral requirements of such a position; that is, if they have led a life of piety and moderation. Such aged widows, whom Chemnitz terms "beguines," would have a home and continued care provided for them by the community. Even such a home, however, is only for women who "are peaceful, conducted themselves well and honorably in their youth, and are worthy of such alms."[61]

Unlike Mary, Anna is an elderly widow, a "prophet" in the temple. For Lutheran preachers she serves as a fine example of how women can serve God and the church. However, her example requires a great deal of interpretation, not only to protect people from "papist" error but also to maintain proper social order and decency among women. Although Wigand is comfortable asserting that Anna lived in the temple, the other preachers are not, insisting rather that she lived nearby. Although she fasted and prayed day and night, this was not ascetic behavior, which would be considered inappropriate in such a pious matron. Rather, her "fasting" was simply moderation in food and drink, not "superstitious" activity meant to gain her heavenly merit. Her role in the temple is also circumscribed: she helped the priests by cleaning and washing clothes, she attended services and the sacraments, and she taught in the girls' school. Even her prophetic participation in the presentation of Jesus in the temple is downplayed: several preachers thought she must only have repeated what Simeon had already said, and confined herself to hymns and prayers. When Anna's example is recommended to women, the sphere is shifted to the home, rather than the church or some other public forum. Even Chemnitz, who specified an order of widows for the church, tightly restricted those who could participate in such an order. The final result is an Anna that resembles a pious, modest, sixteenth-century *Hausfrau* much more strongly than an ascetic widow, a prophet, or a preacher.

The holiday of Mary's Purification, which became an important celebration in honor of the Virgin in the Middle Ages, was maintained by Lutherans in the sixteenth century, despite a number of "superstitious" practices associated with the holiday that were problematic for the reformers. The holiday was retained in the Lutheran calendar primarily because of its significance as a *Herrenfest*— the scriptural text related an important event in Christ's infancy. However, the holiday also remained important in Lutheran regions because of the vitality of social and religious traditions surrounding the churching of parturient women. After the churching ritual(s) of the late medieval church had been "purified" of their superstitious elements—holy water, relics, and blessed candles, the object most explicitly associated with the holiday of Mary's Purification—Lutheran pastors could recommend such rituals to their parishioners as godly and pious activities. While a godly prayer and blessing service could be gladly administered by Lutherans however, the overtones of ritual cleansing of impurity and driving away the power of the devil in churching continued to bother many preachers and were condemned throughout especially the later sermons.

If churching as a ritual activity remained somewhat ambiguous for Lutheran ministers because of persistent popular ideas concerning the ritual, the practice of a six-week confinement for new mothers received universal support among the clergy. A period of confinement was recommended most especially for the health of the mother and new baby, and those who rejected it or were tempted to cut it short were strongly criticized. Preachers condemned those "tyrannical" husbands who pushed their wives into housework and marital duties too soon. They also heaped condemnation upon those stronger women who shortened their own confinement, to the detriment of other women who needed the full period to recover. Like Mary, new mothers were expected to subordinate their own desires to the good of the community, whether in obedience to the law or to social custom. In this context, Mary's example teaches that freedom from the law never means license to do what one pleases: a truly pious man or woman will always sacrifice in order to serve God and the community.

The text that follows Mary's purification, normally read on the Sunday after Christmas, includes Simeon's very important prophecy to Mary of the sword that would pierce her soul, as well as the example of Anna the prophetess. Although Lutherans follow the majority of western interpreters in considering Simeon's prophecy to refer to Mary's pain under the cross of her son, most preachers tend to downplay Mary's pain and sorrow at Christ's passion. Instead, they emphasize that, as Mary represents the church, so it is the church (and thus all Christians) that suffers and grieves at the cross. While in Catholic tradition Mary's association with the image of the church tended to glorify the status of Mary, in Lutheran sermons it seems to have the opposite effect. The church, of which she is the model, becomes more important than she, and her own sufferings as Christ's mother are minimized.

Thus, the picture of Mary that emerges from sermons on these texts can be characterized by subordination: she is humble and obedient to a law of which she is free, for the sake of others and out of respect for God's law; she is willing to be thought impure and in need of purification, despite her true purity as a virgin, again for the sake of others and to avoid scandal; even in the prophecy of her pain and suffering at the death of her son, she is subordinate to the community of Christians, all of whom suffer the prophesied sword as much as she. The image of the prophetess Anna only serves to reinforce the humility of Mary's position: what could be seen as a powerful, public, even ascetic female figure is instead interpreted as a pious, meek, servile widow, who spends her time washing up, teaching girls, and supporting Simeon, who takes the foreground. Lutheran preachers do their best in their sermons on these texts to shape unwieldy feminine images into the "proper" picture of the pious Christian woman, struggling to translate these exceptional figures from another time and culture into role models to which their audiences could relate.

4

Mary in Luke 2:41–52

A Family Visit to Jerusalem

In chapter 2 of Luke's gospel, we find the only biblical record of Jesus' life after his early childhood and before the beginning of his ministry and adulthood. This story records the events surrounding the required trip to the temple in Jerusalem at Passover taken by Mary and Joseph when Jesus was twelve years old. This was the first year that his parents took Jesus along on this journey, which required more than one day in travel. After celebrating the holiday in Jerusalem, Mary and Joseph left the city with their friends and headed home. It was not until the first evening, upon stopping for the night, that they realized that Jesus was not with them. After looking for him among their acquaintances, they returned that night to the city, and spent the next three days searching for their son. Finally, they found him in the temple, sitting among the learned men, talking and listening, surprising them with his maturity. Mary scolded her son for his behavior, but he replied that they should have known he would be in his father's house. His parents did not understand him, but he returned home with them and was an obedient son. Mary "treasured all these things in her heart," and Jesus grew in wisdom and in favor.[1]

This text from Luke 2 was the traditional gospel reading for the Sunday after Epiphany, and thus it appears in the majority of sixteenth-century Lutheran postils.[2] This vignette from Jesus' early adolescence provided a prime opportunity for Luther and his followers to discuss one of their favorite subjects: familial relationships and responsibilities.[3] Mary and Joseph were the good and pious parents who took their child to church and observed religious holidays. Jesus was the obedient son who loved attending church and studying. The crux of the story, that Jesus remained behind unbeknownst to his parents, who then had to search for days to find him, did not produce more than a twinge of defensiveness on the part of several sermon writers. They discuss the issue of parental obedience at length, but on the whole, Jesus is portrayed as the ideal child and it is his parents who take the ambiguous role. They can be seen as good examples, but also make mistakes and display their faulty human nature.

Mary in particular comes in for her share of attention, partly because she plays a greater role than Joseph in the gospel story but also because the Lutheran preachers were concerned to counteract some common Catholic notions of Mary that they viewed as false. Catholic preachers had not used this text as the basis for medieval Mariology, but most Lutheran preachers used every available opportunity for correction. We find in the sermons of Geiler only a few points of significance for Mary. He is very interested, like the later Lutheran preachers, in discussing proper familial relationships: how children should obey and honor their parents; how parents should love their children; even how wives should respect their husbands, the way Mary does when speaking Joseph's name before her own. Joseph himself did not discipline Jesus because he knew that he was God's son, not his own. Mary chided him only out of her great love. Christ was not so much disobedient to his parents, as he was obedient to God and diligent in spiritual matters. Geiler insists that God had ordained this event should happen. Afterward, Jesus returned with Mary and Joseph, and his example of obedience is a great "comfort and lesson" to all children that they should honor their parents.[4] The only point of "wonder" is that Mary did not understand Christ's response, since she also knew he was God's son.[5] Geiler makes no sort of critique against Mary, Joseph, or Jesus, instead relying on the fact that this event was ordained for some purpose in God's greater plan.

Among Lutheran sermons, we see as we move from texts published earlier in the century to texts from the last ten or fifteen years under investigation a decided shift in the treatment of Mary, from a generally positive if fairly limited representation to a more critical and extended one. Throughout this period she is portrayed by Lutheran writers more as a *parent*, while her female role as a *mother* is not emphasized. In general, she is not held up as a model for women in this group of sermons but rather provides a positive example for parents— and all good Christians—to follow or a negative example of behaviors that all listeners or readers should avoid. Authority is a central issue in all of these texts: the authority of parents over their children and its limits, but also (and even more pervasive, although often as a subtext) the authority of the pastor as the divine representative over his congregation. Mary's obedience to religious laws, to her husband, and even to her son's will is used to support the authority of Lutheran pastors in matters both of religion and morality, and over against the authority of the Roman Catholic Church, which Luther and his followers had rejected.

Luther and the Earliest Lutheran Postils

The text that Stephan Roth provides in the *Winterpostille* (1528) for this Sunday's sermon was previously published in 1523, and was given only slight emendations. In this particular sermon, Luther is especially concerned with Mary and how her situation and actions in this story should be interpreted. However, he does not dwell upon her role as "mother," nor does he use her as a special example for mothers. He begins by pointing out that this gospel shows an example of "the holy Cross" and how Christians should behave when they have to carry it.[6] Mary, although she was highly blessed, was not immune to trouble and sorrow. The event of losing her child was probably almost overwhelming to her, and she must have felt that God no longer found her worthy to be the mother of his son. In fact, Luther suggests that God sent these sorrows to Mary on purpose, to teach her not to rely upon herself, saying "I am his mother."[7] Her example, according to Luther, shows us that we must also not rely upon ourselves and our own confidence. Rather we should trust in God, who provides and increases our faith. God humbles the great saints both for their own good and for our benefit. We realize that we are not alone in our troubles, and, in fact, many saints have had to bear worse trials than our own.[8]

But Mary serves as more than an example to comfort us in times of trouble; she provides us with a lesson of what we should *not* do. The reason that Jesus could not be found was that his parents searched for him among "friends and acquaintances" rather than in the temple. The "friends and acquaintances" represent for Luther the teachings of the councils and church fathers, but Jesus will only be found in "that which is his father's," that is, in the word of God.[9] Luther tells his listeners to reject those who continually cry, "The holy councils have decided it, the church has offered it, men have for so long held it, so should we not believe in it?"[10] If Mary herself did not know where to find Christ and mistakenly sought him among friends, how can we think to find him among the teachings of the councils or the learned doctors?: "The bishops and councils have without a doubt not had so much of the Holy Spirit as she, and she failed, so how should they not be in error, since they think to find Christ in other than that which is his father's, that is, in God's word?"[11]

We should not turn to bishops, councils, the pope, or even Mary herself, who could not find Jesus, but instead we must turn to the gospel. When the angel announced to the shepherds that Christ was born, he did not tell them to seek for Mary and Joseph, but rather to look for a babe wrapped in swaddling clothes and lying in a manger. This tells us, according to Luther, that "God does not want to point to any saints, and also not to the mother herself," but rather to a "sure place," that is, the manger.[12] We find Christ "wrapped up" in the Scriptures the way the babe was wrapped in the swaddling clothes and laid in the manger, that is, the sermon, out of which we are fed and nourished.[13] Luther is telling his listeners, in effect, not to seek for their savior through the mediation of Mary and the saints, but rather through God's word and in particular through the interpretation of God's word that they hear their pastor preach.

One of the earliest Lutheran printed postils is the *Indices . . . in Euangelia* of Wittenberg preacher Johannes Bugenhagen (1484–1558) from 1524, which provides short summaries or main points of each gospel lesson for the church year and holidays.[14] For the first Sunday after Epiphany, he suggests two points of importance. The first refers to the actions of Mary and Joseph: what does their trip to Jerusalem show us about the value of the works of the law?[15] Although there is a slightly negative tone in this question, we will see that most of the later sermon writers land squarely on the side of praising Mary and Joseph for following the law that requires them to travel to Jerusalem. The second point refers to Christ: "Christ reveals the divine vocation of parents. He is made subject. Christ was made under the law (Gal. 4) and he obeys his parents, as far as the divine calling allows."[16] This point is also addressed in all the sermons we will see, underscoring how important the issue of authority was for the leaders of the Lutheran church throughout the sixteenth century. However, there is also an ambiguity in the text that must be discussed, which is that obedience to parents is secondary to obedience to God. Discernment is required in deciding when rejection of parental authority for divine authority is appropriate.

The Early Latin Postils

The main themes that we find discussed in Luther's sermon and mentioned by Bugenhagen were taken up by their contemporaries in a series of Latin postils published in the 1530s and 1540s. These collections were addressed to a small, select audience of the well-educated and appear to be intended primarily for the use of pastors or pastors-in-training. Several are clearly not sermons that were preached, but are organized by point, with objections and responses. In this way, it was hoped, the preachers who used these textual tools might "better be able to present [the gospel], to the glory of God, and the benefit of many."[17]

In the *Loci in Evangelia* of Anton Corvinus published in 1536, we hear what becomes a common theme in discussing Mary's and Joseph's attention to the law: although they had been justified by faith, they did not want to offend anyone by not fulfilling the law, and therefore they traveled to Jerusalem. "This is an example of charity."[18] Corvinus briefly outlines the remainder of the lessons contained in this gospel: Mary and Joseph bore a heavy cross after losing their son; Jesus stayed behind and harshly reprimanded his mother to show that the concerns of his heavenly father were greater than those of his earthly parents; but after his time in the temple he returned home with Mary and Joseph and was obedient to them. The only further note of importance is that Mary and Joseph placed a great deal of emphasis on training their son from a young age in God's word. Through their example of taking Jesus to Jerusalem where the law is taught, they hoped to teach all other parents to do the same.[19]

Artopoeus, in his *Evangelicæ conciones dominicarum* of 1537, looks more at the rhetorical teaching strategy of this gospel. We find it displays "demonstrative," "judicial" ("where Christ defends his legitimate status before his parents"), and especially "didactic" genera, whereby Christ teaches us.[20] The "proposition" of the text is that "Mary lost Christ, and found him again. Christ withdrew from his parents, remaining in Jerusalem, and set himself up for us as an example."[21] Mary and Joseph headed home, thinking that Jesus was somewhere among the group and did not discover him missing until they met in the evening. Having lost this "treasure" of their firstborn son and the savior of the world, Mary felt God had punished her for being negligent and careless. Thus, we see that God often tests us by giving and then taking away his gifts. Artopoeus remarks that this is the moment when "that sword of Simeon pierced her soul."[22] But Christ had several important points to teach his parents and us through his actions: parents should be honored, but more obedience is due to God; in the matter of divine callings or concerns (negotio), parents do not have rights over their children, even to question them; however, except in matters of divine importance, children must yield to their parents.[23]

Where Artopoeus is concerned with the freedom of children from their parents in divine matters, Arsacius Seehofer emphasizes the example that Jesus gave in reading, hearing, and teaching God's word. In this gospel, Christ reminds his followers to "excite the people to the study of the divine word," and through his example, Seehofer proposes, he "invites us to a similar work, that we might frequently hear the heavenly word, and learn it diligently."[24] The fact that Jesus remained behind without his parents' knowledge indicates how important this work is, and his harsh and authoritative response to his mother after her "interruption" again stresses the importance of the study and teaching of God's word over obedience to or even recognition of parents.

In a sermon of Philipp Melanchthon we find a repetition of these themes, along with a greater stress on Mary and her participation in the story.[25] Mary, Joseph, and Jesus attended the festival in Jerusalem although they, as already justified, were not *required* to do so. Rather, they provided an example to others in order to promote the ministry of the church. Christ's actions also show us that "the command of God takes priority over the will of the parents," but disobeying one's parents is limited to the cases of when they prohibit "the study of true doctrine, confession, and marriage."[26] Melanchthon does not discuss further the question of marriage here, although it was an important issue for Lutheran reformers and ministers.[27] However, his pairing of marriage with doctrine and confession would seem to indicate that it relates to divine matters and is not simply a social concern.

Most interesting for our study is his fourth point, "concerning the negligence and suffering of Mary." As Melanchthon remarks, the "world" has a different understanding of sin than God does: "it does not recognize how much evil there may be in natural infirmity." However, the saints do not fall into this trap: "they understand the magnitude of their inner weakness, and often a great punishment is experienced after only a little carelessness."[28] As much as "the world" might deny it, the saints themselves know that they "carry around sin" (circumferant peccatum) and when calamities such as the one that befell

Mary occur, they are able to recognize their own faults. Because of this, Mary saw herself as the "second Eve," who had also brought the human race into peril through her negligence. Because she understood what a great sin she had committed, the suffering that she experienced in those three days cannot even be comprehended.[29] Here Melanchthon seems to be suggesting a strict Augustinian view, that concupiscence or "inner weakness" is in itself a sin or necessarily leads one into sin, even if a sin of omission rather than commission.

It is difficult to determine what influence Melanchthon's text had upon his readers or upon later postils. The fact that he calls Mary's negligence a *sin* is somewhat unusual in light of Luther's reluctance to say more than that she erred, and the absence of such a reference in the other texts from this period. Melanchthon is circumspect, moving from a general discussion of "the saints" to Mary, who felt herself that she had sinned and called herself the "second Eve." Her *negligentia* is recognized as sinful because of its results and her concomitant suffering; because even the smallest weakness can cause the greatest evil, Melanchthon is willing to say that Mary sinned. Although this willingness places him in a camp with writers from a later generation, separating him from his contemporaries, there is no virulent tone or explicit anti-Romanist feeling such as that we will occasionally see later.

German and Latin Sermons from Mid-Century

One of the earliest German postils, from 1545, is Corvinus's *Kurtze vnd ainfeltige Außlegung,* which provides both the gospel reading and a "short interpretation" of the text for "poor pastors and house-fathers."[30] Corvinus is concerned to lay out four points that Luke is trying to teach by including the story of the twelve-year-old Jesus in his gospel. First, this story informs us of Christ's office and work: he came as a teacher, one who deals with the Scriptures, and not as a powerful and worldly king.[31] Second, we are taught that parents should raise their children to be honest, respectable, and blessed by God.[32] Mary and Joseph are examples of good parents who follow God's commands by taking their son to church and training him well. The third point follows Luther's interpretation: Mary and Joseph had to bear the cross of losing their son, and Mary in particular was distraught, even to the point of losing her faith. She sought her son for three days but did not find him until she looked in the temple, which teaches that Christ, the hope and comfort of Christians, cannot be found anywhere but in the temple, that is, in God's word.[33] The fourth point stresses that children must be obedient to their parents, except in the case that the parents oppose God's will. As an example, Jesus was both obedient to God when his parents would have hindered him and obedient to his parents after his experience in the temple.

Corvinus spends a significant amount of time in his sermon dealing with the moral issues of proper Christian child rearing and the obedience of children toward their parents. His concern is not so much with Mary as an example, although he mentions that she would have been especially distraught and guilt-ridden upon discovering that her son was missing. Rather, he stresses that Joseph and Mary together are an example to parents, and that Jesus shows children when they should obey their parents and when they owe a higher duty to God. These same points appear in the German postil of Caspar Huberinus, with the addition that children are to be obedient not only to their parents but also to their teachers and rulers, indeed to all their elders. In turn, parents should discipline their children first with words, as when Mary reproached Jesus, before they turn to corporal punishment.[34]

This gospel text provides Johannes Brenz with an opportunity to give "a few words on the education of children [boys]."[35] He emphasizes that the primary reason that today's youth are so troublesome, immodest, and disobedient is that they have only bad examples to follow from their parents and other adults. As he states, "the foremost and best instruction for children is the virtue and piety of parents and adults."[36] Without good examples, it is no surprise that children, already born with sinful natures, do not behave properly and piously. Parents who are bad examples and do not provide proper training for their children disobey God's will, bringing up "slaves of the devil" rather than "citizens of the heavenly kingdom."[37] We can presume that Brenz saw Mary and Joseph as the exemplary pious parents who took their son to church, although he does not state this specifically. What we do learn from the example of Jesus' parents, and Mary in particular, is that children are gifts from God, which he can give or take away, and that we should be satisfied with God's decision in this regard.

Other texts from this period also focus on the responsibilities of parents and children, with slightly varying themes, depending on the intended audience. Leonhard Culmann cites Mary and Joseph as good parental examples: they show us to keep our children from their infancy away from all iniquity, leading them instead to piety and religion, accustoming them to the sacred rites and studious and holy practices.[38] Mary and Joseph did not sin when they lost track of their son, but they did not realize that Jesus owed a greater debt of obedience to God than to them. The words of the apostle Peter are quoted by Culmann, as well as many other postil authors: "It is right to obey God more than men."[39] The fact that Mary and Joseph did not understand the situation and Jesus' words to them gives hope to those who "do not understand all the mysteries of God right away from the beginning."[40] We should indeed imitate Mary, who kept and pondered all these things in her heart.

The demand for obedience to God over obedience to one's parents and other authorities, which we also find expressed in the *Explicationes Piae* (1560) of Hieronymus Weller, should not lead the young person to doubt the authority that his parents have over him. Culmann insists that Christ's "hard response" to his parents should not be taken by youths as an example of "impious rebellion" that they can then follow. Rather, young people should see his example of returning home with his parents as an indication that the proper office of youth is to obey and "to live under the discipline of parents and magistrates."[41] Culmann and Weller seem to realize the difficulties involved in properly interpreting this story for a youthful audience: how does one maintain the youthful freedom from parents who oppose God's "divine business" without compromising parental authority over children? Artopoeus's *Postilla* of 1550, addressed to theology students with texts provided in both Greek and Hebrew, solves this problem by not introducing the matter: boys are to learn from Jesus' example to love reading God's word and attending worship, go to school, avoid bad society, be subject to their parents, and attend to the household and social manners. If they follow this pattern, they will grow up to be worthy and useful men (*frugi homines*), both beloved and dutiful to God and others.[42] He does not suggest that Jesus might also provide an example of disobedience to one's parents.

Johannes Mathesius also expresses a concern for proper familial behavior and duties, on the sides of both parents and children. Because he knows that Mary is a good mother, he insists that beyond bringing Jesus to church and teaching him to obey God's law, she also "accustoms him to work and lovingly cares for him her whole life long."[43] What is more, parents learn from this story that they should baptize their children, teach them the catechism, bring them to church, and teach them useful skills as well as virtues. As Mathesius reminds his readers, children are a blessing from God with which parents are entrusted.

Children, on the other hand, should learn from the example of Jesus. He was obedient to his mother, "in the form of a servant," and was a good carpenter and citizen of Capernaum.[44] Mathesius makes no mention of occasions when disobedience to parents is appropriate but rather insists that children are herein shown that they should be obedient to both their parents and schoolmasters, and take care of them in their old age. They should also gladly pray and thank God, attend sermons, honor ministers, happily study or work, serve everyone, and in general be "willing, chaste, faithful, honest, upright, and discreet."[45] If children follow this somewhat embellished example of Jesus, they will "find favor and grace with God and humanity, and have a long life, happiness, and advancement on earth."[46]

In his more extended postil of 1565, Mathesius repeats the lessons that parents and children should learn from this gospel story. He also takes much more care in pointing out the evils of his own day, suggesting that the example of Mary and Joseph should shame many parents. Jesus and his parents remained in Jerusalem for the full eight days of the holiday, not "running out of church as soon as the gospel reading or sermon is over, as if the church were burning."[47] They did not think it was more important to provide their child with fancy clothing and teach him courtly dancing than to raise him to study and follow God's word. Also, Jesus did not run about, play, or talk during the church service; neither did the sermon "go in one ear and out the other."[48] Those who behave this way, and scorn their parents and rulers, will receive their reward: "they will come into shameful poverty and be brought to ruin, and since they do not do penance, . . . they will finally be paid their due in hellfire."[49] The child that does not learn his lesson of obedience early will pay dearly for his sins, according to Mathesius.

The strong chastisement of parents and children that we hear from Mathesius finds an echo in later Lutheran sermons on this text: Veit Dietrich, in his *Vermanung von der Kinderzucht* of 1567, includes a long litany of complaints against parents, especially those concerned more with money or honor than with pious worship and the instruction of their offspring. He insists that parents think of their children first and not neglect them. However, fulfilling their basic needs should not be a parent's only concern. Parents must be good examples of piety and virtue to their children, but because children are "by nature evil and inclined to sin," parents must also diligently train them and require them to attend church.[50] Here Mary and Joseph are good examples: they not only traveled to the temple in Jerusalem every year, they also brought Jesus with them, teaching him to follow God's law. And as Dietrich reminds his readers, if you expect your children to obey you in matters such as their marriage, you must first teach them to obey God and follow his commands.

Of course, parents are not the only ones who can learn from this story: Jesus is a special example for children, showing that they should gladly go to church and find God's word more precious than all earthly things.[51] But, as Dietrich had complained about parents, so he also complains that children refuse to go to church and instead run wild in the streets. Jesus teaches children that they owe all earthly obedience to their parents, but also that they owe a higher obedience to their Father in heaven. God requires that children obey their parents, and all other earthly rulers along with them, but the things of the heavenly Father are higher and even occasionally demand that one reject all earthly authority, and suffer persecution. However, Dietrich, along with most other pastors who address this issue, does not specify any cases where rejecting worldly authority for the truth of the word would be justified.

Focus on Mary in Sermons from 1570

Up to this point, we have not seen much space devoted to Mary alone, except when the preachers consider her emotional reaction upon losing and searching for Jesus. There are several reasons for this lack of comment: first, writers tend to sound common themes already introduced in earlier works, such as Luther's; second, the duties of parents and the obedience of children are more important themes in the eyes of many sixteenth-century Lutheran pastors; and third, because of the limited space given for each sermon. Most of the postils contain fairly short sermons, while some are simply collections of main themes. This is not the case in the *Außlegung der Euangelien* of Christoph Vischer, published in 1570. Vischer provides three, and sometimes four, sermons for each Sunday and holiday in the year. This makes for a massive volume but also allows Vischer to explore fully a variety of topics, including Mary's role in this gospel story.

Vischer reminds his hearers/readers of Simeon's prophecy to Mary, that a sword should pierce her heart. She was highly blessed and chosen above all other women as a temple of the Holy Spirit, who took her flesh and blood and united it with the divine, but she was also a true "Maria," a poor sad woman.[52] Vischer suggests that, while Luke does not describe her sorrowful actions, we can imagine how she must have wrung her hands and reminded herself that she was responsible for losing the savior of humanity. The devil will have taunted her by saying that although Eve, the "murderer of humanity," cast the whole human race into sin and death, Mary is worse, for through her fault "God no longer has a son through whom he could help the human race."[53] This negative parallel between Eve and Mary is in sharp contrast to the parallel found in the Annunciation texts. In Annunciation sermons, like in much of previous Christian tradition, Eve is portrayed as bad and sinful, while Mary is, conversely, good and pure. Eve causes human suffering and sin, while Mary helps to bring about human salvation, even if only distantly, as Lutheran preachers emphasize. In this case, however, Vischer constructs a situation where Mary calls herself the "second Eve" and feels as though she too were responsible for the destruction of humankind.

Vischer also takes a closer look at the interchange between Mary and Jesus when they meet in the temple. Mary, as a good mother, spoke to her son in a friendly manner, not striking him or cursing, but "gently" and "modestly" addressing him.[54] Although she is a good example for parents in the use of reasonable discipline, she was really in the wrong in this case, acting like the rest of us when we try to bend God to our will. However, Jesus also gives a good example in that he responded to Mary pleasantly and obediently while pointing out his innocence. Children's first obedience is to God, but they should always be respectful and listen to their parents. What Vischer really finds lovely in this story is Mary's attitude of humility toward Jesus after he "publicly shamed her in the temple, before the whole world and the learned teachers"; she patiently accepted his response and thought about it, although she did not understand.[55] She, like all the other saints, showed incomprehension and weakness, and needed to grow from day to day in the understanding and recognition of Christ.[56] This story indicates for Vischer that preachers should, following the example of Christ, discipline publicly those who sin publicly, and listeners should learn from Mary to "suffer punishment patiently," and not grumble over being disciplined in front of others.[57] As long as we remain "docile" like Mary before Christ, God will comfort and patiently support us.[58] Christ serves in this example as a model for preachers, while Mary, his mother, is removed from her position of authority, and is instead praised as the model parishioner, docile and humble before the upbraiding she receives.

Niels Hemmingsen, in his postil of 1571, extends this negative trend even further. He comments that Jesus remained behind in Jerusalem to show that he was not only Mary's son but also God's, and that this divine sonship has a higher priority. His disappearance forced Mary and Joseph to greater care and higher diligence in their parenting and reminded them that they were "poor people by nature."[59] The fact that they did not know immediately that Jesus was missing shows their lack of diligence (vnfleis), which Hemmingsen suggests is no small sin. Mary in her sorrow must have compared herself to Eve, "for just as Eve was tempted through the devil's cunning, and thereby brought the whole human race into misery, so Mary thought that she, through her lack of diligence, had lost the promised savior of the world."[60] And this lack of diligence led Mary and Joseph into error, seeking Jesus among their companions, and only after three days finding him again in the temple among the learned men. In this example Hemmingsen insists that we can see ourselves: through our lack of diligence we neglect the service of God, his worship, and the sacraments, so that when troubles afflict us we do not know where to turn, and we are led into error.

Nicolaus Selneccer characterizes Mary's "error" as twofold: *in defectu*, she neglects her son; and *in excessu*, she worries too much about him, although she knows that he is God. She is an example of those "who do not know a middle way."[61] Her fault lay not in thinking that Jesus was with his father: Selneccer, along with a number of other preachers, comments on the Jewish custom of gender separation during worship that led to the misunderstanding about who had care of Jesus. Rather, as Hemmingsen phrases it, her fault lay in her lack of diligence in caring for her son, and then too much solicitude when he was missing and rediscovered. Selneccer does not insist that Mary sinned, but she is not held up as a great example, other than in her care to educate her son. She does, however, stand in her traditional role of representing the church: "Mary suffers, losing her son. In these things the tribulations of the church are portrayed." Her image is also conflated with the suffering Eve, and the searching lover of the Song of Songs: "I seek him whom my soul loves, I seek him, and I do not find him."[62] It is not until we reach the phrase "and Mary held all these things in heart" that she is again held up as an example for all to follow: we, too, should hear, read, and meditate upon the word of God, putting it into practice in our lives.

The ambiguity of Mary as an example becomes clear in the 1576 postil of Georg Spindler: in some regards she is to be emulated, while in others she is portrayed as weak and almost silly, and quite often in error. Our "dear Mary" travels the long way to Jerusalem, although "females were not so sternly commanded to do so," in order to participate obediently in all "Christian ceremonies."[63] She is a "blessed example" to all parents in that she took her son to church, and "diligently" brought him to hear the sermon, showing all how to raise pious children.[64] Spindler remarks again that it is not surprising that Mary and Joseph lost track of Jesus, for women and men were separated in the temple, but they still should be blamed for "lack of diligence and laziness" in traveling such a distance without noticing his absence.[65] Mary now must have felt terrible and feared that Jesus could be dead: "and such thoughts and ideas will have increased the suffering of her heart, that she will have thought about the example of Eve, 'See, you are now the other Eve, who brings the human race into eternal ruin.' "[66] When she found her son in the temple, she chastised him out of motherly love but also out of "lack of judgment and undeservedly."[67] Her child answered her sharply, that she and Joseph had no place interfering with his service to his father, and they were not in the right to have suffered so much pain and care in the matter.[68]

Georg Walther, in his *Außlegung der Euangelien* of 1579, suggests that

Mary's "error" was greater than simply thinking Jesus was with his father, or mistakenly seeking him among acquaintances. When she confronted Jesus in the temple and did not understand his response to her, it was revealed that she participated in the "delusion" of the other Jews: she had also believed that "her son Jesus would become a great worldly king" who would save his people from Roman rule.[69] By this we see that Mary was not without sin, for otherwise she would have considered what the angel and Simeon had prophesied to her, and understood that Jesus was the Son of God.[70] However, Walther concedes, she can still serve as an example of faith, for although she did not understand, she nevertheless believed and held these words in her heart.

Walther is concerned, as he points out in his preface, to counteract Catholic notions of Mary's role in salvation history. As he writes: "The papists do not want to recognize Christ alone as savior and the one who makes us holy, but next to him they place Mary who must help us."[71] He criticizes the songs and prayers that declare Mary the Comforter of the sorrowful, the Mother of orphans, the Fountain of mercy, grace, joy, and forgiveness. He rejects the notion that Christ somehow needs Mary in order to save humankind, or that we need her to speak for us before the throne of her son. The perceived threat of Catholic teaching had not disappeared in the roughly sixty years since Luther began his attempts to reform the church, and Walther felt the need to express strongly his rejection of the traditional Catholic image of Mary.

There is a clear development in the treatment of the image of Mary in sermons upon this text across the period under investigation. Luther, in his sermon of 1523, is concerned to paint an appropriate and balanced picture of Mary. He points out that this text shows that she could make mistakes and was like the rest of us in relying too much upon herself. She needed a reminder from God that her confidence and faith come from him. Luther wants to bring Mary down to earth, but not to negate a certain honor and status she deserves as the Mother of God. His sermon sets the tone, as well as many of the themes, for a number of the sermons that succeed his own. However, although most sermon writers follow his lead, almost all of them are more interested in the issues of family responsibilities of parents and children than he. The texts aimed primarily at schoolboys emphasize the necessity for children both to study and practice virtue: several authors promise worldly success and rewards for those who follow Jesus' example diligently. Most of the other postil authors balance their comments to both parents and children, insisting that parents must care for the spiritual and educational needs of their children, along with the physical, and that discipline should first be loving correction. Children, on the other hand, owe obedience to the parents who are training them to be good and pious adults, as well as to all other authorities. It is only in the case that divine commands require it that parental authority should be abrogated.

The emphasis on mutual familial responsibilities remains fairly constant in sermons throughout this period, but the tone used when discussing Mary changes rather dramatically. In Melanchthon's sermon of 1548 we find an early precursor to the later, more negative presentations of Mary. He critiques the "world's" view of sin in several ways: sins of omission must be understood to be as evil as those of commission; and even the great saints are sinners, as they in their humility surely understand themselves to be. Mary's example is illustrative: what seemed at first to be merely carelessness, a small error, is shown by its results to be a sin of epic proportion. The fact that she was *human* is enough for Melanchthon to show that she was sinful, for humanity is by its very nature weak and infirm. By her statement to Jesus in the temple we know that she suffered greatly for her sin, and as Melanchthon suggests, she felt herself to be the "second Eve."

This radical change in the interpretation of Mary's person and role does not find an echo in other sermon writers until late in the century, in those sermons published in 1570 and after. However, contrasting Melanchthon's grave and measured tone, these later sermons, while often continuing to use Mary as a good example for their listeners, speak of her with a harshness and negativity not seen before.[72] In these later texts, when Mary is characterized as seeing herself as the second Eve, she is cast as the "murderer of humanity" (*Menschenmörderin*).[73] The strategy of having Mary chastise *herself* as the second Eve, an event that, incidentally, is not recorded in the gospel of Luke, is used to distance the writer from the negative comments he is making about Mary, whose image retained much of its power and impact among lay people, if complaints about their practices are to be believed. The later sermonists also see her other actions in a negative light: she was irresponsible in allowing Jesus to remain behind unnoticed, her concern at his absence was excessive, she did not understand what he said to her despite the prophecies she had received, and she perhaps even participated in the Messiah-delusion of the other Jews.

Although the Lutheran sermon writers were concerned to remove the image of Mary from its Catholic constellation, replacing the powerful Queen of Heaven with a pious and modest mother, obedient under the law and authority, they were able to use her traditional connection with the image of the church to insinuate an ecclesiological critique of the Roman church through this text. This is true in Luther's sermon and in a majority of the others, who are no doubt often echoing Luther. As Culmann expresses it, "Mary erred, therefore the church can err."[74] As Mary was human and made mistakes, so the church councils and fathers could and did make mistakes. In light of this fact, the Lutheran preachers insist that all authority cannot reside in the church or its leadership, but must be found in God's word.

In turn, the ecclesiological critique enables these preachers to claim their own "gospel message" as correct, and to criticize the "false teachings" of the Roman church. However, this did not now mean that all Christians had the freedom to interpret the Bible as they wished or even to use the example of Jesus chastising his parents to rebel against authority. Through this text Luther and his followers could articulate what they saw as the necessary requirements of social control—Jesus was obedient and subject to his parents—while justifying the Protestant break from Roman Catholic hierarchy and authority— Jesus felt in this situation he must be obedient to his heavenly Father and not his earthly parents. To ensure that people, young people in particular, would not take Jesus' example as license for disobedience, all the authors emphasize that it is only when *God* requires it that children can disobey their parents. Several authors specify in which cases it might be appropriate: in matters of faith, of service to God, and occasionally in marriage. Other authors, no doubt unwilling to risk fostering dissent within families, do not address the issue at all, but instead strongly insist that children owe all obedience to parents, schoolteachers, pastors, and magistrates. Preachers, too, were concerned to uphold the integrity of the familial structure as the building block of society: the days in which a child might be encouraged to take monastic vows against the will of his or her parents were over. But preachers did expect to be authorities in many matters, not only for children but also for parents, and this form of dominance would preserve a higher authority for an interpreter of God's word.[75] We even see in the sermons of Christoph Vischer an identification between Christ and the pastor that emphasizes the necessity of congregational obedience to its leader.[76]

It is in the role of "parent," and less that of "mother," that Mary serves an important function in the Lutheran interpretations of this gospel lesson. Her image as a woman is deemphasized, while her role as a parental exemplar becomes central. Mary shows parents that they should raise children lovingly, be good examples, bring them to church, encourage them in education, discipline them with love, and treat them as treasures from God. Even her sorrowful soliloquies while searching for Jesus do not call forth any statements about women or mothers. Possibly this is because her behavior is not seen as particularly or ideally feminine, such as when she takes the main disciplinary role with Jesus. It is more likely, however, that this story raised issues of authority and obedience between parents and children and preachers and their congregations rather than between the sexes for these Lutheran preachers. When Mary is praised for certain qualities, such as her gentleness and friendliness when addressing Jesus, she is a model for parents, not just mothers. When she is praised for her docility and patience in taking correction, she is a model for subjects or members of the congregation, not wives. It was less important for these authors to use the "teachable moment" of this sermon to tutor wives and mothers in appropriate conduct, than it was to promote peace and harmony between rulers and subjects, between the pastor and his congregation, and between parents and children. They could do this by stressing the necessity of training, obedience, and good behavior, while justifying their own authority to teach and adjudicate this behavior despite their rejection of the "parental" role of the Roman Catholic Church.

5

The Wedding at Cana

"Es ward eyne hochzeyt zu Cana . . ." The traditional gospel reading for the second Sunday after Epiphany is taken from John, chapter 2, and recounts the story of Jesus' first miracle. The text relates that "the mother of Jesus was there," while Jesus and his disciples were also invited. When the wine was exhausted, Mary turned to her son, saying, "They have no wine." Jesus' response cries out for interpretation: "Woman, what concern is that to you and to me? My hour has not yet come."[1] The translation of the NRSV does not convey the same harshness as the sixteenth-century German version: "Weyb, was habe ich mit dyr zu schaffen?"[2] "Woman, what do I have to do with you?" Mary apparently did not respond but turned to the servants, telling them, "Do whatever he tells you." Jesus then ordered the servants to fill six stone jars, normally used for the Jewish rites of purification, with water and take some of their contents to the steward. Upon tasting it, the steward called the bridegroom, remarking that normally the good wine is drunk first, but he had saved the better wine for last. This first of Christ's miracles, which "revealed his glory," led his disciples to believe in him.[3]

Sermons on this story appear in most postils—it was a favorite text for preaching on the topic of marriage. This topic, dear to the hearts of many preachers, was an important one for Luther and his followers, in that marriage was the socio-religious institution that took center stage in the Protestant movement. The household was considered to be the basic building block of all society, and, with the rejection of an avowed life of celibacy, marriage became in actuality the only option for the Christian life.[4] Jesus' attendance at the wedding at Cana (despite the text's lack of emphasis on marriage itself) gave vital support to the notion that marriage is a divinely instituted and blessed state, a notion that Lutheran preachers were united in promoting. The fact that Jesus chose a wedding as the site of his first miracle and to begin his life of active ministry indicated the centrality of marriage to the church and the life of its people, both clerical and lay. Many preachers use this opportunity to reject explicitly any Roman Catholic critiques and limitations of marriage, instead insisting that the married life, even with its troubles and "crosses" to bear, is normative for Christians and fulfills God's design.

Mary's role in these sermons is, for the most part, unrelated to the issue of marriage. For those writers whose discussion of marriage includes comments about weddings, however, Mary does play a significant role in that she is a fine, Christian example of how we should help others, especially the poor, in planning and celebrating their weddings. She displays true Christian love and mercy in petitioning her son for help with the supply of wine, thus hoping to avoid any embarrassment to the bridal couple. But it is her interchange with her son that receives the most attention: Jesus' response receives lengthy interpretation, usually based on the traditional understanding that in Christ's public ministry, his divine role and service to his Father take precedence over his human relationships and his normal obedience to Mary.[5] The significance of the rebuke for Luther and his followers is, however, that Christians should not rely on Mary or other intercessors with Christ: this passage completely opposes the efficacy of such prayers. The harshness of Christ's response to Mary is often cited, and she is variously critiqued as overstepping her bounds, and even, in the latest sermons, as sinning in her request.

Despite this negative aspect concerning Mary that appears in most sermons, she is primarily offered as a positive example, not only of love and mercy but also and especially of faithful prayer. Not only does she "pray" to her son to help the young couple, but, instead of becoming angry or losing faith because of his rejection, she continues to hope for his future help. By meekly accepting his rebuke and turning to the servants with the words, "Do whatever he tells you," Mary displays the proper attitude for prayer. She witnesses to her strong faith, and, in exemplary Lutheran fashion, steadfastly holds to the "yes" hidden under the "no" of Christ's harsh words, not turning away in disappointment when she is not immediately granted her petition.

Marriage in the Reformation: A Brief Overview

As I have indicated, marriage became a central focus for Luther and his followers, both because of its positive benefits and role in society, and because of its importance for countering the Roman Catholic emphasis on celibacy as a higher calling. The reformers tended to see marriage and the family as in a state of crisis. In his first treatise on marriage, "On the Estate of Marriage," from 1522, Martin Luther complained that marriage had "universally fallen into awful disrepute," and "pagan books which treat of nothing but the depravity of womankind and the unhappiness of the estate of marriage" were everywhere available. As Steven Ozment observes, Luther is referring to clas-

sical works containing "misogynist and antimarriage sentiments" and to popular bawdy tales that were condemnatory toward women.[6] The clerical origin
of many such sentiments is unmistakable, and Protestant authors published
pro-marriage treatises especially addressed to an audience of former monks
and priests "who had been trained to regard marriage, sexuality, and women
in general as destroyers of their spiritual well-being."[7] Of course, not all those
of the clerical estate who lauded celibacy denigrated marriage—many fifteenth-
century and earlier Catholic writers had also praised the married life and recommended it to their readers. But Protestant authors elevated marriage over
celibacy, finding in marriage a stabilizing force for society and a tool for coun-
teracting the moral and spiritual degeneracy they saw around them.

Protestant authors, like their Catholic forebears, tended to cite the same
three "goods" of marriage delineated by Augustine: "the procreation of children, the avoidance of sin, and mutual help and companionship."[8] Because
marriage, through the family, was the basic building block of society, what
Ozment terms the "cradle of citizenship," the bearing and rearing of children
was the primary purpose and blessing of marriage.[9] The construction of a godly
society was dependent upon the proper inculcation of values and education in
children, as we have seen in the previous chapter. The second good, the avoidance of sin, bespeaks the fact that lust and concupiscence lurk within each
human being, leading to sexual desires that are as basic to our nature as eating
and sleeping. Without marriage, these desires lead one into sin, but within
marriage such desires have their proper and legitimate outlet. Luther compared
the marriage bed to "a hospital in which the disease of raging lust is treated."[10]
Several commentators remark that this view of the naturalness of sexual desires
actually led the reformers to a more positive view of sex and sexuality and a
"genuine break with pre-Reformation views": sex within marriage was not in-
herently sinful, except to the extent that all our actions are sinful, and it need
not be reserved solely for procreation.[11]

While the third good of marriage is "mutual help and companionship,"
this mutuality does not indicate equality. Although Protestant authors praised
marriage highly, it was marriage of a highly patriarchal and traditional order.
Most authors emphasize husbandly authority and wifely submission; in fact,
the submission of all other members of the family to the father, that is, both
children and servants, was required. Women are often praised in treatises and
sermons concerning marriage, but it is as exemplary wives and mothers that
they are so honored. A woman's modesty and domesticity, her devotion to her
husband and family, are her greatest ornaments. But women must be safely
ensconced within the family, under the authority of either a father or a husband; Protestant authors often speak of a woman's vocation as within the
home, not external to it. As Susan Karant-Nunn points out, the praise of marriage does not equal the praise of women qua women.[12] The Lutheran image
of Mary that we have seen so far bolsters this point.

Patriarchal control over marriage and the family also extended to children.
In fact, one of the major changes in the marriage codes in Lutheran territories
was the rejection of clandestine marriages or "secret engagements," thus al-

lowing greater or even total parental control over the marriages of their children. In Luther's opinion, an engagement could only become legally binding when the parents gave their consent. This view was incorporated into Lutheran marriage codes adopted by cities and principalities, and enforced by newly established consistories and marriage courts.[13] While other changes in marriage laws generally accepted in Protestant areas relaxed older restrictions—for example, removal of spiritual affinity as an impediment, the limitation of degrees within which one could not marry, and allowing divorce and remarriage—the tendency was always to support and strengthen the patriarchal family.[14]

Luther's Sermons on the Wedding at Cana

In his sermon in the Lenten postil of 1525, Luther remarks that since he had said enough earlier on the subject of marriage, he would not speak directly on that topic. Instead, he would focus on the message of the text to married people, that is, in what way it provides comfort to them. Christ and his disciples meant to honor marriage by their attendance at the wedding, and Mary even helped with the organization of the wedding, serving as the *braut mutter* for her poor friends, a kind of early wedding coordinator.[15] That Christ performed his first miracle at this wedding indicates that marriage is "God's creation and system"; that it was a wedding of a poor couple who could ill afford even the barest necessities shows how little respected marriage would be in the eyes of the world.[16] Although God never honored the *phariseer stand* in this way (and Luther was fairly certain that the author of said estate was not God, but the devil), modern-day "high priests" were convinced of their superiority over married folks: not only did they not marry as they should, but they often felt themselves too holy even to attend weddings, "as though they were much holier than Christ himself."[17]

But those who are married should be convinced, Luther insists, that marriage is instituted and blessed by God. Christ's help to the poor couple marrying in Cana should also show that comfort and help are always available from God to those who are married—and such comfort is needed, for to "external men" marriage is full of trouble and annoyance. What is difficult and a cross to bear in marriage is really God's "word and work."[18] If one sees it as such, and has faith in Christ, then the "water" of marital troubles will be changed into sweet wine: "For Christ here shows also that he will satisfy what is lacking in marriage . . . as though he said, 'Do you have to drink water, that is, suffer affliction externally and are you becoming acrimonious? Well, I will make you sweet and change the water into wine, and your affliction shall be your joy and happiness.' "[19] Luther implies that only a Christian marriage can be a truly happy marriage, for it is such a marriage that realizes God's pleasure in his good creation.

Next, Luther turns to the issue of weddings: some "sour-faced hypocrites and self-appointed saints" disapprove of the feasting, dancing, and dressing up that accompany such celebrations, but, Luther remarks, "everything has its proper measure," and a wedding is no different.[20] The Bible itself mentions in various places bridal attire, guests, and gifts. Even at this wedding, the wine was not merely to quench the thirst of the guests, for the steward remarked that wine had already been served, but enough had been drunk to "make them happy." If this is a bad thing, then it is Christ and his mother who are guilty, for he presented the wine as a gift, and she asked him for it.[21] But excessive drinking and feasting, such as takes place at many weddings, is still improper; in such cases, a man is not merely trying to be happy (frölich) but wildly drunk (toll und voll).[22] But such people are not human but pigs, and to them Christ would never provide any wine. Likewise with bridal clothing and dancing: all good things are done in moderation.

Turning more directly to the gospel text, Luther remarks that here we are presented with an example of love in Christ and his mother. Mary serves and Christ honors the gathering with his presence and a miracle. But, Luther insists, the example of faith in this text is even more wonderful. We learn that God's grace is given only to those who recognize that they lack it, "for those who are full and satisfied are not fed, but rather those who are hungry, as we have often said."[23] And then, when they recognize their need, God does not quickly come to their aid, but tests their faith and confidence. Thus Mary, "with humble and modest petitions," notifies Christ of the need and hopes for his help.[24] But Christ speaks to her harshly and in an unfriendly manner. What do faithful Christians do when confronted with an unfriendly God, when the only possibility of help has turned away? Mary shows the right way to act: she has no doubt in her heart that Christ is gracious and good, even after she is humbled by his response. Instead of leaving insulted, she orders the servants to follow Christ's commands. Luther insists that all must follow her example, even when one's faith is counter to one's feelings and experiences.

Luther points out another lesson to be learned from this text: that Christ speaks so harshly to his *mother* shows us that there is no authority on earth greater than God's. Parents cannot be obeyed if their commands do not agree with God's will. Likewise, any other authority, whether political or religious, should not be obeyed counter to God's word, for Mary indicates by her speech to the servants, "Whatever he says, do *that* and nothing else."[25] As we saw in the previous chapter, this is an important issue to the reformers: it justifies their own rejection of Roman authority, and yet it is a double-edged sword, undercutting their own conservative emphasis on obedience, both of children and of citizens.

In his following sermon on this text, found in the *Winterpostille* of 1528, Luther rejects the old legend that the bride and bridegroom at Cana were John the Baptist and Mary Magdalene, with John leaving his new wife immediately after the wedding to follow Jesus.[26] It is more useful to pay attention to the lessons we find in this gospel about marriage rather than foolish tales, Luther instructs. Christ and his mother, Mary, both honor marriage by their presence at this wedding, and Christ's miracle indicates a special place for marriage in God's creation. Returning to the theme of marriage versus celibacy, Luther asks, when did Christ ever honor the estate of the Pharisees in such a manner? Why should priests and monks praise themselves so highly? Marriage is far superior to the celibate religious life, and not only because it is clearly instituted and honored by God. It is an estate of "faith," for those who enter into it should be convinced that they are doing God's work and fulfilling their calling. It is an estate of love, for in it one "must and should" help and serve others.[27] The difficulties that must be borne in marriage are also a way for us to "become holy through cross and suffering," for "we must have unhappiness and temptations, either here in life or at our deathbed through the devil."[28] It is far better to suffer during our lives than to have things too easy, as is the case with priests, monks, and nuns. The "easy life" of the religious is misleading: they think they are doing God's will and works, but they are not, and they will pay later.

The second part of this text is concerned with Mary and her role in the story. She is a powerful example of faith, Luther reiterates: instead of reacting with anger to Christ's response or wavering in her faith, she turned to the servants in the certainty that Christ would, through his goodness and love, help the poor bride and bridegroom in their need. She did not, he remarks, use her "motherly rights" over her son, insisting that he do her will, but "believed and considered it certain that he would do it when his time was at hand."[29] And Christians should do likewise, Luther preaches, never fearing that God has forgotten them, or that he might no longer be good and gracious. Instead, they should turn to Christ with all their anxieties, for he will make things right in his own time.

Indeed, not only does Mary's example show Christians how to be faithful, it also shows them the mistake of asking God to grant their petitions on their own schedules. Although she came to her son "in faith and in love" to help her poor friends, as we all should come to God in need, she erred in trying to impose her will on Christ. That is why he responded to her so harshly, indicating that he would do his own will and in his own time. We should learn from this situation that those who claim "the Christian church cannot err, the holy fathers cannot err" are themselves in error: even Mary, the Mother of God and the holiest of people, made mistakes.[30] Christ foresaw, Luther notes, that at certain times his mother would be more highly honored than himself and would be called upon as an intercessor with God. Thus, Christ used this opportunity (along with others found in Scripture) to speak to her harshly, indicating that she cannot serve as an intercessor with him or his Father. He does not mean to imply that Christians should not pray for each other, but that "trust and confidence must be placed in Christ alone."[31] Christ is not the stern judge of the medieval worldview, requiring a "Mother of Mercy" in Mary who shows him the breast that nursed him, demanding and receiving his help for her supplicants.

In his sermon on this text in the 1544 *Hauspostille*, Luther continues to laud the married life over a life of celibacy, sounding increasingly ill tempered. The papists, he argues, "only praise virginity and chastity (although one does not find much of these [virtues] among them)," but we know how the unmarried religious have been punished and chastised by God.[32] In fact, Luther is surprised that the gates of Hell have not simply opened up and swallowed all the monasteries, convents, and religious foundations in the land. The pope and his followers are not able, for some reason, to see and appreciate the "excellent and beneficial example" found in Jesus' attendance at this wedding at the official beginning of his ministry. This example also rules against the Anabaptists and other "rabble" who feel there is a great holiness in abandoning marriage and family and fleeing to the desert. They never ask themselves, "If it is so good to flee into the desert or into a cloister, then why did Christ attend a wedding?"[33] Such lives, although called "holy," are in actuality merely an excuse to live for oneself, in laziness and plenty.

We know from the fourth commandment, contends Luther, that God considers a holy life the one lived within a household, that is, with "wife and child, servant and maid, cattle, fields, craft and livelihood."[34] Even a life as an obedient and pious servant within such a household pleases God more "than all monks' prayers, fasts, masses, and whatever else they praise as high service of God."[35] In fact, Mary's example is especially relevant to servants and their proper attitude. If the wedding (that is, marriage and the household) had been unimportant to Christ, he would never have allowed his mother, the highest and holiest of women, to work and serve at the wedding like a maid. Servants should learn from Mary's example that "when one serves in a home, one is serving God."[36] If they only realized this fact, their servitude would become "a sheer paradise" to them, and a serving girl could say to herself, "I have to cook and do other things, which is the same service that the beloved Virgin Mary gave at the wedding. . . . It is inferior work, but the person is very important and great . . . who realizes that it pleases God."[37]

In these passages, Luther articulates a complex, and very conservative, social perspective. Although he does occasionally say that the husband and wife who live and serve God faithfully will receive blessings—their "water" will be changed to "wine"—he is more insistent that such a life is difficult and involves much suffering. He paints a picture of a man bound by many chains to wife, children, lords, even neighbors and servants, caught in a "prison" of responsibilities and debts. A good Christian will not be freed from such troubles through faith or service to God. Rather, one's perspective on life's troubles and responsibilities will change, seeing in such troubles opportunities to practice Christian love and patience. When the lifestyle that pleases God is accepted, and not rejected in the manner of selfish, "wicked knaves," the chains become light and not only bearable but a true joy.[38]

Lutheran Preachers on the Wedding at Cana and Mary

Later pastors, following Luther's example, did not fail to find much of value in this gospel text. While they were especially interested in marriage and lessons for married people and families, the preachers also focused on two other topics, both of which concerned Mary directly. As in other sermons, preachers continued to find in Mary a positive example for Christians, not only of faith but also of love and hope. The focus on prayer and what we can learn about prayer from Mary is especially strong. In a more negative vein, this text gave preachers the opportunity to discuss divine authority and to reject Catholic notions of saintly intercession and particularly late medieval views of Mary's authority and importance. Capitalizing on the idea found already in Luther's sermons that Mary erred in her request to her son, thus calling upon herself his harsh response, the later preachers asserted not only Mary's errors but her general sinfulness as well.

Marriage, Weddings, and the Family

Why did Christ, his mother, and his disciples attend the wedding at Cana? "From the beginning and creation of the world," recounts Nuremberg pastor Andreas Osiander (1498–1552), "God had not thought to establish or join together any more honorable society or brotherhood, or worthy sect, . . . with which to adorn the heavenly country, than the holy, honorable estate of the married life."[39] Osiander finds biblical support for marriage from the patriarchs to Paul, but sees in this text the greatest significance for the divinely instituted and blessed estate: Christ's own presence and the authority of his first miracle make marriage the standard. Arsacius Seehofer adds that Christ is not only recommending this way of life to all but is also defending marriage against those influential "gentile" thinkers "who impiously call marriage a necessary evil."[40]

Johannes Brenz takes a more careful approach to the issue of marriage than Osiander: he is aware that in a sinful world, even the best of institutions can be misused and degraded. Brenz writes, "if marriage is commended, then teenagers will think that it is acceptable for them to contract marriages with impunity [to satisfy] their desire." However, if one censures such marriages, "the ordinance of God is condemned."[41] As difficult as it is to discuss marriage properly, Brenz concludes that it is still necessary both to explain reasons for marrying and to instruct married people.[42] This gospel lesson is ideal for this purpose, in that *faith* is the key virtue displayed, and faith, according to Brenz, is necessary for a happy marriage: "I cannot teach better than Paul to the Ephesians, who, when he taught that marriage is a sacrament of Christ and the church, taught first that there should be true devotion to religion between spouses."[43] Secondly, of course, Paul taught that "a husband [should] love his wife, and a wife [should] obey her husband." These are the "two principal precepts" that should be remembered and, Brenz remarks in a short aside to other preachers, impressed upon the people.[44] Such precepts are designed to preserve a happy order, for, as Brenz concludes, "if the love of the husband and the obedience of the wife are present, tranquillity is established."[45] Notice that Brenz is promoting *tranquillity*, a virtue of benefit not only to the couple but also to the community, rather than love or even happiness.

While Brenz chooses to focus on the possibility of a blessed life in marriage, other preachers emphasize the burdens and crosses that are found in family life. As Anton Corvinus reminds his listeners, it is because of the transgressions of our first parents that marriage has such a "high heavy cross" laid upon it.[46] In fact, this estate brings so many troubles that if God had not provided comfort, who would be willing to throw themselves into it? But God instituted marriage, and Christ greatly honored it, as we see in this text; thus "under such a cross, pure grace must be hidden."[47] And because of this hidden grace, no one should be frightened away from marriage, despite all the troubles that come with it. If one does not have the inclination to celibacy and would avoid the sins of the flesh, one must marry. "However, if you are given the grace to maintain [virginity]," Corvinus insists, "you should not go into a cloister, but remain under obedience to your parents and the authorities. . . . For a chaste life is good, and to marry is also good, and may also be called a chaste life. . . . But to shirk obedience to parents and authorities is not good."[48] In this passage, it is clear that what worries Corvinus (and others) about the religious life is not virginity or celibacy per se, but rather the rejection of God-given social and parental authority.

Proper marriages preserve and undergird such authority. Caspar Huberinus comments how Christ, by attending the wedding at Cana at the very beginning of his ministry, wanted to restore marriage, "the first and oldest estate," because "everything is dependent upon this estate, and the other two estates, the preaching office and the authorities, come from this estate."[49] This relationship is obviously not apparent to Rome, as Erasmus Alberus (c. 1500–1553) points out in an especially vitriolic sermon against the pope. Proper authority— parents, worldly authorities, even, by extension, God—is subverted in the Catholic system, which is ruled, according to Alberus, not by God but by the devil. Catholic opposition to marriage is one of the most significant indicators of satanic rule, for marriage is the foundation of not only the priestly estate and worldly authority but also of the lives of average citizens and farmers, adds Alberus.[50] Marriage is also related to eternal life, for God takes "little trees, flowers, and roses" from it to plant in his heavenly kingdom: God's children are children of marriage.[51] Christ honored marriage with his presence at the wedding and his first miracle, and Mary and the apostles also were in attendance, thereby helping to honor it. Christ was even born of a betrothed (i.e., legally married) virgin, many preachers reminded their listeners—how is it then that people cannot see the value and divine blessedness of marriage? "Satan blinds the eyes of men, which cannot see nor perceive what an exquisite jewel marriage is," Alberus concludes.[52]

While marriage, serving in Lutheran eyes as a socially conservative institution, was important for maintaining the authority of parents and worldly rulers, it also had a vital religious component. As we have seen, several preachers discuss the importance of Christian faith in marriage, and obviously preachers felt it their duty to instruct their listeners in the morality proper to both weddings and the married life. Despite its classification as a social rather than sacramental institution, marriage remained a vital area of interest and even control for Lutheran churchmen. As Cyriacus Spangenberg (1528–1604) reminded his audience in one *Ehespiegel* wedding sermon, "one should not carry out a marriage without the knowledge of the mother of Christ, that is, without the approval and witness of the holy Christian church. This holy mother should also be present with her prayers and supervision."[53] These prayers of the church will certainly be heard by God, adds Christoph Vischer.[54]

One topic that does not receive a great deal of attention in these sermons is the marriage of ministers: it is mentioned by a number of preachers, but is not the main focus. Spangenberg does indicate in his sermon, along with other critiques of Catholicism, that the apostles' presence at the wedding of Cana proves that marriage is not forbidden to the clergy, as the "papists" think, although he does not address the fact that Christ himself did not marry. The "legend" that the couple marrying at Cana were John and Mary Magdalene, with John leaving his bride immediately, is not mentioned again in these sermons—perhaps the ministers felt that Luther had dealt decisively with that issue, or it was not a common story. Clerical marriage, while an issue throughout the Reformation, was dealt with more frequently in other literature, and it is very likely that the words and instructions addressed to husbands and wives in these sermons were thought to apply equally to clerical and lay marriages alike: chastity and propriety were a duty for *all* Christians.

Mary Models the Theological Virtues

Mary has often served, as recounted in previous chapters, as a model of the virtues of faith and love. She is the ideal of the faithful Christian in her acceptance of the incarnation of Christ, believing the impossible to be true. She expressed true love in visiting and serving Elizabeth, her aged relative. In this text, the Lutheran preachers find again that the mother of Christ modeled both faith and love for their listeners, with the added virtue of hope, leading them to an emphasis upon prayer. The malleability of the image of Mary becomes clearer when studying this aspect of the text: the preachers could find some aspect of Mary's character or behavior to hold up as an example to almost every member of their congregation, and they often took the time to do so.

Mary displayed Christian love by helping the poor couple on their wedding day, especially in asking Christ for help when the wine was exhausted. Many of the preachers laud her charity and urge it upon their listeners: she not only took the bride and groom under her wing by organizing and working at their wedding but she also pleaded with her son on their behalf.[55] Johannes Wigand remarks that here we can see in Mary an example of "justifying love," in that she had great sympathy with the poor couple and did not think it beneath her to help them, and certainly did not expect any remuneration for her support.[56] In fact, Niels Hemmingsen even considers Mary's love to be one of the causes of Christ's miracle: "The cause of such a miracle . . . [includes] the loyal heart of the Virgin Mary, which was very willing and inclined toward help and advice."[57] We learn from Mary, according to Hemmingsen, "to have pity upon other people, and take their need onto ourselves, praying to God the Lord for them."[58] Christian love should be expressed outwardly, toward individuals and the community: we should certainly attend the "honorable weddings" of poor people, be of help to them, and give them gifts.

Although Mary's love is a wonderful Christian example and led her to pray to her son for the young couple, which we all should emulate, it also led her into a bit of trouble. One cannot escape the impression from many sermons that perhaps Mary was *too* zealous in her loving concern, as Christ's harsh response to her might indicate—it pushed her to interfere with his plans. The other elements that Lutheran preachers found problematic in light of their rejection of much of medieval Mariology—Mary taking mercy on the young couple and her intercession with Christ—will be addressed in the following section. What is *not* problematic and is trumpeted by all the preachers is the example of Mary's faith, which is the support for her hope that Christ will help in time of need, despite his seeming rejection of her plea.

In his *Evangelicæ Conciones*, Peter Artopoeus is speaking to an academic audience, and is especially interested in the rhetorical and dialectical aspects of the various gospel texts. He finds this text to be of the "demonstrative" genus in its commendation of marriage, and of the "instructive" genus in teaching about faith and prayer through the example of Mary.[59] Christians learn that their faith will be tried, as Mary's was, but they will not always be rejected. In the end, Mary's plea was granted: the water was changed into wine. Thus, they should not be discouraged, but should continue in faith to pray.[60] This theme is reiterated by many preachers: Mary is a "useful example," according to Brenz, that we should take our petitions to God in prayer, and even if we receive a harsh answer, should "persevere in faith, in prayer, and in obedience to God."[61] She even shows us how to pray, for our own need and for that of others, avoiding the "papist idolatry" of praying to saints, and turning directly to Christ for help.[62]

Why does God sometimes seem to turn his face away from us? "God does not respond immediately to the prayers of the pious, not because he does not hear him, but that he might inflame our faith" and reveal his strength.[63] Mary understood this, which is why, despite Christ's harsh answer to her, she was not frightened or disappointed. She knew, as Corvinus says, that if all appears lost, that is precisely when the Christian must not doubt or despair, "for under such a motionless silence is certain comfort, under such a 'no' an assured 'yes' is hidden."[64] In fact, God wants to help us, but in his own time and at his own pleasure. He wants us to continue to pray without complaint for what we need, for "he is a thousand times cleverer and wiser than we, and he knows better than we when it is time to help, and how he should help."[65]

Mary's faith in Christ, which bears witness to his divinity, makes her "a figure of the Mother of holy Christendom," according to Magdeburg pastor Johannes Baumgarten (1514–78).[66] She tells us with her words to the servants that God does not want us to thirst, but only wants us to do his will, and then we can enjoy everlasting sweet wine. "The holy Christian Church" and Mary, again characterized as a figure of "the Mother of holy Christendom," *both* believe the same thing: "that God the Lord speaks his benediction and blessing over married couples and their households."[67] Her authority as the mother of all Christians everywhere and her faithful witness to Christ combine to create strong evidence in support of marriage as a God-pleasing estate.

Although Niels Hemmingsen does not call Mary a "figure" of the church, he does stress that she is not only a model for the church but also a member of the Christian community. In both capacities she is a faithful witness to Christ, teaching the church "to follow her Lord Jesus Christ and to do everything that he tells her, even if it appears to be totally opposed to her reason."[68] Christoph Vischer suggests that we should make a proverb out of Mary's phrase, "Do whatever he tells you," for it is very wise council. If he "had room for it," Vischer continues, he would also take this opportunity to delineate Mary's fine example for "honor-loving matrons and womenfolk:" Mary did not return harsh words to Christ, but "swallowed them," and instead bore his "unfriendly answer" patiently and meekly. So also should women "accustom themselves from youth on to be meek and patient" with their elders or superiors.[69] But even more importantly, we should all learn from Mary not to give up on prayer, despite any "hard blows" we might have to suffer.[70]

"Woman, What Do I Have to Do with You?"

These words of Jesus to his mother are perhaps the most difficult to understand and interpret in this entire text. What is it about Mary's request or behavior that would cause Jesus to respond to her so harshly? While some exegetes have tried to lessen the sting of this passage, the majority, from the early church fathers to present-day theologians, have accepted these words as a deliberate rebuke to Mary.[71] Geiler presents a traditional Catholic view: Christ's harsh response to Mary indicated, not that her pity or her prayers were misplaced, but rather that his actions in this case would be from his divine and not his human nature. The transformation of water into wine would not be accomplished by his humanity, through which he had "community" with her. This humanity would have its "hour," in his suffering and death, but that time had not yet come.[72] Also, Christ wanted to wait to perform his miracle until the lack of wine should be fully known by all, thus making it evidence to everyone of his power and divine authority.[73] Geiler does not explain why Mary, as a human, should not be able to request something of Christ's divine nature, nor does he indicate if Mary was in error here. Christ's transcendence is what he finds important in this text.

It is clear that medieval interpreters did not find evidence in this text that Mary's intervention was misplaced, or that it might indicate a deeper problem with the notion of saintly intercession. Ironically, although in the text Mary's request is eventually granted, Geiler does not exploit the opportunity to recommend the effectiveness of the prayers of the saints. Luther's followers, although they agree with many of Geiler's conclusions, find in these words, in accordance with Luther, one of the strongest arguments against the intercession of saints in the whole of Scripture. The eventual effectiveness of Mary's prayer is attributed not to her power as an intercessor, but rather to Christ's good will.

Lutheran preachers accepted as a general rule the idea that this text indicates Christ's divine transcendence, in the matter of his miracles and ministry, over his human nature and relationships. Many saw in his addressing Mary as "woman" rather than "mother" a clear indication of this shift. As Osiander suggests, in this matter "she touches heavenly divine work, over which she is no mother, but only over the humanity of Christ."[74] She is "meddling," according to Baumgarten, in things that are appropriate to God alone, which is not allowed even of the mother of Christ.[75] In what "things" is she meddling? The "cares" that she takes on herself—the lack of wine, the situation of the couple, the happiness of the guests—all relate to the cares of married people and their households, cares that belong to Christ alone.[76] When he calls Mary "woman" rather than "mother," it is as though he is saying "Dear Mother, as your own [bodily] son I will gladly be obedient to you," but not in things that belong to God rather than to human authority.[77] Christ will have no master who will tell him what to do or when to do it. He knows, as Eber reminds his listeners, "when it is time to help."[78] We all tend toward the fault of wanting Christ to help us immediately, but we should learn from this interchange not to demand our own will of Christ.

Christ made it clear through his words, according to many preachers, that Mary had no special prerogatives on account of her relationship to him. Her prayers were not more powerful or effective because, in a common phrase, "God is no respecter of persons."[79] In the realm of faith, Mary has no advantage over any other faithful and pious Christian. As Culmann observes, "Therefore it is faith that makes us brothers of Christ [Mark 3]."[80] In fact, Mary realizes that she must rely on Christ's grace and not on their intimate relationship for the realization of her prayers. Vischer suggests that her meek and quiet acceptance of Christ's rebuke and her confident order to the servants prove that she did rely on her faith in Christ's gracious nature, and not on her motherly prerogatives.[81] Brenz, however, criticizes Mary for seeking too much authority over Christ; he agrees that she is not exercising her parental rights but instead is looking for honor from "the Messiah, and desires to be, as it were, an administrative partner of his office."[82]

A number of preachers agree on the fact that Jesus' behavior toward Mary and his harsh response to her do *not* indicate a lack of filial respect and in no way break the fourth commandment. Brenz points out that "there was never a son who honored his mother more than Christ." Christ could not dishonor his mother, for "the law of God is this: 'Honor your parents,' which Christ fulfilled most perfectly."[83] It is Mary's attempt to participate in or somehow command his divine role that calls his harsh response upon her. Christ cannot be a "bad example" to other children, according to Georg Walther, for when we understand the circumstances, we will see why Christ did not speak too harshly to his mother: "his mother went too far over her calling," and wanted him to perform a miracle "to please her and do her honor."[84] Christ shows children that they must obey their parents, but only in the things that are under their authority and do not contradict God's will.

It was obviously wrong for Mary to overstep her authority, and Walther is not afraid to spell this out: like Luther, he says that Mary erred, but he insists that "Mary was also not totally without sin, for otherwise [Christ] would not have given her such hard words."[85] This step seems logically consistent, although in the minds of Lutheran churchmen at least a small difference seems to remain between "error" and "sin." Nicolaus Selneccer addresses the issue in his postil, published in 1575: some people have asked, he explains, if Mary did not sin in speaking to her son. Surely she did right in taking on the needs of the young couple and bringing the problem to Christ's attention? In fact, Selneccer decides, Mary, although right in caring and praying for the young couple, "yields too much to human emotions" in trying to use her motherly authority over her son in "the things of God." In these matters Christ does not allow interference, for that would deprive him of his proper glory.[86] We can learn from this, according to Selneccer, not only to discriminate between the obedience owed to our parents and that owed to God, but we also learn that even the holiest people have weaknesses. Mary is not excused by this fact, however, or else Christ would have to be blamed for blaming her.[87] Is it sin? Selneccer calls it "weakness" (imbecillitas), and later notes that, following her example, we should recognize our "guilt" (culpa) and strive to improve.[88] Martin Chemnitz, in a later postil, suggests that Mary recognized her "infirmity" or "shortcoming" (Gebrechen) and patiently accepted her "punishment" (Straffe) from Christ.[89]

Although the later preachers, in seeking to explain why Mary received such a harsh answer from her son, stress that she deserved the rebuke, few actually use the term "sin." It is enough for their purposes to stress her human weakness and error, in contrast with Christ's self-recognized transcendence and divine power. Why would anyone, all the preachers agree, turn to Mary for intercession with Christ after hearing this biblical text? The break in community between Christ and his mother represented by his words to her reinforce what Luther recognized: there can be no intermediary between sinners and Christ.[90] Several preachers make clear that Christ intended us to realize this fact from his words: "The Lord Christ wanted especially to prevent and curb the abominable, blasphemous, and superstitious custom of the papists, that we [should] not call on nor turn to the holy Virgin Mary or other dead saints, and look for more comfort from them than from Christ himself, the fountain of all grace."[91] We should recognize not only that we should not ask Mary and the saints to intercede for us but also that Mary has no part in our salvation: the office of savior belongs to Christ alone. The many titles given to Mary by Catholics are therefore misleading: honoring Mary as the Queen of Heaven, the Mother of Grace, and the "Salvation of the World" detracts from the true savior, Jesus Christ.[92] Such titles can be especially misleading for uneducated or simple lay folk.

The pericope of the wedding at Cana provides an opportunity for Luther and his fellow preachers to teach their listeners about marriage, what it is and why it is important. One does not need to read too many sermons before it becomes apparent that marriage is thought to be vital both to society and to the church. Marriage, according to these preachers, is the building block and support not only of civil society but also of the heavenly kingdom. It was instituted by God in the Garden of Eden, blessed by Christ with his first miracle, and provides future souls to populate heaven. Its importance can hardly be overstated. It is clear from the few positive references to celibacy in these texts that, despite the official position that celibacy, although a rare gift, is as legitimate a calling as the married life, it was expected that very few would choose or be able to choose such a lifestyle. For almost every Christian, marriage is the lifestyle in which they will live. Not too surprisingly, as we have seen, the views of marriage promoted by these preachers are of a highly patriarchal and traditional sort: Lutheran preachers do not intend to encourage their listeners to flee their daily lives in order to serve God, but rather to embrace their daily cares and burdens as service to God.

The overwhelming focus of these texts is on marriage; several sermons even forgo a mention of the pericope and instead preach simply on marriage. Mary does, however, play an important role in the text, and her actions receive a great deal of attention, both negative and positive. Mary is promoted in many sermons as a good example of the theological virtues of faith, hope, and love. Her faith in Christ's graciousness, her hope for his future help, and her love expressed toward the marrying couple are all lifted up as fine, true Christian virtues for the benefit of listeners. She is especially important as a model for faithful and continual prayer: her faith was tested by Christ's apparent rejection of her plea, but she did not become angry or lose hope.

The texts become more interesting when read for their negative interpretations of Mary and her behavior. Many of the preachers obviously struggle with how to interpret properly the situation presented in the gospel. What is problematic about Mary's request? Why does Jesus respond to her so harshly, calling her "woman" rather than "mother"? How are we to understand her reaction, and Christ's eventual accomplishment of what she had asked? A common traditional interpretation of the text suggests that Christ is beginning his divine mission at Cana; thus, because he owed obedience to Mary only through his human nature, in this context she could not act or command as his mother. Luther and his followers accept this interpretation but add several new elements. First, Mary's attempt to influence Christ's actions in "divine matters" was, at best, a mistake and, at worse, human weakness or even sin. It was not wrong of her to be concerned for her friends, and to pray for them, but rather the problem lay in her attempt to impose her own will and timetable on Christ. Second, Christ's harsh response to Mary indicates a difference between divine and parental authority, but emphasizes especially that neither Mary nor any other saint can serve as an intercessor with Christ. Luther and his followers are convinced they have found proof in this gospel text that the Roman Catholic practice of calling upon Mary for help or intercession is fundamentally wrong: Mary has no advantage over any other pious Christian in matters of faith. The preachers reject the evidence of Catholic practice and medieval tradition, drawing the line in the sand: Mary has no part in our salvation.

6

Other Marian Holidays and *Herrenfesten*

The first five chapters of this study treat the most important Marian holidays that survived in the Lutheran church, along with several other gospel texts in which Mary is a central figure. The remaining texts in which she appears are treated in this chapter. In the Christmas story from Luke 2, Mary played a vital role in the events that took place, but Jesus as the promised Messiah is usually the focus of Christmas sermons. Certain elements significant for this day are important for Mariology, especially her role as the *Theotokos*, the God-bearer. Her importance as the guarantor of Christ's humanity is underscored in these sermons. She plays a more minor role in the remaining texts concerning Jesus' infancy. The sermons on Jesus' circumcision (New Year's Day) rarely mention her, and in both Epiphany and Innocents sermons she appears only infrequently. In the story of Jesus' passion, Mary is mentioned as standing at the foot of the cross and plays a small role in the drama there. The significance of Mary at the cross, so important for late medieval devotion, is minimized in Lutheran sermons, and the growing devotion to Mary as coredemptrix is ignored. Finally, the three important holidays celebrating Mary's conception, birth, and assumption, lacking scriptural evidence and support, are quickly phased out of the Lutheran calendar. Sermons on these days appear only in the earliest postils.

The Christmas Story

In the traditional text for the Christmas holiday, Luke 2:1–20, Mary's centrality for the Christian faith is underscored: she is the mother of the Christ-child, the *Theotokos*. The elements of the story are well-known: in order to register for a census and tax, Joseph and his fiancée, Mary, traveled to Bethlehem, the native city of the Davidic line. There Mary delivered her "first-born son," but because there was no room in the inn, she was forced to deliver in the stable, wrapping the baby in cloths and laying him in the animals' manger. The text also narrates the appearance of legions of angels to some local shepherds, informing them of the birth of the Messiah. When the shepherds came to see Mary and the baby, they recounted what they had seen and Mary "treasured all these words and pondered them in her heart."

Although the significance of this text for Christians rests upon the birth of the Messiah, Mary plays a primary role in the events. She is, in the eyes of traditional orthodoxy, the guarantor of Christ's humanity: christological questions turn of necessity at some point to Mary. Luther and his followers, wanting to stress their orthodoxy on this point and guard against any heretical tendencies, address certain traditional christological themes in their Christmas sermons. Christ was "born of the virgin Mary," in the language of the Nicene Creed, and many pastors strive to educate their listeners on this point. Mary's virginity becomes a special issue in this context, both for the question of Christ's purity and for adherence to traditional readings of biblical texts and prophecies.

Beyond the theological context, Lutheran sermons also address social issues that stem from the Christmas story. The most obvious of these issues is poverty: what kind of lesson can be learned from the poverty and suffering into which Jesus was born? Mary and Joseph are lauded by many pastors for their obedience to the authorities, despite their difficult situation and the impending birth of their child. The shepherds who visit Mary and the baby in the stable are taken as an important example of fidelity to one's vocation, in another swipe at both Catholic and Anabaptist practices. The fact that Mary pondered the angel's message provides an opportunity for Lutheran preachers to praise her faith and again recommend her as an example to their audience.

Mary and Christology

In the sermon for Christmas in his Church Postil of 1522, Luther informs his readers that how this birth exactly occurred is disputed: Did Mary suffer any pain? Did the baby cause her any injury? Luther rejects such disputations, insisting instead that "we should stick with the gospel, which says, 'she bore him,' and by the article of faith that we say, 'who is born of the virgin Mary.' "[1] It was a "true birth," with Mary a "natural mother" and Jesus a "natural son," except, he interjects, for the following conditions: "she gave birth without sin, without shame, without pain and without injury, as she also conceived without sin."[2] Disputation concerning such points is not needed, obviously because Luther already accepts them from tradition as being true. The requirements for a natural birth, that is, that it proves Christ's humanity, are not so great that the traditional view of Mary's experience needs to be rejected. Luther is able to maintain both that Christ had a natural, physical birth as a true human baby, and that Mary experienced no pain or injury: the *purity* of their human natures does not make them less human.[3] In fact, Luther later asserts that Christ is closer to us than Adam and Eve, for they were formed from the earth, while he is born of flesh and blood "like other men."[4]

Why, if the unusual elements of this birth leave it open to question, should Luther want to continue to maintain Mary's freedom from the "curse of Eve"?[5] These elements are not spelled out in the text, so it is not a question of the truth of God's word, but seems rather to be an issue of Luther's adherence to tradition: he has no good reason to doubt the traditional interpretation, but in fact has several good reasons to maintain it. The authority of many councils and church fathers, particularly Augustine, weigh on the side of maintaining not only christological orthodoxy but its concomitant Marian doctrines: Mary as the *Theotokos*, her perpetual virginity, and her freedom from the usual woman's burden of bearing her children in pain. The issue of sexual purity and its connection to sinlessness tie Luther into an Augustinian view of the body and sexuality that makes sense of the following passage: "In order to help this birth [of eternal damnation], God sent another birth that had to be pure and immaculate [in order] to make the impure sinful birth pure. That is the birth of the Lord Christ, his only-begotten son, and therefore he did not want to allow him to be born out of sinful flesh and blood, but he should be born from a virgin alone."[6] In the Augustinian view, concupiscence, the "tinder of sin," is passed through the sexual act, ensuring that God would want to avoid the normal means of procreation in the birth of his own son, who should be pure and free from sin. It is Christ's very purity that has value for us: because he is truly human and yet born without sin, his birth can substitute for ours, allowing us to say, "Therefore Eve the first mother is not my mother, for the same birth must totally die and fade away, since there is no more sin there; there must I place that mother Mary against the mother from whom I was born in sin."[7] Although the point is that Christ's birth replaces our own sinful one, that fact is represented by calling Mary our mother.

Most other Lutheran preachers mention one or more of these christological elements, especially the fact that this text is the source for the creedal statement, "born of the virgin Mary." All the authors who discuss it maintain Mary's perpetual virginity, often arguing, as did Peter Artopoeus, that Mary's virginal condition flies in the face of worldly reason.[8] It also fulfills the Isaianic (7:15) prophecy, "and a virgin shall conceive and bear a son," making Mary's virginity one sign of Christ's true status as Messiah. Luther and his followers do not address in their sermons the debate over the Hebrew word "*almah*" in this passage, and whether it refers to a virgin or simply to a young woman, although Luther argues strongly for the translation "virgin" in other places.[9] Several preachers do recapitulate Luther's stress on the purity of Christ's birth and its significance for our salvation. Corvinus compares the two births: "our birth is impure, sinful, and accursed, but the birth of Christ is pure, innocent, and holy. [If] the condemnation of our birth would be taken away and changed, it must happen through the holy birth of Jesus Christ."[10] This transfer does not happen physically, but rather "spiritually, through the word . . . that the angel said, 'to you, to you (he said) is the savior born.' "[11]

Several preachers stress the uniqueness of Christ's birth rather than focusing on its naturalness and his connection to us. Huberinus emphasizes the miraculous nature of the event: "From the Father [Christ] is born in eternity without a mother; in time he is born of Mary according to humanity, without a natural father; there has never been another child like him born on the earth."[12] Others, such as Leonhard Culmann, despite maintaining Mary's perpetual virginity and other supernatural elements, stress Christ's truly human and natural birth: "the son conceived in her took his substance from the substance of the mother, and thus he was the son of the mother . . . and not a phantasm which she bore."[13] Johannes Wigand stresses both the miraculous divine and human elements of Christ's birth: Christ is the "woman's seed" prophesied in Genesis 3, not the seed of a man, which proves that he is the Messiah, but he was carried and born like any other baby and thus was not a ghost. Mary is the true mother of both God and man, and thus it makes sense that we cannot understand everything about it, including how she could remain a virgin.[14]

Mary as an Exemplary Figure

Luther and his followers considered themselves to be completely orthodox on the point concerning Christ's person and strongly defended themselves against any suggestion of christological heresy. In light of their adherence to tradition, it is not surprising that Lutherans maintained certain doctrines concerning Mary, such as her perpetual virginity, that were seen as directly related to christological truth, as complicated as they might be. Other elements of the Christmas story were also discussed in accord with tradition, ensuring that Lutheran Christmas sermons were, at least in their presentation of Mary, free from anti-Catholic polemic. The portrait of Mary found in the text—the poor, young mother far from home and comforts—was not a problematic image for Lutheran preachers but instead gave them an opportunity to discuss social issues alongside the theological issues of Christ's person.

The most obvious of these issues is poverty. Geiler's exhortation to "simplicity, poverty, and humility" would not have been lost on Luther and his followers.[15] Luther often stressed Mary's poverty and difficult situation in his sermons to excite the emotions of his listeners: the "poor young woman Mary," along with Joseph, probably with no servant, went on foot (the gospel does not mention a donkey) to Bethlehem, patiently suffering the cold. Luther stresses the difference between what she experienced and the respect she should have received as mother of the savior: "think how she was despised on the way to the inn, she who was worthy to be carried in a golden carriage with all splendor."[16] The world cannot recognize nor appreciate God's work, and in fact Christ's pitiful birth not only ensured that he would be rejected by the world, but showed the world's respect and admiration for what it was: hollow and hypocritical. Mary was totally alone, "without any preparation, without light, without fire, in the middle of the night, [she] is alone in the darkness; no one offered her any service that one normally gives to pregnant women."[17] She should have been treated better, for even a beggar or "dishonorable woman" should have been helped and considered at such a time.[18]

What can be learned from this situation? First, Luther says, we learn not to trust the world and what it values. If one is loved and celebrated by the world, one is probably not a true follower of Christ. Concomitantly, he argues, we should learn not to be afraid of suffering, but should instead be comforted by the example of Christ and his mother, who "suffered such need, poverty, and sorrow."[19] Finally, Christ's poverty should teach us "how we should find him in our neighbor, the inferior, and the wretched."[20] Several of Luther's followers also mention this last point, although it does not become the focus of any sermon. Johann Locher, in an early sermon from 1524, suggests that if we want to "show honor to Mary and Jesus," we should serve the poor.[21] Johann Spangenberg recommends to his readers that in order for others to know that "Christ is born in us," we must express ourselves through our actions, helping our neighbors in their need, feeding the hungry, clothing the naked.[22]

A more universally mentioned point is the fine example of obedience given by Mary and Joseph. Again, this emphasis is not new—Geiler also praised Mary and Joseph's obedience to the emperor in traveling to Bethlehem.[23] It is significant, however, that this point is mentioned in almost every sermon in this study. Luther stresses that their compliance with the emperor's order proves them to be "pious, obedient people," especially since Mary's condition would have given her a good excuse not to go. She did not want to give offense to anyone, and thus made the trip, allowing the biblical prophecies to be fulfilled.[24] Corvinus suggests that this example of obedience shows the mistakenness of the Anabaptists, who refuse to obey any prince they consider to be "impious."[25] In fact, Huberinus remarks, if Mary and Joseph were so obedient to a pagan government, how much more we should obey our Christian governments, "who also protect our religion, and allow us to hear God's word and attend proper church services, and maintain Christian policies among us."[26] Although we owe a higher duty to God, reminds Eber, "every subject . . . is responsible before God to be obedient to his rulers in everything that they command and direct that is not against God and his conscience, but only concerning earthly things." This obedience is required because worldly authorities are established by God, whether they are pagan or Christian, pious or not.[27] The concern of many pastors to support the rule of temporal authorities is unmistakable, especially in light of the "Christian freedom" promoted by Luther in his famous tract from 1520 that helped to spark the peasants' revolts in the mid-1520s: Victor Strigel (1524–1569) specifically rejects those who would seek "immunity [from] and lightening of the public burdens under the pretext of Christian freedom."[28]

Mary and Joseph are not the only figures in this story who represent obedience, according to many pastors. The shepherds who announced the message of the angels also display obedience in the sense that they return to their vocations as shepherds after this miraculous experience. Stressing a theme obviously not a part of the earlier Catholic tradition, many preachers praise the example of the shepherds who did not leave their jobs to become monks after their experience, thereby emphasizing the value of work over the supposedly "perfect" life of monks. Wigand suggests that we can learn from the shepherds' example "that in every honorable office, people serve God, and can honor and praise him rightly."[29] He criticizes the Roman church for promoting the idea that only hermits and monks can perfectly serve God, and suggests that in reality a person who leads any life established by God, including "authorities, parents, farmhands, and servants[,] can serve God more than in the cloistered life."[30] A life lived outside the cloister can also be used in service of one's neighbors, remarks Luther. One does not need to change external things, how one dresses, what one eats or drinks, in order to be holy—Christ did not eat or dress differently from his fellows. Such things are merely external, but a "true change . . . [is] that a man would be different in his heart."[31]

The final point involving Mary also has to do with what is in the heart— the phrase "But Mary treasured all these words and pondered them in her heart" (Luke 2:19) led a number of authors to encourage meditation upon the wonders of Christ and his birth. Luther suggests that Mary provides an example of how we should all hear Christ's word, especially in listening to sermons: the words move her heart, and she "seeks diligently after him," confident in the face of the world's opinion that her son is the Son of God.[32] Mary is a great example of faith, according to Johannes Bugenhagen: "This is a holy meditation, a burning faith in the heart."[33] She did not question the words of the shepherds, but allowed her faith to guide her and God's word to comfort her.[34] She accepted God's word as true, emphasizes Strigel, in opposition to Anabaptists and other "fanatics" who expect "divine illumination" in their souls, and reject doctrine and study.[35] The illumination that the shepherds received and she believed, was preached in an angelic sermon, Strigel would say, not directly infused into their hearts.

Mary's faith and acceptance of God's word make her an image of the church, according to Luther: "Mary is the Christian church, Joseph the ministers of the church, who should be the bishops and pastors, if they preach the gospel." The church "holds all the words of God in her heart," so that if one would be a Christian, "he must first find the church." One should not try to "build his own bridge to heaven through his own reason," nor trust a pope or a bishop: it is the "crowd of Christ-believing people" that make up the church.[36] It is Mary (the church), not Joseph (the ministers), that "holds these words in her heart."[37] Luther no doubt trusted that the truth of his own teachings was supported by the faith of the "crowd" of believers.

The Remaining Infancy Narratives

Following Christmas most closely is the festival of Christ's Circumcision, usually celebrated on New Year's Day. Mary's purification—its own holiday—and the remainder of the story of Simeon and Anna, the text for the Sunday after Christmas—are also a part of this narrative (see chapter 3). The text for Epiphany, often called *Obersttag* or *hailigen drey könig tag*, follows the birth narrative in the gospel of Matthew and recounts the visit of the wise men or Magi to Mary's home. The commemoration of the slaughter of the innocents, the day of the *unschuldigen kindlein*, takes up the remainder of Matthew 2 and records the flight of Mary and Joseph to Egypt, as well as Herod's massacre of the children in Bethlehem. In each of these texts, Mary plays a minor role: in the circumcision text she is not mentioned, although she brought Jesus to the temple for the ritual; in the Matthean texts for Epiphany and Innocents, Mary is briefly mentioned, once by name and several other times as Jesus' mother. Luther and his fellow preachers likewise practice great economy is mentioning Mary in sermons on these texts: she appears very infrequently and then usually in conjunction with Joseph as the parents of Jesus. There are, however, several interesting points to mention.

The vast majority of New Year's sermons that treat Christ's circumcision do not mention Mary at all. They are concerned primarily with Christ's fulfillment of the law, despite his freedom from it, and with discussing baptism. Jesus is occasionally called "Mary's son," or "Mary's and God's son," and the "woman's seed." Apart from these indirect references, Mary is mentioned in only two sermons. Culmann remarks that Jesus' parents provide a good example of obedience to God's will, following God's command to circumcise their son without question.[38] Expanding on this point, Christoph Vischer praises Mary and Joseph's obedience to God's command, despite the fact that they knew Jesus was God's divine son, who was purely conceived and born without sin.[39] Their example, he suggests, should make us even more diligent in bringing our children who *are* sinful to be baptized, unlike the Anabaptists, who reject the example of Jesus and his parents.

In the Epiphany sermons, Mary appears slightly more often. Luther and Caspar Huberinus use her appearance in this story as an opportunity to critique the "papist" practice of invoking Mary and the saints. There is a great danger, teaches Luther, that people will decide to see Jesus as they want him to be, rather than as what God's word teaches him to be. It does not please the papists, says Luther, "that [Christ] alone should be the savior," so they also call on Mary and ask her to placate Christ, "the judge [and] hangman." Thus it has come to pass "that everyone has placed more confidence in the intercession of the Virgin Mary and the saints than in the Lord Christ himself."[40] It is no surprise, for where the Word is forgotten, there the devil will enter and lead people to believe in their own thoughts, "for there he knows that he has won and we have lost."[41] But this text teaches us, according to Huberinus, that it is Christ and not Mary whom we should call on and worship: "the wise men worshiped the child alone, and not the mother, threw themselves at his feet, and honored him alone with their gifts."[42]

Although the Magi may have offered their gifts to Christ alone, several sermons comment on the fact that Mary and Joseph also enjoyed these valuable presents. Without the gifts, the family would not have been able to support itself during and after their sudden flight to Egypt: "On the flight and long trip God provided living expenses for the child, his caretaker Joseph, and the Virgin Mary through these wise men." Likewise, it is important for those people with means to help poor, miserable people who cannot afford to send their children to school or training: whoever helps these people also "offers and bestows [help] to the poor baby Jesus."[43] The wise men did not despise Jesus and his family because they were poor, admonishes Culmann.[44] Instead, along with their adoration of Christ, they practiced true charity.

The flight to Egypt inspired more interest in Mary, especially as the narrow escape from Herod's massacre and the difficult trip and life ahead were the first events related to Simeon's prophecy of the sword. Corvinus preaches on this text on the "day of the holy three kings," remarking on the cross that Mary and Joseph had to bear. They suffered from Herod's evil so that they would learn that, although their son was a king, his kingdom was not an earthly one, and "Christ came into the world to suffer."[45] Huberinus calls Mary, Joseph, and the child "martyrs" along with the slaughtered children, "for they were evilly tormented and tortured by the godless," and forced to wander like so many of today's martyrs.[46] But Mary and Joseph were obedient to God once again and did not complain despite their difficulties. Johannes Brenz preaches that this example should teach us to follow God's commands, even if they seem to oppose God's promises.[47] Eventually, after seven years and the death of Herod, according to Brenz, the family was able to return from their Egyptian exile. God saved them "out of their sorrow, and brought them again to Judea," comments Vischer, and will likewise eventually rescue us all from our sorrowful condition.[48]

While Mary and Joseph lived in Egypt they were not inactive, according to Luther and Huberinus. Rather they "preached" about the great miracles that had happened, and "brought others to faith and blessedness."[49] The wise men likewise preached of Christ on their return home, and thus the message of the gospel began to spread. Huberinus credits Mary and Joseph with founding a church in Egypt: "there Joseph and Mary would have, without doubt, revealed the gospel to certain good people, and set up a special little band and church which believed in the baby Jesus and became blessed."[50]

Mary at the Cross

The only mention of Mary in the passion narratives is in the gospel of John, where we find Mary, her sister, and Mary Magdalene standing beneath the cross. John records that Jesus saw his mother and his beloved disciple (usually taken to be John) standing near and commanded them to accept one another as mother and son. From that moment, we are told, John took Mary into his home (19:25–27). From these few verses comes a very extensive tradition concerning Mary as the *Mater Dolorosa*, the sorrowing mother under the cross, that blossomed in literature, song, and art, most especially in the later medieval period. As we saw in the previous section, Simeon's prophecy of the sword piercing Mary's heart was often taken to refer to her suffering under the cross of her son. A number of theologians in the eastern church, beginning with Origen, interpreted the "sword" as doubt that beset Mary at the crucifixion. However, most of the western tradition follows Ambrose, who attributed no doubt to Mary. Rather, he took the "sword" to refer to her foreknowledge of the passion and insists that "while the men were fleeing she stood fearlessly," looking with pity on the wounds her son suffered for human salvation.[51]

In the early church, theologians such as Ambrose and Augustine maintain a separation between Mary's sorrow and Christ's redemptive suffering: although Mary was intimately associated with our salvation through Christ's incarnation and birth, he alone earned our redemption through his death. By the twelfth century, however, some theologians were affirming Mary's role in our salvation through her co-suffering with Christ. Especially important in this regard was the *Mariale super missus est* (or *Mariale*, probably from the late thirteenth century), a work mistakenly attributed to Albert the Great until the 1950s. In this influential work, the author teaches that Mary possessed all graces perfectly, including knowledge of the Trinity, the incarnation, her own predestination, and Scripture. Besides these, she knew *in summo* all human sciences—canon law, astronomy, mathematics, and so on—and was exalted above all the angels. In this context, it is not surprising that the *Mariale* extended to Mary a share in human redemption, calling her the "helper of redemption through her compassion."[52] Thus, under the authority of the name of Albert, Mary's participation in human redemption through her co-suffering with Christ became a commonly accepted mariological doctrine. Influential doctors of the church such as Albert (in his authentic writings), Thomas Aquinas, and Bonaventure did not accept this principle, asserting that Christ is the only savior. Other theologians, however, and especially popular devotional literature continued to attribute to Mary this helping role. By the fifteenth century, Denis the Carthusian could call Mary the "Redemptress of the world" and "salvatrix" through her cooperation with Christ, although he did assert that Christ was sufficient for our salvation.[53]

Sermons and meditations upon Christ's passion remained very popular in the sixteenth century. Lutheran preachers published a number of *Passional büchleins* and often included sermons on the passion narratives in their postils. Mary does not play a large role in these treatments of Christ's passion, primarily appearing only when the Johannine text is treated. Significantly, Luther and his followers are not greatly exercised by any threat from Mary to Christ as the only savior. This would seem to indicate a more limited importance, at least in German-speaking areas, to the idea of Mary as coredemptrix than might have been thought from the popularity of such texts as the *Mariale*. It is possible that the Lutheran pastors felt that the issue was decisively put to rest by their emphasis on Christ as the sole redeemer in other sections of their *Passionals*. However, the idea of Mary as coredemptrix does not play an important role in Geiler's passion sermons, and even Gabriel Biel seems, in the words of Oberman, "restrained" on this point, given "the general preoccupation of the time with this aspect of Mary's function as *coredemptrix*," as well as his own emphasis on Mary's cooperation in Christ's incarnation and work.[54] Despite the widespread interest in Mary as coredemptrix, Luther and his followers were not interested in providing counterarguments to it in their sermons. The contents of their sermons concerning Mary revolve around several common themes: how Christ fulfilled the fourth commandment in his care for and honor of Mary; how the church, represented by Mary, should be cared for by Christians, and especially by pastors, teachers, and rulers; and how Mary suffered great pain, and left us an example of patience and fortitude.

"Woman, Behold Your Son"

On the Saturday before Misericordia, medieval Catholics celebrated *unser lieben Frawen tag des Mitlydens*, the day of Mary's compassion. The theme of Geiler's sermon for this day is the honoring of parents, and he includes a long story, a parable perhaps, of a young man who did not properly honor his parents and paid the price for his behavior. Christ, on the other hand, while hanging on the cross took pains to show honor and love to his mother by recommending her to the care of John. His proper observance of the fourth commandment is a good example for all Christians to follow, while those children who are disobedient and negligent of their poor and aged parents are also poor Christians. Geiler even complains about the linguistic practice of saying "where is *the* father/mother?" rather than "where is *my* father/mother?" as though, he complains, "she were not your mother, and he were not your father."[55]

Curbing such disrespectful behavior and promoting the necessity of honoring and caring for one's parents remained of particular concern to Lutheran preachers. Luther discusses the issue in his *Passio* sermons, which were included in the 1544 *Hauspostille*. We are reminded, he suggests, both by Jesus' words and by John's actions of the fourth commandment. This commandment demands that one honor one's parents "and so God will allow a long life and happiness," proved by the fact that John lived longer than any of the other apostles, "namely sixty-eight years after the resurrection of Christ."[56] We should not be content with this interpretation, for the significance of these acts goes beyond Mary and John, according to Luther. It is a significant enough issue, however, that most of his followers' sermons press the point. The example of good Christian piety found in Jesus' behavior is far too important to ignore, especially by pastors who are interested in conserving and protecting what we might call "family values."

Most of the passion sermons stress the requirement that children honor their parents and care for them in their old age. Christ "perfectly fulfilled the fourth commandment of God for us" and modeled "perfect obedience" to his mother, according to Christoph Vischer. This perfect obedience recompenses for our own disobedience and rebelliousness that, through the influence of the "accursed devil," we have shown to our parents.[57] But despite the effects of sin, good Christian children will care for their parents. The reformer Jakob Andreae (1528–1590), like several other authors who call these words "Christ's last will and testament," thinks that Jesus' example shows us how important it is to arrange for the care of those who are our responsibility before we die, "but especially that we should provide for our poor, comfortless parents."[58]

If good sixteenth-century family values required children to care for their aging parents, especially to preserve them from poverty, family responsibilities also occasionally obstructed obedience to the higher calling of God. We have seen in past chapters how obedience to God, most notably in commitment to the true church and its teachings, outweighed obedience to one's parents. Nördlingen pastor Kaspar Kantz (d. 1544) reminds his listeners here that sometimes "father and mother, wife and children, etc., hinder some people from following Christ." If this happens, he suggests, "they must let [their family] go and recommend them to God," and most especially to "pious people" like John.[59] Johannes Drach also stresses the need for all "penitent and faithful" children to honor their parents but insists that Jesus called Mary "woman" rather than "mother" to remind us that in the Ten Commandments the first table is more important than the second. That is, the commands concerning God take precedence, and "one must obey God more than men."[60] In this context we find a critique of the Catholic notion that Mary aided Christ in our salvation: Vischer teaches that, in calling Mary "woman," Christ wanted to teach us not to "run to Mary for help, or seek comfort from her." He continues, "She contributed absolutely nothing to the salvation of the human race for her part; Christ is the only mediator and throne of grace."[61] Honoring our parents should not lead us either to value obedience to them above obedience to God, or to assign the role of co-savior to Mary.

Caring for "Mother" Church

While Luther thinks that the example of the good son caring for his poor mother is an important one to preach, he is much more interested in the wider meaning of the story. The "narrow," literal significance of the text is not here the most important, for "one should not limit to a few or isolated people what the Lord does and says here on the cross, [for] he embraces the whole world with his work and words, but especially his Christian church."[62] The wider significance of Christ's words to Mary encompasses all Christians, giving them a "common command" that they should be like mother and son to each other, caring for and loving one another. The command rests especially on the authorities of the church: preachers should be like mothers to their parishioners, nourishing them with instruction until they "make fine Christians out of them."[63] Anyone who wishes to be a minister must have a "mother heart" toward the church, or he will not properly care for his sheep and be willing to suffer all the problems facing the clergy. It is just such a "mother heart" that the pope and his bishops lack, according to Luther, and so they would rather be served than serve. Likewise, those who are not called to be preachers should be good and pious children toward the church and willingly allow themselves to be trained and led. Luther complains that more often than not, people, especially the nobility, do not respect their pastors and are not willing to give monetary support to the clergy.[64]

Many other pastors also take this opportunity to remind their listeners that, whatever their vocation, they have something to give to the church. Cyriacus Spangenberg recommends that we "take care of our dear mother, the Christian church, nourish, adorn, and embellish her, protect and help support her, and each should do his best according to his ability."[65] What does taking care of the church involve? Spangenberg suggests that the "worldly rulers" maintain and improve schools and churches, and defend the church from "persecutors of truth" and tyrants. The role of "subjects" is to attend services diligently, live a godly life, and provide "suitable aid" to further the cause of Christ's kingdom.[66] Vischer paints a picture of the "forsaken Christian church," that "poor Mary," who needs protection and support from lords and rulers.[67] Johannes Heune also finds in Christ's words a "secret" meaning: "that preachers and worldly rulers should faithfully cultivate, tend, and protect the church of Christ, so that pure healthy doctrine might be preserved and propagated, and heretics restrained."[68] The church is portrayed as Mary is seen under the cross: poor, weak, alone, in danger and in need of protection from caretakers, preachers, and civic leaders. Far from being a symbol of power, in this context Mary as the church becomes a symbol of weakness, in need of the protection of men.

Mary as the Sorrowing Mother

Despite the equation of the figure of Mary with the weak and helpless church, reliant upon John to care for her, many pastors promote Mary under the cross as a fine example of Christian piety, obedience to God's will, and patience and strength in a time of suffering. These sermons echo some of the praise of Mary found in later medieval sermons. In Gabriel Biel's sermon on the "compassion of the virgin" with Christ, we find Mary portrayed as a great martyr of the church: she maintained both her faith (in fact, she was the only one who was constant) and her "virginal chastity;" she stood without falling or "indecent display," although her heart was pierced by Simeon's sword; and though she believed her son would rise again, "her pain was incomparable."[69] Such extended attention given to Mary and her sorrows in devotional literature and sermons was of concern to Luther and several others, who feared that consideration of Mary might eclipse attention to Christ and his suffering. In his sermon on the "consideration of the holy suffering of Christ" from 1519, Luther complains that people often "carry in a great deal from Christ's departure from Bethany and the pains of the Virgin Mary and come no farther."[70] Such an approach leaves out the most important elements of the passion and does not allow Christ's suffering to enter into our hearts and change us. In fact, Luther does not discuss Mary's suffering and pain again in his postil sermons.

Cyriacus Spangenberg also complains about the excessive devotion to Mary's suffering found in the Catholic Church, which leads Catholics to forget Christ and the "fruits of his suffering." He finds inappropriate the presentation of her "lamentable demeanor": "falling down, pulling out [her] hair, [and] wringing her hands," along with raising a great hue and cry below the cross.[71]

Such devotion is not only of little use, he suggests, it is "idle human dreaming." This is not to suggest, however, either that Mary did not suffer at the cross or that considering such great suffering cannot serve a useful purpose. Spangenberg believes that Mary must have experienced great suffering in her "motherly heart" when she saw her innocent son dying upon the cross. He compares her pain with that of Eve when she learned of the murder of her innocent son Abel, but suggests that Mary bore the pain better because "there has hardly been a stronger, more courageous, and further, manly [*mannhaft*] female on earth, than the beloved holy Virgin Mary."[72] She was able to survive both seeing her son suffer on the cross and hearing the crowd mock and deride him, because she knew that it was God's will and that great good would come of his death. Thus, according to Spangenberg, Christians have a powerful example to follow in Mary, in bearing our crosses with patience and faith in God.

Following the medieval tradition of the "seven sorrows" of Mary, Vischer paints a pitiful picture of the *Mater Dolorosa*: "It would have been no surprise if her heart in her body had completely melted in pain, or exploded into a thousand pieces, and it then would have without doubt wept blood."[73] But she kept the pain within her, says Vischer, for she did not behave wildly, tear out her hair, cry out against the injustice, or wring her hands. Rather than demand revenge from God, she stood "in great patience and steadfast faith," as a "manly and gallant" woman.[74] In fact, she was more "manly" than Peter, who deserted Christ in his last moments and denied him. We also should not be such "tender martyrs" who will desert Christ and give up the cross in order to avoid pain and suffering. Rather, we should follow the example of the virile Mary, who held to God's promise in faith.[75]

Vischer also suggests a parallel between the suffering of Mary at her son's [*Eve !*] death and that of Eve, who must have suffered great fear and pain at seeing her son's "stone-dead" body, when she had never seen a dead man before.[76] Johannes Heune remarks that a sword also pierced the "body and soul" of Eve when she found that Cain had murdered Abel. But, he continues, "Mary's pain and suffering was much higher and greater," for her son was not simply a man but the true Messiah.[77] In fact, Vischer concurs, her suffering was that much greater than Eve's, because she knew Jesus was not only her son but also God's son. Despite this, insists Tileman Hesshusen, "Mary stood fast in faith, like a strong heroine, although the sword that Simeon had prophesied pierced her soul."[78] She knew that they were killing the Messiah, but her faith led her to be obedient to the will of God. She was also prepared for the occasion, according to Hesshusen, because she had studied God's word diligently, especially the Psalms, and knew all the prophecies concerning Christ. Her adherence to Christ's words and to Scripture made her faith stronger than even that of the apostles. We can learn from her, he concludes, to bear our crosses patiently and with obedience.[79]

Once again, Mary serves as an example of patience, obedience, and trusting faith. She is constant under the cross, keeping her faith in God's will for the future. She is also a model of strength, even "manly" courage, in the face both of danger and of suffering. Her courage and faith outshine that of all the others, even Peter, who denied Christ. Despite the references to Mary's manliness, however, her courage is not expressed in terms of rebellion or violence. Rather, her courage is what undergirds her patience and obedience, even her modest reserve. For Mary, although the prototypical mother (hence again her comparison with and superiority to Eve) in suffering at her son's pain and death, is once again the model of female modesty and appropriate behavior. She does not wail and weep, tear out her hair, or wring her hands. Her behavior is portrayed as consistent with her honest, pious, matronly status. Even her strength under the cross, although highly commendable, is not in opposition to her need, as a soon-to-be-childless widow, to be cared for by a man.

Marian Holidays Abandoned in the Sixteenth Century

The last sermons that Luther preached on the festivals of Mary's Conception, Birth, and Assumption stem from the early 1520s. After this time, although Lutherans continued to believe that Mary was conceived, born, and died, the holidays fell into disuse and were even abolished by many ecclesiastical constitutions. In the Osnabrück constitution published in 1543, the Marian holidays of Purification and Annunciation were to be celebrated with a full day, along with Easter and Christmas, while Visitation received half-day recognition. However, "Mary's Assumption shall not be celebrated, since there is nothing certain about it in the Scriptures." Even earlier, Luther had included the Assumption in a list of things that had fallen out of use among the evangelicals.[81] The day of Mary's Conception (December 8) was maintained for some time in Görlitz, but that seems to have been unusual. Sermons for the day appear in only a few postils, Luther's *Festpostille* of 1527 among them. Likewise, Mary's Birth (September 8) was retained in only a few "conservative" church constitutions. Luther preached his last sermon on this day in 1522, although he did not officially condemn it in his "On the Order of Worship" of 1523. This day, along with Assumption, would have to be maintained "for a while" in order not to scandalize the people.[82] The Schweinfurt church constitution of 1543 recommended that pastors should continue to preach on the day of Mary's Assumption (August 15), and the traditional gospel for the day should be maintained, but "otherwise on this festival in the churches the history of Our Lady's Visitation should be celebrated, with singing and reading."[83]

These three festivals had great significance in the later Middle Ages, although they were not completely uncontested. As discussed in the introduction, Mary's immaculate conception was not proclaimed a dogma in the Roman Catholic Church until 1854, and her assumption not until 1950. Theologians argued over whether Mary was conceived completely without sin, or cleansed from sin at some later point. Divergent traditions also developed around Mary's death and assumption. Despite these divergences, however, by the later Middle Ages these three holidays were widely celebrated. It is difficult to estimate people's reaction to the loss of these holidays from the Lutheran church calendar—in some locations the loss may have been minimally felt along with all the other changes that occurred. However, Andreas Zieger notes the reaction of townspeople in Königsberg to criticism of Mary's cult: in 1524 on the festival of the Assumption, Johannes Briesman, the future Lutheran bishop of Samland, preached against devotion to Mary, which created an uproar and forced him to flee to safety in another town.[84] The authorities quickly clamped down on protests, however, and enforced church reform in the entire region. These festivals continued to be celebrated in other areas for a time—we find sermons for these days in several postils from the 1530s and even 1540s. However, their lack of scriptural witness and authority quickly doomed the celebrations of Mary's Conception, Birth, and Assumption among Lutherans.

Mary's Conception: Immaculate or Otherwise

As we have seen, the status of Mary's conception was undetermined and still contested at the time Luther was discussing the issue in his final sermons on the matter. Geiler, although he discusses at length Mary's "eternal" conception in the heart of God, is uncomfortable speaking clearly about her human conception: "What nature conceals in all places, man should also be quiet about." Mary was not conceived through a kiss, as legend has it, but in the "coming together of man and woman, [just] as you and I."[85] This conception is not what people honor on this holiday, according to Geiler. Rather they honor her eternal election and formation in the heart of God, and the "third" conception, which occurred when her soul was created in her body without any original sin.[86] To phrase Geiler's position in Platonic language, we are all ideas in the heart of God, the way a master craftsman plans and knows his creation before it is made. But while God sees a worm as a worm, and a man as a man, he conceived Mary from eternity as "the purest virgin . . . and a Mother of God."[87] From Mary's eternal conception, Geiler moves easily to her immaculate conception, which occurs with her animation.

In his final sermon on the holiday of Mary's Conception, preached in 1520 and included in expanded form in Roth's *Festpostille* of 1527, Luther complains that the debate about her conception has caused a lot of trouble among the monks, even though "there is not a single letter about it in the Gospels or otherwise in the Scriptures."[88] In fact, the text for the day (Luke 11:27–28), although it mentions Mary obliquely, actually discounts any special blessing Mary might have received from being Christ's mother. The woman in the crowd cries out, "Blessed is the womb that bore you and the breasts that nursed you." But Jesus' response to the woman, "Blessed rather are those who hear the word of God and obey it," indicates that human connections are less important than faith considerations. Luther suggests that this response should tell us that "human affect" is rejected by Christ: "The good little woman speaks out of a fleshly, female emotionalism," which "the Lord completely repudiates here and shows us what is more necessary than this, namely to hear God's word and preserve it."[89] Mary herself is made holy not through her physical connection to Christ but rather through her faith.

But Luther does go on in this sermon to consider original sin and how it can be said that Mary is free from it. It is traditional, he remarks, to preach on original sin on this holiday, and Luther provides a traditionally Augustinian view of sin. Original sin is "this whole evil and inclination to evil which all men feel in themselves," leading to pride, anger, jealousy, immorality, and other depravity.[90] We cannot purify ourselves of this sinful inclination, so Christ did it for us through his death. However, even if sinners are saved through baptism, their children still inherit this sin: concupiscence (lust, *begierde*) still infects every conception and birth, for "the flesh of men can never again in this life perfectly regain its purity."[91] The inevitable effects of sin are the reason that Christ wanted to be born of a virgin through the Holy Spirit: only in this way could he avoid the stain of original sin. Mary, on the other hand, was born through the usual means of a father and a mother—what Luther calls the "first conception." During the "second" conception, when the newly created soul informs the body, is the point at which Mary was "purified from original sin and decorated with God's gifts."[92] Although the second conception could not have happened without the first, it is in fact the more important one, for it is at that moment that one is said to begin to live: "So from the first moment that she began to live, she was without all sin."[93] This fact places Mary in the "middle between Christ and other men," and places Luther more to the im- maculist side of the debate.[94] However, Luther insists that one should not make a required article of faith out of this belief or another in Mary's conception, as it is not revealed in Scripture.

Luther's position in the 1527 *Festpostille* is clearly in favor of the immaculate conception, along with Geiler, Biel,[95] and probably the majority of later medi- eval theologians.[96] However, some of Luther's later texts do call into question whether he held this position throughout the remainder of his life. In several sermons in 1532 he mentions that Mary was somehow healed from sin when she conceived through the Holy Spirit, so "that she was without all sin."[97] In a Christmas sermon from 1540, Luther stresses that Christ's sinlessness did not simply come from the Virgin Mary's purity but from the working of the Spirit: Mary was "born from her parents in sin like all men."[98] In a later writing Luther insists that Mary was "saved and purified from original sin through the Holy Spirit" at some point before Christ's incarnation, although he does not specify when this happened.[99] These ambiguous statements do not allow for a definitive answer to the question of whether or not Luther always held to the immaculate conception of Mary, although they do help to clarify the shift in the treatment of the question of Mary's sinlessness by his followers (see chap- ter 1).

The other published Lutheran sermons for the festival of Mary's Concep- tion do not clearly state a position on this issue. Caspar Huberinus comes closest to discussing Mary's conception in relation to her sinlessness. In his sermon on *vnser Frawen empfengknus tag* in his 1554 holiday postil, Huberinus insists that this holiday was instituted for a good reason, but it unfortunately led to great misuse and thus had to be discarded "for the building up of the church."[100] The original purpose of the holiday was to counteract the Eutychian heresy that had arisen in the early church: that Mary "was conceived and born in sin," so Christ must not have taken on her flesh, but rather brought his body from heaven in order to avoid the taint of sin.[101] The verse "blessed is the womb that bore you" is the best defense against this heresy, for it proves that Mary "must have had a pure, holy, blessed body" out of which Christ took his flesh.[102] We also know from the Annunciation that Mary "not only found grace with God but she also became full of grace and the Holy Spirit."[103]

Huberinus also wants to make clear, however, that the grace and sinlessness that Mary enjoyed were not her own possessions, gained by her merit, but were rather gifts of God's mercy. Mary is worthy of praise and honor, but no one should worship or pray to her, as the first commandment teaches. Huberinus recommends that Christians follow a "middle" path in relation to Mary: "We should not despise, scorn, or disparage the Virgin Mary, or withdraw the honor she is due, as the *rottengeister* do; neither should we worship her as an idol" and give to her the honor due only to God.[104] Unlike the other Lutheran pastors, he regrets that the holiday of Mary's Conception had to be discarded "for the good of the church" and is concerned that reforming communities forget to give honor to Mary where honor is due. His concern has some merit, for this is not only the last sermon published on this holiday in Lutheran postils but in the 1550s Mary's position suffered a serious decline in Lutheran preaching.

The two other sermons on Mary's Conception that appeared earlier, both by Corvinus, do not address at all the issues of Mary's conception or sinlessness. Rather, Corvinus is interested in promoting the notion that Mary is blessed, not because of her physical connection to Christ as his mother, but because of her faith. Echoing sermons on the wedding at Cana, Corvinus reminds his listeners that "Christ is not a respecter of persons."[105] In his later sermon, he criticizes the woman in the crowd, saying that although her "meaning was perhaps not evil, yet the emotion was fleshly."[106] It is not human relationships, but whether one believes and keeps God's word that makes one pleasing to God. Elizabeth was right to praise Mary for her faith, rather than her physical closeness to Christ as his mother.

The Birth of Mary

The traditional gospel for the festival of the *Geburt Mariæ* is the listing of Jesus' generations in the first chapter of Matthew. Mary is mentioned as Jesus' mother and the wife of Joseph. The text does not recount Mary's birth, and her birth is not mentioned elsewhere in Scripture. That fact does not make this an insignificant Marian holiday, however—both Geiler and Luther discuss a wide variety of Marian topics in their sermons for this day. Geiler first compares Mary to a star—a propos of the famous hymn *Ave Maris Stella*—recounting a number of characteristics that she and a star have in common: purity, highness, greatness, luster, even power. Because she has more merit, Mary is more powerful than all the other saints: Geiler suggests that in time of need, one should call upon both God and "our Lady."[107] Mary has power over men—

she can come to the aid of those who despair of God's grace—and even over Satan, from whom she can preserve her adherents. Mary may appear small through her humility, but it is only in the way a great star appears small to us through its distance. In reality, she is a great and powerful mediator between God and men, and, as a human, she recognizes "erring men" and will come quickly to their aid.[108] In the following section of the sermon, where Geiler turns to Mary's presentation in the temple, he provides the traditional distinction between the worship reserved for God alone—*latria*—and that due Mary as the highest of all created things—*hyperdulia* (or here *inperdula*).[109] Mary should not be worshiped like God, Geiler warns, but should receive the highest possible honor due her. If Christ is king, Mary as his mother is the queen, whom we should gladly serve. In the remainder of the sermon, Geiler lists the many ways we should honor and serve our gracious queen.

In Luther's sermon, we find a recognition of the power of devotion to Mary, as well as an understanding that a certain devotion is appropriate and should be allowed: "You know, my friends, that the honor that men hold for the Mother of God is cultivated deep in their hearts, and so no one is glad to hear anything against that, but only what increases and makes it greater."[110] Luther quotes Paul to the effect that we are required to honor each other, and "therefore one is also required to honor her, but one should take care that one honors her rightly" and does not place her above Christ.[111] People may retain their honor of Mary, but it should not be made into a requirement. After all, it is not Mary's birth but Christ's that is recorded in this gospel; thus, we should not place our confidence or our trust in her. Mary is not our savior, and in fact we are co-heirs with her to God's kingdom: "and so are we the same [God's children and heirs] as much as the Mother of God herself, and are sisters and brothers of Mary."[112] She may have received a greater grace than we, but that is not from her own merit, but rather from God's mercy. In this light, the hymns *Salve regina* and *Regina coeli* are excessive and misleading. When one calls Mary "the queen of mercy, our life, our sweetness, and our hope," or "Queen of Heaven," it detracts from the honor of Christ.[113] Mary cannot serve as our *fürsprecherin* (intercessor)—a position reserved for Christ alone—but only as a *fürbitterin* (one who prays for us), a role that all the saints play. In fact, he remarks, "your prayer is as dear to me as hers."[114]

Another problem that can occur from excessive attention to Mary and the saints, according to Luther, is that people may forget those who really deserve and need our consideration, that is, the poor. We need to remember the "saints on earth," insists Luther, for "there is no command to honor those saints who have been taken from this life, but there is a command given to you to honor the living Christians in this life, for these are the true saints."[115] What requirements are there to build churches and altars to honor St. Paul or St. Peter? Such money, Luther chastises, would be better used in assisting poor girls than in such "unnecessary honor and service of the saints."[116] Christians should help their poor neighbors before running off to shrines and giving away their money irresponsibly.

This was the final sermon that Luther preached on this holiday, and very few other postils have any sermon for the day of Mary's Birth. Corvinus provides a sermon for this day, along with Mary's Conception, but he primarily discusses the gospel text. He acknowledges that the festival is "unnecessary," like the festivals of Mary's Presentation and Assumption, but remarks that some people still desire to celebrate these days. Such lazy, feast-loving people also need to hear "pure exegesis" of the gospel, so Corvinus provides a sermon for use when it pleases the community and custom.[117] The text is relevant to Mary in that it teaches concerning the incarnation that Christ took his flesh and blood from Mary, against the heresies of the Anabaptists.[118] Her own birth is not mentioned.

Mary's Death and Assumption

Along with Mary's conception, her assumption was not a firmly determined dogma in the sixteenth century. The fact that the holiday did not survive long among Lutherans, however, should not imply that it was not a very popular holiday in the later medieval period. Many of the elements of late medieval Mariology are, in a sense, dependent upon Mary's assumption. The fact that she is fully present in heaven allowed not only continued development of her blessings, honors, and titles but it supported Mary's position as a helper of humankind. Her honored position next to her enthroned son gave her unique access to Christ's mercy and forgiveness. In a common pattern, Geiler opens his sermon on the festival of Mary's Assumption by enumerating the honors given to Mary by God: "God made her an advocate, a helper, an aid, a participant, a lady [over] the world, a queen of heaven, a queen of mercy, [and] the one next to him." She is the advocate for sinful men before God, a strong and powerful speaker for mankind "who has never lost a case."[119] She is a participant in the honor of her son, although this does not make her God, but she is "pure man." Following Ambrose, Geiler calls Mary *regina mundi et domina virgo maria perpetua;* as the "queen of the world" and of heaven we should ask her to pray for us.[120] Mary stands by God, above all angels and saints, or in the words of Bernard, serves as "the neck between the head and the whole body." Geiler even suggests that Mary has "her own throne . . . right next to the throne of Jesus Christ."[121] Excepting only the distinction between God's divinity and Mary's humanity, Geiler's praise and honor of Mary know no bounds.

The traditional gospel text for this day is the story of Mary and Martha, the sisters of Lazarus, in which Jesus commends Mary's attention to his teaching over Martha's hosting and housekeeping duties (Luke 10:38–42). Jesus' mother Mary does not play a part in this history, which becomes an issue for Luther and his followers: there is no biblical evidence for Mary's assumption, which calls its observance into question. Geiler also addresses the issue of how this text is related to the Virgin Mary. In another sermon, he admits that although the literal sense of the text has nothing to do with Mary, the spiritual sense, the allegory, is all about Mary. The text begins *Intrauit Jesus in quodda[m] castellum,* "Jesus entered into a certain fortress" (village, in NRSV). The *castellum* represents Mary, according to Geiler: she is protected by a wall of virginity;

the tower, her humility, protects the wall and is likewise protected by it; also, it is a *quoddam*, or *special* fortress.[122] The story itself can also be applied to Mary, according to Geiler, for the two sisters, Mary (representing the contemplative life) and Martha (the active life), are like two sides of the Virgin Mary's character.

Luther is less convinced that this text is related at all to Mary, Jesus' mother. In his 1522 sermon on the Assumption (the text used in the 1527 *Festpostille*), he remarks that "one cannot know how Mary is in heaven from this gospel," nor is it necessary that we discover everything about the saints in heaven.[123] We know that they live in Christ, to which a number of Scripture passages bear witness, but *how* they live is not for us to know. Therefore, Luther rejects the idea that we can make an article of faith out of some event or teaching not in the Bible: the Bible clearly states what is necessary for us to believe. In this case, "the Scriptures say clearly that Abraham, Isaac, Jacob and all the faithful live; therefore, it is necessary that you believe that the Mother of God lives, but how this happens, that one must entrust to our loving God."[124]

Following Luther's lead, other preachers also began to ignore this holiday. Those postils that include sermons for this day (J. Spangenberg, Sarcerius) adhere to the gospel story and do not mention Jesus' mother. The one exception to this rule is Johannes Brenz: his festival postil includes two sermons on Mary's Assumption, preached in the years 1541 and 1542. He raises questions concerning the traditions of her assumption, tries to provide a proper Lutheran understanding of her position, and insists that the church has a great deal to learn from Mary and that she should not be ignored or discarded. Some people, Brenz relates, say that while Mary's soul is in heaven, her body is sleeping in the earth until the last day. Others think that after her death, her body was assumed into heaven and there was reunited with her soul.[125] Obviously, this event is somewhat uncertain, although not without biblical precedent (for example, the translation of Enoch into heaven). Brenz reaffirms Luther's statement that what is uncertain is not required for belief but is more forthcoming about Mary's current status: "It is most certain that Mary has reached perpetual happiness" and lives with her son in heaven.[126] But how did Mary gain this perpetual happiness? Was it through her virginity, her motherhood of Christ, or perhaps her suffering for Christ's sake? No, insists Brenz, for "blessed are those who hear God's word and guard it" (Matt. 12).

How, then, should Christians treat Mary? She cannot serve as our mediator or savior, says Brenz, for "this majesty applies to Christ alone." But we are required to see her as the "true and holy mother of our Lord Jesus Christ," which should lead us to imitate her virtues.[127] Her virtues include hearing the gospel and believing in Christ as her savior. We also should imitate her modesty and chastity, although Brenz refrains from suggesting that we should imitate her virginity. Instead, he teaches that "virginity was the vocation of Mary, in which she complied with the spirit of God and was perpetually chaste."[128] Chastity will serve those in every calling, whether virginity, marriage, or widowhood. It would be hypocritical to require everyone to remain a virgin, since marriage is also good. Also, virginity in itself is not a recipe for holiness, for some virgins are proud and sinful. Unlike such virgins, Mary was humble and modest, and did not try to usurp another role or office, such as that of apostle. This example should particularly serve wives, for they "should not usurp for themselves the responsibilities of husbands."[129] Finally, we should follow Mary in steadfastly suffering for Christ.

Along with the example of her virtues, Mary can serve a very useful purpose for the church, in that she proves to all people that God keeps his promises. We can understand the relationship that God wants to have with us through the example of Mary: God was merciful and gracious to her, and unconcerned with her lack of status. She was despised, but he chose her to be the most honored of women. Through her the greatness and omnipotence of God are fully revealed, in that he gave his son to be born through her, yet she remained a virgin: "This is impossible in nature and requires the omnipotence of God."[130]

These final holidays of the church year in which Mary played a role reveal various themes that help to complete our investigation of how Mary is presented in sixteenth-century Lutheran sermons. By far the most important of these holidays for Mary's image is Christmas, where Lutheran pastors reaffirm their orthodox understanding of Mary as *Theotokos*, the Mother of God. Although this title falls into disuse among Lutherans—she is more often referred to as Jesus' or Christ's mother—the christological positions conveyed by the acceptance of this title are fully embraced. Mary serves as the guarantor of Christ's true humanity, and Luther and his followers are concerned to guard themselves against any taint of heresy, modern or ancient. In their Christmas sermons they emphasize that Christ is truly human, as well as truly divine, and that he took his flesh and blood from the pure flesh of Mary. As we saw in texts on the Annunciation, Mary was purified of all taint of sin at some point before Christ's conception. Lutherans believe that Mary was a virgin at Christ's birth—Luther and others also maintain traditional elements about the birth, including that Mary suffered no pain—and those who discuss it also continue to hold Mary's perpetual virginity. The benefits of maintaining Mary's virginity and ease of birth—that her virginal, even sinless purity was necessary in an Augustinian context to preserve Jesus from any taint of sin—outweigh any difficulties or tendencies toward heresy from the suspicion that Jesus had anything other than a perfectly normal, human birth.

Beyond the significance of Mary for these theological and christological points, Lutheran preachers also emphasize certain social issues, using Mary and often Joseph as exemplars for their congregations and readers. Mary, along with Christ, suffered poverty, rejection, and many other difficulties. The message here for Christians is that they should not be afraid to suffer in this world, especially for their faith, but also that they should feel called to relieve the suffering and want of others. Despite the attendant suffering, Mary and Joseph were obedient to the decree of the emperor, teaching Christians to observe and obey the rule of temporal authorities, whether Christian or not. Finally, Mary's faith in God's word and promises led to her future blessings, providing another

fine example of faithful living. The social message inherent in these recommendations is unambiguous: be good, obedient, pious, and faithful Christians
and citizens, for this is the will of God; accept suffering when it comes; and
do not reject or rebel against your lot in life. Even the shepherds serve as
examples of those who, despite their involvement in the miraculous happen-
ings at Bethlehem, returned to their lives and original vocations. They did not
give up their families or jobs to become monks, but remained satisfied with
their given situations. Lutheran pastors hoped to inculcate the notion of the
godly, well-ordered, hierarchical society in their listeners, and used Mary and
other biblical figures to help in this project.

The sermons concerning the remaining infancy narratives offer little new
information for our picture of the "Lutheran" Mary. There are some instances
of anti-Catholic polemic, occasional exhortations to help the poor the way the
Magi helped Mary and her family, a certain amount of interest in Mary's sufferings as the beginning of the fulfillment of Simeon's prophecy of the sword,
and indications that the gospel was preached by Mary and Joseph even while
Jesus was still a baby.

Far more important, in light of the developments of the late medieval
church, are the sermons on Christ's passion, and the holidays of Mary's Conception, Birth, and Assumption. The *Mater Dolorosa*, the portrait of the sorrowing mother under the cross, is one of the most influential images of Mary
in the medieval period. The common view of Mary as the coredemptrix of
humankind with Christ was developed from her participation in his suffering
under the cross. Her *com*passion with Christ's passion was thought to give
birth to the church, thus also making her the mother of the church and all the
faithful. For Luther and his followers, however, the significance of Christ's
passion leaves very little room for the participation of his mother: the cult of
Mary as coredemptrix is virtually ignored in Lutheran sermons, and her main
significance is in relation to John, Jesus' beloved disciple. The emphasis in
Lutheran sermons on Mary's role under the cross is upon Christ's fulfillment
of the fourth commandment in his care for Mary, thus stressing the importance
of family values for Lutheran preachers. Good children will care and provide
for their aging parents, the way Christ commended Mary to the care of John—a
necessity in a society without retirement plans or a welfare net. The literal
sense of this text does not limit its meaning, however, and many preachers
emphasize that Mary represents the church, which is also weak and powerless
without the care of its members, especially temporal authorities and pastors.
The view of Mary as a weak and powerless widow contradicts the other important element in these sermons: Mary's example of courage and fortitude in
the face of danger and extreme suffering. She suffered more greatly than Eve
and exhibited more constant faith than the apostles. Her courage made her
"manly" and "virile," albeit in a stoic rather than violent manner. In short,
Mary is the ideal of the faithful, pious, strong but silent matron, manly in her
fortitude and womanly in her chastity, modesty, and mother-love.

The dramatic changes seen in the presentation of Mary under the cross
from the late medieval period to Lutheran sermons in the sixteenth century

are all but absent in the consideration given to Mary's conception, birth, death, and assumption. This absence of change is not due to the Lutheran acceptance of the traditions of these holidays, but rather to the fact that they were quickly phased out of the Lutheran calendar, and very few sermons exist in the postils of the period. The sermons that do commemorate these days, primarily those of Luther from the early 1520s, critique "papist" practices such as the veneration of Mary, prayer to her as an advocate or mediator, and the theological notion of merit. In the few sermons provided for these days, other Lutheran preachers strive to present Mary in the "proper" light, as one who receives God's grace and is praised for her faith, and to reject the excessive praise and error clouding the figure of Mary. The lack of scriptural support for the stories surrounding her conception, birth, and assumption into heaven and thus Lutherans' inability to have any firm belief in them are what finally condemn these holidays in Lutheran observance.

Conclusion

In considering the texts and themes presented in the previous chapters, it is wise to keep in our minds Caroline Walker Bynum's question "for *whom* does this symbol mean?"[1] The subjects of this study, that is, those whose ideas and writings I am investigating, are a relatively small group of male clerics, part of the nascent Lutheran tradition, whose sermons, perhaps preached to an audience, perhaps intended as exemplars, were published. This exceptional group of men has been taken as in some way representative of one, albeit major, strand of Protestant Christianity in the sixteenth century. I have assumed, both for practical purposes and for those reasons outlined in the introduction, that the ideas found in these sermons were widely spread and highly influential, as the large amount of agreement and even repetition within the sermons across the period attests. Thus, these sermons, taken as a whole, can be characterized as presenting orthodox, official opinions of the emerging Lutheran tradition in the sixteenth century.

The opinions found in these sermons concerning the Virgin Mary are the focus of this study. It seeks to answer two main questions: how is Mary presented to the audience in these sermons, and for what purpose(s)? In order to understand the images of Mary presented in the sermons, I have compared the Lutheran views of Mary with the ways Mary was viewed in the medieval Catholic tradition. Both the continuities with the past and the changes or developments in this regard are informative. But the conversation or context in which these Lutheran pastors developed their views of Mary was not solely with the past but also with each other and with their audience. That is to say, Lutheran theology concerning the saints and Mary and the interpretations of Mary's roles were not simply determined by Luther and then passed down through the tradition. In fact, a number of changes occur throughout the sixteenth century, and later pastors express opinions that contradict various views that Luther held.

Finally, the sermons in this study represent a "conversation," although we are privy to only one side, between the preacher and his audience, especially the lay man or woman in the pew, as it were. In this regard, the preachers' opinions concerning Mary as a model and example, either good or bad, are most relevant. Here we find the most direct answer to the question of purpose: the purpose behind the presentation of Mary in these sermons is both pedagogical and hortatory. The ways in which Mary is presented are meant to teach something to the audience—how to believe, how to live, how to behave properly, even how to read the Bible—and then to encourage them to incorporate these ideas into their lives and behavior. Images of Mary found in these sermons help us answer the question, what did it mean for these German Lutheran pastors to be a "good Christian," and, part and parcel of that notion, a good citizen? In my conclusion, I will consider each of these aspects in turn.

Continuity with Tradition

Lutheran preachers maintained certain elements of traditional Marian theology for two primary reasons: first, they thought of themselves as completely orthodox, and, of course, more in accord with the early church than their contemporary Roman Catholics; and second, they promoted what they saw as a literal reading of Scripture, which also included a prophetic understanding of much of the Old Testament. Lutherans accepted the great ecumenical councils of the early church, including both Ephesus and Chalcedon, with their statements about Mary and her importance for Christology. They maintained the title "Mother of God" and, especially in Annunciation and Christmas sermons, emphasized the importance of Mary's virginal purity for the sinlessness and purity of Christ. Luther, in particular, even declared with the tradition that, as Mary had conceived without sin, that is, not in the usual manner, she also gave birth without suffering any pain or difficulty. But, as Christ was completely human, so he had a completely natural birth.

While the virgin birth could be seen as having scriptural support, Mary's perpetual virginity (both *in partu* and post partum) does not. In fact, certain references in Scripture, such as the mention of Jesus' brothers, tend against the idea that Mary remained a virgin. However, once again Luther and his colleagues adhere thoroughly to tradition, maintaining her perpetual virginity, despite some difficulties it caused them in their promotion of marriage over an avowed life of virginity and celibacy. The notion of purity over against the stain and sinfulness of sex, even within marriage, remained powerful in the sixteenth century, and most of the authorities of the early church were in favor of this doctrine. Lutherans managed to find support for marriage through Mary because she herself was married, and because she helped to plan and supervise the wedding at Cana. In several instances, in fact, Mary was used to promote married life against celibacy and the religious life, in that she herself, despite her virginal status, accepted her calling as a wife and mother.

Lutheran preachers also continued to use certain traditional aspects of Marian imagery such as the parallel between Eve and Mary, Mary as a type of the church, and traditional virtues associated with Mary, such as faith and humility. These traditional forms, however, were transformed and, if not entirely new, now conveyed a Lutheran perspective. The parallel between Eve and Mary, which in the medieval period had helped to push Mary into a role of comparison or even equality with Christ and emphasized her participation in salvation, was now used primarily to indicate that Mary was free from the curse that Eve brought upon all women. Several sermons mention Mary's role in making salvation possible, reversing the sin of Eve, but are very careful to reserve any active role to Christ. Mary was merely the "instrument" of God's work, not the one who accomplished the work. Also, when the preachers speak of Mary as a type of the church, the emphasis tends to be taken away from Mary. This is most obvious in sermons on Simeon's prophecy of the sword that Mary would suffer: Mary's co-suffering with Christ's suffering, so significant in the late medieval tradition for Mary's role as coredemptrix, is here mitigated by the suggestion that all Christians suffer together with Mary under the cross. She is less important than the church that she represents. The virtues so important for the medieval image of Mary—her faith, her humility, her chastity—were also stressed in Lutheran sermons. They made her praiseworthy and a great example, but none of these virtues adorned her with any sort of merit or power.

Rejection of the Past

Much of the medieval devotion to Mary was rejected by Luther and his followers. The most obvious element to be removed was the idea that Mary and other saints could serve as intercessors or mediators with God. Christians were encouraged to pray directly to Christ, and to rely on him to answer their prayers and help them in times of need. The intercessory structure found in medieval Catholicism was seen as detrimental to Christ and his role as the sole mediator and savior. Lutherans insisted that there is no evidence in Scripture that saints should play this role for Christians, or that they have any power on their own to help their supplicants. The notion that Mary's merits somehow give her power or that her role as Christ's mother gives her authority over him was decisively rejected: Lutheran preachers stressed that all of Mary's blessings come from God, and she is nothing in herself, as she herself said in her Magnificat. Because Mary has no power to help, prayers should not be addressed to her—even the *Ave Maria* should not be thought of as a prayer, but rather the angel's address to Mary (with the *voll gnaden* now translated as the passive *holdselige*) should be seen to indicate how all of the grace and blessing in the incarnation come from God.

As we saw in the previous section, certain theological changes led to a reimagining of many traditional aspects of Mary's image. Much traditional medieval piety and devotion—that which painted Mary as a powerful mother queen who could impose her will upon her son to help her devotees—was rejected and even ridiculed. The insistence on biblical authority also led to the eventual rejection of Marian festivals not based upon scriptural events: Mary's Conception, Birth, and Assumption. Her immaculate conception and assumption were not defined dogmas at this time, so most Lutheran preachers did not feel it necessary to state their opinions on these points. They did find it necessary, however, to state strongly their opposition to the requirement of a vow of celibacy for the religious life, and the valuation of virginity and celibacy over marriage. And although Lutherans continued to hold to Mary's virginity, they were concerned not to recommend a life of virginity as a vocational choice for their audience. Instead, they used the image of Mary as a wife and mother, and a helper at the wedding of Cana, to impress upon their listeners the value and primacy of the married life. Celibacy, they felt, was not something that could be chosen by the individual, but must be a gift from God—and such gifts were rarely given. Mary could no longer stand as the ideal for the celibate or virginal life.

Developments during the Period

Luther and the early reformers were all reared in and formed by the late medieval Catholic tradition. Despite certain theological objections to the cult of Mary, and concerns that neither she nor any saint detract from the role and majesty of Christ, the earliest reformers maintained a certain attitude of reverence, if not actual devotion, toward Mary. Many statements by Luther support this notion, and the vast literature on the topic of Luther's devotion to Mary proves, if nothing else, that Luther and his near contemporaries were more devoted to Mary than later Protestants. What we find, however, is that the attitude of reverence toward Mary characteristic of Luther and other pastors such as Johann Spangenberg, Caspar Huberinus (who laments that the festival of Mary's Conception has been abandoned), and Johannes Brenz is quickly lost among the younger generation of reformers. This shift is already visible in the postils of Melanchthon but becomes especially noticeable in those sermon collections published in the 1550s and 1560s, which tend to stress Christ and spend little time discussing Mary, and in those published after 1570, which tend to be more critical both of Mary and of Roman Catholicism. These changes are caused not only by the decrease in reverential attitude among those pastors raised in a Protestant rather than a Roman Catholic context but also because of the changing situations with which they were faced, for example, the intra-Lutheran debates and battles over orthodoxy especially in the middle period, and the renewal and resurgence of Roman Catholicism in many areas, particularly through the work of the newly founded Jesuit order. Other scholars have noted the increase in religious tensions among the various confessions beginning around 1570: the process of confessionalization reached a critical juncture in this period as Protestants and Catholics used harsher methods to contain unrest, enforce conformity, and maintain and, if possible, increase their own numbers.[2] As one of the pillars of Counter-Reformation Catholicism was Marian piety, it is no surprise that the Lutheran critique of Mary grew correspondingly harsher.[3]

The most important element of the image of Mary that changed over the sixteenth century was the notion of her sinlessness. The early Lutheran preachers tended to maintain the Augustinian tradition that Mary was free from actual sin, although through God's grace and not through her own power. Luther makes a number of comments about Mary's freedom from sin, and even seems to have held to the immaculate conception, despite certain later ambiguous statements. Huberinus insists that it is the devil who is trying to promote the idea that Mary was not free from sin. Many preachers throughout the period continue to believe the traditional notion that Mary was purified from sin at some point before the incarnation, although they rarely specify what kind of "sin" or impurity they mean. Even in the gospel texts that present Mary and Jesus at odds with each other, the loss of Jesus in the temple and the wedding at Cana (discussed in chapters 4 and 5), Luther is only comfortable saying that Mary erred, and thus we know that the church and its leadership can err.

Few of the later Lutheran preachers discuss Mary's conception and to what extent she was purified of sin before the incarnation, but a number do begin to state that not only did Mary make mistakes, displaying a great lack of diligence in losing her son, but, according to several preachers, she also sinned. In sermons on the wedding at Cana text, Mary is presented as a wonderful Christian model of love and charity. She is especially a good example of faith being expressed in prayer, for she asks her son to help the poor couple. Luther feels that Christ's harsh response to her 1) indicates that Mary has no motherly authority over Christ in his divine mission and thus it is senseless to pray to her to intercede for us with Christ, and 2) imitates the stern face of God that we often see when we come to him with our requests. But Mary models the proper response: she humbly continues to hope and pray for help, knowing that her faith is being tested. While his later followers agree that this text indicates Christ's transcendence over his earthly relations, they also are quicker to criticize Mary for her interference. Several sermons point out Mary's weakness and her emotional response to the needs of the young couple. She overstepped her authority and was punished by her son. Georg Walther tentatively explains: "Mary was also not totally without sin, for otherwise [Christ] would not have given her such hard words."[4]

Later sermons on the loss of the twelve-year-old Jesus in the temple criticize Mary even more harshly. Beginning with Melanchthon, who speaks of Mary's sin as "natural infirmity," yet with dire consequences, the trend among Lutheran preachers is toward a stronger critique of Mary and her actions. The sermons published after 1570 in particular contain harsh comments about Mary, her weakness and her faults, and, occasionally, her sin. At most, she is a good example of how we should take correction and punishment for our faults, even if it is done publicly. As Christoph Vischer instructs his audience, Mary's docility under public correction is a great example. In an interesting twist, several preachers (again, Melanchthon appears to be the first) return to the theme of Mary as the "second Eve," but in this case Mary appears to be even worse and more destructive than Eve. Niels Hemmingsen suggests that Mary must have compared herself to Eve, "for just as Eve was tempted through the devil's cunning, and thereby brought the whole human race into misery, so Mary thought that she, through her lack of diligence, had lost the promised savior of the world."[5] Mary, like all other saints, comes under the scriptural dictum that "all have sinned and fall short of the glory of God."

Moral Instruction of the Laity

As we have seen, one of the primary purposes of the sermon was to provide instruction to the audience. Lutheran preachers wanted to teach their audience how to understand Scripture, that is, what to believe. Just as important, it seems, was teaching their audience how to live, or exhortation. As concerned as Luther and his followers were to reject anything that sounded like works-righteousness—that one could earn merit or grace and hence salvation by what one did—they were as determined to instruct their congregations that what one believes must and will be expressed in the way one lives his life. If Christians put their faith and trust in God, that will determine how they relate to one another and how they live. Thus, a true Christian leads a Christian life, in opposition to someone who, for example, puts his trust in money, or the merits of Mary and the saints, or some other idol. The corollary to this point is, of course, that one should be able to recognize true Christians by seeing how people act and speak, and unfortunately, as Luther and his followers complain, it is clear that true Christians are few and far between. The moral instruction provided in many of these sermons was intended to help remedy this sorry situation.

As Melanchthon wrote in the Augsburg Confession, one way in which the saints remained important for Lutherans was as models of faith and examples of how to live for God. Because saints were not immune from flaws, they could serve as both negative and positive examples. We find that this is the case with Mary: sermons on the pericopes in which Mary plays a significant role often use her to teach the audience about the Christian life. She serves as a positive example of many of the Christian, spiritual virtues that the Lutheran preachers felt were indicative of a Christian life. She also occasionally serves as a negative exemplar, teaching by example how we should *not* behave.

Mary as a Model for All

As Bynum points out, sometimes a gendered symbol is about things other than gender, and that is the case with the image of Mary. The sermons regularly use Mary as a profitable model for all Christians. She is often promoted as a shining example of faith: in believing the words of the angel, despite the inability of her human reason to comprehend them, she exhibited the essential quality of faith, which is an unquestioning trust in the word of God. She was also not afraid to share her faith with others: Mary was the first to preach the incarnation, and her hymn of praise, the Magnificat, is a powerful statement of faith and prayer. She is a model of obedience, following the laws of both her religion in her purification and the government in obeying the registration decree by traveling to Bethlehem, despite her freedom from these laws. She served her neighbor, both through the example of her obedience and her desire not to scandalize anyone through the abuse of her freedom, and also through actual service: she was not too proud to help her elderly cousin Elizabeth and serve as nursery-maid to baby John. In her service and care for her son and his education, she is a fine model for parents: Mary, along with Joseph, brought Jesus along with them to church and took care to instruct him in the Scriptures and proper piety. Just as important, they provided good role models for their son in their virtuous behavior and their devotion to the things of God rather than the things of the world.

The more negative aspects of her image also provide an important model for the preachers' audience. Luther teaches that Mary sought her lost son among friends and relatives without success, when she should have looked first in the temple; thus, we will not find him among the writings of the councils or church fathers, but only in God's word. More directly, Mary is often criticized for her lack of diligence in caring for her son, and then her overly emotional reaction when she found him again. Jesus was respectful to her, always mindful of the fourth commandment, but divine authority takes priority over parental authority: Mary was wrong to chastise her son for obeying God. Although this point is somewhat tricky—no Lutheran preacher wanted to give license to children to disobey their parents when they saw fit—it was important for the reform movement that divine requirements (determined by some authority, such as the ministers themselves) take priority over human authorities. But because of the potential dangers of this idea—after all, they did not want to allow children to run away from their families and responsibilities to join a convent or monastery—most preachers carefully limited the cases in which it could be applied.

In sermons on the text of the wedding at Cana, Mary is again portrayed negatively. Although she is a wonderful example of charity, concern, even of faithful prayer, she meddles in Christ's business. Some preachers suggest that her sin was trying to impose her will on God, or insisting that her son follow her timetable. However, many preachers remind their audience, no one can place demands on God—not even his mother. God is still the "Other," despite his immanence: the human relationships with Mary and with Jesus' other kin so important to the medieval structures of piety have no impact on Christ's "divine business." Mary made mistakes and even sinned like the rest of humanity: she is one of us, rather than above us.

A Special Model for Women

Along with serving as an important model for all Christians, in these sermons Mary also regularly serves as a special model for females, and often particularly for girls. Sermons on the Visitation text stress that along with the virtues of faith, charity, and humility, young people must also be taught social propriety. The proper social behavior is especially important for young women, many pastors insist, for propriety and modesty are inextricably linked to one's honor and reputation, so vital to a young woman's standing. Many people will assume that a girl who does not behave properly is not a virgin, or, even worse, a girl can place herself in dangerous situations by her misbehavior. In order to protect her reputation and her chastity, a girl should attend only pious functions such as church services, but otherwise remain safely at home. When the angel came to Mary to tell her of the incarnation, she was found at home, probably praying, according to many sermons. The image of Mary most popular among Lutheran preachers seems to be of the pious and chaste girl, happy to serve her relatives, but otherwise gladly remaining and working at home. Mary did not leave her family to join a convent, but instead shows all girls how they should be happy in their domestic and familial vocations. The domesticating ideology often found in these sermons gains particular weight when it is declared that Mary, the blessed Mother of God, acted in just these recommended ways.

"Beware of well-traveled young women and untraveled young men!" The repetition of this popular phrase indicates how threatened these Lutheran pastors were by the notion of socially and sexually uncontrolled young women—a threat felt equally strongly by their medieval forebears, as witnessed by their strong critiques of the ravished Dinah.[6] In order for the social structure to remain strong, girls must be both self-controlled in their behavior and demeanor and obedient to the authority of others: these are the elements of Mary's behavior most often stressed to girls. Even more significant, her "feminine" virtues of chastity and modesty are necessary corollaries to her Christian virtues, her faith, humility, and charity; in other words, a truly Christian girl *will be* pious, humble, obedient, chaste, modest, and dutiful.

Jaroslav Pelikan points out that "in every century [Mary] served as the model of patience, indeed of quietistic passivity and unquestioning obedience," a good example for women of how they ought to live, "in submissive obedience to God, to their husbands, and to the clergy and the hierarchy of the church."[7] He adds to this, however, that Mary's role as the *ancilla domini* has often been understood in an active way, and she is concomitantly portrayed as the "Woman of Valor" from Proverbs, especially in the medieval period.[8] Based on the preceding material, I would argue that, for sixteenth-century Lutheran pastors, even Mary's title of the "Woman of Valor," if they ever applied it to her, would take on a passive sense. These sermons consistently strive to reimagine the image of Mary while remaining within the bounds of orthodoxy. This study shows that the combination of the theological changes inaugurated by Luther and the preachers' social conservatism, marked by an insistence on obedience to authorities, completely recast the image of Mary. Gone was the powerful, merciful, mother Queen of Heaven, and in her place remained only the humble, chaste, obedient girl. Her most powerful attribute—her faith—could only be seen and praised as a gift of God. The reverence felt by the early reformers for the Mother of God quickly lapsed into either disinterest or ambivalence.

We should not assume, however, that the "Lutheran Mary," or the image of Mary found in these sermons, is a one-dimensional figure. A number of tensions remained unresolved and ensured that Mary would continue to be a complex symbol, even for those so intent upon breaking the hold of "papist" superstition and doctrine. Mary is still a paradox: virgin, yet mother; human, yet the Mother of God; a humble maid, yet one whose praise would be sung by all generations; a symbol of the church, and yet only one of its members. Robert Scribner reminds us that people can hold conflicting views simultaneously, and that " 'traditional' mentalities" are remarkably persistent.[9] That is one reason why second- and third-generation Lutheran preachers felt the need to continue to train their audiences in the most basic theology and morality. But presenting Mary as a model of faith or even of proper feminine behavior does not exhaust the potential of the symbol, even if one ignores much of the tradition and concentrates solely on her appearance in the gospel texts. The image of Mary often rests somewhat uncomfortably on sixteenth-century Lutheran preachers, for it is more complex and occasionally more subversive than they are willing to admit.

Appendix: Biographies of Lutheran Preachers

ALBER(US), ERASMUS. ca. 1500–1553. Alberus studied in Wittenberg from 1520, first as a student of Karlstadt, and then of Luther. From 1525 to 1527 he taught school in several small towns, then became a pastor and reformer in Sprendlingen. After 1539 he was forced to lead a wandering life, mostly as a result of his frequent disagreements: he served as pastor in Brandenburg, Rothenburg o.T., Wetterau, and Neubrandenburg. He received his doctorate in 1543 and in 1548 became a pastor in Magdeburg. He was a strong critic of the Interim, Rome, the reformed, and Osiander. In 1552 he was again unemployed and living in Hamburg, but in 1553 he was called as superintendent to Neubrandenburg. He died soon after. He was a lifelong strong supporter of Luther and fought any developments in the tradition. He published hymns, satirical works, polemical fables, and sermons. [NDB 1, 123, Gustav Hammann; ADB 1, 219–20, Gaß]

ANDREAE, JAKOB. 1528–1590. In 1541 Andreae entered the university at Tübingen, receiving his baccalaureate degree in 1543 and his *magister* in 1545. In 1546 he married and became a deacon in Stuttgart. During the Interim he was forced back to Tübingen, where he taught boys and continued preaching. In 1553 he received his doctorate and was made the city preacher and superintendent (first "special," then general) in Göppingen. He worked for many years introducing the reform to various places and was a colleague of Brenz. He was involved in disputes over the Eucharist, but eventually sided against Melanchthon and the Swiss and Calvinist parties. In 1562, he became professor of theology at Tübingen, eventually also serving as provost and chancellor. In 1568, he was sent by the duke to Braunschweig-Wolfenbüttel to help introduce reform and build consensus with the north German theologians. From 1568 to 1580 he was involved in formulating the concord, attempting to rid Lutheranism of cryptocalvinism and to institute orthodoxy. He died in Tübingen in 1590. [RTK 1, 501–505, Wagenmann (T. Kolde); NDB 1, 277, Peter Meinhold; ADB 1, 436–441, Henke]

ARTOPOEUS (BECKER), JOHANNES. 1520–1566. Born in Speier, Becker studied in Cologne (from 1538), where he received his *magister*, then at Freiburg from 1540, where he taught the sons of vice-chancellor Mathias Held. He studied philosophy, Greek, and law, receiving his doctorate in both laws (canon and secular) in 1546. He served as a professor of canon law and eventually became rector of the university. He composed panegyrics for both Charles V and Ferdinand I. [ADB I, 614, Steffenh. u. Scherer; NDB 1, 403, Theodor Zwölfer]

BAUMGART(EN) (POMARIUS), JOHANN. 1514–1578. Baumgarten studied in Wittenberg under Georg Major, Luther, and Melanchthon. He taught in Naumberg and then at the Magdeburg Gymnasium, finally becoming the pastor at the Holy Spirit Church there in 1540. He published many catechetical and polemical writings, as well as school dramas and hymns. [NDB 1, 658, A. Elschenbroich; ADB 2, 158, W. Scherer]

BRENZ, JOHANNES. 1498/9–1570. Brenz studied in Heidelberg from 1514, where he heard Luther in the Heidelberg Disputation. He took a call as a preacher to Schwäbisch Hall in 1522 and stayed as a reformer there until 1533. In 1526 he wrote the first *Kirchenordnung* (ecclesiastical constitution) in Hall. In 1530 he attended the Reichstag in Augsburg to assist Melanchthon, and in 1534 was invited by Duke Ulrich to reform Württemburg, including the university in Tübingen. In 1538 he returned to Hall, and in 1550 he was invited to reform Stuttgart. In 1559, at the Stuttgart Synod, he opposed Calvinistic leanings in Lutheran teaching and published the *Große Kirchenordnung* of 1559, influential throughout Germany. His many publications also include the first evangelical catechism, published in 1527. [NDB 2, 598–599, H. Hermelink; ADB 3, 314–316, Hartmann; RTK 3, 376–388, (Hartmann) Bossert]

BUGENHAGEN, JOHANNES. 1484(?)–1558. Bugenhagen studied in Greifswald and received his *magister* in 1503. He taught school in Treptow, and in 1517 the duke commissioned him to write a history of Pommern. He read Luther's 1520 treatise on the "Babylonian Captivity of the Church" and in 1521 traveled to Wittenberg, where he was permitted to lecture on the Psalms in Luther's absence. In 1523 he took the position of city preacher in Wittenberg and was active in the dispute with Zwingli over the Eucharist. His widely distributed *Passional* first appeared in 1524. In 1528 he was called to Braunschweig, and also helped to develop the ecclesiastical constitutions for Hamburg and Lübeck. In 1533 he received his doctorate and in 1534 returned to help reform Pommern. The year 1535 saw his return to Wittenberg, but in 1537 he was called to Denmark by Christian III, who made his new ecclesiastical constitution law in 1539. He remained in Denmark two years, crowning the new king and teaching at the university in Copenhagen. In 1539 he was made the general superintendent in Saxony and in 1542 traveled to Schleswig-Holstein to introduce his ecclesiastical ordinance, but rejected the bishopric there to return to Braunschweig. In the last years of his life (he died in Wittenberg) he was involved in intra-Lutheran conflicts, siding with Melanchthon. [ADB 3, 504–508, J. Köstlin; RTK 3, 525–532, G. Kawerau; NDB 3, Berlin 1957, 9–10, E. Wolf]

CHEMNITZ, MARTIN. 1522–1586. Chemnitz received his education in Wittenberg, Magdeburg, and Frankfurt a.O. After teaching, he returned to Wittenberg in 1545 to study math and astrology, but was soon forced to leave because of the Interim. He was related to Melanchthon through marriage and conducted private studies with him. In

1550 he became the ducal librarian in Königsberg, but fled to Wittenberg in 1554 as a result of the Osiander controversy. In 1554 he was ordained and went to Braunschweig to work with Mörlin. Here he held lectures on Melanchthon's *Loci Communes*, and participated in numerous debates, managing to straddle the fence between the *gnesio* Mörlin and his old teacher Melanchthon. When Mörlin left Braunschweig, Chemnitz became the superintendent. In 1568 he received his doctorate from Rostock and was elemental in founding the university in Helmstedt. Throughout the 1570s he devoted much of his time to Lutheran unity and was one of the major authors of the Lutheran Concord. His postil was published posthumously in 1593. [NDB 3, 201–202, E. Wolf; ADB 4, 116–118, Brecher; RTK 3, 796–804, Johannes Kunze]

CLAIUS (CLAJUS, CLAY), JOHANNES. 1535–1592. Claius studied in Leipzig from 1555 to 1557 and taught in several places until 1569. He then returned to Wittenberg to study theology and received his *magister* in 1570. From 1570 to 1572 he was the rector of a school in Nordhausen, then in 1573 became the pastor in Bendeleben. He was the author of an important grammatical treatise. [NDB 3, 258–259, Otto Basler; ADB 4, 270–272, Eckstein]

CORVINUS (RABE), ANTON. 1501–1553. After attending the Dominican school, Corvinus entered the Cistercian cloister in Loccum in 1519. He studied a short time in Leipzig, then became a monk in Riddagshausen. After reading Luther's writings, he became an evangelical and was ousted from his monastery in 1523. In 1528 he became the pastor at St. Stephen in Goslar, then in 1529 moved to Witzenhausen. Here he wrote his popular *Kurze und einfältige Auslegung*, which appeared 1535–1537. In 1536 he received his *magister* in Marburg. He attended a number of important conferences (including Regensburg) as an advisor to Philipp of Hesse and composed various ecclesiastical constitutions. Eventually he became the regional superintendent in Calenberg-Göttingen and was imprisoned from 1549 to 1552 for his opposition to the Interim. [NDB 3, 371–372, H.H. Harms; ADB 4, 508–509, Brecher; RTK 4, 302–305, G. Uhlhorn]

CULMANN, LEONHARD. 1497/8–1562. Culmann attended schools in Halle, Dinkelsbühl, Nuremberg, Saalfeld, and the universities in Erfurt and Leipzig. He was the teacher at the cathedral school in Bamberg, then served various schools and churches in Ansbach and Nuremberg, becoming the preacher at St. Sebald in 1549. He was the main supporter of Osiander after 1552, although Melanchthon warned him against it. He was forced out in 1555 and in 1556 went to Wiesensteig as pastor. In 1558, he was involved in another argument, this time with Brenz, and he left to be pastor of Bernstatt near Ulm, where he died in 1562. [ADB 4, 639, J. Hartmann]

DIETRICH, VEIT. 1506–1549. Dietrich attended the university in Wittenberg from 1522, living first with Melanchthon and then with Luther, serving as Luther's secretary. In 1529 he received his *magister* and in 1533 was made a deacon. In 1535 he left for Nuremberg to become the preacher at St. Sebald, but he came into conflict with Osiander over the issue of private confession. Dietrich published his notes of Luther's lectures (not always with Luther's permission) and also published Luther's *Hauspostille* (1530–1534). He attended the colloquy at Regensburg and died during the fight against the Interim. [NDB 3, 699, M. Simon; RTK 4, 653–658, T. Kolde; ADB 5, Leipzig 1877, 196–197, Herzog]

DRACONITES (DRACH, TRACH, DRACO, CARLSTADT), JOHANNES. 1494–1566. Drach was active in humanist circles while studying in Erfurt and received his *magister* in 1514. In 1521 he went to Wittenberg to study Hebrew, and he received his doctorate in 1523. He served several parishes in the 1520s, and from 1536 he was a pastor and professor in Marburg, attending the Regensburg Colloquy in 1541. In 1547 he went to Lübeck, and then in 1551 went as *Ratsprofessor* to Rostock, where he was engaged in conflict with Hesshusen. In 1557 he became the city superintendent in Rostock, and in 1560 he left to become bishop in Pommern. He was relieved of this position in 1564, since he spent all his time in Wittenberg. [NDB 4, Berlin 1959, 95, E. Kähler; ADB 5, 371, Fromm]

EBER, PAUL. 1511–1569. In 1532 Eber came to study in Wittenberg with Melanchthon, joining the arts faculty in 1537 after receiving his *magister*. In 1541 he became a professor of Latin. After the Schmalkaldic war he stayed in Wittenberg and was eventually made a professor of theology. In 1558 he succeeded Bugenhagen as pastor. He tried to take a middle position between the Philippist and *gnesio* Lutheran parties. [NDB 4, 225, Robert Stupperich; ADB 5, 529–531, Brecher; RTK 5, Leipzig 1898, 118–121, G. Kawerau]

GRESER, DANIEL. 1504–1591. Greser studied theology in Mainz and Marburg, and was ordained a priest in 1526. He was already familiar with evangelical theology through Erhard Schnepf, preacher in Weilburg. Greser's first evangelical call was in 1532 to Gießen, where he served for ten years. Upon his disagreement with Philipp regarding Philipp's marital problems, he left to be pastor and superintendent in Dresden, where he served until 1589. [NDB 7, Berlin 1966, 49–50, Franz Lau; ADB 9, 641, C. Brockhaus]

HEERBRAND, JAKOB. 1521–1600. From 1538 to 1543 Heerbrand was a student of Melanchthon and Luther in Wittenberg. In 1543 he was made a deacon in Tübingen, but was let go in 1548 during the Interim. In 1550 he received his doctorate in theology and served as superintendent in Herrenberg. He was active with Brenz in several conflicts and councils, and in 1557 returned as a professor of theology to Tübingen. In 1590 he was made chancellor of the university, advisor to the city council, and prior of the Stiftkirche. He wrote an important *Compendium Theologiae* (1573), an evangelical book of doctrine. [NDB 8, Berlin 1969, 194–195, H. Fausel; ADB 11, Leipzig 1880, 242–244, Schott; RTK 7, 519–524, (Wagenmann) Bossert]

HEIDENREICH, ESAIAS. 1532–1589. Heidenreich studied in Frankfurt, then was pastor in Lemberg and in Schweidnitz. From 1569, he served in Breßlau as church and school inspector, assessor of the consistory, pastor at St. Elizabeth, and professor of theology in the gymnasium. He wrote a *Gebets*-postil. [Jöcher 2, 1442]

HEMMING[SEN], NIELS OR NICOLAUS. 1513–1600. Born in Denmark, Hemmingsen attended university in Wittenberg in 1537, paying for his education by tutoring wealthier students. After receiving his master's degree, he returned in 1542 to Denmark, and from 1543 taught Greek at the university in Copenhagen. In 1545 he became a professor of dialectic and also lectured on the Hebrew language. In 1547 he became professor of theology and soon took over the office of vice-chancellor. He was a strong supporter of Melanchthon, and it was because of his influence that the king of Denmark never adopted the Formula of Concord. He was occasionally accused of Calvinism and was eventually released from his post (1579). He left to become a canon at the cathedral in Roeskilde. [ADB 11, 724–725, Prantl; RTK 7, 659–662, Fr. Nielsen]

HESSHUS(EN), TILEMANN. 1527–1588. Hesshusen studied with Melanchthon in Wittenberg from 1553, receiving his *magister*. His feisty personality caused him to change positions often. He served as pastor in Goslar (from 1553); professor and pastor in Rostock (1556); professor and general superintendent in Heidelberg (from 1557); pastor in Bremen (1559); superintendent in Magdeburg (1560–1562); preacher at the court in Neuburg/Donau (from 1565); professor in Jena (from 1569); bishop in Samland (1571); professor in Helmstedt (from 1577). He was a strong supporter of the Formula of Concord, and argued against his former friend, Flacius, over the question of original sin. [NDB 9, Berlin 1972, 24–25, R. Dollinger; ADB 12, 314–316, Gaß; RTK 8, Leipzig 1900, 8–14, Hackenschmidt]

HEUNE (GIGAS), JOHANNES. 1514–1581. Heune studied with Luther in Wittenberg, and from 1537 lived in Leipzig. In 1541 he became rector of a school in Joachimsthal, in 1542 taught in Marienberg, then from 1543 taught in Pforta. He served as a pastor in a village in Silesia, then in Freystadt (for 27 years), then finally from 1577 in Schweidnitz. [ADB 9, 167, H. Kaemmel]

HUBER(INUS), CASPAR. 1500–1553. In 1522 Huberinus matriculated at the university in Wittenberg, probably as a monk. In 1525 he left for Augsburg and was sent by the city council in 1528 to the Bern disputation over the Eucharist, although he held no official office. From 1532 he was supported privately and published critical writings against the Zwinglians. He was sent to Wittenberg in 1535, becoming a deacon and, in 1542, a pastor. He was called through Brenz to be preacher for the Catholic counts of Hohenlohe in Öhringen. Here he was able to push through reforms of church services and the Latin school. He published more than 200 writings. [NDB 9, 701, Gunther Franz; RTK 8, 415–417, T. Kolde; ADB 13, 258–259, Bertheau]

KANTZ, KASPAR. d. 1544. Shortly before 1501 Kantz entered a Carmelite cloister and studied at the university in Leipzig, taking degrees in 1502 (bacc.), 1505 (mag.), 1511 (bacc. biblicus), and 1515 (sent.) He returned home to Nördlingen to become prior, but in 1517 his provincial wanted him removed. He received the support of the city council against his order. He must have been an early supporter of reform, for he published an "*evangelische mess*" in 1522. In 1523 his provincial again attempted to oust him, but the council continued to support him until 1523, when he was banished for announcing in a sermon that he had taken a wife. In 1524 he matriculated in Wittenberg. Eventually he returned to Nördlingen as a schoolteacher, and in 1535 as a preacher. He also published a catechism, hymns, and other pastoral works. [RTK 10, Leipzig, 1901, 23–25, Chr. Geyer]

KELLER (CELLARIUS), ANDREAS. 1503–1562. Keller had lived in a cloister before he appeared in Rottenburg in 1524, giving public sermons against the papacy. He was forbidden to preach, but left to serve at Alt-St.-Peter in Strassburg. In 1524 he became pastor in Wasselnheim, near Strassburg. In 1530 he published his own catechism. In 1536 he left to become pastor in Wildberg, and in 1551 was made superintendent there. [NDB 11, Berlin 1977, 432–433, G. Franz; RTK 10, 203–204, G. Bossert]

LAUTERBACH, JOHANN. 1531–1593. Lauterbach studied with Melanchthon in Wittenberg, then served in the court of the counts of Hohenlohe. In 1553 he became the rector at the university in Heilbronn. An important poet, he also composed hymns. [ADB 18, 75, R. Eitner]

LUTHER, MARTIN. 1483–1546. Luther was a former Augustinian friar and professor at the university in Wittenberg who sparked a major religious reform movement. He is considered the founder of the Lutheran Church. Many of Luther's sermons were transcribed and often published. The sermons of Luther used in this study can mostly be found in the *Festpostille* of 1527 and the *Hauspostille* of 1544.

MAJOR, GEORG. 1502–1574. Major studied in Wittenberg, receiving his degrees in 1521, 1522, and 1523. He taught in Wittenberg until he received a call in 1529 to serve as rector of the gymnasium in Magdeburg. From 1537 he was the preacher of the castle church in Wittenberg, and he was ordained by Luther. He also taught on the arts faculty at the university, and from 1541 on the theology faculty. He joined the Wittenberg consistory in 1542 and in 1544 received his doctorate, giving up his preaching position in 1545 to become a full-time professor. During the Schmalkaldic war, he fled with his family to Magdeburg. In 1551–1552 he served as superintendent in Eisleben, but during this period was involved in a serious controversy over his supposed return to Roman teachings. From Bugenhagen's death in 1558 until his own in 1574 he served as dean of the theology faculty in Wittenberg. [NDB 15, 718–719, Helmar Junghans; ADB 20, Leipzig 1884, 109–111, Wagenmann; RTK 12, Leipzig 1903, 85–91, G. Kawerau]

MAT(T)HESIUS, JOHANN(ES). 1504–1565. Mathesius studied in Ingolstadt, and taught in the Schloß Odelzhausen in 1526–1527. Here he read Luther's "Sermon on Good Works" and joined the reform movement. After studying theology in Wittenberg, he taught in Altenburg from 1529. In 1532 he was called to be rector of the Latin school in Joachimsthal, a silver-mining town in Bohemia. In 1540–1542 he studied again in Wittenberg with Luther and Melanchthon, and after his ordination in 1542 he took another call to Joachimsthal, this time as preacher. From 1545 until his death in 1565 he served as pastor in this community. Around 1,500 of his sermons were printed, especially those relating to weddings and funerals. [NDB 16, 369–370, Herbert Wolf; ADB 20, 586–589, Ledderhose; RTK 12, 425–428, Georg Loesche]

MELANCHTHON, PHILIPP. 1497–1560. Melanchthon was a younger contemporary of Luther who became his most important colleague. Melanchthon's *Loci Communes* dominated Lutheran (and Protestant) theology for much of the century and after. His postils are published in the *Corpus Reformatorum*, volumes 24 and 25.

MÖRLIN, JOACHIM. 1514–1571. Mörlin studied from 1532 in Wittenberg, receiving his *magister* in 1535 and his doctorate in 1540. In 1540 he was called to be superintendent in Arnstadt, but fell out of grace for giving critical sermons and was removed from office in 1543. From 1544 he served as superintendent in Göttingen, but also had problems there and opposed the Interim. He lost this position in 1550. From 1551 he served in Königsberg, where he had a major conflict with Osiander over justification. He was forced to leave Prussia in 1553. He was called as superintendent to Braunschweig and, working closely with Chemnitz, pushed forward Lutheran consensus with the Concord of 1580. From 1568 he was bishop in Samland. [NDB 17, 679–680, Inge Mager; RTK 13, 237–247, Wagenmann (Lezius); ADB 22, 322–325, H. A. Lier]

MUSÄUS (MEUSEL), SIMON. 1529–1582. Musäus studied in Frankfurt a.O., and then in Wittenberg from 1545 to 1547. He taught Greek at a school in Nuremberg, then from 1549 served as pastor in Fürstenwalde in the Neumark. On account of his marriage, the bishop expelled him in 1551, but in 1552 he went as pastor to Crossen. In 1554 he was forced to leave this position for criticizing the city council in his sermons. In this same year he was called to Kosten bei Breslau and also received his doctorate from Wittenberg. In Kosten he fought against the Interim and made enemies of the Catholic clergy, who denounced him and demanded that the city council fire him. He left for Gotha and eventually went to Jena as superintendent and professor, leading the gnesio-Lutheran fight against Wittenberg. From 1561 until his death in 1582 he held a variety of positions and occasionally lived without a position in the cities of Bremen, Lüneberg, Schwein, Gera, Thorn, Coburg, Soest, and, finally, Mansfeld. [ADB 23, Leipzig 1886, 91–92, Schimmelpfennig]

OSIANDER, ANDREAS. 1498–1552. Osiander attended the university in Ingolstadt, where he had humanistic training and studied Hebrew. In 1520 he was ordained a priest in Nuremberg and taught Hebrew at the Augustinian cloister. Here he came into close contact with Luther and other Wittenbergers. In 1522 he was assigned to be preacher at St. Lorenz, and he soon became one of the leaders of the reform movement. In 1525 he married, and he stood with Luther against both the Swiss and the uprising peasants. He enjoyed a period of great popularity and influence, but in the 1530s and 1540s was involved in one of the major intra-Lutheran battles, over the question of requiring personal confession. In 1549 he left to preach in Königsberg and became professor at the university, although he held no academic degree. He was involved in another major conflict in the 1550s, this time over justification by faith. He had many problems with Mörlin, and eventually broke completely with Melanchthon and Wittenberg. He died in 1552; his body was disinterred, and his final gravesite is unknown. [ADB 24, 473–483, M. Möller; RTK 14, 501–509, (M. Möller) P. Tschackert]

PANKRATIUS, ANDREAS. 1529/31–1576. Pankratius probably studied in Wittenberg with Georg Major. He served as deacon in Pressath in the Pfalz, then as preacher in Amberg in the Oberpfalz. He lost his position in 1566 when the duke moved toward Calvinism, and went as preacher, superintendent, and inspector of the gymnasium to Hof in Vogtlande. [ADB 25, Leipzig 1887, 119–221, Wagenmann]

PAULI, SIMON. 1534–1591. Pauli attended the university in Rostock in 1552 but received his magister from Wittenberg in 1555. He was recommended by Melanchthon to the duke in 1558 to be professor of theology in Rostock. Soon the duke called Pauli to be his cathedral preacher and took him along to the Augsburg Reichstag. In 1561 he was named pastor of St. Jacobi and professor of theology in Rostock. In this same year he received his doctorate. He was a close friend of David Chytraeus and was a gnesio Lutheran (i.e., against Melanchthon, cryptocalvinism, and Flacius). He became superintendent of Rostock in 1574. [ADB 25, 273–274, Krause]

RHEGIUS, URBANUS. 1489–1541. In 1508 Rhegius attended the university in Freiburg, studying theology with Eck. He followed Eck to Ingolstadt in 1510, taking his baccalaureate and master's there. He taught rhetoric and poetry, and was crowned poet laureate by the emperor in 1517. He continued his theological studies and was ordained in Constanz in 1519. He received his doctorate in theology in Basle in 1520. After his call to be preacher at the cathedral in Augsburg, he became a reformer and strong supporter of Luther. He was soon forced to leave the city and returned to his home for several years. In 1524 he was called to be preacher in Hall im Innthal, but he soon returned to Augsburg to preach at St. Anna. He married in 1525 and eventually was again forced to leave the city, moving to Celle as court preacher and superintendent. He is considered the reformer of the duchy Lüneberg and published many works in his lifetime. [ADB 28, 374–378, Wagenmann; RTK 16, Leipzig 1905, 734–741, (G. Uhlhorn) P. Tschackert]

SEEHOFER, ARSACIUS. d. 1545. Seehofer studied in Wittenberg with Melanchthon but received his *magister* in 1522 in Ingolstadt. He had to take an oath that he did not follow Lutheran beliefs. However, in the following year he gave a lecture on Paul's letters following Melanchthon's interpretation, and was denounced by the faculty senate and arrested. This caused a great uproar, and led Argula von Grumbach, a noblewoman who sympathized with the reform, to write her famous letter to the university in support of Seehofer. He was finally released after a public disputation of the faculty, and he left for Wittenberg. After a short stay in Prussia, he taught from 1534 in a gymnasium in Augsburg, then in 1536 went as pastor to Leonberg. Later he served as pastor in Winnenden, in Würrtemberg. He published his *Enarrationes evangeliorum dominicalium* in 1538, and it was placed on numerous Roman indexes. [ADB 33, 573–574, Reusch; RTK 18, Leipzig 1906, 124–126, T. Kolde]

SELNECCER, NICOLAUS. 1530–1592. Selneccer studied theology in Wittenberg from 1549, becoming a close friend of Melanchthon. In 1558 he was called to be court preacher in Dresden, and to teach the prince. In 1562 he left to be a professor at the new university in Jena, turning more stringently Lutheran after Melanchthon's death. He was forced out of the university in 1568 under suspicions of cryptocalvinism and went as the general superintendent and pastor to St. Thomas in Leipzig. In 1570 he went as preacher to the court of Julius in Braunschweig-Wolfenbüttel, helping to found the new university in 1571. Here he also had problems with the *gnesio* party and returned to his old position in Leipzig in 1574, where he fought against the Philippists. He was a major player in the development of the Formula of Concord. In 1586 after the death of the elector, the new elector, Christian, supported the Philippist party. Thus, by 1589 Selneccer lost his position and was banned, but in 1590 went as superintendent to Hildesheim, then in 1592 returned to Augsburg. In 1591 Christian died, so he was able to return to Leipzig but could find no position there. He returned again to Hildesheim, where he died in 1592. [ADB 33, 687–692, v. Egloffstein; RTK 18, 184–191 (Wagenmann) Franz Dibelius]

SPANGENBERG, CYRIACUS. 1528–1604. Son of Lutheran pastor Johannes S., Cyriacus studied in Wittenberg from 1542. After receiving his *magister*, he taught at the gymnasium in Eisleben. Upon his father's death, he took over that preaching position. From 1553 he served as deacon in Mansfeld, having quarreled with his father's replacement, Georg Major, over his theory of good works. In 1559 he became court preacher and began working to publish his own and his father's writings. From 1564 he was a member of the Flacian party, which finally led to his exile. His next service was in Sangerhausen, but his opposition to the Formula of Concord led to his further exile in

Strassburg. From 1581 to 1590 he served as pastor in Schlitz, near Strassburg, but was forced to leave. In 1595 or 1596 he returned to Strassburg to renew their music school. [ADB 35, 37–41, Edward Schröder; RTK 18, 567–572, Kawerau]

SPANGENBERG, JOHANN. 1484–1550. In 1508 or 1509 Spangenberg was at the university in Erfurt; he received his baccalaureate degree in 1511, and later his *magister*. He was called to be rector of the Latin school in Stolberg and from 1520 served as a preacher at St. Martins. In 1524 he was called by the council of Nordhausen to be pastor at St. Blasius, and he served there for twenty-two years. He also ran a private school in his home after the city schools were destroyed in the peasants' revolt, then opened a Latin school. In 1546, he was sent by Luther to Eisleben to serve as general inspector. [RTK 18, 565–567, Kawerau; ADB 35, 43–46, Paul Tschackert]

SPINDLER, GEORG. 1525–1605. Spindler studied theology under Cruciger in Wittenberg from 1548. In 1560 he was called to a preaching position in Schlackenwerth in Bohemia. He was involved in the fights against the cryptocalvinists, but after publishing his 1578 postil he was accused of having himself written a Calvinist work. This pushed him to read Calvin's *Institutes*, which helped changed his allegiance. In 1580 he lost his position, wandering until he found a new position in Obernberngau in 1584. He reworked his postil into an explicitly Calvinist vein, publishing it in 1593. [ADB 35, 199–200, Cuno]

STRIGEL, VICTOR(INUS). 1524–1569. Strigel studied in Wittenberg from 1542, receiving his *magister* in 1544. He held lectures here until the Schmalkaldic war forced him out. In 1547 he began lecturing in Erfurt, then went to Jena to help found the university. Here he was involved in a long-term fight with Flacius over the freedom of the human will, siding with Melanchthon. Eventually, after serving time in prison, Strigel was victorious and Flacius and friends were expelled. Strigel was returned to his position in 1562, but in 1563 left for Leipzig. In 1567 he began having troubles in Leipzig over his supposed Calvinist leanings in Eucharistic doctrine, so he left again. After serving for a while in Amberg, he went to the university in Heidelberg, where he died in 1569. [ADB 36, 590–594, P. Tschackert; RTK 19, 97–102, (Wagenmann) Kawerau]

VISCHER (PISCATOR), CHRISTOPH. d. 1597/1600? In 1543 or 44 Vischer received his *magister* in Wittenberg, then went as pastor to Jüterbogk, and eventually to Bensen. In 1552 he was called to be superintendent in Schmalkalden. In 1571 he went as general superintendent to Meiningen and after three years left to be head pastor in Halberstadt. When he died in 1597, he was serving as the general superintendent of Braunschweig and court preacher in Celle. [ADB 7, Leipzig 1878, 51–52, H. Kellner; ADB 40, Leipzig 1896, 30–31]

WALTHER, GEORG. Dates unknown. Walther was a *magister philosophia* and preached in Halle in Saxony. He was in this position when he signed the Formula of Concord in 1580. He is the author of several works. [Jöcher 4, 1800]

WELLER, HIERONYMUS. 1499–1572. Weller studied in Wittenberg, particularly Greek, and received his *magister* in 1518. He taught in Zwickau, but returned in 1526 to Wittenberg to study law and receive his doctorate. After hearing Luther preach, he began to study theology, receiving this doctorate in 1535. In 1539 he was called to be superintendent and inspector of schools in Freyburg. He died in Freyburg in 1572. [Jöcher 4, 1879–1880]

WIGAND, JOHANN. 1523–1587. Wigand studied in Wittenberg from 1539, and in 1541 went as teacher to the Lorenz school in Nuremberg. After three years he returned to his studies in Wittenberg, but during the war (1546) left to preach and teach in Mansfeld. He published many controversial writings, often fighting on the side of Flacius. In 1553 he was chosen to be pastor at St. Ulrich's in Magdeburg, and in 1560 followed Flacius to Jena as professor. Here the two differed over the question of original sin, and Wigand was expelled for being too troublesome. He returned to Magdeburg, then went as superintendent to Wismar in 1562. In 1568 he was recalled to Jena, and the old fight between Wittenberg and Jena broke out again. The *streng* Lutherans were expelled in 1573, and Wigand and Hesshusen left for Braunschweig. Soon Wigand left to teach at the university in Königsberg. In 1575 he was called as bishop in Pomesanien, where he fell into another fight, this time with Hesshusen, now bishop of Samland. Hesshusen was expelled, and Wigand was given his bishopric. [ADB 42, 452–454, Brecher; RTK 21, 270–275, Hauck]

Notes

INTRODUCTION

1. *The Education of Henry Adams*, ed. Jean Gooder (London: Penguin, 1995), 369.

2. Ibid., 368.

3. Mary in Reformation (or Protestant-influenced) art is a popular topic. See, for example (and for bibliography on this topic), Bonnie J. Noble, "The Lutheran Paintings of the Cranach Workshop, 1529–1555," Ph.D. diss., Northwestern University, Evanston, Ill., 1998; Bridget M. Heal, "A Woman Like Any Other? Images of the Virgin Mary and Marian Devotion in Nuremberg, Augsburg, and Cologne, c. 1500–1600," Ph.D. diss., Courtauld Institute of Art, University of London, 2001.

4. Susan Karant-Nunn remarks that "those sermons that did find their way into print were actually few and extraordinary." See "What Was Preached in German Cities in the Early Years of the Reformation? *Wildwuchs* Versus Lutheran Unity," in *The Process of Change in Early Modern Europe: Essays in Honor of Miriam Usher Chrisman*, ed. P. N. Bebb and Sherrin Marshall (Athens: Ohio University Press, 1988), 91.

5. See Larissa J. Taylor, "Out of Print: The Decline of Catholic Printed Sermons in France, 1530–1560," in *Habent sua fata libelli, or, Books Have Their Own Destiny: Essays in Honor of Robert V. Schnucker*, ed. Robin Barnes et al., 121–129 (Kirksville, Mo.: Thomas Jefferson University Press, 1998); Susan Wabuda, " 'Fruitful Preaching' in the Diocese of Worcester: Bishop Hugh Latimer and His Influence, 1535-1539," in *Religion and the English People 1500–1640: New Voices, New Perspectives*, ed. Eric Josef Carlson, 49–74 (Kirksville, Mo.: Thomas Jefferson University Press, 1998).

6. Harold J. Grimm, "The Human Element in Luther's Sermons," *Archiv für Reformationsgeschichte* 49 (1958): 52.

7. The exact origin of the term *"postilla"* is unknown: it may have come from the phrase *post illa verba textus*, which would indicate some kind of explication of Scripture, or it may be a diminutive of *posta*. The earliest us-

age of the word seems to be a biblical commentary of Hugh of St. Cher, the *Postilla in Biblia*, written around 1230–1235. Beryl Smalley points out that even the distinction between *postilla* and *glosa* is hard to determine, but the word *glosa* about this time was taking on a pejorative meaning. See Smalley, *The Study of the Bible in the Middle Ages* (Notre Dame, Ind.: Notre Dame University Press, 1964), 270–271.

8. Bodo Nischan, "Demarcating Boundaries: Lutheran Pericopic Sermons in the Age of Confessionalization," *Archiv für Reformationsgeschichte* 88 (1997): 202–203; Patrick T. Ferry, "Confessionalization and Popular Preaching: Sermons against Synergism in Reformation Saxony," *Sixteenth Century Journal* 28 (1997): 1148–1149.

9. Scribner, "Oral Culture and the Transmission of Reformation Ideas," in *The Transmission of Ideas in the Lutheran Reformation*, ed. Helga Robinson-Hammerstein (Dublin: Irish Academic Press, 1989), 84.

10. Ibid. Scribner notes that preaching had been going through a revival for at least a generation before the Reformation, but suggests that the "scope and intensity of the Reformation preaching revival, as well as its emphasis on the Bible as the sole source of religious truth" distinguish it from the earlier movement (ibid., 84–85). Harold Grimm states the point even more strongly: "The Protestant Reformation would not have been possible without the sermon" (Grimm, 50).

11. Christian Peters remarks, "Auch das es vor allem die Predigt war, die die reformatorischen Prozesse in den Städten in Gang brachte und maßgeblich zu ihrer Dynamik beitrug, gilt den meisten Forschern als gewiß." See his "Luthers Einfluß auf die frühreformatorische städtische Predigt: das Beispiel des Ulmer Kaplans Johann Diepold (gest. vor 1539)," in *Luthers Wirkung: Festschrift für Martin Brecht zum 60. Geburtstag*, ed. W.-D. Hauschild, W. H. Neuser, and C. Peters (Stuttgart: Calwer, 1992), 111–133.

12. Ferry, 1147. For the ecclesiastical ordinances see *Die Evangelischen Kirchenordnungen des XVI. Jahrhunderts*, ed. Emil Sehling (Tübingen: Scientia Aalen, 1979).

13. See Strauss, "The Mental World of a Saxon Pastor," in *Reformation Principle and Practice: Essays in Honour of Arthur Geoffrey Dickens*, ed. P. N. Brooks (London: Scolar, 1980): 161. According to Strauss, visitation records often indicate that church members frequently requested postil preaching over the sermons of their own pastor.

14. Ferry, 1148.

15. Rublack, "Lutherische Predigt und gesellschaftliche Wirklichkeiten," in *Die Lutherische Konfessionalisierung in Deutschland*, ed. H.-C. Rublack (Gütersloh: Gerd Mohn, 1988): 347–348.

16. Luise Schorn-Schütte has shown that the gulf between pastor and congregation became wider in the sixteenth century. Especially in the later decades, most ministers (and this also seems to be true of Catholic priests) came from larger cities or the middle classes of the territorial towns. Ministers serving village parishes were rarely native. See "The Christian Clergy in the Early Modern Holy Roman Empire: A Comparative Social Study," *Sixteenth Century Journal* 29 (Fall 1998): 719ff. Susan Karant-Nunn traces the development of the Lutheran clergy in Ernestine Saxony in *Luther's Pastors: The Reformation in the Ernestine Countryside* (Philadelphia: American Philosophical Society, 1980).

17. Grimm, 50.

18. Luther, although he did not himself write a preaching manual, preferring to publish books of model sermons, mentioned in various places that preaching is both teaching and exhortation—*doctrina et exhortatio* (e.g., WA *Tischreden*, 2, 359, 18–21, no. 2199). Sermons should both instruct with doctrinal content and move the audience to improvement. For the development of preaching theory in Lutheran homilet-

ics, see Beth Kreitzer, "The Lutheran Sermon," in *Preachers and People in the Reformations and Early Modern Period*, ed. Larissa Taylor (Leiden: Brill, 2001), 35–63.

19. The most important doctrinal statements on the saints (including Mary) are Article 21 of the *Confessio Augustana* (1530), the 1531 Apology to the Augsburg Confession (both written by Melanchthon), and Luther's Smalcald Articles of 1537; these three texts are included in the Lutheran Book of Concord, the defining book of confessions for Lutherans. The significant passage of the Smalcald Articles reads: "The invocation of saints is also one of the abuses of the antichrist. . . . [It is not] commanded nor counseled, nor has it any example in Scripture" (pt. 2, art. 2). In the Augsburg Confession, Melanchthon indicates that Lutherans honor the saints in three ways: they give thanks to God for the saints; they strengthen their own faith by observing God's goodness to the saints; and they imitate the saints in faith and also in the virtues appropriate to their vocations. See the discussion in Kolb, *For All the Saints: Changing Perceptions of Martyrdom and Sainthood in the Lutheran Reformation* (Macon, Ga.: Mercer University Press, 1987), 15–16.

20. "[I]t was not until the last decades of the sixteenth century that there came into being an independent theological Mariology (Canisius 1577, Suarez 1590)." Gottfried Maron, "Mary in Protestant Theology," (trans. by David Cairns) in *Mary in the Churches*, ed. H. Küng and J. Moltmann, Concilium 168 (Edinburgh: T. & T. Clark; New York: Seabury, 1983), 42; Peter Canisius, *De Maria Virgine incomparabili et Dei Genetrice sacrosancta libri quinque*, 1577; Francisco Suarez, *De Mysteriis Vitae Christi*, 1592. About one-third of this final work is devoted to Mariology.

21. For a record of the Catholic-Lutheran debate on this topic in the sixteenth through nineteenth centuries, see Hans Düfel, *Luthers Stellung zur Marienverehrung*, Kirche und Konfession, Bd. 13 (Göttingen: Vandenhoeck & Ruprecht, 1968).

22. In fact, many of these works refer only to Luther, probably for the reason cited by Thomas O'Meara: "Luther was more than one of the Reformers: he was the Reformation. . . . [I]t was within his person that the Reformation was enacted in microcosm." See *Mary in Protestant and Catholic Theology* (New York: Sheed and Ward, 1966), 112.

23. Charles Lees, "Archbishop Gawlina, Martin Luther, and the Magnificat," *Mary Today* 56 (1965): 26–28 (cited in William J. Cole, "Was Luther a Devotee of Mary?" *Marian Studies* 21 [1970]: 96–97). Albert Ebneter suggests that it was really Rationalism that killed Marian devotion in the evangelical (i.e., German Lutheran) church, so the witness of Luther "wird zweifellos für viele, Protestanten und Katholiken, eine Überraschung sein." See "Martin Luthers Marienbild," *Orientierung* 20 (1956): 77.

24. Although Preuss does not specifically reject the ecumenical interest in Luther's views on Mary, he does present Luther as rejecting both the immaculate conception and Mary's assumption as unbiblical—a view that exaggerates the evidence. See Preuss, *Maria bei Luther*, Schriften des Vereins für Reformationsgeschichte, Nr. 172 (Gütersloh: C. Bertelsmann, 1954): 8, 16.

25. Friedrich Heiler, "Die Gottesmutter im Glauben und Beten der Jahrhunderte," *Hochkirche* 13 (1931): 198.

26. Ibid.

27. Asmussen, *Maria die Mutter Gottes* (Stuttgart: Evangelisches Verlagswerk, 1950); Schimmelpfennig, *Die Geschichte der Marienverehrung in deutschen Protestantismus* (Paderborn: Ferdinand Schöningh, 1952).

28. Düfel, 26, n. 33.

29. Ibid., 31.

30. See Ebneter, 78–79.

31. See Lansemann, *Die Heiligentage besonders die Marien=, Apostel= und Engeltage in der Reformationszeit, betrachte im Zusammenhang der reformatorischen Anschauungen von den Festen, von den Heiligen und von den Engeln Die Heiligentage besonders die Marien=, Apostel= und Engeltage in der Reformationszeit, betrachte im Zusammenhang der reformatorischen Anschauungen von den Zeremonien, von den Festen, von den Heiligen und von den Engeln* (Göttingen: Hubert, 1938). The great failing of this volume is that the footnotes, although numbered throughout the text, were never published.

32. Beissel, *Geschichte der Verehrung Marias im 16. und 17. Jahrhundert: ein Beitrag zur Religionswissenschaft und Kunstgeschichte* (Freiburg im Breisgau: Herdersche Verlagshandlung, 1910), 100.

33. Lortz, *Die Reformation in Deutschland*, vol. 2 (Freiburg im Breisgau: Herder, 1940), 304.

34. Saturnin Pauleser, *Maria und die Reformation* (Miltenberg, 1951); cited in Cole, 105–106.

35. And books continue to be written on this seemingly inexhaustible topic. For an example see Charles Dickson, *A Protestant Pastor Looks at Mary* (Huntington, Ind.: Our Sunday Visitor, 1998).

36. Groupe des Dombes, *Marie dans le dessein de Dieu et la communion des saints* (Paris: Bayard Éditions & Centurion, 1999); translated as A. Blancy, M. Jourjon, and the Dombes Group, *Mary in the Plan of God and in the Communion of Saints*, trans. M. J. O'Connell (New York: Paulist, 2002). This study and that of the U.S. Lutheran/Catholic dialogue both present well-researched histories of the approach of Catholics and Protestants to Mary in the sixteenth through twentieth centuries: see an evaluation of these two studies in Jared Wicks, "The Virgin Mary in Recent Ecumenical Dialogues," *Gregorianum* 81 (2000): 25–57.

37. Gritsch, "The Views of Luther and Lutheranism on the Veneration of Mary," in *The One Mediator, the Saints, and Mary: Lutherans and Catholics in Dialogue VIII*, ed. Anderson, Stafford, and Burgess, 235–248 (Minneapolis: Augsburg Fortress, 1992); also idem, "Embodiment of Unmerited Grace," in *Mary's Place in Christian Dialogue*, ed. Alberic Stacpoole, 133–141 (Wilton, Conn.: Morehouse-Barlow, 1982). Gritsch's evaluation of "Lutheranism" includes the Lutheran confessions (i.e., Melanchthon and Luther), brief statements on Lutheran orthodoxy and pietism, then a longer section on the nineteenth and twentieth centuries.

38. David F. Wright, "Mary in the Reformers," in *Chosen by God: Mary in Evangelical Perspective*, ed. David F. Wright (London: Marshall Pickering, 1989), 180. O'Meara suggests that Luther's maintenance of nonscriptural points of Mariology (i.e., her perpetual virginity) shows that the Reformation principle of *sola scriptura* in fact was *not* the guiding factor, but rather his "dislike of what seemed papist superstition," that is, anything that interfered with the direct and free mediation of Christ. See O'Meara, 122–123.

39. Oberman, "The Virgin Mary in Evangelical Perspective," *Journal of Ecumenical Studies* 1 (1964): 296.

40. Meinhold, "Die Marienverehrung im Verständnis der Reformatoren des 16. Jahrhunderts," *Saeculum* 32 (1981): 43.

41. See Cole, 201.

42. Ibid.

43. Georg Söll, "Maria in der Geschichte von Theologie und Frömmigkeit," in

Handbuch der Marienkunde, ed. W. Beinert and H. Petri, 93–231 (Regensburg: Friedrich Plestet, 1984).

44. Collegeville, Minn.: Liturgical, 1996.

45. Wright, 161: The Reformers had "limited interest" in Mary. Maron, 41: "For Luther and the Reformers Mary is not a significant theme of theological controversy. Luther's polemic is aimed essentially at the praxis, *the false honor done to Mary.*"

46. Macon, Ga.: Mercer University Press, 1987. See also Max Lackmann, *Verehrung der Heiligen: Versuch einer lutherischen Lehre von den Heiligen* (Stuttgart: Schwabenverlag, 1958); Peter Manns, "Luther und die Heiligen," in *Reformatio Ecclesiae . . . Festgabe für Erwin Iserloh,* ed. R. Bäumer (Paderborn: Schöningh, 1980); Lennart Pinomaa, *Die Heiligen bei Luther* (Helsinki: Luther-Agricola Gesellschaft, 1977); Martin Scharfe, "Der Heilige in der protestantische Volksfrömmigkeit," *Hessische Blätter für Volkskunde* 60 (1969): 93–106; J. M. Weiss, "Luther and His Colleagues on the Lives of the Saints," *Harvard Library Bulletin* 33 (Spring 1985): 174–195.

47. Kolb, "Festivals of the Saints in Late Reformation Lutheran Preaching," *Historian* 52 (August 1990): 615.

48. "Marian Devotion in the Western Church," in *Christian Spirituality: High Middle Ages and Reformation,* ed. Jill Raitt, *World Spirituality: An Encyclopedic History of the Religious Quest,* vol. 17 (New York: Crossroad, 1987): 410.

49. Ibid., 411.

50. "A Lily Ungilded? Martin Luther, the Virgin Mary and the Saints," *Journal of Religious History* 13 (December 1984): 136–149.

51. See Merry Wiesner, "Beyond Women and the Family: Towards a Gender Analysis of the Reformation," *Sixteenth Century Journal* 18, no. 3 (1987): 311–321; idem, "Luther and Women: The Death of Two Marys," in *Disciplines of Faith: Studies in Religion, Politics, and Patriarchy,* ed. J. Obelkevich, L. Roper, and R. Samuel, 295–308, History Workshop Series (London: Routledge & Kegan Paul, 1987); idem, *Women and Gender in Early Modern Europe,* New Approaches to European History (Cambridge: Cambridge University Press, 1993); idem, "Women's Response to the Reformation," in *The German People and the Reformation,* ed. R. Hsia, 148–171 (Ithaca: Cornell University Press, 1988); Susan Karant-Nunn, "Continuity and Change: Some Effects of the Reformation on the Women of Zwickau," *Sixteenth Century Journal* 13, 2 (1982): 17–42; idem, "*Kinder, Küche, Kirche:* Social Ideology in the Sermons of Johannes Mathesius," in *Germania Illustrata: Essays on Early Modern Germany Presented to Gerald Strauss,* ed. Andrew C. Fix and Susan C. Karant-Nunn, 121–140, *Sixteenth Century Essays and Studies,* ed. Charles G. Nauert, Jr., vol. 18 (Ann Arbor: Edwards Brothers, 1992). A book that should also be mentioned in the context of feminist history is Marina Warner's *Alone of All Her Sex: The Myth and the Cult of the Virgin Mary* (New York: Vintage, 1983), originally published in 1976. In a book of over 300 pages, she mentions the reformers only a few times.

52. Wiesner, "Luther and Women: The Death of Two Marys," 303.

53. Ibid.

54. New Haven: Yale University Press, 1996.

55. *Das Marienlob der Reformatoren* (Tübingen: Katzmann, 1962).

56. Pelikan, *Mary Through the Centuries: Her Place in the History of Culture* (New Haven: Yale University Press, 1996), 158–159.

57. It is somewhat ironic that so many studies written in an ecumenical spirit are chiefly concerned with the "Marienverehrung" of the reformers, for, as Stephen Benko asserts: "Protestants err greatly if they consider the problem symbolized by

Mary to be merely one of whether and to what extent the Savior's mother is to be honored by Christians. The theological issue at stake is far more serious and basic, for it involves the question of the fundamental approaches of Protestants and Catholics to the principal issues of Christian theology: (1) the question of whether Scripture alone, or Scripture and tradition together, constitute the sources of divine revelation; (2) the concept of Christology and particularly the question of the Incarnation; and (3) an understanding of the nature of justification and grace." See Benko, *Protestants, Catholics, and Mary* (Valley Forge, Pa.: Judson, 1968), 62.

58. Düfel, 33.

59. John Bossy, *Christianity in the West 1400–1700* (Oxford: Oxford University Press, 1985). See also, among others, Ton Brandenbarg, "Saint Anne: A Holy Grandmother and Her Children," in *Sanctity and Motherhood: Essays on Holy Mothers in the Middle Ages*, ed. Anneke B. Mulder-Bakker, 31–65 (New York: Garland, 1995).

60. Ibid., 9.

61. Pelikan, 47.

62. Warner, 67.

63. "[Paul] declares that all children of Adam—except the Son of the Virgin—are sinners and children of wrath." Anselm of Canterbury, *The Virgin Conception and Original Sin*, trans. Joseph M. Colleran (Albany, N.Y.: Magi), ch. 22. For a more thorough discussion of this topic, see Joseph S. Bruder, *The Mariology of Saint Anselm of Canterbury* (Dayton, Oh.: Mount St. John, 1939).

64. "Tibi, o genitrix vitae, o mater salutis, o templum pietatis et misericordiae, tibi sese conatur praesentare miserabilis anima mea" [Prayer 50; cited in Bruder, 200, n. 73]; "Mundi reconciliatrix" [Prayer 51; cited in Bruder, 208, n.258]. Anselm also refers to Christ as the reconciler of the world.

65. It should be pointed out that this was primarily a debate in western Christendom. Hilda Graef stresses that "the Eastern Fathers simply thought on different lines from the later Western theologians; they used terms like 'immaculate' or 'stainless' much more loosely, taking them to imply only surpassing moral and physical purity, without intending to make any pronouncement about exemption from original sin, which to the Eastern mind meant mortality rather than a moral stain." See Graef, *Mary, a History of Doctrine and Devotion*, vol. 1, *From the Beginning to the Eve of the Reformation* (New York: Sheed and Ward, 1963), 124.

66. See Ton Brandenbarg on representations of St. Anne in "St. Anne and Her Family: The Veneration of St. Anne in Connection with Concepts of Marriage and the Family in the Early Modern Period," in *Saints and She-Devils: Images of Women in the Fifteenth and Sixteenth Centuries*, ed. Lène Dresen-Coenders (London: Rubicon, 1987), 101–128.

67. Graef, vol. 1, 217–218.

68. Eadmer, *Tractatus de Conceptione Sanctae Mariae*, ed. H. Thurston and T. Slater (Friburgi Brisgoviae, 1904), 11; cited in Bruder, 46. This tract was mistakenly attributed to Anselm for a long period.

69. Graef, vol. 1, 231.

70. Ibid., 273.

71. See the *Summa Theologiae*, 3a, q. 27, art. 1–4.

72. *Questio Gulielmi Guarrae, Utrum Beata Virgo concepta fuerit in peccato originali*, ed. in *Bibliotheca Franciscana Scholastica Medii Aevi*, vol. 3, Quaracchi (1904), 10; cited in Graef, vol. 1, 299.

73. The dogma of the immaculate conception, pronounced in 1854 by Pius IX,

essentially follows Scotus's arguments: "the Blessed Virgin Mary at the first moment of her conception by a special grace and privilege of Almighty God, in view of the merits of Christ Jesus, the Savior of the human race, by preservation was pure of all stain of original sin" (*Ineffabilis Deus* 7, cited in O'Meara, 58). This conception, according to O'Meara, refers to animation. For a critique of *Ineffabilis Deus*, see Tavard, *The Thousand Faces of Mary*, 192–197.

74. Oberman, *The Harvest of Medieval Theology: Gabriel Biel and Late Medieval Nominalism* (Cambridge: Harvard University Press, 1963; reprint, Durham, N.C.: Labyrinth, 1983), 285.

75. See, for example, the "*De septem foribus seu festis Beatae Virginis/Die siben Porten oder Feste der Muter Gottes*" of Johannes von Paltz, in his *Werke*, vol. 3, ed. Marius et al., 285–353, Spätmittelalter und Reformation Texte und Untersuchungen, ed. Heiko Oberman (Berlin: Walter de Gruyter, 1989). Paltz argues in favor of the immaculate conception, and declares that this doctrine is the "fundamentum et radix omnium aliarum portarum sive festorum [Mariae]" (315).

76. Oberman, *Harvest*, 294.

77. Ibid., 304–308.

78. Ibid., 308.

79. Ibid., 310.

80. Caroline Walker Bynum, *Jesus as Mother: Studies in the Spirituality of the High Middle Ages* (Berkeley: University of California Press, 1982), 137.

81. Oberman, *Harvest*, 319.

82. Ibid., 322.

83. Scribner, "Ritual and Popular Religion in Catholic Germany at the Time of the Reformation," *Journal of Ecclesiastical History* 35 (1984): 48.

84. Ibid., 50.

85. Ibid., 51.

86. Ibid., 52–53.

87. Ibid., 53, 61.

88. Ibid., 62.

89. See Louis Chatellier, *The Europe of the Devout: The Catholic Reformation and the Formation of a New Society*, trans. Jean Birrell (Cambridge: Cambridge University Press and Paris: Editions de la Maison des Sciences de l'Homme, 1989), which traces the rise of Marian confraternities and their connection with the newly founded Jesuit order. For the medieval origins of the rosary and its association to Marian devotion, see Anne Winston-Allen, *Stories of the Rose: The Making of the Rosary in the Middle Ages* (University Park, Pa.: Pennsylvania State University Press, 1997).

90. Moeller, "Religious Life in Germany on the Eve of the Reformation," in *Pre-Reformation Germany*, ed. Gerald Strauss (New York: Harper & Row, 1972), 14, 25. Moeller suggests that the increased veneration of saints and the development of the system of saintly patronage was tied to a longing for salvation, and an insecurity about it, "an endeavor to bring the mediators between God and man to one's own side, as it were, and to procure a guarantee of salvation" (18–19).

91. Bynum, *Jesus as Mother*, 16–17.

92. See Bynum's chapter "Jesus as Mother and Abbot as Mother"; she points out that maternal imagery was more often used by men than by women in the writings of the high Middle Ages, and it is often applied to Jesus. For example, in a letter Bernard wrote, "If you feel the stings of temptation . . . suck not so much the wounds as the breasts of the Crucified. He will be your mother, and you will be his son" (Bynum, 17).

93. See Rosemary Drage Hale, "*Imitatio Mariae*: Motherhood Motifs in Late Medieval German Spirituality," Ph.D. diss., Harvard University, 1992.

94. Winston-Allen, xi.

95. Ibid., 3–6.

96. Graef, vol. 1, 306–307.

97. "Das Schiff des Heils," in *Geilers von Kaisersberg ausgewählte Schriften*, vol. 4, ed. Philipp de Lorenzi (Trier: Ed. Groppe, 1883), 168.

98. Ibid., 175.

99. Ibid., 337.

100. Paltz was an older contemporary of Luther, who was also active at the congregation in Erfurt; they were briefly in residence at the same time in 1505. He was a popular preacher, and his publications ("bestsellers" of the day, according to Düfel) were in a popular vein. The *Himmlische Fundgrube*, from 1490, is based on a series of four (or more) sermons preached at the time Paltz was promoting the new papal indulgence. The popularity of this work can be seen in that it was reprinted at least twenty times in its first thirty years. The expanded and more scholarly *Coelifodina*, with its *Supplementum*, were published in the early years of the sixteenth century. See the critical editions of these works in *Johannes von Paltz Werke*, 3 vols., in the series Spätmittelalter und Reformation Texte und Untersuchungen, ed. Heiko Oberman (Berlin: Walter de Gruyter, 1983–1989).

101. This text is the gospel for the "festival of the Seven Dolors of the all-holy Virgin Mary," celebrated in the late Middle Ages on the Friday after the third Sunday of Easter. See Paltz's *Werke*, vol. 3, 210, n. 52.

102. "*Die himlische funtgrub*," in *Johannes von Paltz Werke*, vol. 3, 211.

103. Ibid., 212: "O Maria, du aller getreueste muter, erloße uns von der ersten muter, die do gestanden ist bei dem verbotten baum. Zeuch unß zu dir under das kreuze, auf das wir nit betrogen werden von der hellischen schlangen." Note the reference to the Song of Songs 1:3: "Draw me after you."

104. Ibid., 246: "Ich bit dich durch ewig außerwelung, durch dein heilig entpfenknis und durch dein kreuzsteung, kome mir zu hilf an meinem letzten end."

105. See Caroline Walker Bynum's discussion of "The Complexity of Symbols" in *Gender and Religion: On the Complexity of Symbols*, ed. Caroline Walker Bynum, Stevan Harrell, and Paula Richman, 1–20 (Boston: Beacon, 1986); also idem, "Women's Stories, Women's Symbols: A Critique of Victor Turner's Theory of Liminality," in *Anthropology and the Study of Religion*, ed. Frank Reynolds and Robert Moore, 105–125 (Chicago: Center for the Scientific Study of Religion, 1984).

106. Bynum, "Complexity of Symbols," 2.

107. Ibid. For this discussion in Ricoeur, see his "Symbol Gives Rise to Thought," in *Ways of Understanding Religion*, ed. Walter H. Capps, 309–317 (New York: Macmillan, 1972); and idem, *The Symbolism of Evil*, trans. E. Buchanan (Boston: Beacon, 1967).

108. For Turner, see *Forest of Symbols: Aspects of Ndembu Ritual* (Ithaca: Cornell University Press, 1967).

109. Bynum, "Complexity of Symbols," 9. See Geertz, "Religion as a Cultural System," in *Anthropological Approaches to the Study of Religion*, ed. Michael Banton, 1–46 (London: Tavistock, 1966).

110. Bynum, "Complexity of Symbols," 9.

111. Ibid.

112. See Victor Turner, "Social Dramas and Stories about Them," in *On Narra-*

tive, ed. W.J.T. Mitchell, 137–64 (Chicago: University of Chicago Press, 1981). Bynum argues that "women's symbols and myths tend to build from social and biological experiences; men's symbols and myths tend to invert them" (Bynum, "Complexity of Symbols," 13).

113. Bynum, "Complexity of Symbols," 10.

114. Ibid., 2.

115. Ibid., 2–3.

116. Luther felt that preaching should be *doctrina et exhortatio*—both teaching and exhortation to greater piety and better behavior. The use of models, especially biblical figures, was a common feature of *exhortatio* in Lutheran preaching, in fact of preaching generally in the sixteenth century. The humanist interest in classical rhetoric led to a revolution of sorts in styles of preaching for both Catholics and Protestants, with the classical *genus deliberativum*, the mode of speech "in exhortation of the people," becoming the primary form for the sermon. See John W. O'Malley, "Luther the Preacher," *Michigan Germanic Studies* 10 (1984): 3–16; idem, "Content and Rhetorical Forms in Sixteenth-Century Treatises on Preaching," in *Renaissance Eloquence: Studies in the Theory and Practice of Renaissance Rhetoric*, ed. James J. Murphy (Berkeley: University of California Press, 1983): 238–252; Kreitzer, 35–63.

117. E. Jane Dempsey Douglass, *Justification in Late Medieval Preaching: A Study of John Geiler of Keisersberg*, Studies in Medieval and Reformation Thought, ed. H.A. Oberman, vol. 1 (Leiden: E. J. Brill, 1966), 5–6.

I. THE ANNUNCIATION

1. NRSV, Luke 1:31–32.

2. Lansemann, 196–197.

3. Philipp Wackernagel, *Das Deutsche Kirchenlied von der ältesten Zeit bis zu Anfang des XVII. Jahrhunderts*, Vierter Band, *Die Lieder des zweiten Geschlechts der Reformationszeit, von Paulus Eber bis Bartholomæ Ringwaldt, 1554–1584* (Hildesheim: Georg Olms, 1964 [Reprografischer Nachdruck der Ausgabe Leipzig, 1874]): 1066. Hymn no. 1547, "*Am tag der Verkündigung Mariæ*," chosen by Cyriacus Spangenberg for his *Christlichs Gesangbüchlein*, is one example.

4. Lansemann, 24.

5. NRSV, Luke 1:26–38.

6. Bernard of Clairvaux, *Homilies in Praise of the Blessed Virgin Mary*, trans. Marie-Bernard Saïd, Cistercian Fathers Series, no. 18a (Kalamazoo: Cistercian, 1993), 40. The four sermons in this collection are extended meditations on the Annunciation text.

7. Johann Geiler von Keysersberg, *Postill: Uber die fyer Euangelia durchs jor, sampt dem quadragesimal, vnnd von etlichen Heyligen, newlich ussgangen* (Strassburg: Johann Schott, 1522), 33r.

8. Ibid., 33v.

9. Martin Luther, WA 17², *Festpostille 1527*, 399: "Alles, was von flaischlicher empfengknus herkompt, das ist unrain, darumb ist Christus von ainer Jungkfrawen geporen."

10. The events most commonly associated with this date, along with the Annunciation, were the creation of Adam and Eve and the Fall. Christ's crucifixion, completing the parallelism between the first and second Adams, was also thought to have occurred on this date. Authors who discussed all four of these events include Paul

Eber, Georg Major, and Christoph Moller. Moller also thought that other events such as the death of Abel, the sacrifice of Isaac, Lot's escape from Sodom, and the anointing of David all took place on this date. See Lansemann, 124–125.

11. Nicholas Selnecceer, *Epistolarvm et Evangeliorvm Dispositio, qvæ Diebvs Festis B. Mariæ semper virginis, & S. Apostolorum vsitatè in Ecclesia proponuntur & explicantur: Scripta a d. Nicolao Selneccero* (Frankfurt: n.p., 1575), 75: "Fuit enim Maria typus Ecclesiæ." Georg Major, *Ein tröstliche Predigt vber das Euangelium Lucae j. am tage der Verkündigung Marie/ oder des Empfengnis vnsers lieben Heilands vnd Seligmachers Jhesu Christi* (Wittenberg: Hans Lufft, 1549), Nv: "diweil Maria ein furbilde der gantzen Christlichen Kirchen sein sol."

12. Luther, WA 17², *Festpostille* 1527, 399: "DJß ist ain frölich und lieplich Euangelion, . . . denn wir werden hören, wie Maria die junckfraw ain solchen hohen glawben hat, des gleichen wir nicht vil in der schrifft gefunden haben."

13. Ibid.

14. Ibid.: "Das ist ain hoher treflicher glaub, mütter werden und junckfraw bleiben, das ubertrifft warlich sinn, gedancken, dazü alle menschliche vernunfft und erfarung."

15. Cole, 119–120. Luther maintained a belief in the perpetual, physical virginity of Mary throughout his life, considering it an article of faith; see WA 11, 319.

16. Luther, *Festpostille* 1527, 403: "Neyn, Sye hat warlich ain stoß des unglawbens in jr gefült, sonst hette sie nicht gefragt und gesprochen: 'Wie soll das zü geen?' '

17. Ibid., 405: "Maria ist ain Ebraischer name unnd haist bey den Ebreern als vil, als bey uns ein tröpfflein wassers, das an ainem eymer oder krüg behangen bleibt, welchs tröpflein kaine vergleichung hat, wenn es zü dem meer oder gegen aim grossen wasser wirt gerechnet." This is the aspect of Mary's image that Georg Major relates to the church: "die Christliche Kirche eine rechte Maria / ein betrübtes / elendes heufflin in dieser Welt sein werde / welchs viel bitters jamers werde müssen leiden / vnd wenig ruhe vnd gute tage habe / auff das sie darnach in jenem leben mit ewiger herrligkeit bey jrem lieben HErrn Christo Jhesu geschmuckt vnd gekrönet werden möge" (Major, *Ein tröstliche Predigt* [1549], Nv). For more information on the name Mary, see Walter Delius, *Geschichte der Marienverehrung* (Munich: Ernst Reinhardt, 1963), chap. 1.

18. Luther, *Festpostille* 1527, 405–406.

19. Ibid., 408: "Da wirt die braut zur hüren und verleust jre Junckfrawschafft. Denn da hat sie den glauben verlorn und geglaubt, die wercke machen sie selig oder verdampt, und nicht der blosse glaube in Christum."

20. Ibid., 409–410.

21. WA 11, 60: "Si aliquis dixisset non opus esse Mariam adorari, ille hereticus fuisset."

22. WA 52, 625: "So ist es leichtlich abzunemen, was ein solchs Junckfrewlein für einen Stand und wesen füre, das sie jrgendt bey eim freundt gedienet und die deheinen haußarbeyt thun hab wie ein ander Mägdlin, das schlecht, fromm und gerecht ist."

23. The notion that Mary was praying when confronted by the angel is very traditional. Along with her prayers, Geiler suggests that Mary was reading the book of Isaiah, contemplating the holiness of God, and sighing over the future coming of the Messiah. This would have left little time for housework. See Geiler, *Das euangeli buch* (Strassburg: Johannes Grieninger, 1515), 171r.

24. Luther, WA 52, *Hauspostille* (1544), 626: " 'Gegrüsset [spricht er] seist du holdselige' oder begnadete, 'der Herr ist mit dir, du Hochgelobte unter den wey-

bern.' " Heinz Bluhm praises the "inspired translating" of the word *holdselige*, remarking that the word "is a superb German rendering of the idea Luther wished to express." The more philologically correct *begnadete* used by modern translators was also suggested by Luther in his 1544 *Hauspostille* sermon. See Bluhm's "Luther's Translation and Interpretation of the *Ave Maria*," *Journal of English and German Philology* 51 (1952): 198–199.

25. Luther, *Hauspostille* (1544), 627.

26 Ibid., 629: "Darumb, ob wol diß fromm Junckfrewlin allein die muter zu disem kind ist, so gehören wir doch auch unter dises kindlins regiment und Königreich."

27. Ibid., 633: "Und durch solchen glauben allein ist sie auch selig unnd von sünden ledig worden, unnd nicht durch das werck, das sie den Son Gottes hat an die welt gebracht."

28. See Anne Reeve, ed., *Erasmus' Annotations on the New Testament: The Gospels* (London: Gerald Duckworth, 1986), especially 154–155.

29. Andreas Keller, *Ain Sermon auff dem tag der verkündigung Marie gepredigt zü Rottenburg Durch Andream Keller* ([Augsburg: Heinrich Steiner], 1524): B ijr. Hilda Graef writes that *kecharitomene* should be translated "highly favoured [or, privileged] one." Using this greeting gave the angel's message a "highly messianic ring," which also helps to explain why Mary was troubled at the greeting. See Graef, *Mary, a History of Doctrine and Devotion*, vol. 1, 8.

30. Keller, *Ain Sermon* (1524): "das wörtlein / volgnad / soll nit verstanden werden / dy sy von jr selbs sey volgnaden gsein oder volgunst / sondern das alle gnad / gunst von got ist kommen / dann gnad ist nichs anders dann gunst gottes."

31 Ibid.: "auch selbs Luce 2. so er spricht er hat mir grosse ding gethon der da mächtig ist / vnd weytter / er hatt angesehen dye nichtikait seiner dienerin etc."

32. Johannes Brenz, *Pericopæ Euangeliorum qvæ Usitato More in præcipuis Festis legi solent, expositæ per Iohan. Brent.* (Frankfurt: Petrus Brubach, 1557) (Herzog August Bibliothek (Wolfenbüttel); St. Paul, Minn.: Lutheran Brotherhood Foundation Reformation Library, microfiche), 1136–1137.

33. Ibid.: "Hoc non sic intelligendum est quemadmodum hypocritæ explicuerunt, quòd Maria in se ipsa sit cista gratiarum et poßideat tanquàm DEA quædam thesaurum omnium cœlestium bonorum, ex quo distribuat cui uelit."

34. Ibid.: "Gratiosa igitur significat eam, quæ suscepta à Deo in gratiam, et quæ maximum habet fauorem apud Deum."

35. Luther, WA 30², 638. See also the discussion in Bluhm, 200–201.

36. Keller, *Ain Sermon* (1524), B ijr: "vnd dz sy im menschlichen geschlecht ain ainige person ist / über alle deren niemants gleich ist / dz sy mit dem himlischem vater ayn kind / vnd ein solchs kind hat dz für die gantzen welt sünd bezalt hat."

37. Ibid., B ijv: "so sollen wir hie lernen / was do sey das lob Marie der junckfrawen vnd müter gottes / wann hie in dißem grüß wirt es alles begryffen / damit dz wir nit in dem irrchtumb bleiben / da wir byßher in gelegen seyen . . . Singen wir nit vnd haben gesungen jm salue / vnser leben / vnser hoffnung / das dann allain Christo zü gehöret."

38. Brenz, *Pericopæ . . . qvæ Usitato More in præcipuis Festis legi solent* (1557), 1139: "Nam Angelus non idcirco commendauit Mariam tantis præconijs ut eam proponat nobis in mediatricem et reconciliatricem diuinæ Iræ . . . [sed] ut per hæc excitaret in ipsa fidem, qua sequentem promißionem de conceptione et Natiuitate Christi susciperet."

39. Cole, 188–190; also Hans-Ulrich Delius, "Luther und das *'Salve Regina,' "*
Forschungen und Fortschritte 38 (1964), 249–251.

40. Anton Corvinus, *Kurtze vnd ainfeltige Außlegung der Epistolen vnd Euangelien/
So auff die Sonntage vnd fürnemesten Feste/ durch das gantz Jar in der Kirchen gelesen
werden. Für die arme Pfarrherren vnd Haußuätter gestellet/ Durch M. Antonivm Corvinvm* (Augsburg: Valentin Othmar, 1545), 23v: "Leiden kan ich wol / ist auch billich /
das Maria als ain Gotseligs kind gepreiset / gerümet vnnd gelobt / ja als ain Exempel
rechtschaffens glaubens / allen Christen fürgebildet werde / Aber lieber / laß sy doch
ain Creatur bleiben /"

41 Daniel Greser, *Enarratio Brevis et Orthodoxa Evangeliorvm Dominicalivm & Festorum aliquot: authore, Daniele Gresero, Pastore & superattendente Dresdensi* (Frankfurt:
Petrus Brubach, 1567), 619–620: "[Lucas] describit autem non propter personam
Mariæ, ut eam feriando festa eius, et colendo eam propitiam nobis reddamus, ut eius
interceßione peccata nobis remittantur: sicut in Papatu de ea canunt, Nos hac die tibi
gregatos serua uirgo, etc."

42. Johannes Wigand, *Postilla/ Ausslegung der Euangelien, so man durch das gantze Jar auff einen jeden Sontag vnd fürnemste Fest/ in der Kirchen pfleget für zutragen/
Erstmals in Lateinischer Sprach verzeichnet,* trans. Christophorum Obenhin (Ursel: Nikolaus Henricus, 1569), 62: "Der Engel aber leret keines wegs / das man Mariam
anruffen solle Denn die anruffung gebüret allein Gott / man sol allein Gott anruffen /
Deut. 6. Darumb mussen die Papisten freylich tolle vnd vnsinnige Leute sein / welche im salue Regina, vnd in andern Gebetlein Mariam als ein Mitlerin vnd Nothelfferin anruffen."

43. Ibid., 63.

44. Johannes Heune (Gigas), *Postilla der Sontags Euangelien vnd etlicher Festen./
Iohannis Gigantis Northusani* (Alten Stettin: Johann Eichorn, 1570), 102r.

45. Ibid.: "ist Maria voller gnaden / haben sie geschlossen / so ruffet man sie
auch billich vmb hülff an / Aber Maria ist nicht voller gnaden / wie Christus Johan. I
der feine gnade vns mitteilet / vnd vns selig machete."

46. Christoph Vischer, *Außlegung der Euangelien/ so man auff die Sontage in der
Christlichen Kirchen zu handeln pfleget/ Vom Aduent bis auff Ostern/ Darinnen ein jedes
Euangelium in drey/ bisweilen in vier Predigten verfasset ist* (Schmalkalden: Michel
Schmuck, 1570), Sss r: "Diss ist der Gruss Marie / daraus wir nicht ein Gebet
machen sollen / wie die Papisten abends vnd morgens vberal die Aue Marien glocke
leuten lassen / vermeinende damit Marie verdienst vnd vorbitte zu geniessen /
vnd haben die Leute darauff vertröstet / es sey vnmüglich / das dasselbige ort / da
man solche glocke leutet / beschediget werden / viel weniger zu boden gehen
könne."

47. Niels Hemmingsen, *Postilla oder Auslegung der Euangelien/ welche man auff
die Sontage vnd andere Feste/ in der Kirchen Gottes pfleget zu verlesen. Allen getrewen/
fromen Dienern des Euangelij zu gute beschrieben/ vnd auffs new widerumb gemehret/
Durch Nicolaum Hemmingum* (Wittenberg: Hans Krafft, 1571), 25: "Verflucht sein alle
die / so die Creaturn anruffen / vnd die wort der Schrifft felschlich deuten / jre greu-
liche Abgötterey zu bestetigen / mit höchster verachtunge des Sons Gottes / mit
grosser schmach der aller heiligsten Jungfrawen Marie / vnd mit gewisser verderbnis
jrer Seelen seligkeit." Hemmingsen (1513–1600), a Dane, received his education in
Wittenberg and published many of his works in German, and is thus included in this
study.

48. For a brief summary of these early heresies, attested in Epiphanius' *Panarion,* see Graef, vol. 1, 70–73.

49. Nicolaus Selneccer, *Epistolarvm . . . qvæ Diebvs Festis* (1575), 75.

50. Christoff Mollen, *Ein Predig von dem Aue Maria, vnd von anrüffung der Heyligen. Gestellet durch Christoff Mollen von Augspurg/ Euangelischen Kirchendiener zü Gernspach* (Strassburg: Christian Müller, 1575), A ijv: "vnd werden die leut fürnemlich an den orten / da man das Bapstumb wider von newem durch die Jesauiten auff vnd an richtet / zü solchem jrrthum vnd grewel angewisen vnd getriben."

51 Ibid., n.p. (between B iij and C). Mollen also strongly criticizes Martin Eisengrein's book concerning an exorcism performed by the Jesuit Peter Canisius in Alt Oetting that relied heavily on the invocation of Mary. See the article by Lyndal Roper, "Exorcism and the Theology of the Body," in *Oedipus and the Devil: Witchcraft, Sexuality and Religion in Early Modern Europe* (London: Routledge, 1994), 171–198.

52. Georg Spindler, *Postilla. Außlegung der Sontags/ vnd fürnemesten Fest Euangelien vber das gantze jahr/ in gewisse Artickel/ vmb einfeltiger Prediger/ vnd gemeinen Mans willen gestellet/ Durch Georgium Spindler* (Leipzig: Hans Steinman, 1576), 276.

53. Ibid.: "AVch sollen wir den Trost hierbey mercken / das wir alle holdselig / vnd gnade bey Gott haben / die wir nur an Christum gleuben / vnd so selig sind als Maria / denn Christus hat vns die erworben / vnd vns dieselbige in seinem Wort mitgeteilet / vnd im Sacrament versichert."

54. Tilemann Hesshusen, *Postilla [:] Das ist/ Außlegung der Euangelien auff alle Fest vnd Apostel Tage durchs gantze Jar* (Helmstedt: Jacob Lucius, 1581), 93r: "das wir Gott für seine Gaben dancken / das er seinen Son hat lassen Mensch werden / vnd sollen den grund vnsers Glaubens recht lernen verstehen / vnd das treffliche Exempel des Glaubens Marie nachfolgen."

55. Graef, vol. 1, 37–38.

56. Irenaeus, *Against the Heresies*, 3, 22, 4. Cited by Graef, vol. 1, 39.

57. Graef, vol. 1, 246–247. See 1 Corinthians 15:22: "for as all die in Adam, so all will be made alive in Christ."

58. Marina Warner, 245. Luther, in his lectures on Genesis, explicitly condemns this error as leading, through the power of Satan, to the application of this passage to Mary rather than her son, and thus to idolatry. See LW 1, 191–198.

59. Genesis 3:16, NRSV.

60. See for example Warner, *Alone of All Her Sex*, especially 57–59.

61 Keller, *Ain Sermon* (1525), Biijv: "so ist sy gebenedeyt under allen weybern / nit allain von deßwegen / das sy on wee vnd schmertzen geboren hat / vnd auß ist genommen von dem spruch Gen. 3. Der zü Eua gesprochen / in bekummernuß soltu geberen u. auch nit von des wegen das sy on alle befleckung geboren hat / das sy ist magt bliben vor / in / vnd nach der geburt / sonder auch / das sy fruchtbar ist worden vnnd empfangen hat vom hayligen gayst / on alle sünd / vnd dannocht ain leipliche frucht / das da nye kainem weib begegnet / auch in ewigkait kainem begegnen wirt."

62. Ibid.: "Hie wirdt anzaigt das dye frücht jres leybs ist abgesondert von dem flüch der da ist kommen über alle kinder Eue / das sy empfangen werden in sünden / . . . Wir werden alle geboren kinder des zornß."

63. Caspar Huberinus, *Postilla Teutsch/Vber alle Sontägliche Euangelien/ vom Aduent biß auff Ostern/ Kurtze vnd nützliche Außlegung* (Nuremberg: Johann Daubman, 1548), 141r–v: "Derhalben gleich wie der Sathan das weib / vnd also folgends / durch das weibe den mann / den Adam / vnd alle seine nachkommen / verfürte / . . . Also nimbt hie Gott auch ein weibs bildt / der Eua Tochter für sich / vnd last sie den heiligen Geist vberschatten / . . . vnnd bringt also Gott der HErr widerumb zu recht /

durch das weib / der Junckfrawen Mariam / das sie gnade findet bey Gott / vnd durch einen mann / den newen Adam / der Junckfrawen son."

64. Ibid., 143v: "Maria [ist] nicht wie jr mutter Eua / vnd andere weiber / im fluch / vngnad / vnd zoren Gottes."

65. Ibid., 144r–v: "Zum andern, dieweil nun / auß gnaden Gottes / das gefeß / der leib / fleisch / vnnd blut Marie / gereinigt / begnadet / vnd geheiligt ist. . . . Zum dritten / Das Maria die gebenedeyte ist / vnter allen weibern auff Erden / das sie die hochgelobte Junckfraw sein soll / vnter allen weibern auff Erden / vnnd gleich wie Eua ohn zweiffel / noch ein Junckfraw / ein Braut vnd dem Adam vertraut / den fluch eingefürt hat."

66. Ibid., 145r: "Inn summa / Gott der Allmechtig hat diese Junckfrawen herrlich krönnen / vnd jhr ein solchs krentzlin auffsetzen wöllen / welches mit funffzehennerley wolriechenden löblichen blümlin gemachet ist." Using floral and garland imagery in descriptions of Mary was quite popular in medieval literature; the rose garland or chaplet imagery is also common in nonreligious literature and poetry. See Anne Winston-Allen, *Stories of the Rose*, especially chap. 4; also Heimo Reinitzer, *Der verschlossene Garten: Der Garten Marias im Mittelalter*, Wolfenbütteler Hefte 12 (Wolfenbüttel: Herzog August Bibliothek, 1982).

67. Johannes Drach (Draconites), *Ejne Dreifaltige Predigt Des Engel Gabriels. Luce. j. Am tage der Verkündigung Mariæ zu Marpurg ausgeleget* ([Lübeck]: Georg Richolff, 1550) (Herzog August Bibliothek [Wolfenbüttel]; St. Paul, Minn.: Lutheran Brotherhood Foundation Reformation Library, microfiche), Biijr: "du gebenedeiete vnter den Weibern: anzuzeigen / das Maria die seie die von ewickeit dazu erwelet seie / das sie des Messiah mutter seie / dauon er des Weibes Samen genennet seie Ge. 3."

68. Heune, *Postilla* (1570), 102r: "dieweil er sie die Begnadte oder Holdselige nennet / welche den Schlangentreter zur WElt bringen werde / der alles widerumb zu recht bringen sol / was die feindselige Eua mit jhrem vngehorsam vnd fürwitz verschüttet / verrücket vnd verderbet hat / Genesis am 3. Capitel[.]"

69. Vischer, *Außlegung der Euangelien . . . Vom Aduent bis auff Ostern* (1570), n.p.: "Eua war feindselig / hat vns in den schweis gebracht / Du bist holdselig / vnd tregest den Brunnenquell aller holdseligkeit Christum. Sie ist nicht für sich der Gnadenbrunn/ daraus gnade quillet . . . Denn das eignet vnd gebüret allein Christo Jhesu."

70. Ibid., Sss r: "vnd vnter allen Weibern zu dem Jnstrument vnd werckgezeug auserkoren."

71 Hemmingsen, *Postilla* (1571), 25: "Gleich wie Eua verflucht war vnter den Weibern / ja alle Weiber waren verflucht von jrent wegen / also bistu gesegnet durch Gottes gabe vnd gnade."

72. Simon Pauli, *Postilla: Das ist/ Außlegung der Euanglien/ von den fürnemsten Festen der Heiligen/ durchs gantze Jar/ ordentlich vnd richtig nach der Rhetorica gefasset: Neben einer kurtzen erklerung des Textes . . . Das Dritte Teil* (Magdeburg: Wolffgang Kirchner, 1573) (Herzog August Bibliothek [Wolfenbüttel]; St. Paul, Minn.: Lutheran Brotherhood Foundation Reformation Library, microfiche), 101v: "Heut diesen tag / hat des weibes Samen in die flucht geschlagen / vertrieben / vberwunden / vnd vertilgt den Tod / welchen ein Weib in die Welt gebracht."

73. Selneccer, *Epistolarvm . . . qvæ Diebvs Festis* (1575), 79: "III. Ratione innocentiæ. Eua ante lapsum innocens. Maria nunc sanctificata Christum parit, atque ita τ´ o Aue opponitur τ ῆ Euæ, inuersis literis."

74. Johann Spangenberg, *Außlegung der Epistel vnd Euangelien/ von den fürnembsten Festen durchs gantze Jar. Durch Johann Spangenberg* (n.p., 1584), 34r: "Und hat Maria widerbracht / was Eua verloren hett. Vnd hie ist der Vatter versönet worden mit

dem menschlichen Geschlecht / hie ist aller zorn auffgehaben / vnd zugesagt alle gnade vnd barmhertzigkeit / vergebung der sünden vnd das ewige leben / Amen."

75. Joachim Mörlin, *Postilla: Oder Summarische Erinnerung bey den Sonteglichen Jahrs Euangelien vnd Catechism* (Erfurt: Esaias Mechlem, 1587), 56v: "Du wirst allen Weibern auff Erden / auß jhrer Schande wider zu Ehren helffen / daß man jhnen nit mehr wirdt fluchen . . . Ey die Weiber haben sich gleichwol durch Mariam ehrlich wider gelöset vnd vns Christum den Himmelischen Apffel an die Welt gebracht / der vns auß dem Fluch wider zum Segen geholffen."

76. See Graef, vol.1, 147–150.

77. Ibid., 87f., 98–100. Graef suggests that Augustine did not hold to the immaculate conception.

78. WA 17^2, 409: "Auffs erste ist sie voller gnaden, damit sie on alle sünde erkant wirt." The editor of volume 17 suggests that this section is an addition to the text by Roth.

79. WA 52, 633: "Und durch solchen glauben allein ist sie auch selig unnd von sünden ledig worden, unnd nicht durch das werck, das sie den Son Gottes hat an die welt gebracht." For Luther's views on the immaculate conception, see, among others, Ebneter, 78–79; also see the discussion in chapter 6.

80. Keller, *Ain Sermon* (1525), Biijr–v: "das sy on sünd ist gewesen / nit wie Christus / sonder auß gnaden."

81 Huberinus, *Postilla Teutsch* (1548), 27r, "An vnser Frawen empfengknus tag": "wie dan die Eutichiten daraus fürgeben / vnd schliessen wolten / dieweil Maria / wie andere menschen / inn Sünden empfangen / vnd geborn sey / so habe Christus auch ein sündtlich fleisch müssen annemen / so er seinen Leib / auß dem leib Marie habe angenommen / welchen er doch vom Himel / aus der substantz des Vaters genommen hab."

82. Ibid., 28r: "so mus ja Maria einen reinen / Heiligen / seligen Leib haben gahabt / da Christus in der empfengnus vom heiligen Geist / in muter Leib / die ware menscheit an sich genommen hat."

83. Ibid., 144r: "Zum andern / dieweil nun / auß gnaden Gottes / das gefeß / der leib / fleisch / vnnd blut Marie / gereinigt / begnadet / vnd geheiligt ist."

84. Brenz, *Pericopæ . . . qvæ Usitato More in præcipuis Festis legi solent* (1557), 1141–1142: "Nascimur igitur omnes priuati spiritu sancto et subiecti spiritui Satanæ. Sed unus solus Christus conceptus est è spiritu sancto, et attulit secum spiritum sanctum."

85. Wigand, *Postilla* (1569), 63: "Fürchte dich nicht: Solches alles wird vorn anhin gesetzt / auff das man wisse / das Maria ein schwach blöd Mensch / gleich wie andere Leute / gewesen seye / vnd Euangelische tröstung vnd sterckung wol bedurfft habe / auff das nicht jemand dencken möchte / es seye gar kein fehl oder gebrechen an den Heiligen gewesen."

86. In the medieval period, there were a number of authors who denied the immaculate conception, held to Mary's actual sinlessness, but also affirmed a "purification" by the Holy Spirit at the incarnation. For example, Bonaventure affirms that there was an infusion of grace that purified Mary immediately after her ensoulment, so that she was free from all actual sin. But this purification took place in two stages: in the first, she, like other saints, was given the ability to avoid all sin, both mortal and venial; in the second, at the incarnation, she was given the impossibility of falling into sin. See his Commentary on the Sentences, q. 3; cited by Graef, vol. 1, 282–283. Thus, a stress on purification at the incarnation does not necessarily imply a rejection of Mary's actual sinlessness.

87. Hesshusen, *Postilla* (1581), 94r: "Sintemal der heilige Geist / das blut Marie von Sünden gereiniget vnd geheiliget/ . . ."

88. Martin Chemnitz, *Postilla Oder Außlegung der Euangelien/ welche auff die Sontage/ vnd fürnembste Feste/ durchs gantze Jahr in der gemeine Gottes erkleret werden* (Magdeburg: Johann Francken, 1594), 115: "Sonst ist Maria ein Sünderin / gleich als wir / aber das Fleisch / das der HErr von jr angenommen / hat der heylige Geist gereiniget / das es reyn sey."

89. Keller, *Ain Sermon* (1525), c iijv ff.: "Darumb sollen wir nachfolgen jrem glauben / . . . das Cristus auch gaistlich empfangen werde in vnnser hertzen. . . . So dann das hertz durch den glawben in das wort gottes gerainiget ist."

90. Corvinus, *Kurtze vnd ainfeltige Außlegung . . . auff die Sonntage vnd fürnemesten Feste* (1545), 24r: "sy sich erstlich über der red des Engels entsatzte / vnd auch folgendes sich verwunderte [in text margin: Exempel des vnglaubens in Maria.] . . . Widerumb aber höret / das der hailige gaist / das alles außrichten solte / ergibt sy sich gütlich / vnd mit grosser demut / inn Gottes willen / vnd glaubet dem Engel / welchen Gott zu jr gesandt hette."

91. Ibid.: "Dann rechtschaffner glaub hat die art / wie inn Maria gesehen wirdt / das er glaubt dem wort / hanget am wort / bleibt bey dem wort / Vnd wann gleich dz jhenige so das wort sagt / der vernunfft vnbegreiflich ware / ja warumb haisset es sunst glaub / dann das er die ding so man nicht sehen / fülen / oder begreiffen kan / glauben soll?"

92. Leonhard Culmann, *Sacræ Contiones, ac variæ Prædicandorum Euangeliorum formulæ, descriptæ à Leonhardo Culmanno Craylshaimense, ac in tres tomos divisæ* (Nuremberg: Iohannis Montani & Ulrich Neuber, 1550), 116r–v: "Angelus reuocat Mariam ad fidem, ut credat uerbo . . . Maria iam edocta ab angelo obediens est, incipit nunc uerbo credere, humiliat se, parata est ad obedientiam, offert se uoluntati Dei."

93. Ibid., 124v: "Sed Zachariæ interrogatio ex dubitatione et curiositate nascitur. Mariæ non item."

94. Drach, *EJne Dreifaltige Predigt* (1550), B ijr: "Hat aber Maria die mutter Gottes eines Engels predigt durch welchen Gott selbs redet / aus jrem freien willen vnd eigen vermügen nicht verstehen noch glewben können: wie solten denn ich vnd du / aus vnserm freien willen vnd eigen vermügen / dem Euangelio glewben vnd darnach leben können."

95. Ibid., n.p.: "gleich wie Maria sobald Gottes mutter ward / als sie des Engels predigt glewbet vnd bekennet / das wir auch sobald Gottes kinder vnd erben werden / als wir gottes verheissunge von CHRISTO glewben vnd bekennen:"

96. Wigand, *Postilla* (1569), 68: "Solches konte sie mit der Vernunfft nicht fassen / Aber sie stehet auff Gottes Wort / vnd ist mit demselbigen wol zufrieden."

97. Heune, *Postilla* (1570), 104r: "Wer nu die Jungfraw Marien die selige Gottes Gebererin / recht ehren wil / der gleube GOTtes Wort vnd halte sich an Jhesum Christum / wie sie gethan hat / denn die gröste vnd höchste Weißheit ist / dem Wort Gottes gleuben / das fehlet vnd betreuget nicht / denn dreyerley Weißheit ist / ein Menschliche oder Weltweißheit / ein Teufflische / vnd ein Göttliche."

98. Vischer, *Außlegung der Euangelien . . . Vom Aduent bis auff Ostern* (1570), Rrr ijr: "Jedoch nimpt sie jre vernunfft gefangen / vntergibet sich dem gehorsam des Glaubens / weil sie höret / das bey Gott alle ding müglich [sind]."

99. Chemnitz, *Postilla* (1594), 119: "Bey Gott ist kein Ding kein Wort vnmüglich / etc. Derhalben wil ich seyn ein gehorsamer Knecht / eine demütige Magd / ich wil hie von nit disputiren / sondern gleuben / wie du es mir jm wort versprochen vnd zugesagt hast."

100. See for example, Veit Dietrich, *Kinder predig/ von fürnembsten Festen durch das gantze Jar/ gestelt durch Vitum Dietrich* (Nuremberg: Johann vom Berg und Ulrich Neuber, 1546), 61v: "Nun der Engel kombt gen Nazareth / vnd findet das Jungfrewlein Maria allein/ on zweyffel da sie bettet vmb den verheyssenen trost / den weybes samen / der dem Teuffel sein gewalt nemen / vnd das menschlich geschlecht wider soll zu recht bringen."

101. Huberinus, *Postilla Teutsch* (1548), 146v: "[Sie] ist heuslich vnnd eingezogen / da der Engel kombt zu jr hinein / nicht auff der gassen / oder beim tantze." *Häuslich* means both domesticated or home-loving, and economical and thrifty. In this context, I think the first meaning is more suitable.

102. Ibid., 146r–v: "So ist hie Maria ein schön lieblich exempel allen Junckfrawen / vnd Breuten / dann wie der Euangelist hie Mariam rhümet / vnd lobet / Also sollen auch die weibsbilder sonderlich solches bedencken / vnd nachfolgen / Dann zum ersten ist sie glaubig / dieweil sie sagt zum Engel / mir geschehe / wie du gesagt hast / Zum andern / so ist sie schamhafft / sie erschrickt / vnnd entsetzt sich ob dem Engel / ... Zum vierdten / so ist sie züchtig / rein/ vnd keusch / dann sie spricht / ich weiß von keinem Mann / Zum fünfften / so ist sie demütig / dann sie sagt zum Engel / Siehe / ich bin des HErren Magdt."

103. Vischer, *Außlegung der Euangelien ... Vom Aduent bis auff Ostern* (1570), n.p.: "GAr fein ist es / vnd ein schön Exempel vnd beyspiel / oder viel mehr ein artiger schöner Spiegel für alle Jungfrawen vnd Frawen / das der Engel Mariam nicht auff der gassen / in der Spinnstuben / auf der Kirmes vnter den jungen Gesellen / da sie am dicksten gestanden / nicht in Bier oder Weinheusern / angetroffen / sondern daheim in jrem Kemmerlein."

104. Ibid.: "Ehrliche Jungfrawen vnd Matronen sollen dem Exempel Marie folgen / nicht wild / frech vnd vnuerschampt sein / in allen Gelagen ligen / vnd die Gleser vmbstürtzen." The term *umstürzen* has the figurative meaning of "subvert" or "overthrow," and it is clear that Vischer categorizes this sort of female behavior as subversive of the proper social order.

105. Ibid.: "Für gewanderten Jungfrawen vnd vngewanderten Gesellen sol man sich hüten." This phrase is often repeated in sermons for the Visitation; see chapter 2.

106. As Lyndal Roper points out, however, the notion that a woman's work is contained within the house's walls does not at all match the reality that most women faced in the sixteenth century. Whether to obtain and sell household items, visit the markets, or in other occupations, women were required to travel the streets, as well as receive visitors within the home. See *The Holy Household: Women and Morals in Reformation Augsburg*, Oxford Studies in Social History (Oxford: Clarendon Press, 1989), 176–181. We know, especially through Luther's letters, that his wife, Katharina von Bora, was involved in a number of money-making activities, including owning distant property that she managed and occasionally visited.

107. Spindler, *Postilla* (1576), Pppp r: "wie es denn ehrlichen Matronen angeboren ist / das sie erschrecken / wenn sie ein ansehliger Man plötzlich anredet." Mary would also have been afraid if she recognized the man as an angel, for *von natur* heavenly visitors are always frightening to human beings.

2. THE VISITATION

1. NRSV, Luke 1:39–56.

2. Lansemann, 125. It was not recognized as a holiday in the Prussian (1525) or

the Württemberg (1553) *Kirchenordnungen*. In Mecklenburg and Pfalz-Zweibrücken it was celebrated as a half-day festival.

3. Ibid., 126–128.

4. Ibid., 126. Lansemann finds such polemic, above all, in Luther's writings, who especially complains that "Hoc festum a Papa institutum contra Turcas, ut sicut Maria per montana ivit, sic per Turcam pedibus eat et conterat" (Serm., July 1, 1529). The Visitation was first mentioned in the festival catalog of the council of Le Mans in 1247, and it became an official festival of the Franciscans in Pisa in 1263. It was declared a general festival of the church by Urban VI in 1389. See Delius, 166.

5. "Das Fest von der Hymelfart Marie ist durch auß Bäpstisch, das ist: vol Abgötterey unnd one grundt der Schrifft eingesetzt. Derhalben haben wirs in unsern Kirchen fallen lassen unnd den tag dazu behalten, das man die Histori predigen soll, wie Maria uber das Gebirg zu jrer Mumen Elisabeth gangen ist, und was sich da hab zu tragen." In both the Brandenburg and the Nuremberg ordinances, the Visitation was celebrated in the place of Mary's Assumption. See Luther, WA 52, *Hauspostille* 1544, 681. The celebration of the feast of the Assumption is far older than that of the Visitation: it was celebrated in the West on August 15 from the end of the eighth century, and on other dates before that time.

6. See Vischer, *Außlegung der Euangelien/ so man auff die Fest der Apostel/ vnd andere tage/ in der Christlichen Kirchen zuhandeln pfleget. Darinnen ein jedes Euangelium in drey/ bißweilen auch in vier predigten/ gefast ist/ . . .* (Leipzig: Hans Steinman,1575), Ooo ijr. Also see Simon Museaus, *Außlegung der Episteln vnd Euangelien vber gewönliche namhaffte Feste der heyligen Apostel/ Märtyrer vnd Zeugen Christi durchs gantze Jar* (Frankfurt: Nicolaus Bassæus, 1590), 108v.

7. Gerald Strauss, *Luther's House of Learning: Indoctrination of the Young in the German Reformation* (Baltimore: Johns Hopkins University Press,1978), 197. The Hamburg ordinances are from 1568.

8. See Merry E. Wiesner, *Women and Gender in Early Modern Europe*, 122. Wiesner is citing a 1552 ordinance for the girls' school in Mecklenburg.

9. Cornelia Niekus Moore, *The Maiden's Mirror: Reading Material for German Girls in the Sixteenth and Seventeenth Centuries*, Wolfenbütteler Forschungen, bd. 36 (Wiesbaden: Otto Harrassowitz,1987), 91. Porta's *Jungfrauspiegel* presents both biblical examples of young women and a treatise on marriage.

10. Luther, WA 17^2, *Festpostille* 1527, 457.

11. Ibid.: "Damit sind züruck gestossen alle stende und orden, die allein dahin gericht sind, yhnen selbs unnd nichtt andern zü helffen, oder darumb andern dienen unnd güts dienen, das sie darvon wöllen fromm werden."

12. Geiler also sounds this point in a Visitation sermon, along with praise of Mary's humility and her desire to serve others. He does suggest, however, that Mary "gained" or "earned" grace with her great humility: "do hat Maria die müter gotts genod erworben mitt irer grossen demüt" (*Postill* [1522], part 4, 8v).

13. Luther, WA 12, "Predigten des Jahres 1523" (first sermon in the 1527 postil), 609: "die vernunfft hat sy gantz geblendet, dann het sy sollen richten nach der vernunfft, so het sy gesagt 'ey sy kan kain kindt tragen, sy ist noch zu jung.' . . . [D]a lernet die natur des glaubens, das wol mag haissen 'Argumentum rerum non apparentium', das man das sehen sol, das man nit sicht, das hören das man nicht hört."

14. Ibid., 610: "Secht das seind die frücht des glaubens, also geets nach dem glauben, so sindt man sich geschickt im hertzen, wenn man glaubt."

15. Ibid., 612: "darumb ye tieffer du bist, ye geringer du bist, ye heller gottes augen auff dich sehen": Luther's argument against the contemporary usage of humility

is underscored by the popular writings of the nominalist theologian Gabriel Biel (d. 1495): while in the *Collectorium* Biel is careful not to stress any cooperation of Mary in Christ's incarnation, in his sermons the emphasis is instead on her humility, which leads to her special election. Heiko Oberman writes of Biel's sermons that "[Mary] serves as such an inspiring example that everyone who becomes as humble as she may count on God's grace: *facientibus quod in se est deus non denegat gratiam!*" See Oberman, *The Harvest of Medieval Theology*, 301.

16. Luther, *Festpostille* 1527, 461: "das ein mensch wisse, dz er nichts sey und got alle ding sey, von sich nichts halte und von got alles."

17. Ibid., 460: "Wenn das wort einem für die oren kompt, ist anders ein fromm hertz da und das da nach fryde dürstet, da gehet der heilige geist mit ein. Der macht dyß wort im hertzen krefftig und leret Christum recht erkenen, da müß denn züboden geen alle menschliche vernunfft, sinn, witz und verstandt." In fact, Mary's greeting to Elizabeth is not recorded in Luke's gospel. However, Geiler also surmises that this was likely what Mary said (*Postill* [1522], 9v).

18. Luther, *Festpostille* 1527, 460: "gleich wie ein rhor, durch welchs der hailig geyst einfleust und in unsere hertzen kompt. Darumb spricht Sanct Paul zun Galatern, das sy den heyligen geist empfangen haben nicht durch die werke des gesetzs, sondern durch die predige des glaubens [Gal. 3:2]. . . . Auß dem folget, das die nerrisch thun, ja widder Gottes ordnung und eynsetzung, die das eusserliche wort verachten und verwerffen, mainen, der hailig geyst unnd der glawb soll on mittel zü jn kommen, . . . das Got sein heiligen geist on das eusserlich wort nicht geben wil."

19. Ambrose, *Expositio Evangelii secundum Lucam II*, 21 (*Patrologia Latina* 15, 1560): "Discite, virgines, non circumcursare per alienas aedes, non demorari in plateis, non aliquos in publico miscere sermones. Maria in domo seria, festina in publico, mansit apud cognatam suam tribus mensibus." See Luther's "Predigt am Tage der Heimsuchung Mariä in der Schloßkirche," WA 59, 227, fn. 5. (My thanks to Timothy Wengert for this citation.) Geiler suggests that Mary hurried, because those with the spirit always do, unlike "today's virgins," who are easily distracted by men: "Darumb so gieng sye mit ylen. Nitt machet sye stenderling bey den münchen vnd pfaffen/ als vnser jungkfrawen thünd" (*Postill* [1522], 8v).

20. See Luther's 1523 sermon in WA 12, especially p. 610, 11–14 (above) and 4–8 (below): "Arbitror non bene translatum 'cum festinatione', sed Lucas vult indicare ein erbars zeuchtig gebehren virginis, . . . Dicimus 'zeuchtig' u[sw]." In a sermon from 1539 (WA 47, 827–828), Luther provides an explanation for the term *endelich*: "i.e., als ein zuchtigs, feins, reins meidlin und hat den hinder fus nicht lassen stehen."

21. Ibid., 610 (above), 14–16: "und hat sich dannocht so fein eingezogen gehalten unnd zichtig auff dem weg mit dem geberd, das man kain böß exempel von ir nemen möcht."

22. Ibid., (below) lines 7–8: "Exemplo erit omnibus mulieribus et virginibus, zeuchtig mit augen, oren, gebehren u[sw]."

23. Luther, WA 17^2, *Festpostille* 1527, 458: "Weliches der heylige Geist, sonder zweyffel, also hatt schreiben lassenn, anzüzeigen, wie die weybes personen auff der gassen unnd zü strasse züchtig sein sollen unnd niemants ergernus geben mit unzüchtigen geperden."

24. Ibid., 458–459: "Denn das ist der weiber bestes kleinod unnd zierde, eyn züchtigs leben und erbarlichs geperde, Wenn sie den schatz verlieren, so ist es auß mit jn." Similar sentiments can be found in the writings of humanist educators: Juan Luis Vives, in his famous *Instruction of a Christian Woman*, suggests that all the virtues of a Christian woman are summarized under the term "chastity," for she that is

chaste is "fair, well-favored, rich, fruitful, noble, and all best things that can be named, and contrary, she that is unchaste is a sea and treasure of all [ev]ilness" (90). This text, along with others on the education of women, can be found in *Vives and the Renascence Education of Women*, ed. Foster Watson (New York: Longmans, Green, 1912).

25. Luther, WA 17², *Festpostille* 1527, 459: "So ist es doch nit ungleublich, das endtweder Joseph oder ye eine magd mit jr gangen ist, denn es were weiblicher zucht ungemeß, allein uber land zü raisen." Geiler, who claims Bonaventure as his authority in this point, also believes that Joseph accompanied Mary and remained with her (*Postill* [1522], 8v).

26. WA 52, *Hauspostille* 1544, 682–683: "[Lucas] das liebe Junckfrewlin uns allen, sonderlich aber dem Weyber volck, so schön fürmalet in einem krantz, der mit dreyen sonder schönen unnd lieblichen Rosen geschmucket ist. Denn da rhümet er drey sonderliche tugent, deren wir uns auch fleyssen sollen. Die Erste ist der glaub, Die ander ein seer grosse, hohe demut, Die dritte feine unnd züchtige geberde für den leuten." For information on the history of the rose-garland image, see Winston-Allen, *Stories of the Rose*.

27. Luther, WA 52, *Hauspostille* 1544, 683: "Und sonderlich das Weyber volck sich lieber in der Kirchen, bey dem gebett und an der Predig finden lassen denn bey dem Tantz, am Marckt oder anderßwo."

28. Ibid., 685.

29. Ibid., 686: "Die dritte tugent ist, das Lucas sagt, sie sey endelich gangen, das ist: fein züchtig und nicht so auß fürwitz und leichtfertig, wie das jung gesind in die milch, um tantz unnd auff die Kirchweyhe gehet, von einem hauß um andern wescht und allenthalb klapper bencklin auffschlegt und die augen dahin und dorthin wirfft. Das heyssen nicht züchtige Junckfrawen, sonder luder paner [Faulenzerinnen, ed.] Junckfrawen aber und Frawen sollen in jren hewsern bleyben und auff der gassen fein endelich von statten gehen."

30. Ibid.: "Warumb solte ich stets daheym bleyben, wie ein Nonn im Kloster, und nit auch spatzirn gehen, hats doch die Junckfrau Maria thun?"

31. This type of moral commentary is common in sixteenth-century literature, especially in humanist educational material, and was common in earlier literature and sermons as well. Ton Brandenbarg cites two late fifteenth-century lives of St. Anne by Jan van Denemarken, a cleric from the Netherlands, that despite their many other differences from Luther's sermons, sound similar themes in relation to the connection between religious virtues (proper faith, knowledge of Christian doctrine) and good manners, decency, modesty, and chastity (see Brandenbarg, "St Anne and Her Family," 110–111). The morality lessons that Luther draws from Mary's example are echoed at length in Vives's *Instruction of a Christian Woman*, who uses Mary and other Christian virgins as examples for the proper rearing, dress, and behavior of young women.

32. Luther, WA 52, *Hauspostille* 1544, 686: "Mit worten sinds frech und grob, mit geberden unzüchtig, schreyen und toben, als werens thöricht, das heysset denn guter ding sein."

33. Ibid., 687: "weder zucht noch ehr mer bleibet, wie wirs leyder zu unsern zeyten auch sehen, Und derhalb der verdienten straff mit gewarten müssen."

34. Ibid., 688: "Solche tugent sinds wert, das mans auff einen sondern Feyertage, sonderlichen dem jungen volck, fürhalte, auff das yederman lerne from und Gottförchtig sein, unnd sonderlich das Weyber volck sich inn aller zucht, erbarkeyt und demut lerne halten."

35. "The Magnificat," LW 21, 298; also in WA 7, 544.

36. Gerhard Müller points out that "in his interpretation, Luther was not particularly interested in Mary, as the author of the hymn; nor was he primarily concerned here with God's son, whose mother Mary was; his attention was focused instead on God himself." See his "Protestant Veneration of Mary: Luther's Interpretation of the *Magnificat,*"in *Humanism and Reform: The Church in Europe, England, and Scotland, 1400–1643: Essays in Honour of James K. Cameron,* ed. James Kirk, Studies in Church History, subsidia; 8 (Oxford: Basil Blackwell, 1991): 101.

37. LW 21, 301; WA 7, 548–549.

38. LW 21, 308; WA 7, 555: "nit mehr denn ein frolich herberg und willige wirttinn solchs gasts geweszen."

39. LW 21, 309; WA 7, 556: "Aber disz herz Marie steet fest und gleich ynn aller zeit."

40. LW 21, 311; WA 7, 558.

41. LW 21, 321–322; WA 7, 567–568. We find Geiler's suggestions for commemorating this day and honoring Mary quite different: "Neyg dich vor irem bild / oder kneuw daruor / vnd rüff sye an / oder gibe eim armen menschen ein almüßen vmb ir eer willen / Das ist geert Mariam die müter gotts vnd ir müm Elisabeth" (*Postill* [1522], 10v).

42. LW 21, 326; WA 7, 572.

43. LW 21, 327; WA 7, 573.

44. Ibid. Delius remarks in this context, "Der Glaube sucht bei ihr ein Beispiel, der Aberglaube Hilfe." See his discussion of these texts, pp. 211–214.

45. LW 21, 329; WA 7, 575: "Anruffen sol man sie, das got durch yhren willen gebe und thu, was wir bitten, also auch alle andere heyligen antzuruffen sind, das das werck yhe gantz allein gottis bleybe."

46. WA 12, 611: "Aber das ist die recht rainigkait oder junckfrawschafft Marie, das sy allain auff dem herren steet und preyst [perhaps *breyst*; see editor's note 2]."

47. Ibid., 613: "in wem man sy preysen sol: nicht mit vil Salve regina antissen? nain, sunder so. . . . 'Ey das ist also ein grosse gnad, das got das arm maydlein so gnedig hat angesehen und so vil gethan, das ers zu seiner mutter macht.' "

48. WA 52, *Hauspostille* 1544, 689: "Aber mit was verstandt der Bapste, seine Pfaffen, München unnd Nonnen es singen, sehen wir leyder vor augen, das sie nicht einen buchstaben davon verstehen, sonst würden sie sich für der grewlichen Abgötterey hütten."

49. Ibid., 692.

50. Ibid., 691: "die groß Doctorin und Prophetin, die gelerter ist denn alle Apostel und Propheten"; 693: "die liebe Doctorin, das sie seer wenig Schuler werde finden"; 696: "So müssen wir bekennen, das sie ein sondere Meysterin sey, die von hohen sachen wol reden könne"; 698: "das liebe Junckfrewlin mit jrem Exempel und predigt uns vorgehet, das wir nicht hoffertig sein, sonder uns demüttigen und inn aller zucht halten sollen."

51. Brenz, *Pericopæ . . . qvæ Usitato More in præcipuis Festis legi solent* (1557), 1201: "Nec sit maior opportunitas, commoditas, utilitas et neceßitas orandi, quàm cum sumus miserrimi et contemptißimi."

52. Ibid., 1203: "Sed præcipuè [beneficia] spiritualia et æterna. Sicut habes exemplum Mariæ. . . . Non collocat eam in throno regio huius mu[n]di, Sed collocat eam in supremo loco Ecclesiæ inter mulieres, et in cœlesti regno etc."

53. Corvinus, *Kurtze vnd ainfeltige Außlegung . . . auff die Sonntage vnd fürnemesten Feste* (1545), 41: "das rechtschaffner glaub / on folgende wreck / sunderlich damit

dem nächsten gedienet wirdt / nit sein kan / Dan[n] dieweil der glaub Gotes / ver-
haissung ergreifft / vnd wolthat erkennet / vnd derhalben ain hitzig / lebendig / vn[d]
brennend ding im hertzen ist / kan oder mag er nicht verborgen sein."

54. Huberinus, *Postilla/ Deudsch/ Vber alle Fest/ vnd gemeine feyertag/ der Heyligen durchs gantze Jar/ kurtze vnd nutzliche außlegung* (Frankfurt an der Oder: Johannes
Eichorn, 1554), 235r–v: "haben wir hie ein treffentlichs exempel eines waren rechtschaffenen glaubens in Maria / wie der rechte glaub nicht ruhen vnd feyern kan /
sondern bricht von stund an herauß / auß den hertzen / in den mundt / vnnd öffen-
tliche that / dann so bald Maria dem wort des Engels glaubt / feyert sie nit / sonder
machet sich bald vnd eylents auff / vnd schafft nutz / vnd theilet solche erkentnuß
vnnd freud / auch andern mit / dann das ist rechten glaubens art / vnnd eygen-
schafft. . . . Dann ein Christ soll ja sich zu frommen Gottsförchtigen / vrstendigen
leuten begeben."

55. Ibid., 236r: "so grüsset Maria / jre mummen Elisabeth / das ist auch ein
feine demut / vnd art des glaubens / dz wir grußbar vnd dienstbar sein / sich ein
Christ gegen dem andern herunder lasse / vnnd sich demütige mit ehrerbitung /
Rom. 12."

56. Leonhard Culmann, *Sacræ Contiones* (1550), 138v: "Discimus ergo exemplo
Mariæ, nos vicißim gratos Deo ostendere, pro gratuita Dei misericordia, et hæc grati-
tudo est effect[us] fidei, quæ ociosa [odiosa?] esse non potest."

57. Hieronymus Weller, *Altera Pars Annotationvm D. Hieronymi Vvelleri, in Epistolas et Euangelia Dominicalia, quæ à Dominica Trinitatis usque ad finem anni in Ecclesia præleguntur. His Adiectae Sunt Etiam Explicationes Epistolarum & Euangeliorum,
quæ in festis Diuorum legi solent* (Leipzig: Valentin Papae, 1560), 590: "Deinde, ut
dulcißimum illud ac eruditißimum canticum Mariæ in Ecclesia enarretur."

58. Ibid., 590–591: "Postremo, ut exempla fidei, humilitatis et pudicitiæ, in beata
virgine Maria populo proponantur, ut omnes omnium ætatum homines illius pietatem ac uirtutem imitentur."

59. Georg Steinhart, *Ehren Kron/ vnnd Schmuck Christliches Frawenzimmers/ nach
einfeltiger Außlegunge vber das Euangelion/ welchs auff den tag Marie heimsuchung/ in
der Kirchen pflegt gehandelt zu werden/ Luc.1. zusamen gtragen durch Georgium Steinhart*
(Frankfurt: Nicolaus Bassee, 1568), B 2r: "Sondern bringt sie mit einem feinen schönen wolriechenden Ehrenkrentzlein / von dreyerley Blümlein / windtschaffen gemacht / herfür / vnnd setzt jhr dassebige auff das häupt oder stirnen."

60. Ibid., B 2v: "das alle Christen vnd Ehrliebende menschen / jhrem Exempel
nachfolgen möchten."

61. Ibid., C 2r: "Sonderlichen aber / sollen diesem exempel der demut folgen /
das weibsvolck / so etwas von natur zu hoffart gneigter ist / vnnd solches von jhrer
ersten Mutter Heua ererbet."

62. Ibid., between C 5 and D: "Dann es zumal vbel stehet / vn[d] Weibesvolck
wenig ziert entweder auff der gassen gar langsam / als ob man auff nadeln gieng /
. . . oder wie ein hambster lauffen / vnnd die augen gar frech vmb sich hin vnd wid-
erwerffen."

63. Vischer, *Außlegung der Euangelien . . . auff die Fest der Apostel* (1575), after Rrr:
"Das aber Maria nicht in ein Kloster oder in eine wüsten leufft / haus / hoff / vnd jr
eigenthumb verlesset / wie die Widerteuffer / sondern wider heim in jr haus keret /
jres beruffs vnd ampts . . . denn es leret vns / das ein Christ mit gutem frölichen gewissen Gott daheim in deinem hause dienen / angenem vnd gefellig sein kan."

64. Simon Pauli, *Postilla* (1573), 169v: "Meinstu / das du besser seist / denn ein
ander? Pfui dich an / mit deiner schendlichen hoffart / vnd grobem Bawrstoltz.

Christen aber sollen gern grüssen / vnd wenn sie gegrüsset warden / sollen sie
gerne antworten." It is an example of *Bürgerlichen Zucht* to greet one another. Several other sermons (e.g., those by Johann Spangenberg and Joachim Mörlin) mention
the importance of greeting one another, tying it to the maintenance of peaceful coex-
istence.

65. Hemmingsen, *Postilla* (1571), 52–53: "Auff das wir Exempel hetten / der
busse / vnd der barmhertzigkeit Gottes / . . . Darnach das wir jnen in jrem glauben
nachfolgen . . . Vber das / das wir jrem wandel vnd guten sitten nachfolgen."

66. Ibid., 61: "[D]as wir nach dem Exempel der Jungfrawen / dem wort Gottes
gleuben sollen / ob gleich die gantze natur vnd alle Creaturen vns des widerspiels
bereden wollen."

67. Ibid., 64: "AVs dem Exempel Marie sollen wir dis lernen. 1. Vnser elende
vnd nichtigkeit erkennen/ vnd vns in warer busse fur Gott beugen vnd demütigen. 2.
Die wolthaten Gottes gegen vns erkennen. 3. Gott rhümen vnd loben von wegen
seiner wolthaten. 4. Ander Leut durch vnser Exempel zur danckbarkeit reitzen."

68. Luther himself uses this example in several of his early sermons, but it does
not appear in his postil sermons. See "Predigt am Tage der Heimsuchung Mariä"
from 1520 (WA 59, 227–228): "Festinantes itaque, quod pudicarum argumentum est,
domos repetent nec tardiuscule domuitiones capessent. 'Dina filia Jacob egressa, ut
videret mulieres regionis illius,' [et] conspecta a Sichem filio Emor. Materiam prebuit
illiciti incendii in ipsam rapuitque ac vi stupravit. Unde tandem cedes aperta magna
fuit." As the editor of this sermon points out (fn. 5), the opposition of Mary and Dinah is not made by medieval authors such as Thomas Aquinas or Nicholas of Lyra.
For a comparison of Luther's interpretation of the story of Dinah's rape with that of
medieval and patristic interpreters, see Joy A. Schroeder, "The Rape of Dinah: Luther's Interpretation of a Biblical Narrative," *Sixteenth Century Journal* 28 (Fall 1997):
775–791.

69. Corvinus, *Kurtze vnd ainfeltige Außlegung . . . auff die Sonntage vnd fürnemesten Feste* (1545), 41: "Spüret man aber auch, in jrem geen / vnzucht oder leichtfertig-
kait / wie yetz in der jugent vnd junckfrawen vnser zeit / gespürt wirdt? Nain / sun-
det zy geet eylends / vnd endlich / grüsset nyemand / schwetzet mit nyemandt /
sihet sich nit vil vmb / sunder gedenckt nur wie sy zur Elisabeth kommen. . . . Vnd
wann im Alten Testament Jacobs tochter / Dina genannt / mit solcher zucht / erbarkait / vnd gamut / gen Sichem gangen ware / die weiber des Lands zübesehen /
hette sy behalten jr eer vnd Junckfrawschafft."

70. Johannes Mathesius reprimands foolish young women for taking their "Din-
ische spaciergenge," which contradict Mary's example of pious and God-fearing
travel. See his *Außlegung der Euangelien/ von den fürnembsten Festen/ Vom Aduent biß
auff Ostern* (Nuremberg: J. von Bergs Erben & Dietrich Gerlach, 1571), 90v.

71. Huberinus, *Postilla/ Deudsch* (1554), 242r–v: "Da haben nun alle fromme
frawen vnd Junckfrawen einen sondern trost / wo sie von den falschen zungen /
vnnd auß falschen argwon werden verunglimpfft / vnd an jren ehren felschlich
geschmehet / das Gott im Himel auff sie sihet / jr ehr zu letzt rettet / bewaret / vnd
offenbar machete." Huberinus also sets Joseph forth as a good example to bride-
grooms.

72. Culmann, *Sacræ Contiones* (1550), 139r–v: "Et sic docet post susceptum Euangelium uocationem non esse deserendam, et discurrendum esse in orbe, sine certis
sedib[us] et proprijs bonis, relictis parentibus, liberis, coniugibus, consanguineis, ami-
cis."

73. Ibid., 145r: "Virginibus exemplum proponitur in Maria, ne crebro in publico

uersentur, sed ijs se iungant, ex quibus meliores fiunt, discant impendere senioribus honorem, te uerecundiam complecti, sinaque humanæ et officiosæ."

74. Weller, *Altera Pars* (1560), 591: "Atque ita uult Euangelista illustri isto exemplo Mariæ, omnes homines, præcipuè verò sexum fœmineum, ad pudicitiam et integritatem morum inuitare. Nihil enim post pietatem magis commendat hunc sexum, quàm pudicitia."

75. Steinhart, *Ehren Kron/ vnnd Schmuck* (1568), between C 5 and D: "dann wie dass sprichwort heisset / so erkennet man den Vogel an den federn vnd gesange / vnnd den menschen am gesicht vnd gange."

76. Vischer, *Außlegung der Euangelien . . . auff die Fest der Apostel* (1575), between Nnn iijv and Ooo v: "wie offt vnsere Jungfrawen alle kirchmessen / tentze vnd gelag durchstören / vnd vngeacht deß das sie wollen Jungfrawen sein vnd dafür gehalten warden / leichtfertig vnd fürwitzig gar gnug sein."

77. Ibid.: "man sol sich für gewanderten Jungfrawen / vnd vngewanderten Gesellen hüten vnd vorsehen."

78. Ibid., Ppp iir–iijv: "Ihr Jungfrawen lernet von der außerwelten genedeyten Jungfrawen / was jr für lieder singen solt / nicht schampare leichtfertige Buellieder / damit jr den heiligen Geist betrübt vnd von euch jaget / der ein geist der keuscheit vnd reinigkeit ist . . . es stehet Jungfrawen trefflich wol an / wenn sie wenig redden / viel plapperns / waschens vnd redens verstellet ein Weibsbild ausdermassen sehr / wie man sagt: Weiber sein aus der riebe gemacht / darumb klappern sie so."

79. Georg Walther, *Auslegung Der Euangelien so auff die Feiertage vnd furnemeste Feste gelesen werden. Das Dritte Teil* (Wittenberg: Hans Lufft, 1579), 655: "SOlches stehet Gottseligen Jungfrawen nicht zu / denn so schreibet Paulus das sie Custodes Domus / das ist / Hüter des Hauses sein sollen / vnd nicht one sonderliche vrsache viel ausser dem Hause sein / sondern viel mehr jrer Haushaltung warten / die darüber sonst verseumet wird."

80. For example, Simon Pauli, *Postilla* (1573), 167r: "Denn wie eine Schnecke jhr Haus allezeit mit sich tregt / also sollen erbare vnd züchtige Frawen vn[d] Jungfrawen in jren Heusern bleiben / vnd nicht spacieren gehen / wie Dina thut / vnd darüber jre Ehre verschertzet."

81. Brenz, *Pericopæ . . . qvæ Usitato More in præcipuis Festis legi solent* (1557), 1198: "Itaq; neq; Sol neq; cœlestis curia unquàm uidit sanctiorem et excellentiorem conuentum, quàm fuerit hic conuentus in domo Zachariæ."

82. Ibid., 1199: "Itaq; cum non haberent, nec Zacharias, nec Maria aliquam autoritatem emittendi publicos legatos, componit Maria publicam carme[n], quo testatur et suam gratitudinem et ueritatem promißionum Dei, quòd quæ de Christo promissa sunt, iam impleri incipiant."

83. Pauli, *Postilla* (1573), 172v: "Dieweil das Weib am ersten gesundiget / so halten auch die weiber den ersten Synodum des newen Testaments / . . . Es ist dieser Synodus ein gezeugnis / das die Kirche sey ein gering vnd verachtet heufflin/ für der Welt . . ." On the other hand, Paul Eber insists that Zechariah is the foremost authority present at the council, and would be the one providing scriptural counsel: "Diese vnd dergleichen Prophecey / wirt der liebe Zacharias jnen schrifftlich haben außgelegt. Daß also Zacharias / der fürnembsten Person eine ist gewesen bey diesem Synodo." See Paul Eber, *Postilla/ Das ist/ Außlegung der Sonntags vnd fürnembsten Fest Euangelien durch das gantze Jar. . . .* (Frankfurt: Franciscus Basseus, 1578), 71v.

84. Veit Dietrich, *Kinderpredig* (1546), 97v: "ein schöne predig/ inn welcher die Junckfraw Maria vns lehret/ wie wir zu Gottes gnaden mögen kommen."

85. Huberinus, *Postilla/ Deudsch* (1554), 237v: "[es] kan ein Theologische disputa-

tion / vnd gelertes gesprech sein / der Junckfrawen Marie / vnnd der alten frawen Elisabeth / welche beide nicht allein innn jhrem leib schwanger gehen / mit leiblicher frucht / sondern gehen auch Schwanger im glauben / vnd Geist / mit Geistlicher frucht / das seindt rechte gute wreck / von Got gebotten / Exodi 20."

86. Steinhart, *Ehren Kron/ vnnd Schmuck* (1568), B 5r: "Es beschreibet aber der Euangelist nicht allein den glauben der Junckfrawen Marien / sondern wil auch hiemit anzeygen / wie sie zu solchem Glauben kommen sey / nemlich / durch das mündtliche Wort / das jhr durch den Engel verkündiget ist."

87. Ibid., between B 5 and C: "Derhalben sollen wir vns mit allem fleiß vnd andacht / zu dem mündlichen Predigampt vnd Wort Gottes halten / dieweil wir solche schetze hierinnen finden / vnd vns die Enthusiasten vnd Widertäuffer / nicht lassen jrren / die da das mündtlich Wort verwerffen."

88. However, some authors also suggest that Mary was a great reader of Scripture, and this behavior should be emulated—see Johannes Mathesius, *Außlegung der Euangelien/ von den fürnembsten Festen* (1571), 96v.

89. Wigand, *Postilla* (1569), 103–104: "[Sie] hat wöllen halten vn[d] gesellen / zu der recht[n] waren Kirchen vnd Schule[n] / in welcher sie beyde möchte hören vnd lernen / vnd denn auch anzeigen vnd leren / was sie vom Engel gehöret vn[d] gelernet hatte. . . . Auch ist kein zweiffel / Maria wird völligern Bericht vnd Lere von solchen hohen dingen / begeret vnd gefraget haben / welche desmals geschahen / denn Vernunfft kan das nicht fassen."

90. Ibid., 108: "Zum fünfften sol man von Gottseligen Versamlungen lernen / das Frome vnd Gottsfürchtige Leute / zusamen gehen vnd komen sollen / vnd von Gottes Wort miteinander sprach halten."

91. Vischer, *Außlegung der Euangelien . . . auff die Fest der Apostel* (1575), Nnn iijr: "Elisabeth ist die erste Menschen stimme / die erste Predigerin / die von dem herrlichen großmechtigen gnadenschatz redet vnd predigest."

92. Ibid., Nnn iijv: "So ist auch dieser Synodus oder zusammen kunfft der aller erste im newen Testament / darnach alle Concilia / Synodi / Gesprech vnd Versamlungen / so von der Religion handeln / als nach einem compast / angestellet werden sollen vnd müssen / das ist ein rechte grund gute form / muster vnd weise einees Concilij / Zacharias / Elisabeth vnd Maria / sonder zweiffel auch Simeon / Anna vnd andere Christen sind da beysammen. . . . Die colloquenten sind Maria / Elisabeth / Johannes / die Weiber haben hie auch vocem decisiuam, einen machtspruch."

93. Mathesius, *Außlegung der Euangelien/ von den fürnembsten Festen* (1571), 93v: "Denn inn diser aller heiligsten versamlung/ presidiret der recht Legatus a latere, der ewige Sone Gottes."

94. Brenz, *Pericopæ . . . qvæ Usitato More in præcipuis Festis legi solent* (1557), 1190: "Tam etsi enim Maria non sit functa publico ministerio prædicandi Euangelij in Ecclesia, nec sit uel ad Iudæos uel ad gentes ad reuelandum prædicatione sua Christum quemadmodum Apostoli, missa, Ecclesia tamen suas easque maximas utilitates ex Maria accepit."

95. Ibid., 1192–1193: "quòd ipsa sit mater corporalis Christi . . . Et Matth. 12 manifestè docet aliam ess[e] [r]ationem regni sui, quàm ut externæ uel maternitatis, uel fraternitatis, uel etiam filiationis, ut ita loquar, respectus habeatur."

96. Ibid., 1194: "Deinde Maria exhibuit toti Ecclesiæ pulcherrimum exemplum fidei, per quam fidem contingit credenti iustificatio."

97. Ibid., 1196: "Hoc certè excellentius opus est, quàm si fundasset centum monasteria in Iudæa. Nam hæc et si fortaßis piè fuissent instituta, tamen fuissent à Barbaris uastata, Illud autem carmen durabit usq; in finem seculi."

98. Ibid., 1200: "Alij humilitatem hoc loco pro uirtute interpreta[n]tur, sed errant, Maria non est gloriata de sua uirtute aut iusticia, aut meritis coram Deo. Sed humilitas hoc loco significat miseriam, afflictionem, contemptum et abiectionem."

99. See the example of Biel cited by Oberman, 301–302.

100. Corvinus, *Kurtze vnd ainfeltige Außlegung . . . auff die Sonntage vnd fürnemesten Feste* (1545), 41r: "Man laß Glauben / glauben / und wreck / werck sein / das nit ains inn das annder vermengt werde / sunst wurde man auß der frucht ain baum / vnd auß dem baum die frucht machen / wider die leere des Euangelij."

101. Ibid., 41v: "Allain dauor müß man sich hüten / das wir sy nicht anrüffen / an betten / zü Fürsprechen vnd Aduocaten machen / so vns vor Got fürbitten vnd vertretten müssen dann sollichs gehört allain Got zü / wie Sanct Pauls leert."

102. Greser, *Enarratio Brevis et Orthodoxa* (1567), 643: "Sic credendo omnes erimus matres, sorores, et fratres Christi, ut epse Christus dicit, Matth. 12."

103. Huberinus, *Postilla/ Deudsch* (1554), 240r–v: "das were nuhn jhr rechte eher / wann wir sie also selig preyseten / vnnd sie also vns zum Exempel fürstelleten / da würden wir vil mer dardurch gebesseret / dann wann wir sie lang anbeten vnnd anruffen / ohn alle grundt heiliger Schrifft / vnnd ohn alle Exempel / der alten kirchen / der heiligen / gehöret jhr gebürende her / vnd Gott dem HERren / gebüret zur seine eigentliche her / auff das wir nicht vier Personen in der Gottheit anbeten / vnnd anrüffen / wider das erste Gebot / Exod. am 20."

104. Walther, *Auslegung Der Euangelien . . . auff die Feiertage* (1579), 674: "DAraus wir erstlich erkennen / die grosse blindheit der Papisten / welche die Jungfraw Maria gar zu hoch erheben / vnd furgeben / die sey gar one Sünde gewesen / denn wo dem also gewesen / so würde nicht Elisabeth durch den heiligen Geist sagen / das sie durch den glauben selig worden were."

105. Dietrich, *Kinderpredig* (1546), CIv–CIIr: "Zu Hierusalem bey den Juden / thettens die Hohen priester Annas / Caiphas / der könig Herodes / der landrichter Pilatus / die alle treffliche leut / in sonderm ansehen vnd wirden waren. Also heutiges tages ists der Babst / die Cardinel / Bischoffe / Könige / vnd andere grosse Herrn / Die hohen schulen / Doctores / Pfaffen / Münch / die sind dem Euangelio am feyndesten." In his sermon on the Magnificat, Georg Major also stresses that God uses his "arm" and power to defeat not only the devil but also the pope and his followers, as well as sects and heretics. See his *Drey güldene Kleinot des newen Testaments. 1. Das Magnificat Marie. 2. Das Benedictus Zacharie. 3. Das Nunc Dimittis Simeonis* (Wittenberg: Hans Lufft, 1566), [43–79].

106. Simon Pauli, *Postilla* (1573), 164r: "DEr Babst hat dis Fest / darumb verordnet vnd eingesetzt / das man die Jungfraw Mariam wider de[n] Türcken anruffen sol. Denn gleich wie die Jungfraw Maria vber die Berge gegangen / vnd dieselben mit jren füssen zutreten hat / Also solle man sie anruffen / (wil der Babst) das sie mit denselb[n] füssen den Türcken / auch vnter sich trete[n] wolle."

107. Vischer, *Außlegung der Euangelien . . . auff die Fest der Apostel* (1575), Nnn iijr–Qqq ijr: "Aber solche abgötterey vnd Gotteslesterung / der anruffung der verstorbenen Heiligen / habt jr oben am tage Andree aus Gottes Wort gründlich hören widerlegen . . . Sie sagt nicht / man wird mich anbeten für eine Himmelskönigin / Nothelfferin vnd Mitlerin achten / denn solche ehre stehet meinem lieben Kinde allein zu."

108. Pauli, *Postilla* (1573), 164v: "Denn je mehr man Marien im Babstumb wider den Türcken angerunffen/ vnd des rechten nothelffers/ Schlangen vnd Türcken tretters Jesu Christi darüber vergessen hat/ je mehr der Türcke vns getretten/ vn[d] an macht vnd gewalt grösser geworden ist."

109. Bernard of Clairvaux [1090–1153] writes in his Annunciation sermons: "You are told that [Mary] is a virgin. You are told that she is humble. If you are not able to imitate the virginity of this humble maid, then imitate the humility of the virgin maid. Virginity is a praiseworthy virtue, but humility is by far the more necessary. The one is only counselled; the other is demanded." See his *Homilies in Praise of the Blessed Virgin Mary*, 9.

110. As David Wright explains, in Luther's view "Mary [is] an example and no longer an exception—an example both of God's initiative . . . and of human response in humble trust." See his essay in *Chosen by God*, 166.

111. Even if one holds strictly to the doctrine of the immaculate conception, which Luther apparently did not always do, her preservation from sin and its stain is a gift, and not therefore her own doing.

3. THE PURIFICATION OF MARY

1. Lansemann, 131.

2. Graef, vol. 1, 142.

3. It is interesting, however, that iconographic representations from the medieval period usually focus upon Christ and Simeon, rather than Mary. As Susan Karant-Nunn points out, "The artists who created such images did not take as one of their purposes to relate the biblical episode either to the medieval manner of observing Candlemas or to the ceremony that by the fifteenth century parturient women throughout Europe underwent." See "A Women's Rite: Churching and the Reformation of Ritual," in R. Po-Chia Hsia and R.W. Scribner, eds., *Problems in the Historical Anthropology of Early Modern Europe*, Wolfenbütteler Forschungen (Herzog August Bibliothek), Band 78 (Wiesbaden: Harrassowitz, 1997), 114.

4. Ibid., 115. Geiler suggests that Pope Gregory wanted to transform the pagan practice of *Liechtmeß* by allowing the candlelit processions to continue, but instead to honor Mary by this custom. Mary deserved such honor, for she "die gnad vnd barmhertzigkeit allen seelen vnd menschen erwirbet." See Geiler, *Das euangeli buch* (1515), 158r.

5. Lansemann, 131.

6. Bodo Nischan discusses Lutheran defenses of maintaining traditions such as the church calendar with numerous festivals and traditional readings against Calvinist critics: the Saxon pastor Balthasar Meisner (1587–1626) says of the pericopes, "[J]ust because they originated in the old church, it does not follow that they must be eliminated for in and by themselves they provide a useful order." Cited in Nischan, "Demarcating Boundaries": 204 and fn. 24. Although the sermons used in this study do not dwell upon criticism of the reformed, but rather are concerned with debunking "papist" dogma and practice, the citation is relevant. Such traditions were maintained for a reason.

7. Karant-Nunn, "A Women's Rite," 112. See also Robert W. Scribner, "The Impact of the Reformation on Daily Life," in *Mensch und Objekt im Mittelalter und in der frühen Neuzeit: Leben—Alltag—Kultur* (Vienna: Österreichischen Akademie der Wissenschaften, 1990), 315–344.

8. Karant-Nunn, "A Women's Rite," 117–118.

9. Ibid., 118–121.

10. Ibid., 124–125.

11. Luther, "Purificationis Marie Oder am Liechtmessen Fest," *Hauspostille* 1544, WA 52, 148–149: "Solches gebot hat der Bapst vnsern Kindelbetterin auch auffgelegt,

das sie nach dem Kindelbett sich für der Kirche haben müssen einsegnen lassen, Als weren sie unrein und dorfften sonst nicht in die Kirch oder unter die leut gehen. Aber es ist unrecht."

12. Luther, "Die Ander Predigt, Vom alten Simeon im Tempel," WA 52, 164.

13. Karant-Nunn mentions (p. 123) that in the wake of the Reformation some preachers opposed churching, while some women and their husbands also rebelled against the rules of confinement (including its prohibition on sex) and churching, but in general lay men and women, along with the clerical establishment, supported both practices.

14. Arsacius Seehofer, *Enarrationes Evangeliorvm Dominicalium, ad dialecticam Methodum, & Rhetoricam dispositionem accommodatæ . . .* ([Augsburg: Heinrich Steiner], 1539), 53v: "tamen naturalis lex & iustitia docet hoc ut ualetudinis suæ curam agant, & domi se ad tempus contineant, donec conualuerint."

15. Simon Musaeus, *Außlegung der Episteln vnd Euangelien vber gewönliche nam-haffte Feste der heyligen Apostel/ Märtyrer vnd Zeugen Christi durchs gantze Jar* (Frankfurt: Nicolaus Bassæus,1590), 38r: "Darzu etliche Tyrannische Männer auch vrsach geben / wenn sie die Weiber vber jhr vermögen fort treiben / oder sie jrer notturfft berauben." Such husbands were probably also insisting on the resumption of sexual intercourse, which the preachers would find unseemly (or worse), although it is not specifically mentioned in any of these sermons.

16. Mathesius, *Außlegung der Euangelien/ von den fürnembsten Festen* (1571), 89r: "So hat jhnen Gott dargegen jre ruhetage oder wochen verordnet / damit sie jr verschonen / vn[d] die Menner mit jhnen gedult hetten / biß sie sich jrer krefften wider erholeten."

17. Pauli, *Postilla* (1573), 68r: "Vnd [die Menner] solten gedencken / das besser ist / dreymal in der Schlacht im kriege sein / denn ein Kind zur welt geberen / wie jener Philosophus sagete. Sie solten gedencken / das keine Edeler Creatur vnd Geschöpff Gottes auff Erden ist / den[n] eine fruchtbare Frawe / aus welcher das Menschliche geschlecht gebawet / vnd als aus einem paradis / der Himel gepflantzet wird."

18. Ibid., 68r–v: "Wer hat denn schuld am Tode vn[d] am Blute dieser armen Weiber? Niemand / denn jhre eigene Tyrannische Menner / vnd die starcken Pferdeweiber / welche mit jrem Exempel andern bösen Mennern vrsach geben / das sie jre schwache Frawen zur erbeit treiben vnd schlagen."

19. Musaeus, *Außlegung der Episteln vnd Euangelien* (1590), 38r: "Darumb thut der Bapst vnrecht / daß er der Christen Kindbetterin auffleget / daß sie nach jhrem Kindlbeth sich für der Kirchen müssen lassen einsegnen / welches (wie gesagt) allein die Jüden im alten Testament bindet."

20. Although Lutherans tended to paint all Catholics with the same tarred brush, in fact preachers such as Geiler had made these same points before: the "work" of marriage is not sinful or impure, but this law (which does not bind us today) serves to remind us that we sin every day. See Geiler, *Postill* (1522), 29r–30r.

21. Vischer, *Außlegung der Euangelien/ . . . Vom Aduent bis auff Ostern* (1570), n.p. (between C and D): "Wil jetzt der geweiheten Kreuter / Saltzes / Wasser / vnd mancherley abergleubischen segens geschweigen. Nein / Gott hat seine lieben Engel auff die armen Sechswöchnerin bescheiden / die warten jnen auff denn dienst."

22. Ibid., Dd iij r: "Also sollen wir vns auch zum raht der frommen vnd zu der Gemeine halten / gerne im Hause Gottes / vnter dem hauffen derer sein / da man Gott lobet vnd preiset."

23. Ibid.: "Christliche / fromme / erbare / tugentreiche Matronene oder Weiber /

sollen auch aus dem exempel Marie lernen / das sie jrer selbs verschonen / jrem leibe / als einem Tempel des heiligen Geistes / seine gebürende reuerentz vnd ehrer-bietung erzeigen / vnd sich eine zeitlang nach der geburt innen halten . . . [Dd iiij r] [auch] das sie mit jrem Kindlein / ausgangs jrer Sechswochen / Christlich vnd erbar-lich zur Kirchen gehen / dem getrewen Gott von hertzen dancken / das er nicht al-lein jr Kindlein in jrem leibe wunderbarlich erhalten / [sondern auch] wider des Teuf-fels wüten vnd toben gnediglich behütet."

24. Mathesius, *Außlegung der Euangelien/ von den fürnembsten Festen* (1571), 89r: "Will eine darzu öffentlich für sich vnd jre kindlein bitten lassen / stehet auch jeder-man frey . . . Da eine aber vmb kelt vnd schwachheit willen / jr kindlein nicht mit sich zur Kirchen nimpt / der wil ich hie jr gewissen auch nicht beschweren / denn es ist eine freye Ceremonien."

25. Ibid., 90r: "Derhalben will ich euch Eltern vermanet haben / nemet euch ewer Kinder trewlich an / betet alle Jar vnnd teglich für ewre Kinder / ziehet sie Christlich auff / haltet sie zur Predigt vnnd Sacrament / damit sie Gott hie vnnd dort in ewigkeit loben vnd preisen. Vom Blasius liecht vnd andern mißbreuchen / wöllen wir auff dißmal nicht redden / wir dancken vnserm lieben Gott / der vns daruon erle-digt hat." The term "Blasius lights" refers to the consecrated candles held in a crossed position over the heads or throats of the faithful by a priest in the "blessing of St. Blasius." The traditional feast day for Blasius (or Blaise) in the west is February 3, thus the connection of those candles to the lights used in Candlemas celebrations. St. Blasius, a legendary martyred bishop in the early church, supposedly cured a boy choking on a fishbone and so was considered to protect against diseases of the throat [Catholic Encyclopedia, vol. 2, 1907]. Also popular was holy water blessed on the feast of St. Blasius, common from the thirteenth century. It was thought to cure illnesses, especially of the throat, in humans and cattle, and to protect geese and poultry from thieves. See Scribner, "Ritual and Popular Religion in Catholic Germany at the Time of the Reformation," 63.

26. Mathesius, *Außlegung der Euangelien/ von den fürnembsten Festen* (1571), 94v: "Was aber die werde Jungfraw Maria belangen / wil sie hiemit allen Christen ein gut exempel vn[d] lere geben / das wir vmb lieb / fried / glimpf / einigkeit / vnnd er-gernuß zuuermeiden / alle gute sitten / vnd feine Ceremonien / vnd löbliche gebreu-che / willig vnd gerne ehren vnnd halten helffen / da wir es schon nicht schuldig weren."

27. Hesshusen, *Postilla* (1581), 72r: "Das der Bapst mit seinen München fürge-ben hat / als weren die Kindelbetterin vnreiner denn sonst / vnd weren vnter des Satans gewalt / vnd hat mit geweiheten vnd gesegneten Kreuteren vnd Kertzen / den Satan vertrieben / vnd mit Weihwasser die Sechswöcherin reinigen wollen / ist ein recht Affenspiel gewesen / aus dem alten Testament genomen / mit grossem jrthumb vnd Aberglauben. . . . Das ist aber Christlich vnd löblich / das gottselige Ma-tronen / die Gott mit leibes frucht gesegnet / wenn sie jre Wochen ausgehalten / vnd zu jrer gesundheit wider komen sind / sich zur Kirchen finden."

28. Chemnitz, *Postilla* (1594), 64.

29. Ibid.: "Daher auch da Einleyten der Kindbetterin im Bapstthumb geblieben ist / wiewol auch diese Ceremonien wie fast alle andere gute Ordnungen / mit vielem Gottlosen Wesen vnd abergleubischen Mißbreuchen ist befudelt vnd verderbt wor-den."

30. Karant-Nunn, "A Women's Rite," 132.

31. Origen, Hom. 14 on Luke; cited in Graef, vol. 1, 45.

32. Graef, vol. 1, 81.

33. Geiler, *Postill* (1522), 13v: "Vnd das ist ouch geschehen. dan[n] do der herr am crütz gestorben ist / do hatt Maria die müter gottes grossen schmertzen gelitten in irem hertzen / vß dem mitliden so sye hott gehaben von dem liden vnsers herren. vnd also großen schmertzen / das sye ein grössere marterin gewesen ist weder kein ander marterer. Deßhalben das sye gelitten hatt in dem vnlidelichsten teil . . . Maria die müter gottes hott gelitten im hertzen."

34. Luther, *Winterpostille 1528*, WA 21, 52: "denn von Maria lesen wir nicht, das sie leiplich sey gemartert und gepeiniget worden."

35. Ibid.: "sondern meynet betrübnis und hertzeleyd, das da würde Mariam ubergehen."

36. Both Geiler and Luther remark that this "blessing" is in fact simply a greeting, and should not be construed as anything more. See Geiler, *Postill* (1522), 13r; Luther, WA 21, 48.

37. Luther, *Festpostille 1544*, WA 52, 74: "Denn solche boßheyt der welt hat sie sehen unnd erfaren müssen, und sie nicht allein, sonder die gantz Christliche kirch."

38. Corvinus, *Loci in Evangelia cvm Dominicalia tum de Sanctis, ut uocant, ita adnotati, ut uel commentarij uice esse possint, nunc primum autore Antonio Coruino publicati. Cum præfatione M. Adami Vegetij Fuldensis* (Warburg: Eucharius Agrippina, 1536), b iiiv: "Et Mariæ hic uentura crux præciditur, ut ne inopinatum ac nouum aliquid accidere sibi existimet, si quando aliter ac uelit tractari filium suum uideat."

39. Artopoeus, *Evangelicae Conciones Dominicarvm tocius anni, per Dialectica et Rhetorica artificia breuiter tractatæ. Subnexis Epistolarum argumentis* (Wittenberg: n.p., 1537), 24r: "Hæc due cohærent, Habere Christum, et ferre crucem, seu animam transfigi gladio."

40. Culmann, *Sacræ Contiones* (1550), 52v: "Hæc translata à Maria ad pios omnes docent, quantis doloribus afficiuntur pij, quando uident Christum contemni ac reijci."

41. Mathesius, *Kurtze Ausslegung der Sontags Euangelien vnnd Catechismi* (Nuremberg: Berg and Neuber,1563), E iiv: "Maria aber vnnd die liebe Christenheyt / werden grosse angst / trübnuß vnnd hertzenleid haben / Darumb das die Welt sich mit gewalt wider Jhesum Christum wirdt rotten vnnd aufflehnen / Psalm.2."

42. Wigand, *Postilla* (1569), 93: "Er warnet sie aber darumb zuuor / auff das sie nachmals / wenn sich solches begeben vnd zutragen / nicht abfalle / kleinmütig vnd verzagt werde."

43. Vischer, *Außlegung der Euangelien/ . . . Vom Aduent bis auff Ostern* (1570), biiijr: "Vnd dieweil die gute alte Priester die beysorge treget / Maria möchte jr die gedancken machen / sie wolte auff lauter Rosen gehen / . . . vnd nimmermehr kein betrübnis oder hertzleid vnd bekümmernis an / damit sie hernachmals nicht zurück pralle / wenn jr der glaube in die hand kömmet."

44. Chemnitz, *Postilla* (1594), 180: "Als jhnen nun Joseph vnnd Maria solche gedancken einbilden / bey diesem jhrem Kindlein / da tritt Simeon hinzu / vnd machet die Glossa uber den Text."

45. Ibid., 179: "darüber Marien, das ist, der Kirchen Gottes / ein Schwerdt durch die Seele werde dringe[n]."

46. Cited by Marina Warner, 218. Interestingly, Lutheran sermons on Christ's passion referring to Mary under the cross will occasionally refer to her stoic, faithful, even courageous stance. However, sermons on Simeon's prophecy of the sword do not convey this image of Mary. See the section on Mary under the cross in chapter 6.

47. A number of Lutheran preachers believe that she was a widow for eighty-four years, which would have placed her actual age somewhere over one hundred.

Luther's bibical translation reads: "Und es war eine Prophetyn, Hanna . . . die war wol betaget und hatte gelebt sieben jar mit yhrem mann von yhrer Jungfrawschafft an, und war nu eine witwe bey vier und achtzig jaren."

48. Brenz, *Evangelien= Predigten von Johann Brenz, weiland Propst in Stuttgart*, Erster Band: *Die festliche Hälfte des Kirchen-Jahres*, trans. L. de Marées (Cottbus: Gotthold-Expedition, 1877), 60: " 'Sie kam nimmer vom Tempel und dienete Gott mit Fasten und Beten Tag und Nacht.' Also war sie abergläubisch? Mit nichten, sondern fromm."

49. Ibid.: "Sie hat nämlich gefastest—nicht zur Sühne für ihre Sünden, nein, gefastet, d.h. nüchtern gelebt."

50. Ibid.: "endlich, um nicht ihrem Leibe durch Ueppigkeit Anlaß zur Sünde zu geben."

51. Corvinus, *Kurtze vnd ainfeltige Außlegung . . . auff die Sonntage vnd fürnemesten Feste* (1545), 17r: "Hie soll[e]n nun alle Frawen / Witwen vnd Junckfrawen / ain Exempel nemen / das sy im erkantnuß Christi / in güttem wandel / in rechtgeschaffnem gotsdienst / diser Han[n]a nach folgen. . . . [D]er glaub lebendig vnd thätig sein müß."

52. Spangenberg, *Postilla. Euangelia, & Epistolae, qvae Dominicis & Festis diebus per totum Annum in Ecclesia proponuntur, per Quæstiones piè ac synceriter explicata, & imaginibus exornata. Item eadem Evangelia, et Precationes, quas Collectas uocant, quibus utitur Ecclesia, Carmine Elegiaco reddita* (Frankfurt: C. Egenolphus, 1553), 44v: "Arbor ipsa fuit bona, bonos igitur fructus produxit."

53. Mathesius, *Postilla Oder Ausslegung der Sontags Euangelien vber das gantze jar* (Nuremberg: Neuber and Von Bergs Erben, 1565), 42r: "Denn da das land volls Krieg vnd auffrhur war . . . helt sich dise Christliche Widwe zum Tempel / vnd dienet vnserm Gott mit glaubigem hertzen / vnd lebet nüchtern vnd messigklich / wartet des stiftes / vnd dienet dem Tabernackel / wie ein Kirchewidwe / leret die Meydlein / vnd bettet tag vnnd nacht zu vnserm Gott."

54. Ibid.: "[Sie] höret Simeonis des grossen Doctors zeugnuß vnd gesang / . . . vnd glaubet jres Pfarrners seligen worten / vnnd fehet an Gott zu loben vnnd dancken / vnnd singet jren Psalm mit den andern Frawen / vnd zeuget darneben von disem Kindlein / das es der rechte Messias vn[d] erlöser sey."

55. Ibid., 42v: "Lasset vns Manne Simeones sein / vnnd fleissige hörer des worts Gottes / Jr Frawen seyt fromme Annen / gehet fleissig zur Kirchen / lebet messig vnd züchtig / bettet daheim mit ewern kinderlein vnd gesinde / . . . Tröstet euch mit Gottes wort / redet vnd singet daruon in ewern heusern / gehet zum heyligen Sacrament / harret Gott auß in gedult."

56. Wigand, *Postilla* (1569), 95: "ein Prophetin / Das ist / sie hat gewust die verheissungen / vnd zugleich mit anderen auff die zeit des zukünfftigen Messiae vleissig achtung geben / auch andere von denselbigen errinnert."

57. Ibid.: "Es war aber gebreuchlich / das etliche Weiber bey dem Tempel zu Jerusalem woneten / die da den Leuiten die Kleider / derer sie zu dem Gottesdienst in Tempel gebrauchten / wüschen."

58. Eber, *Postilla* (1578), 47v: "vn[d] nichts desto weniger waren sie fleissig im Tempel / höreten Predigt / vnd vbeten sich in Gottes Wort / hielten an im Gebett / vnd das das fürnembste war / hielten sie auch Jungfrauwen Schul."

59. Ibid.: "haben sie gefastet / das ist / sich eyngezogen vnd messig gehalte[n] mit essen vnd trincken."

60. Chemnitz, *Postilla* (1594), 187: "Deß sollen nun fromme Gottselige Weiber zum Trost sich erinnern/ vnd des also gebrauchen/ daß sie hieraus lernen/ das sie auch/ eben so wol als Manns Personen zum Reich des HERRN Christi gehören."

61. Ibid., 191–192: "Daher ist bey vns auch die Ordnung der Bagginen / . . . daß man sonderliche Heuser von Alters her darzu verordnet hat. . . . Vnd da ists fein verordnet / was man für Personen in solche Bagginen Heuser nem[en] sole / nemlich / die friedsam sein / vnd sich in jhrer Jugend ehrlich vnnd wol gehalten haben / vnd solche Allmosen wirdig sein."

4. MARY IN LUKE 2:41–52

1. NRSV, Luke 2:41–52.

2. A small minority of postils use a different gospel text for this Sunday's lesson, such as Jesus' baptism in John 1. See, for example, the 1584 postil of Victor Strigel.

3. The history of the family in sixteenth-century Germany is a well-discussed subject. It was also an issue of note for concerned individuals at that time. As Steven Ozment remarks, "[A]ccording to contemporary observers, marriage and the family were in a crisis in late medieval and Reformation Europe" (p. 1). New laws and courts were being introduced to deal with family matters, and religious groups accused each other of being opposed to "family values." See Ozment's *When Fathers Ruled: Family Life in Reformation Europe* (Cambridge: Harvard University Press, 1983). For a discussion of the importance of this issue in Lutheran preaching, see Eileen Theresa Dugan, "Images of Marriage and Family Life in Nördlingen: Moral Preaching and Devotional Literature, 1589–1712" (Ph.D. diss., Ohio State University, 1987).

4. Geiler, *Postill* (1522), 22r: "Das hott der herr gethon zü einem trost / vn[d] einer leer allen kinden, das sye sollend lügen vor allen dingen / dz sye vatter vnnd müter in eren zucht vnd reuerentzlicher eererbyetung warnemen."

5. Ibid.: "Das was wol ein wunder / das Maria die müter gottes das wort nitt hon verstanden / die do wysset / dz er keinenn andren vatter hatt / den[n] allein got den vatter."

6. WA 12, 409.

7. Ibid., 410: "Noch sihestu, wie Got yhr hertz blosz und nacket aufszeucht, das sie nun nicht kan sagen 'Ich bin sein mutter.' "

8. Ibid., 412: "Also demuttigt der almechtig God die heyligen und helt sie yn yhrem erkentnis. . . . Dieweyl wir aber sehen, das es der junckfrawen und andern heyligen auch also ist gangen, so haben wyr dennoch ein trost, das wyr nicht vertzagen."

9. Ibid., 414: "Drumb gilts nicht, wenn man sagt, man muss glewben, was die Concilia beschlossen odder was Hieronymus, Augustinus und andere heyligen veter geschrieben haben, sondern man mus ein ort anzeygen, da man Christum finde und keyn anders, nemlich, das er selb anzeygt und sagt, er musse sein in dem das seynis vaters ist, das ist, niemandt wirt yhn finden anderswo denn ym wort Gottis."

10. Ibid., 415: "Denn da schreyen sie ymmer on auffhören als weren sie unsinnig 'Ey das haben die heyligen Concilia beschlossen, das hat die kirch gebotten, das hat man so lange zeyt gehalten, sollen wyr denn nicht dran glewben?' "

11. Ibid.: "Dis Bischoff und Concilia haben on zweyffel des heyligen geysts nicht soviel gehabt als sie, hat sie denn gefeylet, wie solten denn yhene nicht yrren, weyl sie Christum meynen anderswo zu finden denn ynn dem, das seyns vaters ist, das ist ynn Gottis wort?"

12. Ibid., 418: "das uns Got auff keynen heyligen wil weysen, auch zu der mutter selb nicht, denn das kan alles feylen, drumb muss er uns ein gewiss ort anzeygen, da Christus ligt, das ist die krippen."

13. Ibid.: " 'Christus ist ynn der schrifft eyngewickelt durch und durch, gleych

wie der leyb ynn den tuchlen'. Die krippen ist nu die predigt, darynn er ligt und verfasset wirt, und daraus man essen und futter nympt."

14. Bugenhagen, *Indices qvidam Ioannis Bvgenhagii Pomerani in Euangelia (ut
uocant) Dominicalia, Insuper usui temporum et Sanctorum totius anni seruientia.
Ab Ipso
Avtore Iam primum emissi et locupletati* (Wittenberg: Johann Lufft, 1524); this is almost
the same text as his *Postillatio Ioan. Bvgenhagii Pomerani in Euangelia, usui temporum
et Sanctorum totius anni seruientia, ad preces Georgij Spalatini scripta. Habes Hic et Concionum et meditationum copiosißimam syluam, quisquis es, cui cordi est pietas* ([Mainz:
Johann Schöffer,1524]).

15. Bugenhagen, *Indices* (1524), n.p.: "1. Ascendunt Hierosolymam sancti Maria
et Ioseph etc. Quid igitur prosunt legis opera?"

16. Ibid.: "2. Christus præfert uocationem diuinam parentibus Fit subditus.
Christus factus est sub lege (Gala. 4) et parentibus obedit, quatenus diuina uocatio
sinit."

17. Introduction by Bugenhagen to Artopoeus's *Evangelicae Conciones* (1537), ii:
"meliora præstare possunt, ad gloriam Dei, et salutem multorum."

18. Corvinus, *Loci* (1536), b v v ff.: "Ioseph ac Maria quanquam iustificati per
fidem iampridem essent, eoque lege opus non haberent, tamen ne cui sint offendi-
culo, proficiscuntur & ipsi ad estum Iudæorum Hierosolymam. Exemplum charitatis
est."

19. Ibid., n.p.: "Maria & Ioseph Christum Hierosolymam ubi tradebatur lex, per-
ducentes, docere omnes parents uolunt, uti statim ab ipsis incunabilis liberos suos in
uerbo domini institui curent / propterea quod aetas illa in quamlibet sequax sit materiam." Gerald Strauss, when discussing "Pedagogy and the Family," suggests that it
was a commonplace for Lutheran preachers and writers of the sixteenth century to
stress the necessity for parental instruction of children in the home. They continued
to hold this ideal, even when taking practical measures to remove religious instruction from the purview of parents and to place it under the state and church. See
Strauss, *Luther's House of Learning*, 108–131.

20. Artopoeus, *Evangelicae Conciones* (1537), 31v: "EVangelium est generis De-
monstratiui facti, et habet admixtum genus iudiciale, ubi defensit se Christus coram
parentibus, Status legittimi. Et est generis Didascalici, ubi Christus nos docet." For a
discussion of sixteenth-century uses of the classical theories of rhetorical genera, see
John W. O'Malley, "Luther the Preacher," *Michigan Germanic Studies* 10 (1984): 3–16.

21. Artopoeus, *Evangelicae Conciones* (1537), 31v–2r: "Propositio. Maria perdidit
Christum, et inuenit rursum. Christus se subduxit a parentibus remanens Hieroso-
limæ, et statuit se nobis pro exemplo."

22. Ibid., 32v: "Hic persodit eius animam Simeonis ille gladius." See chapters 3
and 6 for more information on Simeon's prophecy of the sword.

23. Artopoeus writes, "Pater, Deus est, mater homo est. Ergo Deo magis quàm
hominibus obediendum est. Acto. 5" (ibid., 33v).

24. Arsacius Seehofer, *Enarrationes Evangeliorvm* (1539), 36r–v: "exemplo ipsius
Christi seruatoris nostri accendamus populum ad studium uerbi diuini. . . . Tali etiam
exemplo nos ad simile opus inuitat, ut cœleste uerbum frequenter audiamus, & se-
dulo addiscamus."

25. Although Melanchthon was not an ordained preacher, he did hold lectures
on the Bible and also preached Latin sermons on the appointed gospels and lessons,
usually for the foreign students in Wittenberg. These sermons comprise Melanchthon's postils, and can be found in the *Corpus Reformatorum*, primarily in volumes 24

and 25. Some of this material, including the sermon that follows, was published in the sixteenth century. For more information, see Timothy J. Wengert, "The Biblical Commentaries of Philip Melanchthon," in *Philip Melanchthon (1497–1560) and the Commentary*, ed. Timothy J. Wengert and M. Patrick Graham (Sheffield, Eng.: Sheffield Academic Press, 1997), esp. pp. 129–130.

26. Philipp Melanchthon, *In Evangelia qvæ Vsitato more diebus dominicis & festis proponuntur, Annotationes Philippi Melanthonis, Recognitæ et auctæ, adiectis ad finem aliquot conciunculis* (Wittenberg: Johann Lufft, 1548), 38v: "Mandatum Dei anteferendum est uoluntati parentum. . . . ut quando parentes prohibent studium ueræ doctrinæ, confeßionem, coniugium. Rursus extra hunc casum debetur obedientia parentibus."

27. For a discussion of issues surrounding marriage and changes in marriage practices demanded and idealized by Lutheran reformers, see chapter 4, and the following: Ozment, *When Fathers Ruled*, and Lyndal Roper, *The Holy Household*. Thomas Robisheaux discusses the impact (or lack thereof) of Lutheran ideas on marriage in the countryside in "Reformation, Patriarchy, and Marital Discipline," chap. 4 of *Rural Society and the Search for Order in Early Modern Germany* (Cambridge: Cambridge University Press, 1989).

28. Melanchthon, *In Evangelia . . . Annotationes* (1548), 39r: "Qvartvs. De negligentia et dolore Mariæ. . . . Mundus non intelligit esse peccata, nisi externa ciuilia peccata. Non agnoscit quantum malum sit naturalis infirmitas . . . Sed sancti intelligunt magnitudinem huius interioris imbecillitatis, et sæpe experiuntur ingentes pœnas sequi leuem negligentiam."

29. Ibid., 39r–v: "Ita hic Maria agnouit suam negligentiam, . . . conferebat se cum Eua, quæ antea perdiderat genus humanum, nunc ipsa cogitat se alteram Euam esse, quæ amisso filio rursus perdiderit genus humanum, cogitauit omnia miracula, quibus Deus ipsam ad curam huius filij excitauerat. Cum igitur uideret quantum peccatum esset hæc negligentia, necesse est fuisse ingentes dolores toto triduo, quorum magnitudinem nemo hominum intelligit."

30. Anton Corvinus, *Kurtze vnd ainfeltige Außlegung . . . auff die Sonntage vnd fürnemesten Feste . . . Für die arme Pfarrherren vnd Haußuätter gestellet* (1545). This is not a translation of his earlier Latin postil.

31. Ibid., 23v: "So hat er vns dannocht mit disem geschicht wöllen züuersteen geben / was sein Ampt vnd werck . . . / Nemlich / das er würde die Schrifft handlen / vnd mit hailsamer leere vmbgeen."

32. Ibid., 24r: "Zum andern / leernet diß Euangelium / wie die eltern jre kinder zür erbarkait vnd Gottseligkait ziehen sollen."

33. Ibid., 24v: "[S]y nicht allain jres kindes / sonder auch jres glaubens gegen Gott beraubt wirdt / . . . Sy fand nicht trost bey den gefreündten oder bekandten / auch in der Statt nit, sonder im Tempel. Also auch wir / wenn wir fallen in trübsall / . . . sollen wir nyrgent anders / dann bey Christo hülf vnd trost [finden?] / der sich in dem Tempel / das ist / in seinem wort / allzeit will finden lassen."

34. Huberinus, *Postilla Teutsch* (1548), n.p.: "Soll man die kinder zum gehorsam aufferziehen / das sie nit allein den Eltern / sonder auch jhren Lehrmeistern / Oberkeyt / vnd alten leuten fein vnterthenig / willig / vnd ehrbietig seyen . . . vnnd sie allweg zuuor mit worten / vnterrichten / vnnd straffen / wie hie Maria spricht / mein Sun warumb hast du vns das gethon / auff das die Eltern zuuor fleyssig die sach erforschen / mit worten / ehe sie mit schlegen die kinder vber eylen."

35. Brenz, *Pericopæ Euangeliorum quæ Singvlis Diebvs Dominicis publicè in Ecclesia recitari solent, expositæ per Ioannem Brentivm* (Frankfurt: Petrus Brubach, 1556) (Her-

zog August Bibliothek [Wolfenbüttel]; St. Paul, Minn.: Lutheran Brotherhood Foundation Reformation Library, microfiche), 149: "Et hac occasione dicenda nobis sunt pauca quædam de puerorum educatione." His use of *educatione* seems to carry the connotations of the German *erziehung* (upbringing), as it is translated by Ludwig de Marées in the 1877 edition of these sermons. This sermon by Brenz is actually from 1542 and was included by Michael and Jakob Gretter in their collection of Brenz's sermons published in 1556.

36. Ibid.: "Præcipua enim et optima puerorum institutio est parentum et maiorum honestas et pietas."

37. Ibid., 152: "Quare danda est opera unicuique patrifamilias, ut educet cœlo ciues, et non Satanæ mancipia."

38. Leonhard Culmann, *Sacræ Contiones* (1550), 57r: "Vnde monemur, piorum parentum esse, ab ipsis cunabulis liberos abstrahere ab omni iniquitate, adducere autem ad pietatem et religionem. Imò assuescere ritibus sacris, et moribus studijsque sanctis."

39. Ibid., 57v: "Sicut et Petrus dixit: Oportet Deo plus obedire q[uam] hominibus."

40. Ibid., 58r: "Vnde docemur neminem animum despondere, si non protinus ab initio intelligat omnia Dei mysteria."

41. Ibid.: "Et descendit cum eis, etc. Audiant et animo recondant hæc iuuenes, et discant filij dei exemplo, proprium esse iuuenum, debitumq[ue] offitium obedire, et sub disciplina uiuere parentum ac magistrorum."

42. Petrus Artopoeus, *Postilla Euangeliorum, & Epistolarum Dominicarum, & præcipuorum Festorum totius Anni, per scholasticis, & nouellis Prædicatoribus, Breues Annotationes* (Basel: Heinrich Petri, 1550), G 7v–[8r]: "Filiorum item tria sunt officia, Ea docet puer Iesus: Ascendere cum parentibus Ierosolymam, id est, à puerò ad pietatem consuescere, audire uerbum Dei, interesse pijs cæremonijs. Sedere in medio doctorum, audire eorum doctrinam, interrogare de incognitis. Ire in scholam, Discere Bonas, fugere Malas artes, Adiungere se ad bona sodalicia, Vitare mala consortia. Redire cum parentibus domum, et subdere se illis, applicare auditum uerbum Dei ad pium usum uitæ. Secundum Deum obedire parentibus, assuescere ad œconomiam, politiam, et ad certum, honestumque uitæ genus. Inde adolescent frugi homines, Deo et hominibus dilecti et officiosi, ut puer Iesus."

43. Mathesius, *Kurtze Ausslegung* (1563), n.p.: "[Sie] gewehnet es [ihr kindlein] zur arbeyt / vnd sorgt hertzlich für es jr lebenlang."

44. Ibid., F iijr: "Jm hause ist er seiner Mutter gehorsam . . . vnd gehet inn knechtes gestalt / vnnd wirdt ein Zimmerman vnd Bürger zu Capernaum." As Johannes Wigand remarks, instruction about the household economy should include both practical and moral aspects. He calls the home the "workshop, in which children should be led and instructed in all fear of God, propriety, honor, and virtues" ("sie sey ein Werckstat / in welcher die Kinder in aller Gottsfurcht / Zucht / Erbarkeit vnd Tugenden sollen angefüret vnd vnterwiesen werden.") Wigand, *Postilla* (1569), 153.

45. Mathesius, *Kurtze Ausslegung* (1563), F iijv–F iiij: Children should "gerne betten / Gott dancken / zur Predigt gehen / die Kirchendiener inn ehren halten / ihren Eltern vnd Schulmeystern im HERRen gehorsam sein / vnd sie in jrem alter ernehren / vnd versorgen helffen / vnd sollen gerne studieren / oder arbeyten / jederman dienen / willig / Züchtig / trew / warhafftig / redlich vnd verschwigen sein."

46. Ibid.: "So werden sie gunst vnd gnade bey Gott vnd den menschen finden / langes leben / glück vnd fürderung auff erden haben."

47. Mathesius, *Postilla* (1565), 52r: "Wie nun Joseph vnd Maria zu Kirchen gehen

/ bleyben sie allda gantzet acht tage / erharren des segens / lauffen nicht bald nach dem Euangelio / oder wenn die predigt auß ist / auf der Kirchen / als brennet sie."

48. Ibid., 53r: "Christus helt sich zum Predigstuel / stecket sich nicht in winckel vnd treybet schalckheyt / spielt vnnd rasselt nicht / . . . vnd lesset [nicht] jm die predigt zu einem ohr ein / zum andern wider auß gehen."

49. Ibid.: "sie sollen zu schendtlicher armut kommen / vnnd an den bettelstab gedeyen / vnd da sie nicht busse thun / . . . entlich im hellischen fewer bezalt werden."

50. Veit Dietrich, *Vermanung/ Von der kinderzucht / auss dem Euangelio / Luce am 2. Durch: M. Vitum Dieterich* (Nuremberg: U. Neuber, 1567), n.p.: "[Kinder sind] von natur böß / vnnd zur sünden geneigt."

51. Ibid.: "Also stehet das Exempel vom Kindlin Jesu dar zur lere für die Jugent / das sie dem kindlein Jesu nach / sich halten / auch in der kirchen sich gern finden lassen / vnd Gottes wort jhnen lieber lassen sein / denn alles was auf Erden ist."

52. Christoph Vischer, *Außlegung der Euangelien . . . Vom Aduent bis auff Ostern* (1570), q v: "gott hat die Königliche Jungfraw Maria / seines lieben sons Mutter / vber alle massen hoch geehret / . . . der heilige Geist hat jr fleisch vnd blut an sich genommen / vnd dasselbige vnzertrennlich mit seiner Götlichen natur vereinigt vnd vereinbaret hat." But "sie ist eine recht Maria / ein betrübtes armes Weibsbild." The Hebrew name means "bitterness" or "bitter sea."

53. Ibid., q iir: "Gott hat nu keinen Sohn mehr / damit er dem Menschlichen geschlechte helffen köndte / Darumb bistu tausent mal ein ergere Menschenmörderin denn Eua."

54. Ibid., r v: "setzet sie jn zu rede . . . vnd doch mit freundlichen / sanfftmütigen / bescheidenen worten."

55. Ibid., r iijv: "Gar schön ist es von Maria / das sie von der strafe nicht vnwillig wird / das er sie so öffentlich im Tempel / für aller welt / auch den grawen heubtern / beschemet / sondern sie tregt es gedultig / vnd dencket jm fein nach / wie Lucas ferner saget: Vnd sie verstunden das wort nicht / das er mit jnen redet."

56. This theme is also articulated in the postil of Johannes Heune, which in other respects is indistinguishable from postils of the 1550s and 1560s. He emphasizes the responsibilities of parents to discipline and children to obey in church, school, and home. The fact that neither Mary nor Joseph fully understands Jesus' defense of himself causes him to remark that they were affected, "like all saints," with "great weakness and ignorance" ("Da geben sich Maria vnd Joseph zu fried / wiewol sie solche antwort nicht volkömlich verstehen / wie denn bey allen Heiligen grosse schwacheit vnd vnwissenheit mit vnterleuffet / u[sw].") Heune, *Postilla* (1570), 38r.

57. Vischer, *Außlegung der Euangelien . . . Vom Aduent bis auff Ostern* (1570), r iijv: "Hieraus sollen wir lernen / das Prediger / dem Exempel Christi nach / straffen sollen / was zu straffen ist / vnd wer da öffentlich sundiget / den sollen sie öffentlich straffen / . . . Zuhörer sollen lernen von Maria / das sie gedultig die straffe leiden / vnd nicht darüber murren oder gruntzen sollen / das sie so öffentlich gestrafft werden."

58. Ibid., r iiijr: "Sondern er wil mit euch gnedige gedult vnd mitleiden tragen / wie hie mit Maria / so fern jr nur dociles seid."

59. Hemmingsen, *Postilla* (1571), 151: "Zum vierden / auff das sie beide / Joseph vnd Maria / durch solche Göttliche zucht erinnert würden / vnd ernstlich bedechten / was für arme Leute sie von Natur weren."

60. Ibid., 152: "Denn gleich wie Heua durch des Teuffels List verfüret ward / vnd das gantze Menschlich Geschlecht in ewige not brachte / Also gedachte die Jung-

fraw Maria / das sie durch jren vnfleis den verheissenen Heiland der Welt verloren hette."

61. Nicolaus Selneccer, *Evangeliorvm et Epistolarvm Omnivm, quæ Dominicis et Festis Diebvs in Ecclesia Christi proponi solent, Harmonie, Explicationes, & Homiliarum Pars Prima. A 'Prima Dominica Aduentus, vsque ad Dominicam, quæ Quadragesima, siue Inuocauit nominatur* (Frankfurt: n.p., 1575), 477: "Quid igitur errauit? Errauit in defectu, inquis, negligens puerum: Errauit in excessu, nimis solicita de puero, quem Deum esse sciebat. Exemplus hoc quidem est ijs, qui medium non norunt." This same point is made in Johann Spangenberg, *Außlegung Der Episteln vnd Euangelien / von Aduent, biß auffs Ostern Durch Johann Spangenberg/ in Fragstück verfasse* (n.p., 1584), 42r.

62. Selneccer, *Evangeliorvm . . . Pars Prima* (1575), 487 [478]: "Maria dolet, amisso Filio. Hîc tribulationes Ecclesiæ depinguntur. Labor itineris, lacrymæ multæ, lucta in corde, Euæque, nouus dolor repetitus concurrunt, et accedit triste desiderium, de quo in Canticis scriptum est: Quæsiui, quem diligit anima mea, quæsiui illum, et non inueni: Surgam erto eundo de loco ad locum, et circumibo ciuitatem per vicos et plateas, et quæram quem diligit anima mea."

63. Spindler, *Postilla* (1576), L iij: "vnd ob wol solchs den weibsbildern so ernstlich nicht geboten war / wil doch die liebe Maria niemands ergernis geben / sondern Christliche Ceremonien mit jhrem gehorsam gerne erhalten."

64. Ibid.: "Weil aber jhr liebes kindlein zwölff jahr alt war / vnd nun ins dreyzehende jahr gieng / nemen sie es mit zu kirchen / vnd lassens mit fleis auff die Predig hören / allen Eltern zum seligen exempel / daraus sie lernen köndten / wie sie fromme kinder erziehen solten."

65. Ibid.: "da sie bey ein fünff meil wegs gereiset hatten / dadurch denn der eltern vnfleis vnd nachlessigkeit vermercket wird."

66. Ibid., L iijv: "Vnd solche gedancken vnnd einfelle werden die schmertzen deß hertzens gemehret haben / das sie an Eua exempel wird gedacht haben / Sihe du bist nu die andere Eua / die das menschliche geschlecht in ewig verderben bringt."

67. Ibid.: "vnd die Mutter straffet jhr kind / aus mütterlicher trewe / doch aus vnuerstandt vnd vnschüldiger weise."

68. Ibid., L iiijr: "Also wil das kind vngestraffet sein / in dem was es recht thut / vnd seine Mutter vnd Joseph müssen vber den schmertzen vnd kümmernis vnrecht haben."

69. Georg Walther, *Auslegung der Euangelien / so an den Sontagen gelesen werden. Das erste Teil / vom Aduent bis auff Trinitatis* (Wittenberg: Hans Kraffts Erben, 1579), 283: "denn sie mit den andern Jüden auch in dem wahn gewesen / jr Son Jhesus würde ein weltlicher grosser König werden / der sie von dem Römischen Reich wider erlösen vnd freymachen."

70. Ibid.: "damit sie genugsam zuerkennen gegeben / das sie nicht aller dinge one Sünde gewesen / sonsten würde sie betracht haben / wie sie den Son empfangen / vnd was jr der Engel von jm gepredigt in der empfengnis."

71. Ibid., b r: "Die Papisten mögen Christum nicht alleine für den Heiland vnd Seligmacher erkennen / sondern neben jhm setzen sie Mariam das sie vns müsse darzu helffen."

72. This is not an issue that can be broken down along Lutheran confessional lines: it is not only the "Philippists" who take up Melanchthon's themes in these sermons, but *all* Lutheran sermon writers whom I have read, including, for example, Nicolaus Selneccer, who was interested in distancing himself from any Philippist connection.

73. See note 52.

74. Leonhard Culmann, *Sacræ Contiones* (1550), 65r: "Quod si erravit Maria. Ergo et Ecclesia potest errare."

75. Gerald Strauss suggests that "the real object" behind stressing the authority of parents, especially the father, over children, "was to inculcate in the population habits of submission and obedience leading beyond parents to the higher authorities governing state and church" (Strauss, *Luther's House of Learning*, 119). While this seems to imply hypocritical manipulation on the part of religious and political authorities, I am sure that the vast majority of sermon writers who addressed issues of authority genuinely believed that the stability and prosperity of society depended upon proper relationships of obedience and authority within the home.

76. See Vischer, fn. 57.

5. THE WEDDING AT CANA

1. NRSV, John 2:4. Graef states that the Greek "Gynai, ti emoi kai soi?" is most obviously translated as "Woman, what have I to do with you?" However, many Catholic exegetes have variously translated this passage to downplay its harshness; e.g., the Douai version, following the Vulgate, has "Woman, what is that to me and to thee?" Most of the early church fathers, Thomas Aquinas, Newman, and most contemporary Mariologists and exegetes interpret this passage as a rebuke to Mary from her son, emphasizing Christ's transcendence over his former earthly relations during his public ministry. See Graef, vol. 1, 19–20.

2. *Das Euangelion auff den andern Sontag nach Epiphanie, Johannis ij*, from Luther's *Fastenpostille*, 1525. See WA 17², 60.

3. The full text is John 2:1–11 (NRSV).

4. As a number of scholars have remarked, the Protestant reformers were the first to value marriage over a life of celibacy. The vast majority of people should marry, since they are not given the gift of chastity, a gift given by God only rarely. See the discussion in Ozment, *When Fathers Ruled*, chap. 1. It appears that some reformers, including Luther, believed that women were *never* given the gift of lifelong celibacy. See his sermon "am tag Johannis des heiligen Aposteln und Euangelistens Evangelion Johannis xxi" (WA 17², 347), cited by Susan Karant-Nunn, "*Kinder, Küche, Kirche*: Social Ideology in the Sermons of Johannes Mathesius," 127.

5. Geiler interprets Jesus' response "Als ob er spräch. Was gost du mich an in dißem stuck / dz ich sol ein wunderzeiche[n] würcken / welchs wunderzeichen würcken ich nitt hab von menschlicher natur / die ich hab / sonder von göttlicher natur . . . Dorumb was hab ich mitt dir züschaffen frow / oder was hab ich mit dir gemeynschafft[?]" See his *Postill* (1522), 24v.

6. Ozment, 3.

7. Merry E. Wiesner, *Women and Gender in Early Modern Europe*, 22.

8. Ibid. See Augustine, *On the Good of Marriage*, 24 (32), who identifies the three goods as procreation, chastity, and the sacramental bond.

9. Ozment, 9.

10. "Ein Sermon von dem ehelichen Stand," WA 2, 168–169; cited in Karant-Nunn, "*Kinder, Küche, Kirche*," 129–130.

11. Lyndal Roper, "Luther: Sex, Marriage and Motherhood," *History Today* 33 (December 1983): 35.

12. Karant-Nunn, "*Kinder, Küche, Kirche*," 131. The praise of women "qua women" found a certain place in the *querelle des femmes* literature of the early modern

period, but not beyond it. It should not, in fact, be expected in sermons, which have as their goals teaching piety and religion, and exhorting to better morality and behavior.

13. Thomas Robisheaux, "Peasants and Pastors: Rural Youth Control and the Reformation in Hohenlohe, 1540–1680," *Social History* 6 (1981): 282–285.

14. See Joel F. Harrington, *Reordering Marriage and Society in Reformation Germany* (Cambridge: Cambridge University Press, 1995). Harrington argues that the main characteristic of Protestant marriage reform is a social conservatism. Although divorce was allowed in most Protestant areas, it was rarely granted by the courts, and usually only in cases of adultery and malicious desertion.

15. Luther, sermon on "Das Euangelion auff den andern Sontag nach Epiphanie Johannis ij," *Fastenpostille*, WA 17^2, 61: "Dazu ist seyne mutter da, also die solche hochzeyt ausrichtet, das es scheynet, es seyen yhr arm nehisten freundlin odder nachbarn gewesen, das sie hatt müssen der braut mutter seyn."

16. Ibid.: "Denn er bestettigt damit, das die ehe Gottis werck und ordenung ist, es sey auch wie veracht odder geringe es wölle fur den leutten."

17. Ibid.: "Noch meyden, verwerffen und lestern sie den selben und sind so heylig, das sie nicht alleyn selbs nicht ehlich werden, wie sie wol bedurfften und sollten, sonder iur ubriger heylickeyt auch bey keyner hochzeyt seyn wöllen, alls die viel heyliger sind denn Christus selbs."

18. Ibid., 62: "Denn daher kompts auch, das so viel muhe und unlust ym ehestand ist nach dem eusserlichen menschen, Das alles, was gottis wort und werck ist, also gehen mus, das es dem euserlichen menschen saür, bitter und schweer sey, soll es anders seliglich seyn."

19. Ibid.: "Denn das zeyget auch Christus hiemit, das er will erfullen, was ynn der ehe mangel hatt . . . als solt er sagen: müsset yhr wasser trincken, [d.h.] trübsal leyden nach dem eusserlichen wesen und wird euch saür? wol an, ich wills euch susse machen und das wasser ynn weyn verwandeln, das ewr trübsall soll ewr freude und lust seyn."

20. Ibid., 63: "So fern doch, das solchs alles seyne masse habe und eyner hochzeyt ehnlich sey . . . Das hierynn niemand sich keren soll an die saür sehende heuchler und selberwachsene heyligen, wilchen nichts gesellet, denn was sie selb thün und leren und nicht wol leyden sollten, das eyne magd eyn krantz tregt odder sich eyn wenig schmuckt."

21. Ibid.: "Sie sind drumb nicht des teuffels gewesen, ob ettlich dises weynes haben eyn wenig uber den durst getruncken und sind frölich worden, sonst wirstu Christo die schuld müssen geben, das er ursach mit seym geschenck dazu geben hat, und seyne mutter hatt drumb gebeten, Das beyde Christus und seyne mutter his sunder sind, wo die saür sehende heyligen sollten urteilen."

22. Ibid., 64: "man auch nicht sucht frölich zu werden, sondern toll und voll zu seyn."

23. Ibid., 65: "Denn sie speyßet nicht, die voll und satt sind, sondern die hungerigen, wie wyr nü offt gesagt haben."

24. Ibid.: "Das sihe hie ynn seyner mutter. Die fulet und klagt yhm den mangel, begerd auch hülff und rad von yhm mit demütigem und sittigem antragen."

25. Ibid., 67: "Und sollen festiglich gleuben, das es nicht der kirchen gepott sey, wie sie rumen und liegen, was ausser und uber gottis wortt gepotten wird. Denn Maria spricht: Was er sagt, das, das, das thut und keyn anders."

26. Luther, "Am Andern Sontage nach der erscheinung Christi, Euangelion Johannis. ij," *Winterpostille* 1528, WA 21, 57. Geiler indicates that this legend is found in

the writings of Jerome, but "man kans nitt eygentlich wissen" of its veracity. See Geiler, *Postill* (1522), 24r.

27. Luther, "Am Andern Sontage nach der erscheinung Christi, Euangelion Johannis. ij," *Winterpostille* 1528, WA 21, 58–59: "so ist der ehestand ein stand des glaubens . . . so ist es ein stand der liebe, nicht der fleischlichen liebe, sondern, darynne eines dem andern aus liebe dienen, ratten und helffen mus und sol."

28. Ibid., 59–60: "Alhie solten wir Gotte dancken, das er uns ein creutz hette auffgelegt, denn wir müssen yhe durchs creutz und leiden selig werden, wir müssen unglück und anfechtung haben, es sey entweder hie ym leben odder am todbett durch den Teuffel."

29. Ibid., 63: "Sie gebrauchte hie nicht yhr mütterlich recht gegen yhrem sone, denn sie yhm wol solchs zu thuen hette gebieten künnen, sondern gleubets und hielts gewis dafur, das ers thuen würde, wenn nu seine zeit furhanden were."

30. Ibid., 64: "Dis exempel ist fast wol zu mercken widder die, die da sagen, die Christliche kirche künne nicht yrren, die heiligen veter künnen nicht yrren, Ja wol hie sehet yhr das widderspiel auch an dem allerheiligsten menschen, an Marien der mutter Gottes, die on zweiffel ein grössern, sterckern glauben hat gehabt denn yrgend ein heilige, noch yrret sie hie."

31. Ibid., 65: "Auch hat Christus dazu mal gemarckt und verstanden, das man mit der zeit seiner mutter mehr ehre geben und uschreiben würde denn Christo selbs, nemlich, das man sie würde fur eine mitleryn und fürsprecheryn halten zwischen Got und uns, dem furzukomen feret er sie nicht allein hie, sondern an andern ortten mehr hart an, damit er anzeiget,, das es nicht umb sie zu thuen sey, sondern umb yhn . . . Christus verbeut hie nicht, das wir nicht fur einander bitten sollen, sondern das vertrawen und zuversicht mus allein auff Christum gestellet sein."

32. Luther, "Am Andern Sontag nach dem Obersttag, Euangelion Joh. 2," WA 52, 110–111: "Sonderlich aber wissen ewr liebe, wie der Ehstand unter dem Bapstthumb seer ist geringert worden, Und allein die junckfrawschafft und keuschheyt (der man doch nicht vil drinn gefunden) gepreyset. Wie aber Gott die Ehlosen geystlichen widerumb bezalet und gestraffet hab, wissen wir zü gütter maß."

33. Ibid., 111: "Aber da ist keiner gewest, der diß liecht het können sehen und sagen: Wenn es denn so güt ist, in die Wüsten gehen oder in das Kloster lauffen, warumb ist doch Christus auff die hochzeit gangen?"

34. Ibid., 112: "wo hochzeyt, das ist: Vatter und Mütter ist, da muß ein haußhalten sein, da wirdt weyb unnd kindt, knecht und magd, vich, Acker, handwerck und narung sein."

35. Ibid.: "Knecht und magd im hauß auch also, wenn sie thün, was jre herrschafft sie heyst, so dienen sie Gott, und so ferrn sie an Christum glauben, gefelt es Gott vil baß, wenn sie nur ein Stuben keren oder Schüch außwischen, denn aller München betten, fasten, Meßhalten, und was sie mer für hohe Gottes dienst rhümen."

36. Ibid., 114: "wenn man im hauß dienet, das es Gott sey gedienet."

37. Ibid.: "Denn solt nit ein magd im hauß, die kochen und anders thün muß, solches sich trösten und frewen unnd sagen: Das ich kochen und anders thün muß, das ist eben der lieben Junckfrawen Maria dienst auff der hochzeyt gewesen, die kochet auch und sahe, wie es alles wol verrichtet wurd. Ein geringes werck ist es. Aber die person ist seer hoch und groß und thüts auch der ursach halb, das sie waiß, das es unserm Herrn Gott wolgefelt."

38. Ibid., 116: "Denn da ist einer gefangen mer denn mit zweintzig stricken. Von solchen stricken machen die argen Büben sich loß und leben nach jhrem eygen willen."

39. Andreas Osiander, *Ain schöne Sermon / Geprediget zü Nüremberg von Andreas Oseander / prediger zü S. Lorentzen am Sontag Misericordia Domini auff dy Euangelium Johannes. Secundo. u[sw]*, (N.p., 1523), B r: "das gott im anfang vn[d] schöpfu[n]g der welt / kain erlichern gesellschafft oder brüderschafft / vn[d] kain wirdigen seckt hat gewyßt auffzürichten / vnd züsam[m]en fügeu[n] / das im zü seinem götlichen lob / liepplicher / vnd fruchtparlicher wurd dz himelschlich vaterland zü zieren / als den hailigen eerlichenstand des eelichen lebens/"

40. Seehofer, *Enarrationes Evangeliorvm* (1539), XLv: "Hactenus autem ordo iste apud multos non infimæ classis homines præter meritum male audiuit, huic enim apud gentiles iniqui fueru[n]t maximi uiri, qui matrimonium impie uocarunt necessarium malum."

41. Brenz, *Pericopæ Euangeliorum . . . Singvlis Diebvs Dominicis* (1556), 166: "Na[m] si co[m]mendatur matrimoniu[m], existima[n]t adolesce[n]tiores sibi impunè licere pro sua libididine matrimoniu[m] co[n]trahere. Si uituperatur, condemnatur ordinatio Dei."

42. Ibid.: "Attamen neceßitas exigit, ut ratio co[n]iugii explicetur et co[n]iuges erudia[n]tur."

43. Ibid., 170: "Non possum melius docere quàm Paulus ad Ephesios, qui cùm doceat, matrimonium esse Sacramentum Christi et Ecclesiæ, docet primum inter coniuges debere esse uerum studium Religionis."

44. Ibid.: "Deinde iubet maritum diligere uxorem, et uxorem obedire marito. Hæc sunt præcipua præcepta."

45. Ibid.: "Si adest dilectio mariti, et obedientia uxoris, constat et tranquillitas."

46. Corvinus, *Kurtze vnd ainfeltige Außlegung . . . auff die Sonntage vnd fürnemesten Feste* (1545), 26v: "[E]s wirdt im ersten büch Mosi angezaigt / wie vmb der übertrettung willen vnser ersten Eltern / disem stand ain hoch schwär Creütz auffgelegt worden sey."

47. Ibid.: "Demnach müssen wir nun hie leernen / dieweil Gott solchen stande selber eingesetzt / vnd durch Christum so herrlich gezieret hat / das derhalben vnnder sollichem creütz / eytel gnad verborgen sein müsse."

48. Ibid.: "Ist dir aber gnad gegeben züenthalten / solt du darumb nicht in ain Closter geen / sonder vnder dem gehorsam deiner Eltern vnnd Oberkait bleiben / . . . Dann keüsch leben ist gütt / Freyen ist auch güt / vnd mag auch ain keüsch leben gehaissen werden / . . . Aber den Eltern vnd der Oberkait gehorsam entziehen / ist nicht güt."

49. Huberinus, *Postilla Teutsch* (1548), n.p. (before Niii): "[Christ] kommen sey / nemlich der aller ersten / vnnd eltesten Stand . . . widerumb zu recht brechte . . . dieweil doch alles an disem stande gelegen ist / vnd die andern zwen stend / Predig ampt / vnnd Oberkeyt / auß disem stand kommen."

50. Erasmus Alberus, *Ein Predigt vom Ehestand / vber das Euangelium / Es war ein Hochzeit zu Cana etc.* (Magdeburg[?]: Christian Rödinger, 1550), C r.

51. Ibid., Ciiv: "Denn Gott nimpt jm aus dem Ehestand Bewmlein / Blümlin vnd Rosen / die er in sein Ewiges Reich setzet vnd pflantzet."

52. Ibid., Ciijv: "Der Satan verblendt der Menschen augen / das sie nicht sehen noch mercken / wie ein köstlich kleinot der Ehestand sey." Johannes Wigand notes, "Sonst hat der Herr Christus auch den Ehestand gezieret / das er hat aus Maria wöllen geboren werden / da sie dem Joseph vertrawet war" (*Postilla*, 167).

53. Cyriacus Spangenberg, *Ehespiegel: Das ist/ Alles was vom heyligen Ehestande / nützliches / nötiges / vnd tröstliches mag gesagt werden. Jn Sibentzig Brautpredigten* (Strassburg: Samuel Emmel, 1573), 95r: "Wir werden hye auch vermanet / das man

den Ehestandt / ohn wissen der Mütter Christi / das ist / ohn bestätigung vnd be-
zeügnuß / der heyligen Christlichen Kirchen / nicht vollziehen soll. Dise heylige
Mütter / soll mit irem Gebett vnd auffsehen / auch dabey sein."

54. Vischer, *Außlegung der Euangelien . . . Vom Aduent bis auff Ostern* (1570), before t: "Wenn man nu den Herrn Christum zur Hochzeit gebeten / so sol man auch
Mariam die Mutter Christi dazu laden / das ist / der Christlichen Kirchen gemeines
Gebet für sich thun lassen / welchs Gott / laut seiner verheissung vnd zusagung /
gewislich erhören wil."

55. See, among others, Corvinus, *Loci,* between b and c; Culmann, *Sacræ Contiones,* 69v; Hemmingsen, *Postilla,* 172.

56. Wigand, *Postilla* (1569), 165: "Es wird aber in Maria ein Exempel der rechtschaffenen lieb gesehen / die da begert diesen armen Eheleutlein zu helffen vnd
handreichung zuthun / vnd verachtet nicht den schlechten vnd geringen vorrhat /
dieser armen Leutlein / Sondern sie hat ein hertzliches mitleiden mit jnen."

57. Hemmingsen, *Postilla* (1571), 172: "VRsach solches mirackels ist viererley /
. . . 4. Das getrewe Hertz der Jungfrawen Marie / welche zu helffen vnd zu rathen
gantz willig vnd geneigt war."

58. Ibid., 177–178: "VOn Maria sollen wir lernen / vns vber andere Leute erbar-
men / vnnd jrer nodturfft vns annemen / Gott den HERRen für sie bitten / das er
den Armen mit seinem segen beistehen wölle."

59. Artopoeus, *Evangelicae Conciones* (1537), 35v: "EVangelium est generis De-
monstratiui rei, ubi commendantur nupciæ, et miraculum Christi. Generis Didascalici, ubi fidem et orationem in Maria docemur."

60. Ibid., 36v: "Peroratio Maria assequitur sua uota. Aqua in uinum conuertitur.
Dominus quamuis nobis durus apparet, non tamen repellit nos in oratione. Ipse scit
horam exaudiendi."

61. Brenz, *Pericopæ Euangeliorum . . . Singvlis Diebvs Dominicis* (1556), 174–175:
"[I]n hodierno Euangelio [Maria] præbet nobis utile exemplum ad consequendam pe-
titionem nostram in oratione ad Deu[m]. . . . Obseruabile exemplum, quo admonemur
ut perseueremus in fide, in oratione et in obedientia Dei."

62. Alberus, *Ein Predigt vom Ehestand* (1550), E r: "Hie sehen wir auch / was das
rechte Gebet sey. Besten heist / Wenn wir vnserm HERRn Gott vnsere not furbrin-
gen. Welches wir leider im Bapstumb nicht verstanden haben / da wir meineten / das
vnnütze geblepper vnd Götzen anruffen / were das rechte Gebet."

63. Ibid., 175: "Deus enim non respondet statim precibus pij, non q[ui] non ex-
audiuerit eum, sed ut accendat fidem nostrum."

64. Corvinus, *Kurtze vnd ainfeltige Außlegung . . . auff die Sonntage vnd fürnemesten Feste* (1545), 27r: "Ja wenn sich die sach dermassen liesse ansehen / als solte dir
alle hülff versagt sein / so solt du gleich wol nicht zagen oder zweifflen / dann vnder
solchem still schweigen ist ain gewisser trost / vnder solchem nain / ist ain gewisses
ja verborgen."

65. Paul Eber, *Postilla* (1578), 77v: "Aber er wil helffen / wenn es jm gefellig ist /
nicht wenns vns gelegen ist . . . daß er viel tausent mal klüger vnnd weiser sey denn
wir / vnnd daß er mehr wisse denn wir / wenn es zeit zu helffen sey / vnd wie er
helffen sol."

66. Johannes Baumgarten, *Eine Predigt Vom Ehestande / vber das Euangelium von
der Hochzeit zu Cana in Galilea* (N.p.: 1568) (Herzog August Bibliothek [Wolfenbüttel];
St. Paul, Minn.: Lutheran Brotherhood Foundation Reformation Library, microfiche),
between A and B: "Welches Maria (die ein Figur der Mutter der heilige[n] Christen-

heit ist) mit jrem waren glauben vnd bestendigem bekentnis . . . krefftiglichen bezeu-
get."

67. Ibid., between C and D: "Dieweil denn Maria die Mutter des HERRN / vns als eine Figur der Mutter der heiligen Christenheit vorgebildet wird / vnd die heilige Christliche Kirche / beyd im Alt vnd Newen Testament eben das gleubet vnd helt von Christo / das do helt vnd gleubet die Mutter Gottes Maria / Nemlich / das Gott der HErr seine Benediction vnd Segen / vber die Ehelichen vnd jre Haushaltunge spricht."

68. Hemmingsen, *Postilla* (1571), 174: "Gibt vns eine gemeine lere in der Kirchen / welcher fürbild vnd gliedmas die Jungfraw Maria gewesen ist. Was hat denn die Christliche Kirche hieraus zu lernen? Das sie mit der heiligen Jungfrawen Maria den Dienern vnnd allen Christen befehle / jrem HErrn Christo zu folgen / vnd zu thun alles was er sie heisset / ob es gleich jrer vernunfft scheinet gar zu wider sein."

69. Vischer, *Außlegung der Euangelien . . . Vom Aduent bis auff Ostern* (1570), n.p. (after t): "Darneben müssen wir auch dem trewen raht Marie folgen / vnd vns daraus auch ein sprichwort machen / Alles was er euch saget / das thut. . . . Wenn wir raum dazu hetten / solten wir auch dauon sagen / das die heilige Königliche Jüngfraw Maria / allen ehrliebenden Matronen vnd Weibsbildern zum exempel . . . [sie] gedultig vnd sanfftmütig die vnfreundliche antwort duldet vnd vertregt: Also sollen sich Weibsbilder vnd Jungfrawen von jugend auff dazu gewehnen / das sie sanfftmütig vnd gedultig sein / jren öbern etwas vertragen."

70. Ibid., t iiijr: "Wir sollen aber Marie das Meisterstuck ablernen / die den harten puff gedultig ausstehet / . . . nicht vom Gebete ablest / sondern den harten bissen verschlunget."

71. Graef, vol. 1, 20.

72. Geiler, *Postill* (1522), XXIIIIv: "[Jesus said:] was gost du mich an in dißem stuck / dz ich sol ein wunderzeiche[n] würcken / welchs wundereichen würcken ich nitt hab von menschlicher ntur / die ich hab / sonder von göttlich[n] natur . . . Do- rumb was hab ich mitt dir züschaffen frow / oder was hab ich mit dir gemeynschafft . . . Do zü so ist mein stund noch nit hye / das ich wil eigen mein menschliche natur / die ich von dir hab. wen[n] das würt erst geschehen so ich wurd liden vnd sterben."

73. Ibid.: "[I]ch sol vnd wil warten der zeit / bitz dz der vol gebrust vnd mangel erschinet / vnd dz der selb mangel vn[d] gebrust yederman offenbar ist / vnd das man deßhalben mercken kan . . . das es ein groß wnnderzeichen ist."

74. Osiander, *Ain schöne Sermon* (1523), Aiijr: "[W]aru[m]b nenet er sy weyb vn[d] nit müter (daru[m]b) dan[n] sy begeret hym[m]lische götliche werck / über die was sy kain müter / nur über die me[n]schait Christi."

75. Baumgarten, *Eine Predigt Vom Ehestande* (1568), between A and B: "menge sie sich in die dinge / die der Gottheit alleine zu zueigenen sein / das kan die Gott- eit in Christo niemand / auch seiner leiblichen Mutter nicht gönnen."

76. Ibid., Cijv-Ciijr: "das Christus der HErre selbst die Haus sorge der Ehelichen / die Göttlichen zuuersthen / auff sich genommen / vnd jm die allein wil vorbehal- ten haben . . . vnd solche sorge keinem andern gönnen / auch seiner eigen Mutter selber nicht." Huberinus also sounds this theme in his *Postilla Teutsch*, between m and n.

77. Ibid., Ciijv: "Also solt er sagen: Liebe Mutter / als dein leiblicher Son wil ich dir gerne gehorsam sein / vnd thun was ich meiner natürlichen Mutter zuthun vorp- flicht vnd schuldig bin. Aber das do belanget etwas vber das was Menschlich / als

geben do nichtes ist / oder Wein zapffen aus einem ledigen Vas do nichtes jnnen ist
. . . Warlich das eigent keinem Menschen / sondern gehöret eigentlichen Gott zu."
[Cf. Acts 5:29]

78. Eber, *Postilla* (1578), 77r: "[Christus spricht] ich weiß wol / wenn es zeit ist
zu helffen."

79. Culmann, *Sacræ Contiones* (1550), 70r: "Deus personarum respector non
est." See also Corvinus, *Loci*, between B and C; his *Kurtze Auslegung*, 27; cf. Acts 10:
34 (NRSV): "God shows no partiality."

80. Culmann, *Sacræ Contiones* (1550), 70r: "Ergo fides facit nos Christi fratres.
Mar. 3."

81. Vischer, *Außlegung der Euangelien . . . Vom Aduent bis auff Ostern* (1570), tiijv.

82. Brenz, *Pericopæ Euangeliorum . . . Singvlis Diebvs Dominicis* (1556), 173: "Vbi
uero Maria no[n] eum tantum honorem quærit, qui debetur parentibus, sed etiam
ambit honorem Meßiæ, et cupit esse quasi socia administran[n]di eius officij."

83. Ibid., 172–173: "[N]ullus unquam filius plus honorauit matrem suam
quàm Christus. Lex enim Dei est: Honora parentes, quam impleuit Christus per-
fectißimè."

84. Walther, *Auslegung der Euangelien . . . an den Sontagen* (1579), 312: "[Christ]
hat derhalben das ansehen / als habe er gar zu hart geantwortet / vnd er gebe damit
andern Kindern ein böses Exempel / das sie dergleichen jre Veter vn[d] Mütter also
vnfreundlich beantworten vnd anfaren / Aber wo man die vmbstende ansihet so be-
findet man / das er nichts zuuiel noch zu hart geantwortet / denn seine Mutter zu
weit gegangen it / vber jhren Beruff / vnd Christo in sein Ampt gefallen / vnd gleich
begeret / das er auff jr suche[n] solte ein wunderzeichen / jr zu gefallen vnd ehrn
thun." Johannes Mathesius suggests that Mary asked Jesus to perform this miracle,
not necessarily for her own benefit, but because she had seen Jesus turn water into
wine before, when he was a child. See his 1565 *Postilla*, 54r. Johannes Wigand also
intimates that Jesus had helped Mary before through his divine power, as they had
been very poor while he was growing up. See his 1569 *Postilla*, 165.

85. Ibid., 314–315: "so sey Maria auch nicht gentzlich ohne Sünde / denn sonsten würde er nicht also jhr harte wort gegeben haben."

86. Selneccer, *Evangeliorvm . . . Pars Prima* (1575), 530: "Quæritur hîc à nonnullis
de Mariæ compellatione ad Filium, num peccauerit? Certè Maria rectè facit, quod
neceßitatibus amicorum afficitur, et quòd eas ad Filium defert. . . . In eo autem Maria
nimium humanis affectibus indulsit, primùm, quòd materna fiducia et autoritate
vteretur erga Filium in rebus Dei, id quod Filius in diuinis rebus admittere nolebat,
quandoquidem gloriæ Christi detraheret."

87. Ibid.: "Ex his due discimus: Prius est, de agnoscenda imbecillitate etiam
sanctißimorum. Maria enim non excusatur, quasi nunquam humanis affectibus in-
dulserit, alioqui Christus culpandus esset, qui eam culpauit. . . . Posterius est de dis-
crimine obedientiæ erga Deum, et erga parentes."

88. Ibid., 531: "Delinquentes igitur non molestè feramus obiurgationem, nec res-
ponsatores simus, sed agnoscamus culpam et emendemus in melius."

89. Chemnitz, *Postilla* (1594), 269.

90. Osiander, *Ain schöne Sermon* (1523), Aiiiv: "So nur cristus der ewig got vnd
herr hat sölichs seiner lieb[e]n müter marie also zü erfrag[e]n vn[d] wissen / vnd jr
beger oder bitt darbey abgeschlagen/vn[d] ain anzaigung geben / dz er selbs on gebet-
ten vn[d] ongemandt den sünder erhören will / so der sünder ain gerecht hertz vnd
gemüt im glaben zü im tregt."

91. Vischer, *Außlegung der Euangelien . . . Vom Aduent bis auff Ostern* (1570), t iiijr:

"Sonderlich hat der Herr Christus dem grewlichen / Gotteslesterlichem vnd abergleu-
bischem gebrauch des Bapsthums stewren vnd wehren wollen / das wir nicht die heilige Jungfraw Mariam / oder andere verstorbene Heiligen / anruffen oder anlangen /
vns mehr trostes zu jnen / denn zu Christo selbs / dem Brunnen der gnaden verse-
hen."

92. Hemmingsen, *Postilla* (1571), 173: "Darumb haben die Abgöttische / aber-
gleubische Leute lesterlich vnd vnrecht gehandelt / das sie die Jungfrawen Mariam
eine Königin der Himel nenneten vnd verehrten / Jtem / sie anrieffen als jre Fürsprecherin / jr Leben / süssigkeit / Mutter der Gnaden / vnd das Heil der Welt. Denn
man soll der Maria kein teil der Erlösunge zuschreiben."

6. OTHER MARIAN HOLIDAYS

1. Luther, *Das Euangelium ynn der Christmeß*, WA 10¹ I, 66–67: "aber wyr sollen
bey dem Euangelio bleyben, das do sagt, sie habe yhn geporn, und bey dem artickell
des glawbens, da wyr sagen: der geporn ist von Marien der iungfrawen."

2. Ibid., 67: "on das sie on sund, on schand, on schmertzen vnnd on vorserung
geporn hatt, wie sie auch on sund empfangen." Geiler says of the birth: "Jr solle[n]
mercke[n] dz Maria dz kind gebore[n] hat on hebame[n] / vn[d] on alle[n] schmer-
tze[n] / da wz kein winde[n] / kein angst od[er] not. Nitt anders wed[er] ein glast vo[n]
der sonne[n] durch ein glaß ynstreimet / vnd das glaß vngeletzt bleibt. Also hat Maria
gebore[n] Cristu[m] Jesum / vnuerruckt jrer schloß / vn[d] ist iunckfraw blibe[n] vor
der geburt / in der geburt vnd nach der geburt / wer anders von jr glaubt d[er] wer
ein ketzer." (*Das euangeli buch* (1515), 164r) Luther avoids such questions as how a
human baby can pass through a womb like light passing through a window by avoiding such metaphors altogether.

3. Luther, *Das Euangelium ynn der Christmeß*, WA 10¹ I, 68: "Natur ist an yhm
unnd seyner mutter reyn geweßen, ynn allen glidenn, ynn allenn wercken der glider."

4. Luther, "Am heyligen Christag das Euangelion Luce am ij. Die erste predigt,"
Festpostille 1544, WA 52, 39: "das Gottes Son ist mensch worden, Nicht wie Eva noch
wie Adam, der auß erden ist gemacht worden, Sonder ist uns noch neher gefreundet,
sintemal er auß dem fleisch unnd blüt der Junckfraw Maria geborn ist wie andere
menschen."

5. Luther, WA 10¹ I, 67: "Der fluch Eue ist nit ubir sie gangen, der da lautt: ynn
schmertzen solltu deyn kindern geperen . . ."

6. Luther, "In der Christnacht Messe," *Festpostille* 1527, WA 17², 304: "Diser geburt zühelffen hat Got geschickt ain andere geburt, die da rain und unbefleckt sein
müste, solte sie die unraine, sündliche geburt rain machen, Das ist nun dise geburt
des herrn Christi seines aingebornen sons, Und darumb hat er jn auch nit wöllen
auß aim sündlichen flaisch und blüt lassen geboren werden, sonder er solt von ainer
junckfrawen allain geborn werden."

7. Ibid., 305–306: "Da ist nu Heua die erste mütter nymmer meyne mütter,
denn die selbige gepurt müs gar sterben und vergehen, dz nicht mehr sünde da ist,
Da müs ich wider die mütter, von welcher ich bin in sünden geporen, dise mütter
Mariam setzen."

8. Artopoeus, *Evangelicae Conciones* (1537), 14v: "Mater permansit uirgo, contra
naturam et rationem."

9. See WA 47, 704; 11, 71; 11, 320; 36, 145f., among other citations. To find a full
discussion of this point by Luther in translation (along with notes), see LW 45, 206–
213 ("That Jesus Christ Was Born a Jew"). For more information on the debates con-

cerning the term, see John F. A. Sawyer, *The Fifth Gospel: Isaiah in the History of Christianity* (Cambridge: Cambridge University Press, 1996), esp. 65–82.

10. Corvinus, *Kurtze vnd ainfeltige Außlegung . . . auff die Sonntage vnd fürnemesten Feste* (1545), 14r: "Vnser geburt ist vnrain / sündtlich vnd verdampt / Die geburt Christi aber / ist rain / vnschuldig / vnd hailig. Sol nun das verdamnuß vnser geburt / gewandelt vnd weg genom[m]en werden / So müß es durch die hailigen geburt Jesu Christi geschehen."

11. Ibid.: "gaistlich / durchs wort . . . Da der Engel sagt / Eüch / Eüch (sagt er) ist der Hayland geboren."

12. Huberinus, *Postilla Teutsch* (1548), n.p.: "Vom Vatter ist er in ewigkeit geborn / on ein mutter / Inn der zeyt / ist er / nach der menscheit / von Marie geboren / on einen natürlichen Vatter / dergleichen kinder ist keines auff erden nye geborn worden."

13. Culmann, *Sacræ Contiones* (1550), vol. 3, 30r: "quia filius in ipsa conceptus substantiam suam de substantia matrix acceperat, atq; ideo filius matris erat, illa q; suum proprium filiu[m], non phantasma quodam genuit."

14. Wigand, *Postilla* (1569), 67.

15. Geiler, *Postill* (1522), 9v: "In de[m] selben stall (sprich ich) gebar Maria die müter gottes iren erstgeborne[n] sün. Do solt ich eüch ermanen zü einfalt / armüt / vnd demüt."

16. Luther, *Kirchenpostille 1522*, WA 10¹ I, 63: "Denck, wie sie unterwegen ynn herbergen voracht geweßen, die doch wirdig war, das man sie mit gulden wagen und aller pracht gefurtt hette."

17. Ibid., 65: "Szondernn alda on alle bereyttung, on liecht, on fewr, mitten yn der nacht, ym finsternn alleyn ist [sie], niemand beutt yhr eynigen dienst ann, wie man doch naturlich pflegt schwangernn weybern."

18. Luther, *Hauspostille 1544*, WA 52, 38: "Denn obgleych die junckfraw Maria ein bettlerin oder mit züchten zü reden, ein unehrliche fraw gewesen, die die ehr het hindan gesetzt, so solt man doch zür solchen zeyt, jr zü dienen, willig unnd geneygt sein."

19. Luther, *Festpostille 1527*, WA 17², 302: "Hieraus sollen wir lernen, das es uns auch nit bewegen sol, ob wir gleich arm, elend und von der welt verlassen sind, Denn hye haben wir ein grossen trost, hat Christus der schepffer aller dynge unnd seyne liebste mütter yhnn solchem elend müssen ligen . . . dieweyl wir sehen, das der herre Christus solche not, armut und elend gelitten hat."

20. Luther, *Festpostille 1522*, 10¹ I, 139: "seyn armut lere, wie wyr yhn sollen finden ynn unßerm nehsten, dem geringsten und durfftigen."

21. Johann Locher, *Eyn lieplicher Sermon Colligiert an dem heyligen Christag / Gemainem man / durch das/ gantz Jar vast trostlich / Wie man das Kindlein Jhesum süchen soll* (Zwickau: Georg Gastel, 1524), B v: "Darumb welt yr Marie vnnd Jhesu Ere erzeygen / so mügt yrs noch heüt bey []ags thün-Wie ynn den armen."

22. Johann Spangenberg, *Außlegung der Episteln vnd Euangelien / von Aduent, biß auffs Ostern* (N.p., 1584), 26r: "Wobey erkennt man es / daß Christus in vns geboren ist? Wenn wir vns aller vnser güter eussern / vns vnsers nechsten noth / angst / jammer vnd ellende annemen / den hungerigen speisen / den durstigen trencken / den nacketen kleiden / den krancken besuchen / u[sw]."

23. Geiler, *Das euangeli buch* (1515), 164r: "Das ander stücklin des euangeliu[m]s ist marie ghorsame vnd Josephs. Wa sie seind vff gangen von dem Galileischen land . . . sich zü bekenne[n] vnd[er]worffen sein dem keiser."

24. Luther, *Festpostille 1527*, WA 17², 301: "Disem Kaiserlichen gepot was Joseph und Maria auch gehorsam, ertzaigeten sich wie ander fromme, gehorsame leutte, zo-

gen hin gehn Bethlehem. . . . Maria dieweil sich schwanger war und der gepurt nahe, hette sich fur solcher reyhse wol künden entschuldigen, aber sie thüts nicht, wöllen nit ergernus geben den andern."

25. Corvinus, *Loci in Evangelia* (1536), before b: "Egregius locus contra Anabaptistas, qui obedientiam impijs principibus non debert, contendunt hoc tempore."

26. Huberinus, *Postilla Teutsch* (1548), n.p.: "Also sollen wir auch von jhr den gehorsam lernen / vnser Oberkeit willig / vnd bereit sein / auch mit gferligkeyt vnsers leibs / guts / vnd lebens / dann das sind wir schuldig / dann thut Maria / einer Heydnischen Oberkeyt / solchen gehorsam, wie vil mehr sollen wirs einer Christlichen Oberkeit leisten / die vns / auch vnser Religion schützet / vns zu lasset Gottes wort zuhören / den rechten Gottesdienst zubegehn / vnd ein Christich Policey vnter vns erhaltet."

27. Eber, *Postilla* (1578), 29v: "Zum dritten / wirt vns hie ein fein Exempel geben / vnd fürgeschrieben / daß ein jeder Vnderthaner / er sey wer er wölle / vor Gott schüldig ist / seiner Obrigkeit gehorsam zu seyn / in alle dem / das sie jm gebeut vnd befihlet / das nit wider Gott vnd sein Gewissen ist / sondern allein zeitliche sachen betreffend."

28. Victorinus Strigel, *Postilla Sive Explicationes Evangeliorum, quæ diebus Dominicis vsitato more in Ecclesia proponuntur, Scriptæ à Victorino Strigelio. Et nunc primùm editæ, opera & studio Christophori Pezelii, Sacræ Theologiæ Doctoris* (Neustadt an der Haardt: Matthæus Harnisch, 1584) (Herzog August Bibliothek [Wolfenbüttel]; St. Paul, Minn.: Lutheran Brotherhood Foundation Reformation Library, microfiche), 98: "Sic Ioseph & Maria obtemperant Magistratus edictis, & non defugiunt officia politica, vt exemplo suo nos doceant, ne prætextu libertatis Christianæ affectemus immunitatem & publicorum onerum leuatiatiionè."

29. Wigand, *Postilla* (1569), 78: "Daher lernen wir / das in einem jeglichen ehrlichen ampt / die Menschen Gott dienen / jn recht ehren vnd preisen können."

30. Ibid., 79: "Derhalben ist gar kein zweiffel / das man in allem anderen Leben / von Gott verordnet / die Oberkeit / Eltern / Knecht vnd Hausgesinde mehr Gott könne dienen / denn in dem Klosterleben."

31. Luther, *Hauspostile* 1544, WA 52, 61: "Das aber ist die rechte enderung, umb welcher willen Christus ist kommen, das ein mensch innen im hertzen anderst werde."

32. Ibid., 59: "Das ist nu ein Exempel, an welchem man mag sehen und lernen, wie man Gottes wort recht soll hören. Sie bewegets in jrem hertzen, das ist: sie trachtet jhm fleyssig nach, . . . und so die gantze welt dawider gewest wer, so het ihrs doch niemandt benemen noch außreden können, sie würd jren Son für den Son Gottes und der gantzen welt heiland gehalten haben." Again we hear echoes of the Song of Songs.

33. Johannes Bugenhagen, *Indices . . . in Euangelia* (1524), A Vr: "Maria autem [exemplum fidei] etc. Hæc est meditatio sacra, et ardens in corde fides."

34. Wigand, *Postilla* (1569), 78.

35. Strigel, *Postilla* (1584), 116: "Porrò Mariæ exemplum palàm refutat fanaticos spiritus, qui fingunt ocioso animo expectandas esse cœlestes illuminationes, & repudiant doctrinam, studia, & exercitia docendi & discendi, sicut sæpe audiuimus impiè clamantes Anabaptistas."

36. Luther, *Kirchenpostille* 1522, WA 10[1] 1, 140: "Maria sey die Christliche kirche, Joseph der kirchen diener, alßo da seyn sollten die Bischoff und pfarrer, wenn sie predigeten das Euangelium. . . . Die Christlich kirche behellt nu alle wort gottis ynn yhrem hertzen unnd bewigt dieselben, hellt sie gennander und gegen die schrifft.

Darumb wer Christum finden soll, der muß die kirchen am ersten finden. . . . Nu ist die kirch nit holtz vnd steyn, ßondernn der hauff Christglewbiger leutt, tzu der muß man sich hallten und sehen, wie die glewben, leben und leren; . . . Darauß folgt, es sey unsicher und falsch, das der Bapst odder eyn bischoff will yhm alleyn geglewbt haben und sich fur eynen meyster außgibt; denn dieselben yrren alle und mügen yrren."

37. Ibid., 141: "denn nit Joseph, ßonndernn Maria behelt diße wortt yn yhrem hertzen."

38. Culmann, *Sacræ Contiones* (1550), vol. 3, 59r.

39. Vischer, "Am Newen Jars tage," in *Außlegung der Euangelien . . . Vom Aduent bis auff Ostern* (1570), between d and e: "das sie (vngeacht dessen / das jr pfleg vnd natürlich Kind auch zugleich des lebendigen ewigen Gottes lebendiger ewiger Son / nach seiner Göttlichen Geburt / vnd nach seiner Menschlichen geburt von dem heiligen Geist empfangen / vnd von jr der heiligen Jungfrawen Maria / ohne Sünde geboren war / vnd demnach seiner Person halben keiner Beschneidung bedorffte) das liebe newgeborne Kindlein Jhesum / am achten tage seines alters / nach Gottes befehl beschneiden lassen."

40. Luther, "Am Oberstag, Euang. Matthei am andern," in the *Hauspostille* 1544, WA 52, 89: "Das gefelt [die Papisten] an jhm nicht, das er allein soll der heyland sein. . . . Item sie rüffen die Junckfraw Marien an, das sie jhnen den Son versönen wölle, Meinen, solches anrüffen und fürbitt soll jhnen auch ein heyland sein . . . [da] Christus sei ein Richter, ein Hencker, ein Stockmeister. . . . Daher ists im Bapstthumb kommen, das yederman mer vertrawens auff die junckfrawen Maria und der heyligen fürbitt denn auff den Herrn Christum selb gestellet hat."

41. Ibid.: "So gehets, wo man nicht beim wort bleybt, Darumb ist dem Teuffel sonderlich vil dran gelegen, wie er uns vom wort reyssen und ausser dem wort auff eygne gedancke füren möge. Denn da weyß er, das er gewonnen unnd wir verloren haben."

42. Huberinus, *Postilla Teutsch* (1548), n.p.: "die Weisen / das kindlin allein / vnd nit die Mutter darzu anbeten / für dasselbig niderfallen / vnnd mit jhren schanckungen es allein ehren."

43. Luther, WA 52, 92: "Auff solch flucht und weyte rayse schaffet Gott durch dise weysen dem kindlein, seinem pfleger Joseph und der junckfrawen Maria ein zerung. . . . Derhalb wer armen, unvermöglichen, Hartseligen leuten mit gelt und güt hilffet, . . . Der opffert und schenckt dem armen kindlein Jesu."

44. Culmann, *Sacræ Contiones* (1550), vol. 3, 77v.

45. Corvinus, *Kurtze außlegung . . . an den fürnemsten Fästen* (1545), 14v: "Wölche flucht on allen zweiffel / gemeltem Joseph vnd Marien nicht ain gering Creütz gewesen ist . . . Christus war inn dise welt zü leiden geben."

46. Huberinus, *Postilla / Deudsch* (1554), 75r–v: "die heilig Junckfraw Maria / vnd Joseph sich mit jrem vnschuldigen Kindlin haben leiden müssen / Solche sind wol auch rechte Marterer / dann sie werden von den Gottlosen wol so vbel geplagt vnd zermartert."

47. Brenz, *Pericopæ Euangeliorum . . . Singvlis Diebvs Dominicis* (1556), 103: "Discamus igitur primùm exe[m]plum obedientiæ: debemus enim præceptis Dei obedire sine tergiuersatione. Nam fieri solet, ut præcepta Dei uideantur co[n]tra promissa eius."

48. Vischer, *Außlegung der Euangelien . . . Vom Aduent bis auff Ostern* (1570), n.p. (after g): "Also wil er vns trewe Leute in vnserm elende erwecken . . . Wie er hie Joseph / Mariam / vnd Christum / aus jrem elende erlöset / vnd widerumb in Judeam gebracht hat."

49. Luther, *Hauspostille* 1544, WA 52, 602: "Denn an dem ist kein zweyffel, Maria und Joseph und villeicht andere mit jnen . . . von dem grossen wunder, das mit disem Kind geschehen, gepredigt unnd andere zum glauben und seligkeyt bracht haben."

50. Huberinus, *Postilla / Deudsch* (1554), 80r: "vnd da wirdt on zweiffel / Joseph / vnd Maria / bey etlichen guten leuten / das Euangelion geoffenbaret haben / vnd ein sonder heufflein / vnd Kirchen angericht haben / welche an das Kindlin Jesum geglaubt / vnd selig worden sind."

51. Ambrose, *De Inst. Virg.*, 49; cited in Graef, vol. 1, 82.

52. Borgnet edition, v. 37, q. 150 (p. 219): "adjutrix redemptionis per compassionem." Cited in Graef, vol. 1, 273.

53. *On the Praise and Dignity of Mary* 2, 8; cited in Graef, vol. 1, 320.

54. Oberman, *Harvest of Medieval Theology*, 303. David Steinmetz points out in his study of Johannes von Staupitz (d. 1524), the Augustinian vicar-general who served as confessor to and influence upon Luther, that Staupitz also does not stress Mary as a co-redeemer with Christ, although he suggests that her sufferings at the cross bear fruit in the birth of the church—it is at the cross that Mary, now the bride of Christ, becomes the mother of the faithful. See Steinmetz, *Misericordia Dei: The Theology of Johannes von Staupitz in its Late Medieval Setting*, Studies in Medieval and Reformation Thought, ed. Heiko A. Oberman, vol. 4 (Leiden: E. J. Brill, 1968), 147–150.

55. Geiler, *Postill* (1522), 37r: "Und wann du noch jnen frogen wilt / so sprich / Wo ist mein vatter? Wo ist mein mütter? Nitt sprich / wo ist der vatter . . . Oder wo ist die Mütter? . . . Als ob sye nit sein mütter wer / vn[d] er nit sein vatter wer."

56. Luther, *Passio. Die Zwölfft Predig*, in *Hauspostille* 1544, WA 52, 810: "Man sol Vater und mutter in ehren haben, so wölle Got langes leben und alles glück widerfaren lassen, Wie denn Johannes, der hie solches gutes wercks halb gerhümet wirt, lenger denn andere Apostel gelebt hat, nemlich 68 jar nach der Aufferstehung Christi."

57. Vischer, *Christlich vnnd Einfeltige Auslegung der Sieben Wort vnsers lieben HErrn Jhesu Christi / die er am stamm des heiligen Creutzes / kurtz vor seinem köstbarlichen / thewren / aller heiligsten vnd aller krefftigsten Tode / geredt hat. Gestellet in Sieben Predigten/* . . . (Schmalkalden: Michel Schmuck, 1566), between E and F: "Also erfüllet er volkömlich für vns das Vierde Gebot Gottes / leistet seiner lieben Mutter volkomenen gehorsam / Büsset vnd bezalet damit für vnsern vngehorsam vnd wider spenstigkeit / die wir die zeit vnsers lebens / aus des leidigen Teuffel anstifftung / vnsern lieben Eltern erzeiget haben."

58. Jakob Andreae, *Passional Büchlein/ Das ist/ Die Historia des bittern vnd thewren leiden vnd sterbens/ auch der frölichen Aufferstehung vnsers HErrn Jhesu Christi / nach den vier Euangelisten / geprediget vnd ausgeleget in der Pfarrkirchen zu Wittenberg /* (Wittenberg: Johann Krafft, 1577), 76r: "sonderlich aber / da wir arme trostlose Eltern hetten / versorgen sollen."

59. Kaspar Kantz, *Die historia des leydens Jesu Christi nach den vier Euangelisten. Vnd auch von der Juden Osterlamm / mit trostlicher außlegung. 1538* (Wittenberg: Jörg Rhaw, 1538), G iiij r: "Dann vatter vnd mütter / weib vnd kinder u[sw.] verhindern manchen menschen ann der volg Christi / wer nun solchs merckt / der müß sie faren lassen vnd Gott befelhen . . . vnd sie fromen leüten befelhen / wenn er nit mer kan bey jhn bleiben."

60. Drach, *Die Passio Jesu Christi außgelegt Doctor Joannes Draconites* (Frankfurt: Cyriacus Jacob, [1544]), after R: "Er nennet sie aber darumb weib / daß in Gottes

sachen die erste Tafel hoher sol geachtet werden denn die andere . . . Denn man müß
Gott mehr gehorchen denn menschen."

61. Vischer, *Christlich vnnd Einfeltige Auslegung der Sieben Wort* (1566), G r: "Er
wil auch vns lehren / das wir nicht sollen zu der heiligen Jungfrawen Maria vmb
hülffe lauffen / oder sie vmb trost ersuchen / Sie hat zu der erlösung des Menschlichen geschlechts lauters nichts für jre Person geholffen / Christus ist der einige
Mittler vnd Gnadenthron." The only other reference I found to Mary's role in salvation is somewhat oblique: Selneccer criticizes the "blasphemy of the Jews" [*blasphemia
Iudæorum*] by which Mary is called *Tthluima*, or *matrem crucifixi* [mother of the crucified one]. He insists that it is the crucified Christ who is our glory and life. See his
Distributio Historiæ Passionis, in Selneccer, *Evangeliorvm et Epistolarvm Dominicalivm,
Explicationis Pars Secunda. A 'Dominica Quadragesimæ siue Inuocauit, vsque ad Resurrectionis diem solennem: continens Historiam Paßionis Domini nostri Iesu Christi* (Frankfurt: n.p., 1575), 356.

62. Luther, *Passio. Die Zwölfft Predig*, WA 52, 810: "Denn was der Herr hie am
creutz thut und redet, sol man nicht einziehen auf wenige oder einzehliche personen,
Er fasset mit seinem werck und worten die gantze welt, sonderlich aber seine Christlich Kirchen."

63. Ibid.: "einen gemeinen befehl sein gegen alle Christen unnd die gantze Kirche, das wir alle unter einander . . . sollen sein wie Mutter und Sun . . . In sonderheit
aber weil der Herr das wörtlin mutter und Sun füret, sihet er auff das Kirchen Regiment, das ist: auff bede theyl, Erstlich auff die, so das wort füren, und darnach auff
die zuhörer. Denn gleich wie ein muter das kindlein nehret und sein wartet mit allem
fleiß, biß es erstarcket, also thun die rechtschaffenen Prediger auch, haben mühe
und arbeit, biß sie das volck unterrichten und feine Christen auß jnen machen."

64. Ibid., 811.

65. Cyriacus Spangenberg, *Passio. Vom Leiden vnd sterben vnsers Herrn / Heilands
vnd Seligmachers Jesu Christi / etliche schöne vnd nützliche Predigten/ Durch M. Cyriacum Spangenberg / Prediger im Thal Mansfeld. Auffs newe vbersehen/ Vnd vier kurtze Pre-
digten/ darin die gantze Passion begriffen / darzu gethan* (Eisleben: Urban Gaubisch,
1564), Hh 5r: "Darnach werden wir auch alle mit einander durch das Exempel vermanet / das wir vns vnserer lieben Mutter / der Christlichen Kirchen annemen sollen /
sie nehren / zieren / schmücken / schützen / fördern helffen / vnd ein jeder nach
seinem vermögen das beste darbey thun."

66. Ibid.: "Die weltliche Oberkeit sollen Schulen vnd Kirchen helffen erhalten
vnd bessern / vnd wider die verfolger der Warheit / vnd Tyrannen / jren von Gott
befohlen Gewald / zu schutz vnd rettung der armen Christen gebrauchen. Die Vnter-
thanen sollen nach jhrem vermögen / mit vleissigem zuhören / vnd Gottseligem leben / vnd zimlicher handreichung / das Reich Christi helffen befördern."

67. Vischer, *Christlich vnnd Einfeltige Auslegung der Sieben Wort* (1566), G iiij:
"Fürsten, Herrn / vnd grosse Potentaten / sollen sich der armen Mariæ / der verlas-
senen Christlichen Kirchen / trewlich annemen / jrer pflegen vnd warten / darob
sein."

68. Heune, *Postilla* (1570), 141v: "dann hierinnen lauter Geheimnis stecket . . .
das Prediger vnd weltliche Regenten / die Kirchen Christi trewlich bawen / weiden
vnnd schützen sollen / daß reine gesunde lehr erhalten vnd propagiret, vnd Ketzern
geweret werde / u[sw]."

69. Gabriel Biel, *Sermo[n]es Gabrielis Biel Spire[]sis de festiuitatib[us] gloriose uirginis Marie. Passio[n]is d[omi]nice Sermo historialis notabilis atq[ue] preclarus venerabilis*

domini Gabrielis Biel Artium Magistri: sacre theologie Lice[n]tiati (Haguenau: n.p., 1515), E 3v: "nihil sedum: nihil indecens exterius gessisse: nequaq[ue] obliuiscens in tantis anguistijs: et fidei catholice / et virginalis pudicitie. Dolore[m] e[ni]m suum incomp[ar]abilem: et fides quam de filij sui resurrect[i]one habuit temp[er]auit vtcu[i]q[ue] ne deficeret."

70. Luther, "Sermon von der Betrachtung des heyligen leydens Christi," WA 2 (with changes in WA 21, 164–165), 136: "Der art seynd, die mitten yn der passion weyt auß reyßen und von dem abschied Christi zu Bethanien und von der Junckfrawen Marien schmertzen viel eyntragen und kummen auch nit weyter."

71. C. Spangenberg, *Passio* (1564), Hh 3r–v: "Jm Bapsthumb hat man alhie in diesem stück viel wort gemacht / von der mitleidung vnd jemerlichen schmertzen der heiligen Jungfraw Marien / vnd von jhren kleglichen geberden / niderfallen / Haar ausreifen / Henden ringen / Hertz klopffen / Amacht vnd Zetergeschrey / Vnd hat man diese ding so sehr getrieben / das man auch des HErrn Christi / vnd der frucht seines Leidens darüber vergessen / vnd nur die Jungfraw Maria beweinet hat / Das ist wenig nütz gewesen / vnd darzu eitel Menschen gedicht." A number of earlier writers had also followed (pseudo?-)Bernard on this point, who insisted that Mary maintained her "virginal modesty [*junkfreuliche sitigkeit*]" under the cross. See, for example, Johannes von Paltz, "Die himlische funtgrub," *Werke*, vol. 3, 211 (and fn. 58).

72. Ibid., Hh 3v: "Dennoch (sage ich) so ist widerümb kein stercker / behertzter / noch Mann haffter Weibsbild auff Erden kaum gewesen / als die liebe heilige Jungfraw Maria." As the Greek word for courage, *andreia*, incorporates the word for man, so often in the Christian tradition (and pagan tradition as well) a courageous woman was considered "manly." This is especially true of female martyrs, but also of female ascetics and virgins. See the article by Elizabeth Clark, "Devil's Gateway and Bride of Christ: Women in the Early Christian World," in *Ascetic Piety and Women's Faith: Essays in Late Ancient Christianity*, Studies in Women and Religion, vol. 20 (Lewiston: Edwin Mellon, 1986), especially 43–46. Mary had been deemed "manly" also in the medieval tradition: Paltz refers to her as *ritterlich* under the cross ["Die himlische funtgrub," 211.]

73. Vischer, *Christlich vnnd Einfeltige Auslegung der Sieben Wort* (1566), F v: "Nicht wunder were es gewest / jr hertz im leibe wer jr für leid zerschmoltzen / oder auff tausent stücke zersprungen / wie es denn sonder zweiffel Blut geweinet."

74. Ibid.: "Sondern sie lest Gott die rache / stehet in grosser gedult vnd standthafftigem Glauben . . . [F ijr] Noch ist sie so mannlich vnd ritterlich."

75. Ibid.: "Das alles ist vns zur Lehre vnd Exempel fürgeschrieben / das wir nicht so zarte Merterer sein sollen / die wir vmb Christi willen nichts leiden oder dulden / vnd vns nur allein zu jm bekennen wolten / wenns vns wol gehet / im Creutz aber wolten wir einen weiten von jm geben."

76. Ibid., F ijr: "Da Eua jren lieben Son Abel stein todt für sich hat ligen sehen / da ist jr sonder zweiffel weh vnd bang gewest / weil sie zuuor keinen todten Menschen gesehen."

77. Heune, *Postilla* (1570), 141r: "vnser Mutter Euæ drang auch ein Schwerdt durch Leib vnd Seel / . . . da sie erfuhr daß Cain Abel ermordet hatte / Aber Mariæ schmertz vnd leid ist viel höher vnd grösser gewesen / sie stehet vnter dem Creutz / sihet daß jhr lieber Son der ware Meßias mit Händen vnd Füssen angenagelt vnd also zugerichtet ist."

78. Hesshusen, *Funffzehen Passion Predigten. Vom Leiden vnd Sterben vnsers HErrn vnd Heilandes Jesu Christi*, in *Postilla* (1581), 74r: "Aber Maria stehet da fest im Glauben / wie eine starcke Heldin / ob jr wol das Schwert / dauon Simeon hatte geweissaget / durch jre Seele drang."

79. Ibid., 74v.

80. Hermann Bonnus, "Die Kirchenordnung für die Landkirchspiele des Fürstenthums Osnabrück," in *Nach seinem Leben und seinen Schriften*, ed. B. Spiegel (Leipzig: Roßberg'sche Buchhandlung, 1864), 136: "Pasche, Pinxten, Weinachten, Ascensionis, Nie Jahrsdag, Epiphaniae, Purificationis, Annunciationis Mariae, Joannis Babtistae scholen gantz gefieret werden. Dessglieken ock Visitationis Mariae, Vp Marien Magdalenen dag schal Vormiddage alleine dat Evangelium gepredigt werden. . . . Marien Himmelfahrt schal nidt gethiret werden dwile nicht gewisses daruve steit in der schrifft."

81. Lansemann, 131, referring to Luther's 1530 "Vermahnung an die Geistlichen, versammelt auf dem Reichstag zu Augsburg." Festivals for *Maria Himmelfahrt* and *Mariæ Geburt* were stricken from some church calendars (notably in Prussia) as early as 1524–25. See Andreas Zieger, *Das Religiöse und Kirchliche Leben in Preussen und Kurland im Spiegel der evangelischen Kirchenordnungen des 16. Jahrhunderts*, Forschungen und Quellen zur Kirchen- und Kulturgeschichte Ostdeutschlands, ed. Bernhard Stasiewski, Bd. 5 (Köln Graz: Böhlau, 1967), 5–6.

82. Lansemann, 132: "Auch Assumptionis Mariae (Mariae Himmelfahrt, 15. Aug.) fiel in Wittenberg. Zwar sagte Luther in der Schrift 'Von Ordnung Gottesdienst' 1523 davon (wie von Nativitatis), man müsse es noch eine Zeit lang bleiben lassen."

83. "Aber sonst sol an disem Feirtage in der Kirchen die Historien von vnser Frawen Fest, Visitationis genannt, mit singen vnd lesen gehalten werden." Cited in Lansemann, 133.

84. Zieger, 18–19.

85. Geiler, *Das euangeli buch* (1515), 174r: "Wan[n] was die natur verdecket an allen orten / das sol der mensch auch stil halten. . . . Also ist vnser liebe frauw auch menschlich empfangen nit von dem kuß / als thorechte menschen dauon reden sund[er] in beiwesen man[n] vn[d] frauwe[n] / als ich vn[d] du."

86. Ibid., 172v: "Zü dem dritten ist Maria empfange[n] / da dz leiblin Marie geformiert ist gewesen / vnd die seel geschöpfft hat im leib / on erbsünd."

87. Ibid., 173v: "Also hat er Maria von ewigkeit empfangen / das sie die reinest iunckfraw solt sein / vn[d] ein müter gottes." The notion of Mary's eternal predestination is an important aspect of Gabriel Biel's Mariology, but it does not surface in the works of Duns Scotus, the great formulator and defender of the immaculate conception. See Oberman, *Harvest of Medieval Theology*, 294–295.

88. Luther, *Festpostille* 1527, WA 17², 280: "sintemal nit ein büchstaben davon steht im Euangelio oder sunst in der schrifft."

89. Ibid., 281: "Das gütte weibichen redet aus eim fleischlichem weibischem affect, . . . die verwirfft der Herr hie gantz und zaiget uns an, was da nöttiger ist denn diß, nemlich Gottes wort hören und dasselbige bewaren."

90. Ibid., 284: "die erbsünd nychs anders ist denn dise gantze boßhait und naigung zum bösen, welliche alle menschen in jn [selbst] fülen, die da geboren ist zur hoffart, zoren, neyd, unkeuschait unnd andern lastern mere."

91. Ibid., 286: "Das ist aber dye gantze ursach, denn das flaisch der menschen kan nymmer mer yn disem leben volkommlich züseiner rainigkait kommen, so das es on lust und sündtliche begirde were, Derhalben künden die elternn one solche lust und begirde nicht kinderempfahen noch gepern."

92. Ibid., 288: "so das im ein gyessen der seele sie auch zügleich mit von der erbsünnde sey gerainniget worden und mit Gottes gaben getzieret."

93. Ibid.: "Und also den ersten augenblick, da sie anfieng zü leben, was sie on alle sünde."

94. Ibid.: "Also helt die Jungkfraw Maria gleich das mittel zwyschenn Christo und andern menschen." This is not exactly Duns Scotus's thesis, for Duns stresses (primarily by the argument of fitness) that Mary was *preserved* by Christ from any original sin, rather than *restored* to grace. Luther's "sey gerainniget worden" may only be a manner of speaking rather than a technical explanation—it is difficult to judge, as evidenced by the number of scholars who have disagreed on Luther's views on Mary's conception. See, for example, Algermissen, Heiler, Schimmelpfennig, and Cole in favor of Luther holding, throughout his life, the immaculate conception of Mary; see H. Preuss and Delius in favor of Luther's position shifting. Luther does speak of Mary as "in Erbsünden empfangen" (WA 17^2, 287) but distinguishes between the physical conception (act of the parents) and the animation by the soul, at which point the person is in existence. The *reinigung* of which he speaks refers, it seems, to the original sin present in the body. Thomas Aquinas denies Mary's immaculate conception because of just this point: it makes no sense to attribute either sin or grace before a person exists, i.e., before animation; therefore sanctification must take place *after* animation (see his *Summa Theologiae*, 3a. q. 27.) Max Thurian suggests that, when Luther speaks of Mary having original sin, he is referring both to her body before its union with her soul and to the presence of the effects of original sin in Mary's body (i.e., fatigue, etc.). See Thurian, *Mary, Mother of the Lord, Figure of the Church* (London: Faith, 1963); also E. Stakemeier, "De Beata Maria Virgine ejusque cultu juxta reformatores," in *De Mariologia et oecumenismo* (Rome: Pontificia Academia Mariana Internationalis, 1962), 435.

95. Biel clearly defends Mary's immaculate conception against its detractors, especially Gregory of Rimini. In his *Collectorium* Biel does not clarify whether for Mary "the *fomes peccati* is totally extinguished or rather neutralized by an abundance of grace" at her animation or at the moment she conceived Christ by the Holy Spirit. However, in his sermons he makes it clear that Mary's soul is created with sanctifying grace. See Oberman, *Harvest*, 295–296.

96. Staupitz, along with Augustinians generally in the fifteenth and sixteenth centuries, also accepted the doctrine of the immaculate conception, despite the earlier opposition of important Augustinian theologians such as Giles of Rome and Gregory of Rimini. Unlike some other late fifteenth-century theologians, however, Staupitz is concerned to minimize any Pelagian dangers in the doctrine of Mary's preservation from sin: he emphasizes that it is through God's grace rather than her merit. See Steinmetz, 145–147.

97. *Hauspostille* 1544 (Christmas, 1532), WA 52, 39: "dass sie ohne alle Sünd gewesen ist."

98. Sermon on Christmas Eve, 1540, WA 49, 173: "Ideo describitue, quod natus ex virgine, nec tantum sic, quia Maria ist auch nicht zu rein, quia nata a parentibus in peccato ut alii homines."

99. *Vom Schem Hamphoras und vom Geschlecht Christi*, 1543, WA 53, 640: "[Maria ist] ein heilige Jungfraw, die, von der Erbsunde erlöset und gereiniget, durch den heiligen Geist." Ebneter thinks that because this statement falls in the context of a defense of the incarnation, Luther means that Mary was purified at that point. Others (e.g., Schimmelpfennig) believe that this phrase still supports the immaculate conception. See Ebneter, "Martin Luthers Marienbild," 78–79.

100. Huberinus, *Postilla / Deudsch* (1554), 26v: "Es ist one zweiffel dises fest / vnnd feiertag / von den alten nicht vergebens eingesetzt worden / wiewol nichts so gut inn der kirchen je angericht worden ist / da nicht zu letzt darinnen ein grosser mißbrauch erwachsen / vnd eingerissen ist worden / So mus man nhu das gut behalten zur aufferbawung der Kirchen / vnd das böß hinweg thun."

101. Ibid., 27r: "dan die Eutichiten daraus fürgeben / vnd schliessen wolten / dieweil Maria / wie andere menschen / inn Sünden empfangen / vnd geborn sey / so habe Christus auch ein sündtlich fleisch müssen annemen / so er seinen Leib / auß dem leib Marie habe angenommen / welchen er doch vom Himel / aus der substantz des Vaters genommen hab / sonst hette er vns / mit einem sündtlichen fleisch erlösen mussen / wo er seinen leib / aus Maria leib genommen hette."

102. Ibid., 28r: "so mus ja Maria einen reinen / Heiligen / seligen Leib haben gahabt."

103. Ibid., 35r: "Derhalben so hat Maria nit allein gnad bey Gott funden / sondern sie ist auch vol der gnaden vnd des heiligen Geists worden / Luc.I."

104. Ibid., 35v: "[Wir] sondern im mittel bleiben / Wir sollen die Jungkfrawen Mariam nicht also gering achten / verachten / verkleinern / vnd jhr gebürende ehr nit entziehen / wie die rottengeister thun / so sollen wir sie auch nit für eine Abgöttin halten."

105. Corvinus, *Loci in Evangelia* (1536), n.p.: "Christus ut personarum respector non est."

106. Corvinus, *Kurtze außlegung . . . an den fürnemsten Fästen* (1545), VIr: "Die mainung dises weiblins war villeycht nicht böß / aber doch der Adfect war flayschlich."

107. Geiler, *Das euangeli buch* (1515), 178v: "Ja du solt got an rüffen vnnd vnser frauw in der not vnd in allen andern nötten / vnnd anfechtungen was dir zü handen gat."

108. Ibid., 179v: "Sie hat vns zu[m] vereinien gegen gott dem herren / wann sie ist ein mitlerin zwischen Got vnd dem sünder. . . . vnnd wer weisset mee die irrigen menschen den Maria / darumb so rüff sie an / sie wil dir zehilff kumen."

109. Ibid.: "wir diene[n] de[n] Künig [God] mit de[n] höchste[n] dienst / so wir möge[n] / vn[d] heißt latria / Aber d[ie] künigin [Mary] diene[n] wir mit de[n] höschte[n] / so vnd[er] de[n] creature[n] gedient / vn[d] geeret werde[n] mag vn[d] heisset inperdula."

110. Luther, "Sermon von der Geburt Mariä," WA 10³, 313: "Jr wißt, mein freünd, das gar tieff in die hertzen der menschen gebildet ist die ere die man thüt der mütter gotes, also auch das man nicht gern dawider hört reden, sonder allain meret und grösser macht." This sermon from 1522 is the text used by Roth in Luther's *Festpostille* of 1527.

111. Ibid.: "Darumb ist man ir auch ain eer schuldig, aber da sehe man zü, das man sy recht ere, . . . [und] das man [nicht] meer hat die hertzen auff sy gestelt dann auff Christum selbst."

112. Ibid., 315: "so wir doch von Christo Christen haissen, das wir an jm allain hangen sollen vnnd sollen gotes kinder und erben sein, vnnd so seind wir gleich als vil als die müter gotes selbs und sein Marie schwester und brüder."

113. Ibid., 321–322.

114. Ibid.: "dein gebet ist mir gleich als lieb als jrs."

115. Ibid., 317: "Dann die hailigen die von disem leben genommen seind, der ist dir kainer züeeren gebotten, aber die hie seind, die seind dir geboten züeeren, die lebendigen Christen im leben, die da die rechten hailigen seind."

116. Ibid., 318: "Sehet mit dem güt hett man manchen armen jungkfrawen künden aushelffen, das ist nun alles nach bliben mit der unnotlichen ere und dienst der hailigen."

117. Corvinus, *Kurtze außlegung . . . an den fürnemsten Fästen* (1545), 48v–49r: "WJewol diß Fäst vnnötig / vn[d] nicht vil vrsache hat / darum[b] mans billich feyre / wölchem dann auch Assumptio vnnd Presentatio Marie fast gleich ist / Habe ich dannocht diß Euangelion / denen zügefallen wöllen außlegen / die zü vilen feyren lust haben / auff das sy neben jrem vnzeitlichen müssiggange / doch die raine außlegung des Euangelij haben / so sy pflegen zü lesen inn jren Gemainden vnnd Kirchen / Sy mügen darnach auff gemeldt Fäst / diß oder ain anders brauchen / nach jrem wolgefallen."

118. For the Anabaptist (or, more exactly, Melchiorite and Mennonite) understanding of the incarnation, see Sjouke Voolstra, "The Word Has Become Flesh: The Melchiorite-Mennonite Teaching on the Incarnation," *Mennonite Quarterly Review* 57 (April 1983): 157–160, and his *Het woord is vlees geworden: de Melchioritisch-Menniste incarnatienleer* (Kampen: J. H. Kok, 1982). Menno Simons and others believed that they were protecting Christ from any taint of sinful flesh by insisting that his body did not come from Mary, but rather from heaven. The doctrine of the immaculate conception is, of course, another solution to this problem.

119. Geiler, *Das euangeli buch* (1515), 189v: "Got hat sie gemacht: Ein fürsprecherin/Aduocatem, Ein helfferin/Auxiliatrice[m], Beistenderin/Assistricem, Theilhafftig/Participem, Ein fraw d[er] welt/D[o]n[i]ma [!] mu[n]di, Ein künigin des hirnels/Regina[m] celi, Ein künigi[n] d[er] barmhertzikeit/Reginam misericordie, Die nest bei im / Proximam . . . Got hat gemacht Mariam ein fürsprecherin des gantzen menschlichein heils gegen im vn[d] Maria ist nit ei[ne] schlechte fürsprecherin / besunder ein crefftige vnnd ein gewaltige / Also das sie nie kein sach verlore[n] hat."

120. Ibid., 191r: "Aber Maria ist nit got / Sie ist ein luterer mensch . . . [S]prech Ambrosius also (regina mundi et domina virgo maria perpetua) O künigin der welt / vnd fraw junckfraw Maria bit für vns."

121. Ibid., 191v: "sie sich zwischen got vnd allen heilige[n] / wie der hals oder die gurgel sei zwischen dem houpt vnd dem gantze leib . . . Maria hab ein eigen thron / vff dem sie sitze / der sey geordinet gleich nebe[n] dem thron Jesu Christi."

122. Geiler, *Postill* (1522), 17r: "Die erst vrsach dorumb das wort castellum bedeütet Mariam die müter gottes / ist / qui castellu[m] circundatur muro. das castell würt vmbgeben mit einer muren. Vnd Maria die müter gotts ist vmbgeben mit der muren der jungkfrawlicheit" (etc.).

123. Luther, "Sermon von der Himmelfahrt Marie," WA 10³, 268: "Darumb kan man auß disem Euangelio nitt haben wie Maria im hymel sey, und es ist auch nit von nöten, ob wir gleich nit alles außscherpffen künden, wie es mit den hailigen zügee im hymel."

124. Ibid., 269: "Aber hie sagt die schrifft klar, das Abraam, Isaac, Jacob und al glaubig leben, darumb ist es nötig, das ir glauben das die müter gotes leb, wie aber das zügee, das befelch man dem lieben got."

125. These are the two main traditions concerning Mary's assumption that stem from the dormition legends of the fifth and sixth centuries. See Stephen J. Shoemaker, "Mary and the Discourse of Orthodoxy: Early Christian Identity and the Ancient Dormition Legends," Ph.D. diss., Duke University, Durham, N.C., 1997.

126. Brenz, *Pericopæ . . . qvæ Usitato More in præcipuis Festis legi solent* (1557), 1236: "Certißimum autem est, q[ui] Maria consecuta sit perpetuam fœlicitatem, et uiuat cum Christo filio suo."

127. Ibid., 1239: "Hæc enim maiestas ad solum Christu[m] pertinet. . . . Sed primum debemus honestè de ipsa sentire, quòd sit uera et sancta mater Domini nostri Iesu Christi. Deinde debemus imitari uirtutes eius."

128. Ibid., 1240: "Virginitas fuit uocatio Mariæ, in hac obsecuta est spiritui Dei, et fuit casta perpetuo."

129. Ibid., 1246: "Præterea est exemplum modestiæ etiam in hoc, quòd et si mater Christ fuit, tamen non usurpauit sibi alienum officium, uidelicet Apostolicum. Sic uxores non usurpent sibi officiæ maritorum."

130. Ibid., 1245: "Hoc est naturæ impoßibile, et requirit omnipote[n]tiam Dei."

CONCLUSION

1. See the introduction, 19–21.

2. R. Po-Chia Hsia outlines the Catholic plan to missionize Germany, largely through the services of the newly founded Jesuit order; see *Social Discipline in the Reformation: Central Europe 1550–1750* (London: Routledge, 1989), 39–50, 81. Marc Forster notes that "rising confessional tensions after about 1570 had serious consequences in German cities." Even in Speyer, the focus of his study, where the various religious confessions tended to live together peacefully, the 1570s and 1580s saw increased conflict and violence, largely due to the arrival of the Jesuits. See *The Counter-Reformation in the Villages: Religion and Reform in the Bishopric of Speyer, 1560–1720* (Ithaca: Cornell University Press, 1992), 117–120.

3. Hsia, *Social Discipline*, 54: "The rites of Counter-Reformation Catholicism underpinned Hapsburg imperialism. Four central motifs in this Austrian piety were devotion to the Eucharist, faith in the crucifix, Marian piety, and the veneration of saints."

4. Walther, *Auslegung der Euangelien . . . an den Sontagen* (1579), 314–315: "so sey Maria auch nicht gentzlich ohne Sünde / denn sonsten würde er nicht also jhr harte wort gegeben haben."

5. Hemmingsen, *Postilla* (1571), 152: "Denn gleich wie Heua durch des Teuffels List verfüret ward / vnd das gantze Menschlich Geschlecht in ewige not brachte / Also gedachte die Jungfraw Maria / das sie durch jren vnfleis den verheissenen Heiland der Welt verloren hette."

6. For medieval interpretations of the story of Dinah, see Schroeder, "The Rape of Dinah: Luther's Interpretation of a Biblical Narrative."

7. Pelikan, 83–84.

8. Ibid., 85.

9. Scribner, "Reformation and Desacralisation: From Sacramental World to Moralised Universe," in *Problems in the Historical Anthropology of Early Modern Europe*, ed. R. Po-Chia Hsia and R. W. Scribner, Wolfenbütteler Forschungen (Herzog August Bibliothek), Band 78 (Wiesbaden: Harrassowitz,1997): 89.

Bibliography

PRIMARY SOURCES

(The WF signature numbers refer to the books catalogued at the Herzog August Bibliothek in Wolfenbüttel, Germany.)

Adler, Kaspar. *Ein Gnadenreich vnd Gottseliges Newes Jahr/ Von dem Neugeborenen kindlein/ vnserm eynigen Mitler vnnd Heylandt Jhesu Christo/ vber den Tröstlichen Spruch Esaie/ Vnns ist ein Kindt geboren/ vnnd ein Sohn ist vnns gegeben/ Vnnd vber das alte Christliche liedt/ Ein Kindelein so löbeleich u[sw.] Allen Christen zum trost auß Göttlicher heyliger Schrifft* . . . Nuremberg: Joachim Heller, 1556. WF sig: 386.7 Theol. (10).

Alberus, Erasmus. *Ein Predigt vom Ehestand/ vber das Euangelium/ Es war ein Hochzeit zu Cana etc.* Magdeburg?: Christian Rödinger, 1550. WF sig: Ts 393 (2).

Andreae, Jakob. *Passional Büchlein/ Das ist/ Die Historia des bittern vnd thewren leiden vnd sterbens/ auch der frölichen Aufferstehung vnsers Herrn Jhesu Christi/ nach den vier Euangelisten/ gepredigt vnd ausgeleget in der Pfarrkirchen zu Wittenberg/.* Wittenberg: Johan Krafft, 1577. WF sig: 421.5 Theol. 4° (2).

Artopoeus, Petrus. *Evangelicae Conciones Dominicarvm tocius anni, per Dialectica et Rhetorica artificia breuiter tractatæ. Subnexis Epistolarum argumentis.* Wittenberg: n.p., 1537. WF sig: QuH 146 (3).

———. *Postilla Euangeliorum, & Epistolarum Dominicarum, & præcipuorum Festorum totius Anni, per scholasticis, & nouellis Prædicatoribus, Breues Annotationes.* Basel: Henrichus Petri, 1550. WF sig: 988.7 Theol.

Baumgarten, Johann. *Eine Predigt Vom Ehestande/ vber das Euangelium von der Hochzeit zu Cana in Galilea.* N.p., 1568. Herzog August Bibliothek (Wolfenbüttel); St. Paul, Minn.: Lutheran Brotherhood Foundation Reformation Library. Microfiche. Yv 572.8° Helmst. (5).

Bernard of Clairvaux. *Homilies in Praise of the Blessed Virgin Mary.* Trans. by

Marie-Bernard Saïd. Cistercian Fathers Series, no. 18-A. Kalamazoo, Mich.: Cistercian Publications, 1993.

Biel, Gabriel. *Sermo[n]es Gabrielis Biel Spire[]sis de festiuitatib[us] gloriose uirginis Marie. Passio[n]is d[omi]nice Sermo historialis notabilis atq[ue] preclarus venerabilils domini Gabrielis Biel Artium Magistri: sacre theologie Lice[n]tiati.* Haguenau: n.p., 1515.

Brenz, Johannes. *Ain Sermon von den hailigen/ gepredigt zü Schwebischen Hall/ durch Johannem Brentz/ an sant Jacobs tag M.D.xxiij.* [Augsburg: Philipp Ulhart d.Ä.], 1523. WF sig: Yv 2298.8° Helmst.

——. *Evangelien Predigten von Johann Brenz, weiland Propst in Stuttgart.* Erster Band: *Die festliche Hälfte des Kirchen–Jahres.* Translated by Ludwig de Marées. Cottbus: Gotthold-Expedition, 1877.

——. *Pericopæ Euangeliorum quæ Singvlis Diebvs Dominicis publicè in Ecclesia recitari solent, expositæ per Ioannem Brentivm.* Frankfurt: Petrus Brubach, 1556. Herzog August Bibliothek (Wolfenbüttel); St. Paul, Minn.: Lutheran Brotherhood Foundation Reformation Library. Microfiche. C 529a Helmst. 8°.

——. *Pericopæ Euangeliorum qvæ Usitato More in præcipuis Festis legi solent, expositæ per Iohan. Brent.* Frankfurt: Petrus Brubach, 1557. Herzog August Bibliothek (Wolfenbüttel); St. Paul, Minn.: Lutheran Brotherhood Foundation Reformation Library. Microfiche. J 54 Helmst. 8° (1).

——. *Werke: Eine Studienausgabe.* Edited by Martin Brecht, Gerhard Schäfer, and Frieda Wolf. Tübingen: J. C. B. Mohr (Paul Siebeck), 1970.

Bretschneider, C., and H. Bindseil, eds. *Corpus Reformatorum.* Vol. 24–25, *Postilla Melanthoniana,* by Philipp Melanchthon. Braunschweig: C. A. Schwetschke and Sons, 1856.

Bugenhagen, Johannes. *Historia des Lidendes vnde der Vpstandinge vnses Heren Jhesu Christi/ vth den veer Euangelisten/ dorch D. Johan. Bugenhagen Pamern uppet nye vlitigen thosamende gebracht. Ock de Vorstöringe Jerusalem vnde der Jöden/ up dat körteste begrepen..* Magdeburg: Christian Rödinger, 1546. WF sig: G 331.8° Helmst. (1).

——. *Indices Qvidam Ioannis Bvgenhagii Pomerani in Euangelia (ut uocant) Dominicalia, Insuper usui temporum et Sanctorum totius anni seruientia. Ab Ipso Avtore Iam primum emissi et locupletati.* Wittenberg: Ioannes Lufft, 1524. WF sig: 919.135 Th. (2).

——. *Postillatio Ioan. Bvgenhagii Pomerani in Euangelia, usui temporum et Sanctorum totius anni seruientia, ad preces Georgij Spalatini scripta. Habes Hic et Concionum et meditationum copiosißimam syluam, quisquis es, cui cordi est pietas.* [Mainz: Johann Schöffer, 1524]. WF sig: C 51. Helmst. 8° (2).

Chemnitz, Martin. *Postilla Oder Außlegung der Euangelien/ welche auff die Sontage/ vnd fürnembste Feste/ durchs gantze Jahr in der gemeine Gottes erkleret werden.* Magdeburg: Johann Francken, 1594. WF sig: 345 Theol. 2°.

Claius, Johannes. *Explicationes Evangeliorvm, quae Dominicis Diebvs per totum annum proponuntur. Cum præfatione D. Pavli Eberi.* Wittenberg: Laurentius Schuuenck, 1568. WF sig: P 1439. 8° Helmst.

Corvinus, Anton. *Kurtze außlegung der Episteln vnnd Euangelien/ so auff die Sontag/ von Osteren bisz auffs Aduent gepredigt werden. Für die armen Pfarrherren vnd Haußuätter/ gestellet durch Antonium Coruinum.* [Augsburg: Valentin Othmar], 1545. WF sig: 434.9 Th.2° (1).

——. *Kurtze außlegung der Episteln vnd Euangelien/ so an den fürnemsten Fästen im gantzen Jar gepredigt werden. Für arme Pfarrherren vnd Haußuätter gestellet/ durch Antonium Coruinum.* [Augsburg: Valentin Othmar], 1545.

_____. *Kurtze vnd ainfeltige Außlegung der Epistolen vnd Euangelien/ So auff die Sonntage vnd fürnemesten Feste/ durch das gantz Jar in der Kirchen gelesen werden. Für die arme Pfarrherren vnd Haußuätter gestellet/ Durch M. Antonivm Corvinvm.* Augsburg: Valentin Othmar, 1545. WF sig: 434.9 Th.2° (1).

_____. *Loci in Evangelia cvm Dominicalia tum de Sanctis, ut uocant, ita adnotati, ut uel commentarij uice esse possint, nunc primum autore Antonio Coruino publicati. Cum præfatione M. Adami Vegetij Fuldensis.* Warburg: Eucharius Agrippina, 1536. WF sig: C 454 Helmst. 8° (3).

Culmann, Leonhard. *Sacræ Contiones, ac variæ Prædicandorum Euangeliorum formulæ, descriptæ à Leonhardo Culmanno Craylshaimense, ac in tres tomos divisæ.* Nuremberg: Iohannis Montani & Ulrich Neuber, 1550. WF sig: 735.1–3 Th.

Dietrich, Veit. *Kinderpredig/ von fürnembsten Festen durch das gantze Jar/ gestelt durch Vitum Dietrich.* Nuremberg: Johann vom Berg und Ulrich Neuber, 1546. WF sig: C 565 Helmst. 8° (2).

_____. *Vermanung/ Von der kinderzucht/ auss dem Euangelio/ Luce am 2. Durch: M. Vitum Dieterich.* Nuremberg: U. Neuber, 1567. WF sig.: Alv.: Aa 148 (1).

Drach (Draconites), Johannes. *Ejne Dreifaltige Predigt Des Engel Gabriels. Luce. j. Am tage der Verkündigung Mariæ zu Marpurg ausgeleget.* [Lübeck]: Georg Richolff, 1550. Herzog August Bibliothek (Wolfenbüttel); St. Paul, Minn.: Lutheran Brotherhood Foundation Reformation Library. Microfiche. 502.7 Th. 2° (55).

_____. *Die Passio Jesu Christi außgelegt Doctor Joannes Draconites.* Frankfurt: Cyriacus Jacob, [1544]. WF sig: G 331 Helmst. 8° (2).

Eber, Paul. *Postilla/ Das ist/ Außlegung der Sonntags vnd fürnembsten Fest Euangelien durch das gantze Jar. Deß Ehrwirdigen vnd Hochgelehrten Herrn Pauli Eberi/ der H. Schrifft Doctorn/ Weilandt Superintendenten zu Wittenberg. Auffs fleissigste nachgeschrieben/ zusammen gefast/ vnd der gemeynen Christenheit zu gut/ jetzundt zum Ersten in Druck verfertiget/ Durch Iohannem Cellarivm Bvdissinvm.* 2 Teile. Frankfurt: Franciscus Basseus, 1578. WF sig: Alv.: V 399.

Geiler von Keysersberg, Johann. *Das euangeli buch.* Strassburg: Johannes Grieninger, 1515.

_____. *Postill: Uber die fyer Euangelia durchs jor, sampt dem quadragesimal, vnnd von etlichen Heyligen, newlich ussgangen.* Strassburg: Johann Schott, 1522.

_____. *Predig d[er] Himelfart Ma[rie].* Strassburg: J. Grüninger, 1512.

_____. "Das Schiff des Heils." In *Geilers von Kaisersberg ausgewählte Schriften,* ed. Philipp de Lorenzi, vol. 4. Trier: Ed. Groppe, 1883.

Greser, Daniel. *Enarratio Brevis et Orthodoxa Evangeliorvm Dominicalivm & Festorum aliquot: authore, Daniele Gresero, Pastore & superattendente Dresdensi.* Frankfurt: Petrus Brubach, 1567. WF sig: 680.38 Theol.

Heerbrand, Jakob. *Ein Predig/ Von der Keuscheit. Am andern Sontag nach Epiphania gehalten zu Tübingen.* Tübingen: Alexander Hock, 1578. WF sig: Alv. Eh 136 4° (22).

Heidenreich, Esaias. *Gebets Postilla/ Darinnen mit fleis Euangelischer Lehr/ Trost/ vnnd Seufftzen gezeiget wird: Gestellet/ vnd auffs New vbersehen/ Durch Esaiam Heidenreich/ der heiligen Schrifft Doctorem.* Leipzig: Georg Deffner, 1586. WF sig: Alv.: Ba 73 8°.

Hemmingsen, Niels. *Postilla oder Auslegung der Euangelien/ welche man auff die Sontage vnd andere Feste/ in der Kirchen Gottes pfleget zu verlesen. Allen getrewen/ fromen Dienern des Euangelij zu gute beschrieben/ vnd auffs new widerumb gemehret/ Durch Nicolaum Hemmingum.* Wittenberg: Hans Krafft, 1571. WF sig: Alv.: Aa 109.

Hesshusen, Tilemann. *Postilla [:] Das ist/ Außlegung der Euangelien auff alle Fest vnd Apostel Tage durchs gantze Jar.* Helmstedt: Jacob Lucius, 1581. WF sig: C 354 Helmst. 2°.

Heune (Gigas), Johannes. *Passion vnd Triumph vnsers Herrn vnd Heylands Jhesu Christi Geprediget zur Schweidniß in der Schlesien/ Anno 1576. zu guter Nacht/ Von Johanne Gigante Northusano.* Frankfurt an der Oder: Johan Eichorn, 1577. WF sig: P 1470 Helmst. 8° (3).

————. *Postilla der Sontags Euangelien vnd etlicher Festen. Iohannis Gigantis Northusani.* Alten Stettin: Johann Eichorn, 1570. WF sig: G 212.2° Helmst. (2).

————. *Vonn den lebendigen Heiligen auff erden/ eine Predigt Iohannis Gigantis Northusani.* Frankfurt an der Oder: Johann Eichorn, 1569.

Huberinus, Caspar. *Postilla Teutsch/Vber alle Sontägliche Euangelien/ vom Aduent biß auff Ostern/ Kurtze vnd nützliche Außlegung.* Nuremberg: Johann Daubman, 1548. WF sig: C 622a 8° Helmst. (1.2).

————. *Postilla/ Deudsch/ Vber alle Fest/ vnd gemeine feyertag/ der Heyligen durchs gantze Jar/ kurtze vnd nutzliche außlegung.* Frankfurt an der Oder: J. Eichorn, 1554. WF sig: C 624.8° Helmst.

Kantz, Kaspar. *Die historia des leydens Jesu Christi nach den vier Euangelisten. Vnd auch von der Juden Osterlamm/ mit trostlicher außlegung.1538.* Wittenberg: Jörg Rhaw, 1538. WF sig: C 852 Helmst. 8° (1).

Keller, Andreas. *Ain Sermon auff dem tag der verkündigung Marie gepredigt zü Rottenburg Durch Andream Keller.* [Augsburg: Heinrich Steiner], 1524.

Kempffen, Ambrosius. *Euangelien vnd Epistlen des Neüwen Testaments/ nichts auszgelassen/ vnnd das fruchtbarest auß Sanct Johanns heymlichen Offenbarung/ vnd den Geschichten der Aposteln außzogen/ Mit den Historien vnd Propheceyen des Alten Testaments/ wie das Neüw im alten figuriert/ vnd Christus vnser seligmacher/ vnd die Aposteln zü vil malen des meldung thün/ in alle tag des gantzen jars eingetheylt/ also das alle tag ein besundere Lection auß dem Alten Testament/ Euangelium vnd Epistel auß dem Neüwen gesetzt/ kein wort so von der kirchen geordnet/ verendert/ bey dem klaren Text/ on alle glosen/ bliben/ kein wort darzü/ noch daruon thon/ wie Gott geheyssen hat/ Du solt nichts zü/ oder von meinen worten thün/ wie die Vorred das klärlich anzeyget. Mit schönen figuren des Neüwen vnnd Alten Testaments/.* Colmar: Bartholomeus Grüninger, 1543. WF sig: 461.1 Theol. 2°.

Lauterbach, Johannes. *Evangelia Totivs Anni, Compendiosa Expositione in vsvm scholasticæ iuuentutis descripta, à Iohanne Lauterbachio P[oeta]. L[aureatus]. Summarische Beschreibung der Euangelien durchs gantz Jar/ der Schül jugent sehr dienlich.* Frankfurt: Ludovici Lucius, 1563. WF sig: 221.1 Theol. (4).

Linck, Wenceslas. *Ein nützlicher Sermon aus dem zehenden capital Luce/ was das beste sey/ oder des Menschen seligkeit/ auff den tag der himelfart Marie gepredigt zu Nürnberg durch D. Wentzeslaum Lincken im 1536.jar.* Nuremberg: Johan Petreius, 1536. WF sig: 127.17 Theol. (1).

Locher, Johann. *Eyn lieplicher Sermon Colligiert an dem heyligen Christag/ Gemainem man/ durch das/ gantz Jar vast trostlich/ Wie man das Kindlein Jhesum süchen soll.* Zwickaw: Georg Gastel, 1524.

————. *Vom Aue Maria Leuthen den glaubigen vast fürderlich.* [Zwickau: Jörg Gastel], 1524. WF sig: 106.4 Theol. 4° (2).

Luther, Martin. *D. Martin Luthers Werke.* 62 vols. Weimar: Böhlaus, 1883–.

Major, Georg. *Drey güldene Kleinot des newen Testaments. 1. Das Magnificat Marie. 2. Das Benedictus Zacharie. 3. Das Nunc Dimittis Simeonis.* Wittenberg: Hans Lufft, 1566. WF sig: Yv 455.8° Helmst. (1).

———. *Ein tröstliche Predigt vber das Euangelium Lucae j. am tage der Verkündigung Marie/ oder des Empfengnis vnsers lieben Heilands vnd Seligmachers Jhesu Christi.* Wittenberg: Hans Lufft, 1549. WF sig: K 287.4° Helmst.

Mathesius, Johannes. *Außlegung der Euangelien/ von den fürnembsten Festen/ Vom Aduent biß auff Ostern.* Nuremberg: J. von Bergs Erben u. Dietrich Gerlach, 1571. WF sig: C 670a.8° Helmst.

———. *Kurtze Ausslegung der Sontags Euangelien vnnd Catechismi.* Nuremberg: Berg und Neuber, 1563. WF sig: C 669.8° Helmst.

———. *Postilla Oder Ausslegung der Sontags Euangelien vber das gantze jar.* Nuremberg: Neuber und Von Bergs Erben, 1565. WF sig: C 364.2° Helmst. (1).

Melanchthon, Philipp. *In Evangelia qvæ Vsitato more diebus dominicis & festis proponuntur, Annotationes Philippi Melanthonis, Recognitæ et auctæ, adiectis ad finem aliquot conciunculis.* Wittenberg: Iohannis Lufft, 1548.

Mörlin, Joachim. *Postilla: Oder Summarische Erinnerung bey den Sonteglichen Jahrs Euangelien vnd Catechism.* Erfurt: Esaias Mechlem, 1587. WF sig: 365 Th. 2°.

Mollen, Christoff. *Ein Predig von dem Aue Maria, vnd von anrüffung der Heyligen. Gestellet durch Christoff Mollen von Augspurg/ Euangelischen Kirchendiener zü Gernspach.* Strassburg: Christian Müller, 1575. WF sig: 206.6 Th. (23).

Musaeus, Simon. *Außlegung der Episteln vnd Euangelien vber gewönliche namhaffte Feste der heyligen Apostel/ Märtyrer vnd Zeugen Christi durchs gantze Jar.* Frankfurt: Nicolaus Bassæus, 1590. WF sig: Alv. Bb 161 2°.

Osiander d. Ä., Andreas. *Gesamtausgabe.* Edited by Gerhard Müller. Gütersloh: Gerd Mohn, 1975.

———. *Ain schöne Sermon/ Gepredigt zü Nüremberg von Andreas Oseander/ prediger zü S. Lorentzen am Sontag Misericordia Domini auff dy Euangelium Johannes. Secundo. u[sw].* N.p., 1523.

Paltz, Johannes von. *Werke.* 3 vols. Spätmittelalter und Reformation Texte und Untersuchungen, ed. Heiko A. Oberman, vols. 2–4. Berlin: Walter de Gruyter, 1983–1989.

Pankratius, Andreas. *Vber der Sontäge Epistel vnd Euangelia/kurtze Summarien vnd Gebetlein/Allen liebhabern Jhesu Christi/In sonderheit aber/den Christlichen Eltern/ sampt jren Kindlein vnd Haußgesind/zu lieb vnnd dienstgestellet. Jetzt von newem widerumb vberschen/vnd mit etlichen Episteln vnd Euangelien gemehret.* Nuremberg: Valentin Geißler, 1572. WF sig: Alv.: Dd 62 (1).

Pauli, Simon. *Postilla: Das ist/ Außlegung der Euanglien/ von den fürnemsten Festen der Heiligen/ durchs gantze Jar/ ordentlich vnd richtig nach der Rhetorica gefasset: Neben einer kurtzen erklerung des Textes . . . Das Dritte Teil.* Magdeburg: Wolffgang Kirchner, 1573. Herzog August Bibliothek (Wolfenbüttel); St. Paul, Minn.: Lutheran Brotherhood Foundation Reformation Library. Microfiche. C 715 Helmst. 8° (1).

Porta, Conrad. *Jungfrawenspiegel. Faksimiledruck der Ausgabe von 1580.* Edited by Cornelia Niekus Moore. Nachdrucke Deutscher Literatur des 17. Jahrhunderts, ed. Blake Lee Spahr, bd. 76. Bern: Peter Lang, 1990.

Rhegius, Urbanus. *Ain predig von der hailigen junckfrauwen Catharina/ Doctoris Urbani Regij Thümpredigers zu Augspurg/ gepredigt im M.D.XXI. Iar.* Augsburg: Siluanus Otmar, 1521.

Seehofer, Arsacius. *Enarrationes Evangeliorvm Dominicalium, ad dialecticam Methodum, & Rhetoricam dispositionem accommodatæ . . .*[Augsburg: Heinrich Steiner], 1539. WF sig: Yv 1309.8° Helmst. (2).

Selneccer, Nicolaus. *Evangeliorvm et Epistolarvm Omnivm, quæ Dominicis et Festis Diebvs in Ecclesia Christi proponi solent, Harmonie, Explicationes, & Homiliarum*

Pars Prima. A 'Prima Dominica Aduentus, vsque ad Dominicam, quæ Quadragesima, siue Inuocauit nominatur. Frankfurt: n.p., 1575. WF sig: 541 Theol. (1).

―――. *Evangeliorvm et Epistolarvm Dominicalivm, Explicationis Pars Secunda. A 'Dominica Quadragesimæ siue Inuocauit, vsque ad Resurrectionis diem solennem: continens Historiam Paßionis Domini nostri Iesu Christi.* Frankfurt: n.p., 1575. WF sig: 541 Theol. (2).

―――. *Epistolarvm et Evangeliorvm Dispositio, qvæ Diebvs Festis B. Mariæ semper virginis, & S. Apostolorum vsitatè in Ecclesia proponuntur & explicantur: Scripta A D. Nicolao Selneccero.* Frankfurt: n.p., 1575. WF sig: 542 Theol. (2).

Spangenberg, Cyriacus. *Ehespiegel: Das ist/ Alles was vom heyligen Ehestande/ nützliches/ nötiges/ vnd tröstliches mag gesagt werden. Jn Sibentzig Brautpredigten.* Strassburg: Samuel Emmel, 1563. WF sig: Th 4° 62.

―――. *Passio. Vom Leiden vnd sterben vnsers Herrn/ Heilands vnd Seligmachers Jesu Christi/ etliche schöne vnd nützliche Predigten/ Durch M. Cyriacum Spangenberg/ Prediger im Thal Mansfeld. Auffs newe vbersehen/ Vnd vier kurtze Predigten/ darin die gantze Passion begriffen/ darzu gethan.* Eisleben: Urban Gaubisch, 1564. WF sig: Alv. Aa 104 8° (1).

Spangenberg, Johann. *Außlegung der Episteln vnd Euangelien/ von Aduent, biß auffs Ostern Durch Johann Spangenberg/ in Fragstück verfasse.* N.p., 1584. WF sig: C 393.2° Helmst.

―――. *Außlegung der Epistel vnd Euangelien/ von den fürnembsten Festen durchs gantze Jar. Durch Johann Spangenberg.* N.p., 1584. WF sig: C 393.2° Helmst.

―――. *Postilla. Euangelia, & Epistolae, qvae Dominicis & Festis diebus per totum Annum in Ecclesia proponuntur, per Quæstiones piè ac synceriter explicata, & imaginibus exornata. Item eadem Evangelia, et Precationes, quas Collectas uocant, quibus utitur Ecclesia, Carmine Elegiaco reddita.* Frankfurt: C. Egenolphus, 1553. WF sig: C 779–780.8° Helmst.

Spangenberg, Johann, and Cyriacus Spangenberg. *Vier vnd dreissig Leich predigten/ Aus dem heiligen Euangelisten LVCA.* Wittenberg: Peter Seitzen Erben, 1556. WF sig: Yv 202.8 Helmst. (1.2).

Spindler, Georg. *Postilla. Außlegung der Sontags/ vnd fürnemesten Fest Euangelien vber das gantze jahr/ in gewisse Artickel/ vmb einfeltiger Prediger/ vnd gemeinen Mans willen gestellet/ Durch Georgium Spindler.* Leipzig: Hans Steinman, 1576. WF sig: 207.1 Theol. 2°.

Steinhart, Georg. *Ehren Kron/ vnnd Schmuck Christliches Frawenzimmers/ nach einfeltiger Außlegunge vber das Euangelion/ welchs auff den tag Marie heimsuchung/ in der Kirchen pflegt gehandelt zu werden/ Luc.1. zusamen gtragen durch Georgium Steinhart.* Frankfurt: Nicolaus Bassee, 1568.

Strigel, Victorinus. *Postilla Sive Explicationes Evangeliorum, quæ diebus Dominicis vsitato more in Ecclesia proponuntur, Scriptæ à Victorino Strigelio. Et nunc primùm editæ, opera & studio Christophori Pezelii, Sacræ Theologiæ Doctoris.* Neustadt an der Haardt: Matthæus Harnisch, 1584. Herzog August Bibliothek (Wolfenbüttel); St. Paul, Minn.: Lutheran Brotherhood Foundation Reformation Library. Microfiche. Alv. Ei 161 4°.

Suarez, Francis. *The Dignity and the Virginity of the Mother of God: Disputations I, V, VI from The Mysteries of the Life of Christ.* Translated by Richard J. O'Brien. West Baden Springs, Ind.: West Baden College, 1954.

Vischer, Christoph. *Außlegung der Euangelien/ so man auff die Sontage in der Christlichen Kirchen zu handeln pfleget/ Vom Aduent bis auff Ostern/ Darinnen ein jedes*

Euangelium in drey/ bisweilen in vier Predigten verfasset ist. Schmalkalden: Michel Schmuck, 1570. WF sig: 422.6 Theol. 2°.

————. *Außlegung der Euangelien/ so man auff die Fest der Apostel/ vnd andere tage/ in der Christlichen Kirchen zuhandeln pfleget. Darinnen ein jedes Euangelium in drey/ bißweilen auch in vier predigten/ gefast ist/* . . . Leipzig: Hans Steinman, 1575. WF sig: 422.8 Theol. 2°.

————. *Christlich vnnd Einfeltige Auslegung der Sieben Wort vnsers lieben HErrn Jhesu Christi/ die er am stamm des heiligen Creutzes/ kurtz vor seinem köstbarlichen/ thewren/ aller heiligsten vnd aller krefftigsten Tode/ geredt hat. Gestellet in Sieben Predigten/* . . . Schmalkalden: Michel Schmuck, 1566. WF sig: Alv. Eh 136 4° (5).

————. *Ein Predig/ dem Stiffter vnd Christlichem heiligen Ehestandt zu lob vnd ehren/ Auch allen jungen Eheleuten zur lahr/ trost vnd heilsamen vnterweisunge/ Gethan zu Schweinfurdt/* . . . Schweinfurt: Valten Kröner, 1562. WF sig: 1164.71 Theol. (4).

Wackernagel, Philipp. *Das Deutsche Kirchenlied von der ältesten Zeit bis zu Anfang des XVII. Jahrhunderts. Dritter Band. Die Lieder des ersten Geschlechts der Reformationszeit von Martin Luther bis Nicolaus Herman, 1523–1553*. Hildesheim: Georg Olms, 1964. [Reprografischer Nachdruck der Ausgabe Leipzig, 1874].

————. *Das Deutsche Kirchenlied von der ältesten Zeit bis zu Anfang des XVII. Jahrhunderts. Vierter Band. Die Lieder des zweiten Geschlechts der Reformationszeit, von Paulus Eber bis Bartholomæ Ringwaldt, 1554–1584*. Hildesheim: Georg Olms, 1964. [Reprografischer Nachdruck der Ausgabe Leipzig, 1874].

Walther, Georg. *Auslegung der Euangelien/ so an den Sontagen gelesen werden. Das erste Teil/ vom Aduent bis auff Trinitatis*. Wittenberg: Hans Kraffts Erben, 1579. WF sig: C 800 Helmst. 8°.

————. *Auslegung der Euangelien so auff die Feiertage vnd furnemeste Feste gelesen werden. Das Dritte Teil*. Wittenberg: Hans Lufft, 1579. WF sig: Alv.: V 508.

Weller, Hieronymus. *Hieronymi Vvelleri Theologiae Doctoris, in Epistolas et Evangelia Dominicalia, Explicationes Piae, Breves, Ervditae. His Additae Svnt Enarrationes in Aliqvot Epistolas & Euangelia, quæ in diuorum Festis legi solent*. Leipzig: Valentin Papae, 1560. WF sig: Yv 449 Helmst. 8°.

————. *Altera Pars Annotationvm D. Hieronymi Vvelleri, in Epistolas et Euangelia Dominicalia, quæ à Dominica Trinitatis usque ad finem anni in Ecclesia præleguntur. His Adiectae Sunt Etiam Explicationes Epistolarum & Euangeliorum, quæ in festis Diuorum legi solent*. Leipzig: Valentin Papae, 1560. WF sig: YV 449 Helmst. 8°.

Wigand, Johannes. *Postilla/ Ausslegung der Euangelien, so man durch das gantze Jar auff einen jeden Sontag vnd fürnemste Fest/ in der Kirchen pfleget für zutragen/ Erstmals in Lateinischer Sprach verzeichnet*. Translated by Christophorus Obenhin. Ursel: Nikolaus Henricus, 1569. WF sig: Alv. Bb 159 2°.

Wirth, Johann. *Grundtliche vnd Warhafftige Erklerung vnd Außlegung der Historien oder Evangelions/ uon der Entpfengniß Christi/ oder Verkündigung Marie/ Mit gründtlicher Widerlegung aller Grewel vnd Jrthumb/ so im Bapstumb darauß entstanden vnd herkommen/ vnd noch nicht ganz vnd gar außgerott seind*. Frankfurt: Peter Braubach, 1557. WF sig: J 205.4° Helmst. (6).

SECONDARY SOURCES

Abray, Lorna Jane. "The Laity's Religion: Lutheranism in Sixteenth-Century Strasbourg." In *The German People and the Reformation*, ed. R. Po-Chia Hsia, 216–232. Ithaca: Cornell University Press, 1988.

Algermissen, K. "Mariologie und Marienverehrung der Reformatoren." *Theologie und Glaube* 49 (1959): 1–24.

Althaus, Paul. *Forschungen zur Evangelischen Gebetsliteratur.* Gütersloh: G. Mohn, 1927; reprint, Hildesheim: Georg Olms, 1966.

Anderson, H. George, J. Francis Stafford, and Joseph A. Burgess, eds. *The One Mediator, the Saints, and Mary: Lutherans and Catholics in Dialogue VIII.* Minneapolis: Augsburg Fortress, 1992.

Ashley, Kathleen, and Pamela Sheingorn, eds. *Interpreting Cultural Symbols: Saint Anne in Late Medieval Society.* Athens: University of Georgia Press, 1990.

Asmussen, Hans. *Maria die Mutter Gottes.* Stuttgart: Evangelisches Verlagswerk, 1950.

Baxandall, Michael. *The Limewood Sculptors of Renaissance Germany.* New Haven: Yale University Press, 1980.

Beck, Hermann. *Die Erbauungsliteratur der Evangelischen Kirche Deutschlands,* vol. 1, *Von Dr. M. Luther bis Martin Moller.* Erlangen: Andreas Deichert, 1883.

Beissel, Stephan. *Geschichte der Verehrung Marias im 16. und 17. Jahrhundert: ein Beitrag zur Religionswissenschaft und Kunstgeschichte.* 2 vols. Freiburg i. Br.: Herdersche Verlagshandlung, 1910.

Benko, Stephen. *Protestants, Catholics, and Mary.* Valley Forge, Pa.: Judson, 1968.

Beumer, Johannes. "Die marianische Deutung des Hohen Liedes in der Frühscholastik." *Zeitschrift für katholische Theologie* 76 (1954): 411–439.

Bluhm, Heinz. "Luther's Translation and Interpretation of the *Ave Maria.*" *Journal of English and German Philology* 51 (1952): 196–211.

Blumenfeld-Kosinski, Renate, and Timea Szell, eds. *Images of Sainthood in Medieval Europe.* Ithaca: Cornell University Press, 1991.

Bossy, John. *Christianity in the West, 1400–1700.* Oxford: Oxford University Press, 1985.

Brooks, Peter Newman. "A Lily Ungilded? Martin Luther, the Virgin Mary, and the Saints." *Journal of Religious History* 13 (December 1984): 136–149.

Brown, Peter. *The Cult of the Saints: Its Rise and Function in Latin Christianity.* Haskell Lectures on History of Religions, New Series, ed. Joseph M. Kitagawa, no. 2. Chicago: University of Chicago Press, 1981.

Brown, R. E., et al. *Mary in the New Testament.* Philadelphia: Fortress, 1978.

Brückner, Annemarie, and Wolfgang Brückner. "Zeugen des Glaubens und ihre Literatur: Altväterbeispiele, Kalenderheilige, protestantische Martyrer und evangelische Lebenszeugnisse." In *Volkserzählung und Reformation: Ein Handbuch zur Tradierung und Funktion von Erzählstoffen und Erzählliteratur im Protestantismus,* ed. Wolfgang Brückner, 520–565. Berlin: Erich Schmidt, 1974.

Burke, Peter. *Popular Culture in Early Modern Europe.* New York: Harper & Row, 1978. Reprint, London: Scolar, 1994.

———. "Popular Culture Reconsidered." In *Mensch und Objekt im Mittelalter und in der Frühen Neuzeit: Leben—Alltag—Kultur,* 181–191. Veröffentlichungen des Instituts für Realienkunde des Mittelalters und der Frühen Neuzeit, nr. 13. Vienna: Verlag der Österreichischen Akademie der Wissenschaften, 1990.

Bynum, Caroline Walker. *Jesus as Mother: Studies in the Spirituality of the High Middle Ages.* Berkeley: University of California Press, 1982.

———. "Women's Stories, Women's Symbols: A Critique of Victor Turner's Theory of Liminality." In *Anthropology and the Study of Religion,* ed. Frank Reynolds and Robert Moore, 105–125. Chicago: Center for the Scientific Study of Religion, 1984.

Bynum, Caroline Walker, Stevan Harrell, and Paula Richman, eds. *Gender and Religion: On the Complexity of Symbols.* Boston: Beacon, 1986.

Caloren, W.H.F. " 'The Virgin Mary in a Reformation Theology': A Reply." *Canadian Journal of Theology* 7 (July 1961): 176–181.

Cameron, Euan. *The European Reformation.* Oxford: Clarendon, 1991.

Camille, Michael. *The Gothic Idol: Ideology and Image-making in Medieval Art.* Cambridge New Art History and Criticism, ed. Norman Bryson. Cambridge: Cambridge University Press, 1989.

Campi, Emidio. *Zwingli und Maria: Eine reformationsgeschichtliche Studie.* Zürich: Theologischer Verlag, 1997.

Carroll, Michael P. *The Cult of the Virgin Mary: Psychological Origins.* Princeton, N.J.: Princeton University Press, 1986.

Chatellier, Louis. *The Europe of the Devout: The Catholic Reformation and the Formation of a New Society.* Translated by Jean Birrell. Cambridge: Cambridge University Press and Paris: Editions de la Maison des Sciences de l'Homme, 1989.

Chrisman, Miriam Usher. "Lay Response to the Protestant Reformation in Germany, 1520–1528." In *Reformation Principle and Practice: Essays in Honour of Arthur Geoffrey Dickens,* ed. P. N. Brooks, 33–52. London: Scolar, 1980.

Cole, William J. "Was Luther a Devotee of Mary?" *Marian Studies* 21 (1970): 94–202.

Davis, Natalie Zemon. *Society and Culture in Early Modern France.* Stanford: Stanford University Press, 1965.

Delius, Hans–Ulrich. "Luther und das 'Salve Regina.' "*Forschungen und Fortschritte* 38 (1964): 249–251.

Delius, Walter. *Geschichte der Marienverehrung.* Munich: Ernst Reinhardt, 1963.

Dörfler-Dierken, Angelika. *Die Verehrung der heiligen Anna im Spätmittelalter und früher Neuzeit.* Forschungen zur Kirchen– und Dogmengeschichte 50. Göttingen: Vandenhoeck & Ruprecht, 1992.

Douglass, E. Jane Dempsey. *Justification in Late Medieval Preaching: A Study of John Geiler of Keisersberg.* Studies in Medieval and Reformation Thought, ed. H. A. Oberman, vol. 1. Leiden: E. J. Brill, 1966.

Dresen–Coenders, Lène, ed. *Saints and She-Devils: Images of Women in the Fifteenth and Sixteenth Centuries.* Translated by C.M.H. Sion and R.M.J. van der Wilden. London: Rubicon, 1987.

Düfel, Hans. *Luthers Stellung zur Marienverehrung.* Kirche und Konfession, Bd. 13. Göttingen: Vandenhoeck & Ruprecht, 1968.

Dugan, Eileen Theresa. "Images of Marriage and Family Life in Nördlingen: Moral Preaching and Devotional Literature, 1589–1712." Ph.D. diss., Ohio State University, 1987.

Dupuy, B.-D. "La mariologie de Calvin." *Istina* 4 (1958): 479–490.

Ebneter, Albert. "Martin Luthers Marienbild." *Orientierung* 20 (1956): 77–80, 85–87.

Ellwein, Eduard. "Das Reformatorische Bild der Maria." *Zeitwende* 24 (1953): 494–501.

Ferry, Patrick T. "Confessionalization and Popular Preaching: Sermons against Synergism in Reformation Saxony." *Sixteenth Century Journal* 28 (1997): 1143–1166.

Forster, Marc R. *The Counter-Reformation in the Villages: Religion and Reform in the Bishopric of Speyer, 1560–1720.* Ithaca: Cornell University Press, 1992.

Gawthrop, Richard, and Gerald Strauss. "Protestantism and Literacy in Early Modern Germany." *Past and Present* 104 (1984): 31–55.

Gold, Penny Schine. *The Lady and the Virgin: Image, Attitude, and Experience in Twelfth-Century France.* Chicago: University of Chicago Press, 1985.

Gorski, Horst. *Die Niedrigkeit seiner Magd: Darstellung und theologische Analyse der*

Mariologie Martin Luthers als Beitrag zum gegenwärtigen lutherisch/römisch-katholischen Gespräch. Frankfurt am Main: P. Lang, 1987.

Graef, Hilda. *Mary, a History of Doctrine and Devotion.* Vol. 1, *From the Beginning to the Eve of the Reformation.* New York: Sheed and Ward, 1963.

————. *Mary, a History of Doctrine and Devotion.* Vol. 2, *From the Reformation to the Present Day.* New York: Sheed and Ward, 1965.

Grimm, Harold J. "The Human Element in Luther's Sermons." *Archiv für Reformationsgeschichte* 49 (1958): 50–60.

Hagenmaier, Monika. *Predigt und Policey: Der gesellschaftspolitische Diskurs zwischen Kirche und Obrigkeit in Ulm 1614–1639.* Nomos Universitätsschriften, Geschichte, Band 1. Baden Baden: Nomos, 1989.

Hale, Rosemary Drage. "*Imitatio Mariae:* Motherhood Motifs in Late Medieval German Spirituality." Ph.D. diss., Harvard University, 1992.

Harrington, Joel F. *Reordering Marriage and Society in Reformation Germany.* Cambridge: Cambridge University Press, 1995.

Heiler, Friedrich. "Die Gottesmutter im Glauben und Beten der Jahrhunderte." *Hochkirche* 13 (1931): 172–203.

Hendrix, Scott. "Masculinity and Patriarchy in Reformation Germany." *Journal of the History of Ideas* 56 (1995): 177–193.

Hsia, R. Po-Chia. *Social Discipline in the Reformation: Central Europe 1550–1750.* London: Routledge, 1989.

Hsia, R. Po-Chia, and R. W. Scribner, eds. *Problems in the Historical Anthropology of Early Modern Europe.* Wolfenbütteler Forschungen (Herzog August Bibliothek), Band 78. Wiesbaden: Harrassowitz, 1997.

Johnson, Elizabeth A. "Marian Devotion in the Western Church." In *Christian Spirituality: High Middle Ages and Reformation,* ed. Jill Raitt, 392–414. World Spirituality: An Encyclopedic History of the Religious Quest, vol. 17. New York: Crossroad, 1987.

Karant-Nunn, Susan. "Continuity and Change: Some Effects of the Reformation on the Women of Zwickau." *Sixteenth Century Journal* 13 (1982): 17–42.

————. "*Kinder, Küche, Kirche:* Social Ideology in the Sermons of Johannes Mathesius." In *Germania Illustrata: Essays on Early Modern Germany Presented to Gerald Strauss,* ed. Andrew C. Fix and Susan C. Karant-Nunn, 121–140. Sixteenth Century Essays & Studies, ed. Charles G. Nauert, Jr., vol. 18. Ann Arbor: Edwards Brothers, 1992.

————. *Luther's Pastors: The Reformation in the Ernestine Countryside.* Transactions of the American Philosophical Society, vol. 69, part 8. Philadelphia: American Philosophical Society, 1980.

————. "What Was Preached in German Cities in the Early Years of the Reformation? *Wildwuchs* Versus Lutheran Unity." In *The Process of Change in Early Modern Europe: Essays in Honor of Miriam Usher Chrisman,* ed. P. N. Bebb and Sherrin Marshall, 81–96. Athens: Ohio University Press, 1988.

————. "A Women's Rite: Churching and the Reformation of Ritual." In *Problems in the Historical Anthropology of Early Modern Europe,* ed. R. Po-Chia Hsia and R. W. Scribner, 111–138. Wolfenbütteler Forschungen (Herzog August Bibliothek), Band 78. Wiesbaden: Harrassowitz, 1997.

Kittelson, J. M. "Successes and Failures in the German Reformation: The Report from Strasbourg." *Archiv für Reformationsgeschichte* 73 (1983): 153–175.

Kolb, Robert. "Festivals of the Saints in Late Reformation Lutheran Preaching." *The Historian* 52 (August 1990): 613–626.

————. *For All the Saints: Changing Perceptions of Martyrdom and Sainthood in the Lutheran Reformation.* Macon, Ga.: Mercer University Press, 1987.

Kreitzer, Beth. "The Lutheran Sermon." In *Preachers and People in the Reformations and Early Modern Period*, ed. Larissa Taylor, 35–63. Leiden: Brill, 2001.

Küng, Hans, and Jürgen Moltmann, eds. *Mary in the Churches.* Concilium 168. Edinburgh: T. & T. Clark and New York: Seabury, 1983.

Lansemann, Robert. *Die Heiligentage besonders die Marien-, Apostel- und Engeltage in der Reformationszeit, betrachte im Zusammenhang der reformatorischen Anschauungen von den Zeremonien, von den Festen, von den Heiligen und von den Engeln.* Göttingen: Hubert, 1938.

Mackenzie, Ross. "Calvin and the Calvinists on Mary." *One in Christ: A Catholic Ecumenical Quarterly* 16 (1980): 68–78.

Matter, E. Ann. *The Voice of My Beloved: The Song of Songs in Western Medieval Christianity.* University of Pennsylvania Press Middle Ages Series, ed. Edward Peters. Philadelphia: University of Pennsylvania Press, 1990.

Mayberry, Nancy. "The Controversy Over the Immaculate Conception in Medieval and Renaissance Art, Literature, and Society." *Journal of Medieval and Renaissance Studies* 21 (Fall 1991): 207–224.

Meinhold, Peter. "Die Marienverehrung im Verständnis der Reformatoren des 16. Jahrhunderts." *Saeculum* 32 (1981): 43–58.

Michalski, Sergiusz. *The Reformation and the Visual Arts: The Protestant Image Question in Western and Eastern Europe.* Christianity and Society in the Modern World, ed. Hugh McLeod and Bob Scribner. London: Routledge, 1993.

Moeller, Bernd. "Einige Bemerkungen zum Thema: Predigten in reformatorischen Flugschriften." In *Flugschriften als Massenmedium der Reformationszeit: Beiträge zum Tübinger Symposion 1980*, ed. Hans-Joachim Köhler, 261–268. Spätmittelalter und Frühe Neuzeit: Tübinger Beiträge zur Geschichtsforschung, eds. Volker Press and E. W. Zeeden, Band 13. Stuttgart: Ernst Klett, 1981.

————. "Religious Life in Germany on the Eve of the Reformation." In *Pre-Reformation Germany*, ed. Gerald Strauss, 13–42. New York: Harper & Row, 1972.

————. "Was wurde in der Frühzeit der Reformation in den deutschen Städten gepredigt?" *Archiv für Reformationsgeschichte* 75 (1984): 176–193.

Moore, Cornelia Niekus. *The Maiden's Mirror: Reading Material for German Girls in the Sixteenth and Seventeenth Centuries.* Wolfenbütteler Forschungen, Bd. 36. Wiesbaden: Otto Harrassowitz, 1987.

Mulder-Bakker, Anneke B., ed. *Sanctity and Motherhood: Essays on Holy Mothers in the Middle Ages.* New York: Garland, 1995.

Müller, Gerhard. "Protestant Veneration of Mary: Luther's Interpretation of the *Magnificat*." In *Humanism and Reform: The Church in Europe, England, and Scotland, 1400–1643: Essays in Honour of James K. Cameron*, ed. James Kirk, 99–111. Studies in Church History, subsidia, 8. Oxford: Basil Blackwell, 1991.

Nischan, Bodo. "Demarcating Boundaries: Lutheran Pericopic Sermons in the Age of Confessionalization." *Archiv für Reformationsgeschichte* 88 (1997): 199–216.

Oberman, Heiko A. *The Harvest of Medieval Theology: Gabriel Biel and Late Medieval Nominalism.* Cambridge: Harvard University Press, 1963; reprint, Durham, N.C.: Labyrinth, 1983.

————. "The Virgin Mary in Evangelical Perspective." *Journal of Ecumenical Studies* 1 (1964): 271–298.

Oftestad, Bernt Torvild. "Lehre, die das Herz bewegt: Das Predigtparadigma bei Martin Chemnitz." *Archiv für Reformationsgeschichte* 80 (1989): 125–153.

O'Malley, John W. "Content and Rhetorical Forms in Sixteenth-Century Treatises on Preaching." In *Renaissance Eloquence: Studies in the Theory and Practice of Renaissance Rhetoric*, ed. James J. Murphy, 238–252. Berkeley: University of California Press, 1983.

——. "Luther the Preacher." *Michigan Germanic Studies* 10 (1984): 3–16.

O'Meara, Thomas A. *Mary in Protestant and Catholic Theology*. New York: Sheed and Ward, 1966.

Opitz, Claudia, H. Röckelein, G. Signori, and G. Marchal, eds. *Maria in der Welt. Marienverehrung im Kontext der Sozialgeschichte 10.–18. Jahrhundert*. Zurich: Chronos, 1993.

Ozment, Steven. *When Fathers Ruled: Family Life in Reformation Europe*. Cambridge, Mass.: Harvard University Press, 1983.

Pelikan, Jaroslav. *Mary Through the Centuries: Her Place in the History of Culture*. New Haven: Yale University Press, 1996.

Peters, Christian. "Luthers Einfluß auf die frühreformatorische städtische Predigt: das Beispiel des Ulmer Kaplans Johann Diepold (gest. vor 1539)." In *Luthers Wirkung: Festschrift für Martin Brecht zum 60. Geburtstag*, ed. W.-D. Hauschild, W. H. Neuser, and C. Peters, 111–133. Stuttgart: Calwer, 1992.

Preuss, Horst Dietrich. *Maria bei Luther*. Schriften des Vereins für Reformationsgeschichte, Nr. 172. Gütersloh: C. Bertelsmann, 1954.

——. "Luthers Hauptgedanken über Maria, die Mutter des Herrn." *Luther: Mitteilungen der Luther Gesellschaft* 26 (1955).

Robisheaux, Thomas. "Peasants and pastors: rural youth control and the Reformation in Hohenlohe, 1540–1680." *Social History* 6 (1981): 281–300.

——. *Rural Society and the Search for Order in Early Modern Germany*. Cambridge: Cambridge University Press, 1989.

Roper, Lyndal. " 'The Common Man,' 'the Common Good,' 'Common Women': Gender and Meaning in the German Reformation Commune." *Social History* 12 (1987): 1–21.

——. *The Holy Household: Women and Morals in Reformation Augsburg*. Oxford: Basil Blackwell, 1989.

——. "Luther: Sex, Marriage and Motherhood." *History Today* 33 (December 1983): 33–38.

——. *Oedipus and the Devil: Witchcraft, Sexuality, and Religion in Early Modern Europe*. London: Routledge, 1994.

Rothkrug, Lionel. "Popular Religion and Holy Shrines: Their Influence on the Origins of the German Reformation and Their Role in German Cultural Development." In *Religion and the People, 800–1700*, ed. James Obelkevich, 20–86. Chapel Hill: University of North Carolina Press, 1979.

Rublack, Hans-Christoph. "Augsburger Predigt im Zeitalter der lutherischen Orthodoxie." In *Die Augsburger Kirchenordnung von 1537 und ihr Umfeld*, ed. Reinhard Schwarz, 123–158. Schriften des Vereins für Reformationsgeschichte, ed. Gustav Adolf Benrath, Bd. 196. Gütersloh: Gerd Mohn, 1988.

——. "Lutherische Predigt und gesellschaftliche Wirklichkeiten." In *Die Lutherische Konfessionalisierung in Deutschland*, ed. H.-C. Rublack, 344–395. Schriften des Vereins für Reformationsgeschichte, ed. Gustav Adolf Benrath, Bd. 197. Gütersloh: Gerd Mohn, 1988.

——. " 'Der wohlgeplagte Priester': Vom Selbstverständnis lutherischer Geistlichkeit im Zeitalter der Orthodoxie." *Zeitschrift für Historische Forschung* 16 (1989): 1–30.

Rublack, Ulinka. "Pregnancy, Childbirth and the Female Body in Early Modern Germany." *Past and Present* 150 (1996): 84–110.

Sauder, Gerhard. "Erbauungsliteratur." In *Hansens Sozial-geschichte der Deutschen Literatur vom 16. Jahrhundert biz zur Gegenwart*, vol. 3, ed. Rolf Grimminger, 251–266. Munich: Carl Hansen, 1980.

Schilling, Heinz. *Religion, Political Culture, and the Emergence of Early Modern Society: Essays in German and Dutch History*. Translated by Stephen G. Burnett. Studies in Medieval and Reformation Thought, ed. Heiko A. Oberman, vol. 50, 205–245. Leiden: E. J. Brill, 1992.

Schimmelpfennig, Reintraud. *Die Geschichte der Marienverehrung im Deutschen Protestantismus*. Paderborn: Ferdinand Schöningh, 1952.

Schnabel-Schüle, Helga. "Distanz und Nähe: Zum Verhältnis von Pfarrern und Gemeinden im Herzogtum Württemberg vor und nach der Reformation." *Rottenburger Jahrbuch für Kirchengeschichte* 5 (1986): 339–348.

Schorn-Schütte, Luise. "The Christian Clergy in the Early Modern Holy Roman Empire: A Comparative Social Study." *Sixteenth Century Journal* 29 (Fall 1998): 717–731.

Schroeder, Joy A. "The Rape of Dinah: Luther's Interpretation of a Biblical Narrative." *Sixteenth Century Journal* 28 (Fall 1997): 775–791.

Schütz, Werner. "Jakob Andreae als Prediger." *Zeitschrift für Kirchengeschichte* 87 (1976): 221–243.

Schützeichel, Heribert. " 'Das berühmte und denkwürdige Lied der heiligen Jungfrau:' Calvins Auslegung des Magnificat." In *Creatio ex amore: Beiträge zu einer Theologie der Liebe: Festschrift für Alexandre Ganoczy zum 60. Geburtstag*, ed. Franke et al., 300–311. Würzburg: Echter, 1988.

Scott, Joan Wallach. "Gender: A Useful Category of Historical Analysis." In Scott, *Gender and the Politics of History*. Gender and Culture, ed. Carolyn G. Heilbrun and Nancy K. Miller. New York: Columbia University Press, 1988.

Scribner, Robert W. "Cosmic Order and Daily Life: Sacred and Secular in Pre-Industrial German Society." In *Religion and Society in Early Modern Europe, 1500–1800*, ed. Kaspar von Greyerz, 17–32. London: George Allen & Unwin, 1984.

———. "The Impact of the Reformation on Daily Life." In *Mensch und Objekt im Mittelalter und in der Frühen Neuzeit: Leben-Alltag-Kultur*, 315–344. Veröffentlichungen des Instituts für Realienkunde des Mittelalters und der Frühen Neuzeit, nr. 13. Vienna: Österreichischen Akademie der Wissenschaften, 1990.

———. "Oral Culture and the Transmission of Reformation Ideas." In *The Transmission of Ideas in the Lutheran Reformation*, ed. Helga Robinson-Hammerstein, 83–104. Dublin: Irish Academic Press, 1989.

———. "Pastoral Care and the Reformation in Germany." In *Humanism and Reform: The Church in Europe, England, and Scotland, 1400–1643: Essays in Honour of James K. Cameron*, ed. James Kirk, 77–97. Studies in Church History, Subsidia, 8. Oxford: Blackwell Publishers for the Ecclesiastical History Society, 1991.

———. "Practice and Principle in the German Towns: Preachers and People." In *Reformation Principle and Practice: Essays in Honour of Arthur Geoffrey Dickens*, ed. P. N. Brooks, 95–117. London: Scolar, 1980.

———. "Ritual and Popular Religion in Catholic Germany at the Time of the Reformation." *Journal of Ecclesiastical History* 35 (1984): 47–77.

———. "Ritual and Reformation." In *The German People and the Reformation*, ed. R. Po-Chia Hsia, 122–44. Ithaca: Cornell University Press, 1988.

Sheingorn, Pamela. " 'The Wise Mother': The Image of St. Anne Teaching the Virgin Mary." *Gesta* 32 (1993): 69–80.

Shoemaker, Stephen J. "Mary and the Discourse of Orthodoxy: Early Christian Identity and the Ancient Dormition Legends." Ph.D. diss., Duke University, Durham, N.C., 1997.

Shuel, James A. "The Virgin Mary in a Reformation Theology." *Canadian Journal of Theology* 6 (October 1960): 275–283.

Söll, Georg. "Maria in der Geschichte von Theologie und Frömmigkeit." In *Handbuch der Marienkunde*, ed. Wolfgang Beinert and Heinrich Petri, 93–231. Regensburg: Friedrich Plestet, 1984.

Sparn, Walter. "Preaching and the Course of the Reformation." In *The Transmission of Ideas in the Lutheran Reformation*, ed. Helga Robinson-Hammerstein, 173–183. Dublin: Irish Academic Press, 1989.

Stacpoole, Alberic. *Mary's Place in Christian Dialogue*. Wilton, Conn.: Morehouse-Barlow, 1982.

Stakemeier, E. "De Beata Maria Virgine ejusque cultu juxta reformatores." In *De Mariologia et oecumenismo*, 423–478. Rome: Pontificia Academia Mariana Internationalis, 1962.

Steinmetz, David C. *Misericordia Dei: The Theology of Johannes von Staupitz in its Late Medieval Setting*. Studies in Medieval and Reformation Thought, ed. Heiko A. Oberman, vol. 4. Leiden: E. J. Brill, 1968.

Strauss, Gerald. *Luther's House of Learning: Indoctrination of the Young in the German Reformation*. Baltimore: Johns Hopkins University Press, 1978.

———. "The Mental World of a Saxon Pastor." In *Reformation Principle and Practice: Essays in Honour of Arthur Geoffrey Dickens*, ed. P. N. Brooks, 155–170. London: Scolar, 1980.

———. "Success and Failure in the German Reformation." *Past and Present* 67 (1975): 30–63.

Tappolet, Walter. *Das Marienlob der Reformatoren*. Tübingen: Katzmann, 1962.

Thurian, Max. *Mary, Mother of the Lord, Figure of the Church*. London: Faith, 1963.

Warner, Marina. *Alone of All Her Sex: The Myth and Cult of the Virgin Mary*. New York: Vintage, 1983.

Weinstein, Donald, and Rudolph Bell. *Saints and Society: The Two Worlds of Western Christendom, 1000–1700*. Chicago: University of Chicago Press, 1982.

Wengert, Timothy J., and M. Patrick Graham. *Philip Melanchthon (1497–1560) and the Commentary*. Sheffield, Eng.: Sheffield Academic Press, 1997.

Wicks, Jared. "The Virgin Mary in Recent Ecumenical Dialogues." *Gregorianum* 81 (2000): 25–57.

Wiesner, Merry E. "Beyond Women and the Family: Towards a Gender Analysis of the Reformation." *Sixteenth Century Journal* 18, no. 3 (1987): 311–321.

———. "Luther and Women: The Death of Two Marys." In *Disciplines of Faith: Studies in Religion, Politics, and Patriarchy*, ed. J. Obelkevich, L. Roper, and R. Samuel, 295–308. History Workshop Series. London: Routledge & Kegan Paul, 1987.

———. *Women and Gender in Early Modern Europe*. New Approaches to European History. Cambridge: Cambridge University Press, 1993.

———. "Women's Response to the Reformation." In *The German People and the Reformation*, ed. R. Po-Chia Hsia, 148–171. Ithaca: Cornell University Press, 1988.

Winston-Allen, Anne. *Stories of the Rose: The Making of the Rosary in the Middle Ages*. University Park, Pa.: Pennsylvania State University Press, 1997.

Wright, David F. "Mary in the Reformers." In *Chosen by God: Mary in Evangelical Perspective*, ed. David F. Wright, 161–183. London: Marshall Pickering, 1989.

Zeeden, Ernst Walter. *Katholische Überlieferungen in den Lutherischen Kirchenordnungen des 16. Jahrhunderts.* Katholisches Leben und Kämpfen im Zeitalter der Glaubensspaltung, Vereinsschriften der Gesellschaft zur Herausgabe des Corpus Catholicorum, 17. Münster in Westfalen: Aschendorffsche Verlagsbuchhandlung, 1959.

Zieger, Andreas. *Das Religiöse und Kirchliche Leben in Preussen und Kurland im Spiegel der evangelischen Kirchenordnungen des 16. Jahrhunderts.* Forschungen und Quellen zur Kirchen- und Kulturgeschichte Ostdeutschlands, ed. Bernhard Stasiewski, Bd. 5. Köln Graz: Böhlau, 1967.

Index